EDUCATIONAL ADMINISTRATION TODAY

EDUCATIONAL ADMINISTRATION TODAY

DONALD E. ORLOSKY
University of South Florida

LLOYD E. McCLEARY
University of Utah

ARTHUR SHAPIRO
University of South Florida

L. DEAN WEBB
Arizona State University

Charles E. Merrill Publishing Company
A Bell & Howell Company
Columbus   Toronto   London   Sydney

Published by
Charles E. Merrill Publishing Company
A Bell & Howell Company
Columbus, Ohio 43216

This book was set in Souvenir
Production coordinator and text designer: Mary Henkener
Cover design: Cathy Watterson

Library of Congress Catalog Card Number: 83-63015
International Standard Book Number: 0-675-20110-1
1 2 3 4 5 6 7 8 9—89 88 87 86 85 84
Printed in the United States of America

CONTENTS

PART IV   Leadership in the Real World

15   Promoting Constructive Change, 313

FOREWORD

One of the by-products of space exploration and the electronic revolution is an unprecedented awakening of state and national interest in education. This awakening is in large part a culmination of forces that preceded these two revolutionary developments, but these developments brought the problems of education more forcibly to the attention of the public and made the need for solutions much more compelling. The preceding forces, whose educational effects have collected at an alarming rate, include the extensive accumulation of scientific knowledge, shifts in world orientation and national interest, concentration of population, increasing amalgamation of cultural and ethnic groups, rapid and sweeping changes in the occupational structure, and an awakening sense of human rights and societal responsibilities. These forces have given rise to educational problems of great magnitude. It is in this setting that the work of the administrator is viewed by the authors.

The increasing sensitivity of the public to state and national concerns has brought the schools to the fore as a state responsibility, putting them in the arena of state politics. State legislatures are increasingly taking on responsibilities that formerly belonged only to local boards of education. Today it is not unusual for programs of study to be shaped largely by state mandate. In addition, testing programs, devised and controlled by the state, are being used to evaluate student progress and to decide who shall receive high school diplomas. These programs may well lead to evaluation of the school itself.

Increased awareness of human rights and institutional responsibilities is making the teaching profession sensitive to issues in student discipline, hiring and firing, school accidents, evaluation, conduct on field trips, student dress and grooming, and countless other areas that in times past would have been ignored. As a result, school administrators are hedged by an assortment of possible litigations. They must be aware of and understand legal aspects of education to a far greater degree than ever before. The unionization of the profession has reinforced this necessity.

The diversification of the student body, largely attributable to the increasing amalgamation of the population, has influenced the development of programs to satisfy its various needs and interests. This development has run head-on into national and industrial demands for a more scientifically oriented work force. The encounter is resulting in state legislative action to reshape the comprehensive program of the public schools into a more academically oriented one.

Public concern over the quality of its educational system has also raised serious questions about the competence of the profession itself. Demands for higher student achievement are being translated into public insistence that teachers themselves be evaluated in terms of the achievements of their pupils. That this movement will result in state programs that evaluate individual schools as well as teachers is becoming increasingly likely. Such evaluations will involve administrators and will require a new type of competence: the ability to objectively observe and diagnose teacher performance.

From these movements and developments, a new type of leadership is emerging. This leadership is thoroughly versed in school finance, school law, all levels of politics, educational programs, evaluating teachers and other personnel, curriculum development, court decisions, educational policy making, and public relations. It possesses a sense of direction and skills in social and personal interaction; it takes pride in its professional knowledge and competence and at the same time realizes that it works with personnel whose knowledge in many areas of practice is equal to or superior to its own; it shapes positive public opinion about the status and direction of public education.

This volume addresses the essentials of this seminal leadership, its knowledge base, and its characteristics and responsibilities. The reader will find a clear and succinct treatment of the concepts and principles of effective leadership presented in the concrete terms and exemplified in practical situations.

B. Othanel Smith

PREFACE

The work of school administrators and the factors that define their role require constant examination. Yet schools do not hold still to permit the precise study that enables generalizations and formulas for school management to be perfected. The study of school administration requires that factors impinging on or even dictating the work of schools be revised, identified, understood, and considered as administrative practices are developed. These factors are often complex and always require synthesis into practical application and action when administrators perform responsibly. The dynamic nature of these characteristics create a task for administrators that is fraught with pitfalls and problems that are often handled with an uneasy resolve.

A few illustrations make the truth of this instability quite evident. For example, school law and teacher evaluation illustrate the changing rules under which school administrators must operate. School law is a sea of change in which precedents are set and legal decision overturned. These decisions are in many areas such as due process, student rights, desegregation, and sexual bias. Teacher evaluation has been important for purposes of retention, but with responsibility for certification shifting more to school districts and issues such as merit pay emerging, the old rules of the game are changing. This text discusses these new contexts and issues, which are paramount in the operation of today's schools.

In addition to these changes, some fundamental elements and structures continue to form the framework on which sound school leadership is based. The decentralized characteristics of the nation's schools, that is, a stronger state than federal role, and the relationship between local school boards and the school administrators are two areas that have remained relatively constant. It is important to understand and acknowledge the valuable lessons we have learned from experience that have established these workable characteristics of the schools. Thus, the context of the schools that has been inherited from the past and the changing patterns of school leadership that have emerged in the present are combined in this text.

To serve this purpose the book has been divided into four parts. Though each part tends to stand alone, the chapters provide a cohesive sequence that gives continuity across the four parts of the book's organization. The four parts compartmentalize the knowledge, theory, and practice of school administrators into distinct areas that require different kinds of expertise. Administrators assume several roles, and what we consider the four major roles comprise the four parts of this text. These roles can be called Theoretician, Legal and Financial Expert, Supervisor, and Problem Solver. Such titles only suggest the general area of behavior of the administrator. The details and more specific problems resolved through administrative leadership are elaborated in the text, but even a text that delineates the features of each of these roles is smaller than life. A text can only be illustrative. Nevertheless, the explanations are drawn from research, expert opinion, and the lives of the authors to bring to the reader a presentation of practice and theory in the schools.

Part I describes the fundamental characteristics of school administration by presenting information about educational politics, school organization, control, policy development, staffing, staff development, and administrative roles and responsibilities.

Part II focuses on the administrator's role in developing and maintaining effective schools. This section identifies the characteristics of effective schools as reported in the current literature and then discusses the application of this research in developing personnel and curriculum development activities that are most likely to be productive.

Part III discusses legal and financial aspects of school administration. This segment provides an introduction to how the legal system affects schools and explains the federal and state court systems. Important legal decisions that dictate school responsibilities are provided to supply critical knowledge and also to illustrate the philosophy that underlies the actions of the courts and the role schools are perceived to assume as one of society's institutions. Discussions about school finance also explain the structure and the approach to obtaining monetary support for the schools. The account is extended to include the subtleties that are part and parcel of tax reform and distribution of the tax base for school support. The responsibilities of administrators to understand how money is raised and the rationale for its distribution are included.

Part IV discusses how school administrators deal with bureaucracy, promote school-community relationships, address conflicts and controversy, and engage in constructive change. All of these topics call for an understanding of the situation that confronts the administrator and a clarification of the options available. That application of the art of administration is dealt with in which the style and communication skills of the administrator are blended with idiosyncrasies of the situation to provide effective leadership. It is in this area that the administrator utilizes personal creativity and professional knowledge to establish the climate, image, and attitudes that characterize the schools.

This text was written for those who plan to serve as administrators in schools. This book should also benefit those who do not become administrators by helping them to better understand the work of school administrators. If a reader of this text will place himself or herself in the role of the administrator, then the realities of the work of school administration should be more vivid, albeit vicarious, as the problems, knowledge, and solutions described in this text unfold. This book can serve several purposes depending on individual expectations, backgrounds, career plans and working situations. But for all readers, a greater awareness of the practice of school administration and an appreciation for the complexities of that work should evolve.

This book is the result of the combined effort of many people, including those whose research and writings in the field of school administration have contributed to the knowledge on which this book is based. Each author also relied on assistance from others who provided a number of vital services in the production of this book. Special thanks go to Dr. Blanche Sherman Hunt for her editorial assistance, Victoria McCleary for her research, and Lois Kinkaid and Lillie Biggs for their typing. Futhermore, the administrative support and assistance of Vicki Knight from Charles E. Merrill was essential in completing this book. The authors assume full responsibility for the contents of the book even though excellent ideas were often incorporated from those who helped in the final writing.

Donald E. Orlosky
Lloyd E. McCleary
Arthur Shapiro
L. Dean Webb

PART I
The Foundation

It is important in the early stages of the study of school administration to grasp the basic principles, tenets, and the responsibilities that school administrators must understand. The administration of schools calls for some responsibilities that are similar to those assumed by administrators in other enterprises, but also for some behaviors that are unique to the field of education. These differences help distinguish the roles of school administrators from the roles of other administrative positions. Certain questions are important to raise and answer in this regard. For example, what differences arise in administration because of the nature of the goal? In the case of the schools, the proper goal is an educated graduate whose performance reflects well on the schools and who also finds a personal and productive niche in society. In what way is this young human being, obviously unfinished at this stage of life, different from the product that comes off the assembly line of a factory or from a product that is worn until threadbare and discarded? What administrative behavior makes the greatest impact of schools on human lives and at the same time reflects the importance of organization, evaluation, and structure characteristic of good administration in all productive organizations? This uniqueness of school administration requires a good foundation of knowledge and an understanding of the work of school administrators. Part I addresses this concern by an opening discussion of school administration and continues with an elaboration of the special responsibilities that arise in the politics of educational administration, the particular roles and responsibilities of administrators, and finally the importance of strengthening the performance of schools through the staffing procedures.

1

Life has no meaning except in terms of responsibility.
- Reinhold Niebuhr

School Administration

Administration consists of applying rational thinking to organized activity. This application of rational thinking gives rise to the science of administration and a search for basic principles. Administration is concerned with values because it must encompass goals, purposes, and choices among alternatives. In questions of control and governance, educational administration becomes intimately involved with politics as it applies to policy making and policy implementation. Administration, as considered here, exists in organizations, and thus is concerned with people. However, the administrator's concern for people involves more than questions of organization. Education is the shaping of human character, and educational administration is confronted with moral and ethical questions not always found in other types of administration. Finally, the administrator, as a person, brings to the administrative act a view of human nature and a set of values and action patterns that can be labeled as administrative style. This total mosaic of administration has been called "the highest order of human activity" by some.

In all industrialized societies, organizations and administration are pervasive. Despite the foibles and transgressions attributable to organizations and their administration, they are the best means to achieve collective ends in a regular, predictable fashion. Since organizations and administration occur in all areas of human activity, it seems reasonable to assume that a body of knowledge and practice is common to administration wherever it exists. To a degree this is so, and it is appropriate to treat and study administration as a general class of activities. Some aspects of administration, however, defy general treatment, and thus administration is categorized into business, public, medical, educational, and other specialties. For purely scholarly purposes, administration might be approached as a rational investigation of general principles and of general and special components, although, as will be shown, there are problems in this method. Nonetheless, there is a distinctive set of organizational functions and activities to allow concentrated study of administration as a discipline and as a practice.

Administration and Management Terms and Meanings

The terms *administration* and *management* do not have precise meanings. Care must be taken when they are encountered to determine their context and their referent(s). *Administration* and *management* are frequently treated as synonymous and interchangeable terms (McFarland 1974, 6–7). However, for both practical usage and conceptual analysis, distinction between these terms is necessary.

In education, those with "line" authority, beginning with assistant principals and continuing with their superiors, are referred to as *administrators*. In business, the term *business manager* is universally used for those whose responsibility is over business affairs. The distinction derives from the designation of positions in business where first-line officers are labeled *managers*, higher level personnel are labeled *administrators*, and top level personnel are labeled *executives*. Supposedly, a manager deals with the purely operational aspects of accomplishing a particular set of tasks: supervising workers, organizing work activities, and resolving immediate problems that interfere with efficient achievement of goals. Administrators supervise managers, deal with longer range problems, and execute policy. Executives engage in long-range planning, set overall policy and direction, and handle the complex relationships of the organization with its external environment.

Usage as a means of definition is not workable because, in education, administrators do engage in management; and in business, the functions ascribed to managers, administrators, and executives are not definitive. The corporate game of titles interferes with conceptualizing about function. Successful business ventures involve all levels of "management" in planning, while "managers" at all levels do make decisions, and so on. Later chapters delineate function, as generally applied in educational practice, and clarify managerial and administrative concepts, as employed there.

The inductive approach, which involves working from the details of practice to general principles, reveals a lack of tight definition of *management* and of *administration*. A deductive approach is of somewhat more assistance, but here also is a lack of precision. Although the distinction is not universally accepted, *management* can be thought of as a subset of *administration*. A first approximation is to alter the term *management* to the term *technical-managerial*. *Managerial* in this sense refers to the specialized, quantitative, means-oriented activities by which administators go about planning, coordinating, supervising, decision-making, monitoring, and evaluating. Though technical-managerial skills are basic to sound administration, they are not synonymous with admistration. Administration can be conceived as encompassing three interrelated but reasonably restrictive sets of acts: (1) technical management, (2) organizational leadership and direction, and (3) long-range planning and policy-making.

Administration as Process and as Discipline

At the simplest level administration can be explained as a process that includes planning, deciding and implementing decisions, monitoring implementation, assessing results, and replanning. Each phase of the process for a given condition may be very complex, extend over a long time period, and require sophisticated knowledge and skills.

Example: A school principal initiated curriculum changes due to faculty dissatisfaction with the content of the language arts programs, student apathy with the subject, and some parental complaints. After consulting with the central office and school faculty, the principal appointed a committee that surveyed other programs, studied national curriculum projects, and used external consultants. This committee examined the social studies and science areas, evaluated student work, and analyzed the content of existing curricula. The committee determined to prepare a systematic plan to introduce critical thinking skills across the three subject areas and to revise their content substantially. At this stage parents, students, and central office staff became part of the planning process.

The first phase of the administrative process, *planning*, required a lengthy time period—over eighteen months. The principal completed the entire administrative process cycle within this first phase of the larger cycle. The principal (1) *planned* the steps to be undertaken; (2) *decided* who was to be involved, to do what; (3) *implemented* decisions by setting out the work to be done, for example, by arranging resources for materials and consultants; (4) *monitored* progress by obtaining feedback on activities and reports of results; (5) *assessed* results; and (6) *replanned* additional activities as the work progressed. As the first planning cycle ended, the decisions and their implementation (the second phase of the overall management process) required a comparable repetition of the cycle. Monitoring of the trial project and full implementation of the program required an additional three years.

This example illustrates the application of disciplined thought and practice. From the distinctions made between management and administration, one might infer the technical-managerial, the organizational leadership, and perhaps the policy-making acts required of this principal.

However, there is more to the story. Several critical events occurred during this process. First, there was considerable disagreement within the faculty. An intense interpersonal conflict resulted that created staff morale problems. During this period, the principal was accused of engineering changes already decided upon by a clique within the faculty. Then, the science curriculum specialist of the central office questioned the inclusion of the science program in the project. The proposed content included questions of morality in science. The science specialist thought that pressures would arise from the creationists to include their teachings in the science curriculum. Finally, a conservative group demanded to review the reading lists and teaching outlines since they understood that the program would include contemporary readings concerning social issues. In addition to attending to interpersonal conflicts within the faculty and the differences with the science specialist over district curriculum policy, the principal presented and defended the project to the Board of Education and held meetings with interested community groups.

In this school of almost two thousand students the principal also maintained daily operation: overseeing guidance, student activities, special education, teacher in-service training, and eight other departments; carrying through an annual school plan that included installation of microcomputers and reorganization of an alternative school subunit; and performing certain district-wide assignments. The administrative skills of organization, time management, conflict resolution, human relations, and program design were vital in handling this problem. This illustrates the need for the professional study of administration in its general dimensions, in its educational application, and in conditions which are unique to education. Conditions that make educational administration a unique branch of general administration are taken up in the next section. However, it should be clear that educational administration is not a profession to be learned on the job, and that its successful practice requires a significant knowledge base.

Administration as People and as Career

As well as being seen as process and as a field of disciplined study, the term *administration* is encountered in two additional ways. First, *administration* frequently is used to denote collectively those who administer a specific organizational unit. For example, one refers to the administration of a school or district as entering the negotiation process with the teachers' bargaining unit, or the administration as preparing a plan for reorganization. This use of the term is not a frivolous one. As seen from the example already provided, no single individual could perform all of the administrative duties implied by the conditions in the situation presented. There is frequent reference in the literature to the administrative team (American Association of School Administrators 1981; Erickson 1977; Wynn 1976). The use of *administration* as a collective term implies leadership shared within a group to fulfill the total administrative requirements of a given organization. The organization needs a common knowledge base along with complementary specialized competencies shared within the administrative group and the skills and dispositions to work cooperatively. Effectiveness of most principals, superintendents, and other administrative heads depends upon their abilities to select, organize, and lead the administrative team.

The term *administration* is also used to denote a career. This aspect is treated in the final section of this chapter. Within the public schools approximately 80 percent of all administrators move into other posts from the elementary principalship or the assistant principalship. Thus, there are career routes and career patterns of which the aspiring educational administrator should be aware: what it means to pursue a career; what career opportunities exist inside and outside the public schools, internationally as well as nationally; how one maps a career; and what professional associations and other means of enhancing one's professional life are important to a productive and satisfying career in administration.

Administration as Educational Administration

There is an emerging science of administration in which common practices and generalizable theories apply to business, government, military, church, or education. A rapidly expanding technology, highly useful across many types of organizations, is associated with administration. However, there is much that is unique to educational organizations: the mission, the socio-economic-political conditions, the clients served, the programs offered, the functions performed, and the organizational structures that result.

Mission: Goals, Purposes, and Clients

Despite disagreement over specific purposes and priorities, the mission of any administrative effort is to enhance the capabilities of the learner, employee, or worker. In this sense, the military, industry, and other organizations as well as schools, engage in educational efforts; but both public and private schools for the young differ in at least two important ways. First, they are educating in the interest of the learner. Educators generally agree that schools should educate the young to live well in their environment and to have the ability to improve it. The influence of narrow community interests sometimes pressures schools to restrict the curriculum or to offer specific training programs to the exclusion of others. Often parents become concerned about teaching that exposes their children to values and practices in conflict with their own. Principals report problems dealing with sex education, multicultural education, economic theories, and even the placement of certain handicapped learners or pregnant young women in regular classrooms. In such matters educational administration clearly differs from administration of any other type.

A second difference in educational administration derives from the relative immaturity of the learner. Schools have a mandate to educate all young members of society, whatever their entry level skills, aspirations, interests, and motivations. With the immature, readiness to accept and profit from schooling becomes the responsibility of the school. Other institutions, even private schools, may exclude clients. It becomes the responsibility of the school to instill in the young a readiness to accept and profit from education.

Political Milieu of Educational Administration

Schools are organized by a political system which has given them a unique governance structure. This attempts to accommodate the interests and pressures of parents, teachers, suppliers, publishers, real estate brokers, pundits, and special interest advocates, and sometimes the ambitions of political figures (Kirst 1970). Conflict management and conflict resolution, consensus building, and the skills of deliberation are required at every level. Moreover, educational administration has not diversified, so that few specialists with these skills exist. Under these conditions, every educational administrator can expect to encounter a variety of interests and pressures from the political milieu unaided by specialists (March 1978).

The Learning Process and Program

Promoting learning is the ultimate purpose and primary responsibility of educational administration. This profession confronts the complexities of learning and of the teaching-learning process. The administrator could better meet this responsibility if teaching and learning were restricted to well-defined intellectual skills practiced in a classroom. However, learning is not such a simple matter. The administrator must promote the highest quality of learning for each student, assure that emotional growth occurs, enhance the love of learning itself, and intercede when learning is judged inadequate. But to make learning vital to the learner, the school must offer, and be prepared to defend, experiences that depart from the desires of the parents and the preconditioned attitudes and understandings of learners themselves. Another characteristic of learning is that it does not occur in isolation. To exploit what is learned in school and to extend the experiences provided there, the educational administrator needs to work with community leaders and agencies. The administrator also must work with the faculty to clarify the unique purposes of the school and to take advantage of the educating experience of home, church, neighborhood groups, recreational programs, mass media, and the example of adults, all of them powerful learning influences.

The three foci of concern are formal instruction, concomitant learning, and external community experiences requiring administrative expertise unique to education. Activities in each of these areas can go seriously astray unless they are coordinated so the faculty and the administrative team work together. Effective school administrators must be able to design programs and to articulate them to a variety of publics.

Organizational Structure

Educational organizations are frequently referred to as "organized anarchies." The governance structure and the obligation of the public schools to accept all children impose the need to attend to a wide variety of publics and clientele, and even make of education an ideological battleground. Perhaps the most demanding condition of organization that affects the administration of schools is people. Teaching is labor-intensive with costs determined by salaries that approximate 80 percent of school budgets. The clients are children and youth, who can be thought of as the raw materials and products, as crude as that analogy might seem. Finally, the technology is that of learning and change in people (Lortie 1976).

Organizational structures are hierarchical; but authority structure, work flow, and other features conform only roughly to classical bureaucratic models. School organization has been characterized as "loosely coupled" rather than bureaucratic (Meyer and Rowan 1977; Weick 1976; Hannaway and Sproul 1979). School units are relatively small, geographically scattered, and insulated from external influences and controls. Futhermore, administration at all levels does not intrude into daily teaching activities to any great extent; neither supervision nor direction is as close or controlling as in industry, business, hospitals, or the military. These distinguishing characteristics of organizational structure have particular relevance to questions of educational quality, accountability, change, and the professional role of administrators.

Historical Developments and Emphases

The practice of educational administration is several centuries old. The formal study of educational administration began around the turn of this century, but the "professionalization" of the field was not well underway until after World War II. The emergence of a field of scholarly study, with some semblance of an authoritative knowledge base, research orientation, and methodologies of inquiry occurred only within the past three decades. A brief overview of the development of the field of educational administration provides a perspective for examining the current status and future directions of the field.

Theory and Practice. Schools remained organized in relatively small units, except for high schools in large cities, until the 1920s. Small schools with few or no special programs or services and with stable, homogeneous neighborhoods required few administrative services. Principals taught, kept records, and performed tasks involving discipline, ordering and distributing supplies, meeting with parents, and managing the opening and closing of school. The first national organization for elementary school principals was established as a department of the National Education Association (NEA) in 1921; for secondary school principals, in 1927. At that time no formal training was required for an administrative post, and less than 5 percent of members in these organizations held master's degrees. An association of superintendents had been organized in 1867. In 1937 this became the American Association of School Administrators (AASA). However, AASA still does not actively seek to include school principals, and there is no single organization that represents all educational administrators.

School size began growing after World War I and continued until the 1970s, when declines in school population began to affect public and parochial systems heavily. Yet even after forty-five years of steady growth in the size of school units (1920–1965), over 65 percent of all high schools in the country still had fewer than five hundred students. By 1977, more than one-third of the high schools had between one and two thousand students, and over 12 percent had enrollments of more than two thousand students (Byrne, Hines, and McCleary 1978, 37).

Size was not the only factor affecting practice. The admission of a diverse student population required diverse goals and programs, a variety of support services, and a host of specialists, both in teaching and in service. Also, complexity in organizational elements reflected complexity in society which had, and is continuing to have, enormous impact upon schools.

Changes in activities at district central office, state agency, and federal levels were even more dramatic than in school units. Federal expenditures in education in 1950 were under 300 million dollars, but by 1983 reached over 14 billion dollars. State agencies changed in parallel fashion. For example, the number of state agency professional employees grew an average of 1200 percent from 1950 to 1980. One small state had five professional employees in 1950; at this writing it has over three hundred. District central offices were altered by deliberate movement to consolidate small districts into larger ones; more than sixty thousand districts in 1950 were combined into fewer than fifteen thousand today. In response to these changes, administrative practice altered significantly and irreversibly in a relatively short period. Size of organization, multiple purposes, specialization of personnel, sophistication of methods and treatments, and introduction of technology all complicated administrative practice.

The National Society for the Study of Education (NSSE) devoted a yearbook to educational administration in 1946 and another in 1964. The two are dramatically different. The earlier work was written entirely by educationists. There are no references to theory, and few to research, philosophy, history, or concepts from the behavioral sciences. Each of these areas of study could have contributed to an understanding of the almost overwhelming forces then in the process of altering educational practice. In the 1964 yearbook, only one chapter treats a topic (the preparation of educational administrators) dealt with in the 1946 book. By a heavy emphasis upon organizational theory and the contributions of the social and behavioral sciences, the 1964 yearbook signals that the insularity of educational administration was ended.

One section of the 1964 yearbook deals with the ferment in educational administration. It notes three 1947 events as contributing factors to change: "(a) The Kellogg Foundation received a recommendation from its education advisory committee that school administration was a field which deserved Foundation support; (b) the planning committee of AASA included in its statement of goals for the association the initiation of studies and programs looking toward further professionalization of the superintendency, and (c) the professors of educational administration formed an organization which was to focus on the scientific study of administration, the elements of leadership, and the dissemination of practices encountered in the preparation of school administrators" (National Society for the Study of Education 1964, 15). These three events indicated an awareness of the need for professionalization of educational administrators.

The ferment in educational administration was caused by recognition of the field's potential to reconstruct itself, of the role for scientific study, and of the need for substantive preparation programs. The accomplishment of these goals has been the focus of debate, research, and attempts to influence the direction of study and practice into the present period. The nature and relationship of theory and practice are central to the question.

Alfred North Whitehead states succinctly that ". . . the term Profession means an avocation whose activities are subjected to theoretical analysis, and are modified by theoretical conclusions derived from that analysis. This analysis has regard to the purposes of the avocation and to the adaptation of the activities for the attainment of those purposes." He continues, "The antithesis to a profession is an avocation based upon customary activities and modified by the trial and error of individual practice. Such an avocation is a Craft . . . ." (Whitehead 1933, 72-73). There are critics today, both inside and out of education, who assert that educational administration is still more a craft than a profession.

The study of educational administration and the preparation programs which grew rapidly from 1945 to 1960 (institutions offering preparation programs numbered more than three hundred by 1960) were heavily practice-oriented. College courses were formed around aspects of "the job" as described by administrators and defined as "subjects" by professors. Hollis Moore characterized the content of preparation programs as "largely folklore, with little research into the process or theory of administration" (NSSE 1964, 14). Administration of all types is practice-oriented in the sense that it focuses on action and pragmatism is the stereotypical attitude of administrators. The logical and practical approach to the need (without a codified knowledge base) to prepare large numbers of administrators was to study and teach "current best practice."

Practice, then, dominated the field of educational administration; and the mastery and emulation of current best practice was a primary standard of competence. This condition did, and to some extent still does, inhibit progress. It limits inquiry and speculation about what is attainable under present, or short-term, conditions. A field based upon craftsmanship assumes a static, or at best slowly evolving, art and relies upon occasional flashes of insight and technical invention to advance. Research, on the other hand, permits speculative inquiry coupled with controlled testing and criticism so the eventual adoption of concepts and techniques suitable for practice has a theoretical basis.

The critical factor in an applied field such as educational administration is the relationship of theory and practice, for one cannot prosper without the other. John Dewey speculated about "where we draw so that there shall be steady and cumulative growth of intelligent, communicable insight, and power of direction [in education]." He insisted that "educational practices provide the data, the subject matter, which form the problems in inquiry . . . ." They are also the final test of conclusion reached." (Dewey 1938, 10). He noted that the human sciences are particularly relevant for method as well as substance, but he cautioned that, "Remoteness is found whenever there is a lack of vital connection between field work, practices, and research work" (Dewey 1938, 43). He desired that a dynamic tension exist between the discipline and the public served.

For educational administration, however, Dewey's point about the relationship of a discipline to its field of practice creates difficulties. No one discipline supplies the range of method and substance; and no single set of clients (schools, school districts, state agencies, policy-making groups, etc.) provides the full range of settings for research and uses all of its results. Talcott Parsons and Gerald Pratt would partially resolve this dilemma by seeking a reasonable consensus about (1) the object of clinical interest; (2) a definition of the desirable state of the object of clinical interest, including specification of values; (3) identification of clinical problems; and (4) a mobilization of knowledge relevant to the clinical problems (Parsons and Pratt 1975). The following section examines how the discipline of educational administration has defined its field of inquiry.

Concepts and Formulations. Educational administration did not suddenly "emerge from the wilderness" upon realizing that its neglected theory and research needs were woefully inadequate, even misdirected. The shift in perspective was not sudden, although the general acceptance of the point of view and the formation of what might be termed a movement give that appearance. Significant antecedents stressed description over prescription and distinguished fact from value. The movement was undoubtedly delayed by the Great Depression and World War II, and even deterred during the 1950s by the rapid growth of the public schools. The field of business and public administration underwent a similar change, for all three studies had a common source. When the *Administrative Science Quarterly* was founded in 1956 by the Graduate School of Business and Public Administration, Cornell University, editor James Thompson foresaw: "When we look back in 1966, it may be obvious that administration was at a pre-science stage in 1956. Yet if the name of the journal proves to be premature, it was not lightly chosen. It expresses a possibility of developing an administration science and a conviction that progress is being made and will continue" (1956, 1). Business, public and educational administration set upon the same course at much the same time.

The antecedents began after the turn of the century with the work of Frederick W. Taylor (1915) followed by H. L. Gantt (1919) who was one of Taylor's disciples. Taylor formulated a science of production by analyzing tasks to be performed. His method, an inductive approach, used time and motion studies. Gantt, using Taylor's methods, mapped work flow and developed the well-known Gantt charting in current use. The core of systems analysis and the techniques of automation and programming are clearly traceable to Taylor's work. Henri Fayol ([1916] 1949) in France was using a deductive approach to analyze functions of administration by observing organizational needs for planning, coordinating, deciding, and organizing. His work led to the organization chart, the logical analysis of administrative tasks, and the fixing of formal lines of authority and communication to provide for administrative structure. Max Weber cannot be excluded from early theorists, for his sociological explanation of organizations produced a formal bureaucratic model still used in some organizational analyses.

All of the individuals noted in the preceding discussion based their analysis on an impersonal view of the organizational member and the administrator. Worker and administrator were cogs for the organizational machine. The humanist reaction appeared rather quickly with the work of Mary Parker Follet (Metcalf and Urwick 1940) and the extensive Western Electric studies of Roethlisberger and Dickson (Roethlisberger 1939). The latter produced the concept of the Hawthorne effect (improved output from the fact of being studied), which the experimental designer of today must struggle to control. The writings of Follet, Roethlisberger, and Weber are useful reading for the contemporary administrator.

These humanists found a complex and fascinating human system operating alongside the technical system and profoundly affecting its functioning. Their early studies led directly to recent work of Maslow (1954) and Argyris (1973). Maslow, from a psychological point of view, postulated a hierarchy of human needs with self-actualization at the apex. Herzberg (1966) followed the Maslow principle of a hierarchy of needs with evidence to support lower level (hygienic or security) and higher level (job or motivational) factors affecting productivity and satisfaction. Argyris was primarily concerned with how the individual and individual needs fit organizational requirements. He advocates restructuring organizations to maximize satisfaction for the member and productivity for the organization. Although we have moved ahead of the story, antecedents did exist that are directly traceable to the development of the field of administration.

A general encompassing theory to treat administration *qua* administration seemed within reach by the mid-1950s. In fact, the first issue of the *Administrative Science Quarterly*, already noted, contained an article by Edward H. Litchfield (1956) which for a time provided optimism that this had been achieved. He advanced a series of "fundamental propositions" around which he proposed a general theory of administration, but subsequent research based upon them proved disappointing. (Reasons for this are taken up in the next section of this chapter.) The works of two other theorists also should be read by the serious student of administration. They are Chester I. Barnard's *The Functions of the Executive* (1938) and Herbert A. Simon's *Administrative Behavior* ([1945] 1965).

Barnard, who was president of New Jersey Bell Telephone Company, viewed organization as a cooperative system and administration as an integral part of that system, separable only for analytical purposes. He began with basic propositions that a formal organization can only exist when individuals (1) are willing to cooperate, (2) are trying to achieve mutually compatible purposes, and (3) are being linked together through an identifiable, stable system of communications. After an extensive analysis, including an intriguing proposal that an informal organization must precede formal organization, Barnard examined the functions and methods of administrators in formal organization. In addition to contributing his concepts of informal organization and of communication structure, he treated value considerations in administrative decision-making and the moral component of administrative behavior.

Simon based a comprehensive theory of administration on decision-making. Simon viewed rationality and, unlike Barnard, value-free judgment as essential. The task at hand was to guide action, and he proposed that rational decisions were the key to organizational effectiveness. So the administrator's function was to extend the rationality of decisions and actions. Simon also focused upon the concept of role and role playing; each member of an organization was to fulfill an ascribed role, screening out personal and other considerations. According to Simon, all aspects of administration could be understood in terms of the nature and quality of decisions made. Further, he contended that administrative behavior was the only basis of data about administrative leadership. His conception of decision-making was extended and applied to educational administration by Daniel Griffiths (1958). Griffiths' conception of administrative behavior was employed in education by Ralph Stogdill (1963) as leader behavior. Stogdill's series of studies included development of the Leader Behavior Description Questionnaire (LBDQ), a widely used instrument in studies of administration in education, business, and the military.

Current Emphases and Future Directions. The discussion has attempted to make the points that: (1) administration requires a disciplined, scientific approach to achieve orderly development of administrative thought; (2) concepts and formulations we might term G-factors are applicable to administration generally; (3) special conditions that we might term S-factors, distinguish types of administration; and

(4) the search for a general theory has produced considerable theory building efforts. Although a general theory has not been attained, the search has produced useful concepts and formulations. The latter might well be termed "middle-range theories" because the ordering of concepts for speculation about their relationships can become powerful tools for additional research; they also are of practical use to administrators in thinking about educational problems. For example, the concept of the role expectations is useful in analysis of role conflict. Most principals and superintendents have experienced conflict and personal discomfort from differing expectations about the administrator's role. To assess dispassionately the expectations of teacher, parent, students, board of education member, colleague, superior, or interest group representative is important in making appropriate judgments about one's role. Role theory leads to helpful understanding of these relationships.

The most useful current areas of research in educational administration for educational administrators are briefly noted here. No analysis is made of each, nor is each treated in the detail required for a full understanding. The purpose here is to identify significant areas of scholarly study for the practicing educational administrator.

Organizational Theory. The specification of positions and the school and district role to be played by occupants of a position form the structure of organization. Authority, power and influence, delegation and responsibility attach to positions. The structure in an organization can be understood in terms of such concepts as line and staff, unity of command, span of control, and work flow. Within any school or district, informal relationships develop as individuals carry out formal responsibilities. These take on a structure in terms of regularity of interpersonal contacts, content of communications within the informal structure, flow of influence, identity of subgroups and informal leaders, psychological concomitants of relationships, and resulting organizational climates. The relationships between the formal and informal structures are particularly important in schools because each influences the other, affecting both organizational productivity and individual satisfaction.

Change is another aspect of organizational theory, and at least four distinct formulations of change have been identified and employed in schools. These are action research or responsive model (Goodlad 1975), linkage model (Berman and McLaughlin 1975), change agent model (Havelock 1973) and staff development or OD model (Schmuck 1977). In each of these models the school principal has been shown to be central to the occurrence of change.

Organizational studies of schools, have begun to depart significantly from approaches in studies of other types of organizations. Already noted are works treating schools as loosely-coupled systems. Jerald Hage (1965) proposed an axiomatic theory of organizations in which he related four means variables (complexity-specialization, centralization-authority hierarchy, formalization-standardization, and stratification-status system) with four ends variables (adaptiveness-flexibility, production-effectiveness, efficiency-cost, and job satisfaction-morale). Hage's theory holds that there are always "trade-offs" because increasing one variable automatically decreases another; for example, an increase in complexity automatically means a decrease in centralization. This organizational dilemma has particular meaning to schools as programs or specialists are added, and as highly controlling evaluation schemes are introduced.

Leadership Theory. The study of leadership has been as persistent as that of the study of organization, for they are interrelated. Administrators are designated leaders of organizations but a great deal of administrative work could not be labeled as leadership. On the other hand, many administrators transcend prescribed functions to accomplish extraordinary changes in schools and communities. Leadership, according to Lipham and Hoeh (1974), is "that behavior which initiates a new structure in interaction with a social system; it initiates change in goals, objectives, configurations, procedures, input, processes, and ultimately the outputs." The social system might be the classroom, a school department, school, school district, or community. The social system can be thought of as the domain wherein individuals are influenced by leader behavior. Other dimensions, such as scope (the range of issues or values over which a leader exercises influence); weight (the degree of influence a leader has in a given situation); and credibility (how others view and receive leadership attempts) are primary dimensions of leadership, useful to estimate leader potential.

As with the study of organization, so many variables are involved in theory that leadership can best be understood in quite specific conditions. The often-used illustration is that of the administrator who has led effectively in one school or district but has failed after moving to another. Obviously, leadership traits or sets of skills which succeed in one complex setting may fail in another. This happens partly because leadership depends upon talents existing within the organization. The leader's success also varies according to the point of view from which it is measured. For instance, the leader's ability to "initiate structure" and to "show consideration" are complex primary aspects of successful leadership. Yet it has been shown in numerous studies of principals and superintendents that subordinates prefer leaders who emphasize consideration over initiating structure, although superiors prefer leaders who emphasize initiating structure over consideration.

The exercise of leadership in education often occurs as the administrator establishes relationships between the school or school district and other agencies. Therefore, it would be a mistake to think of leadership as being exercised only within an organization. In a recent meeting, one principal from the Washington, D.C. area reported on the number and types of external proposals and requests made to her school in a month. She indicated that one of her heaviest expenditures of time was with agencies and interest groups that wished the school to take on some project. From Sacramento, a principal reported that one of his most time-consuming efforts was in getting community groups to assist the school with problems which could only be solved through community cooperation.

The NASSP has initiated a group of National Assessment Centers to aid school districts and universities in assessing potential school administrators. In simulation exercises trained assessors rate applicants on twelve dimensions of competence. These twelve, identified during seven years of development work in cooperation with the American Psychological Association, are problem analysis, leadership in leaderless group situations, judgment, oral and written communication, organizational ability, personal motivation, sensitivity, range of interests, decisiveness, stress tolerance, and educational values. These twelves areas appear to be critical to successful performance by school administrators.

Even with such an ambitious approach as that of NASSP, it is recognized that other competencies might be important in a given situation, and that organizational conditions are not included in this type of assessment. This recognition earlier led to contingency models (Fiedler, Chemers, and Mahar 1976) in attempts to measure leadership style and match leadership styles to organizational variables. Fiedler (1967) identified three organizational variables as important: leader-member relations, task structure, and leader-position power. Fiedler's research reports are poignant descriptions of efforts to study leadership. Two of his titles are: "Style or Circumstance: The Leadership Enigma" and "Leader Experience and Performance: Another Hypothesis Shot to Hell." Even though such study may not provide definitive solutions to specific problems, much is known about leadership in formal organizations such as schools which can serve the administrator in making reasoned judgments.

Decision Theory. One of the earlier comprehensive theories of administration (Simon [1945] 1965) proposed that administration's essential function was to make decisions and that all questions relating to administration could be understood in terms of decisions made, processes of research beforehand, and effects afterward. This theory has led to examination of decision-making as a process or a set of interrelated steps: problem awareness, problem definition, identification of alternative solutions, selection and testing of an alternative, evaluation of effects, and a renewal of the process where needed. Decision theory underlies a number of systems management techniques such as: (1) program evaluation and review technique, critical path method (PERT-CPM); (2) planning, programming, budgeting systems (PPBS); (3) a variety of needs assessment techniques; and (4) management by objectives (MBO). Decision theory has also stimulated the development of strategies to include the variety of groups and specialists whose involvement is necessary to solve educational problems. This development began with action research (Corey 1953) and has led to the change strategies already noted.

Process formulations from decision theory assume a rationality in decision-making that is often unwarranted. In education the openness of the system, the mix of laypersons and professionals, the values of individuals and groups, and reliance upon consensus pose unique difficulties. The administrator is often, therefore, a manager, a negotiator, coordinator, or a facilitator of decisions.

Given these considerations, educational administrators must make judgments about the types of decisions they encounter. For routine decisions, procedures and authority are clear. Such routine decisions may initiate a program, clarify responsibilities, allocate resources, or resolve a misunderstanding. More involved and creative decisions call for significant departures from current practice. It is under such circumstances that the management techniques and strategies for change are of particular importance. Abbott (1974) identified five critical skills which he argues are essential to competent decisions. These are the abilities (1) to differentiate among types of decisions; (2) to obtain adequate information to make the decision; (3) to involve the appropriate people at the proper time and in the appropriate manner; (4) to set priorities and initiate action at each stage; and (5) to anticipate intended and unintended consequences. To this list should be added the ability to assess progress and evaluate results.

Social Systems Theory. The fact that schooling is predominantly a human enterprise and only secondarily a technical one has made the humanist approaches appealing to educational administrators. Individuals in one organization, such as a school, have duties and responsibilities assigned them; but no management system can prescribe all the details of daily work for each person. An informal person-to-person communication system quickly develops to clarify how to perform duties and how to coordinate activities. The "grapevine" forms, subgroups and informal leaders appear, and an infrastructure of interpersonal contacts interprets and conditions the operation of the formal structure. The informal and formal structures intertwine to form the social system. One of the authors, for example, regularly maps contacts in the informal communication structure. The method, using matrix analysis, is useful to organize teaching teams and identify team leaders, clarify work assignments, examine breakdowns in communication and work flow, and assist in assigning administrators and supervisors to work groups.

The social system approach to organizational studies goes beyond concern for the formal structure. The social system includes all individuals who interact regularly to influence organizational life. The boundaries of a school social system are not limited to the faculty, support staff, and administrators as depicted on an organizational chart. The social system includes students, secretaries, custodians, parents, volunteers, central office staff, and others. Depending upon the issues and activities, the social system changes over time. The school administrator has influence over who is included or excluded, over issues and activities, and over the extent of involvement, but does not have absolute control.

Social systems theory is useful in understanding conditions relating to organizational health (Miles 1964). Each individual in an organization relies upon others for information from which attitudes, work standards, and public opinion are formed. Individuals derive much of their satisfaction from the informal relationships of the social system rather than from the formal relationships or the work itself. Jointly held opinions and attitudes result in an organizational climate which is a major influence on commitment, goals, and willingness to cooperate. Administrative styles which, ignoring the social system, depend heavily upon formal lines of communication and "go by the book," do not achieve high morale and productivity except through the accident of having strong natural leaders in an organization. The creative energy and the innovative ideas for problem solving and change, which generate and surface through the formal social structure, largely maintain the vitality of an organization.

Other Theory Formulations Relative to Administration. This review of attempts to devise a general theory of administration, and the review of organization theory, decision theory and social system theory, do not exhaust the body of theory and knowledge which has contributed to an emerging science of educational administration. In the review, passing reference has been made to other theory formulations which have become sterile and relatively unproductive in generating new knowledge, but still have conceptual value to educational administration. Among these are role theory and systems theory. Theory formulations less central than those reviewed, nevertheless provide useful constructs from their developing state. Among these, values theory and communications and information processing theory will be discussed in later chapters.

Theory Uniquely Appropriate to Educational Administration. Educational administration focuses its attention on the education of all individuals who are helped in learning through formal schooling processes. Therefore, the nature of learning, the design of educational programs and delivery systems, program evaluation, curriculum development, instruction, and the legal-political system of education are substantive areas of administrative study. Each has theory formulations going well beyond the constructs usually treated in teacher preparation programs. Teacher preparation and experience are not sufficient grounding for the educational administrator. Theory provides conceptual formulations and the potential for further theory development which are required if formal schooling is to thrive. Without such a base in theory and knowledge, the educational administrator becomes a processing agent without substantial professional expertise.

In the area of learning theory, for example, significant departures are being made from the Stimulus-Response (S-R) bond and gestalt schools of psychology through research and developing theory of human learning. Ausubel (1970) has proposed a learning theory partially based upon the concept of advanced mental organizers which has altered the understanding of readiness and has influenced selection of content and sequencing of learning tasks. Bloom (1976) has set forth propositions he refers to as mastery learning, including the simple, but empirically substantiated, concept of time-on-task. Learning styles have been linked to teaching styles in assessing why many normal youngsters are not learning effectively in school. These interrelationships were probably first meaningfully analyzed by Gage (1964), who took psychology to task for producing learning theory which could not be translated into teaching theory. Joyce and Weil (1972) examined paradigms of teaching from a sound psychological base of learning theory. Their work was predated by a highly useful volume *Conceptual Models in Teacher Education: An Approach to Teaching and Learning* (Verduin 1967). Knowles's (1978) noteworthy work distinguished characteristics of adult learning and led to changes in school-connected programs for adult learners. This brief notation of knowledge growth within just one area of educational administration indicates the need for serious, concentrated study for those who aspire to become administrators.

Current Emphases and Future Directions

The history of educational administration can be characterized as having identifiable periods in which practice is strongly influenced by a dominant perspective. Goodlad (1978) described three such periods. He labeled the first charismatic-autocratic; it was replaced by an emphasis upon technical-managerial principles; in its turn, the second is now being replaced by a pragmatic, school-based leadership approach. Button (1966) described five distinct "doctrines" of educational administration. He concluded that the current period is one marked by the application of behavioral science concepts, and he expressed the view that "the next doctrine of administration will be indigenous." He believed that this doctrine would probably be built upon "knowledge of schools and administration and of educational policy." Both Goodlad and Button see, with good reason, a shift in emphasis in educational administration now occurring.

Beginning in the 1970s and continuing with increasing frequency into the current decade, practitioners and scholars in education have voiced concern about the locus and the methodologies of inquiry in education, particularly in educational administration. The logical-positivistic, empirical approaches have produced abstract concepts which have too little meaning in specific situations. Inquiry has been guided mainly by concepts adopted from the behavioral sciences. Denton (1970) was one of the first to question the dominant research paradigm in educational administration. He argued that the knowledge needed could only be obtained through intensive study of individuals in terms of ordinary experience using ordinary language. He sought a phenomenological approach rather than a positivistic approach. To use "ordinary" terms read *positivistic* as: "empirical, controlled, experiential, theory-based, and quantitative"; read *phenomenological* as: "clinical, field-based, experiential, process-focused, naturalistic, and qualitative."

The phenomenological approach to the study of educational administration has surfaced in several ways. Eisner (1979) treats the design of educational programs using methodologies of art criticism because he maintains that teaching is more an art than a science. Guba and Lincoln (1981) produced a book on naturalistic approaches to program evaluation and these authors deal with a variety of phenomenological methods arguing that such methods provide more useful results. In educational administration, Griffiths (1979, 41–62) cites studies which indicate the uniqueness of schools and institutions of higher education and then concludes, "New theories are likely to be highly specific and focused on particular types of organizations. The search for a general theory of administration will be long delayed" (Griffiths, 58).

There is reason to believe as Button proposes, that the study of educational administration will become more indigenous. There is also reason to believe that the study will become more naturalistic. A part of the argument hinges upon the fact that competent inquiry and appropriate methods for naturalistic inquiry in education are developing. There should no longer be the need to base research in educational administration purely upon behavioral science research, although those sciences and educational administration will continue a mutual interest in constructs and methodologies. The substance and focus of inquiry, however, will alter substantially.

In addition, there is evidence that some unpredictable conditions in the applied sciences complicate scientific inquiry in educational administration. Cronbach reminds us that "generalizations decay. At one time a conclusion describes the existing situation well, at a later time accounts for rather little variance and ultimately it is valid only as history. . . .The more open a system, the shorter the half-life of relations within it are likely to be" (1975, 122).

From studies in information processing, McNabb (1983) provides evidence that information from one domain is difficult to translate and apply in another. Likewise, he gives further support for Cronbach's observation; for there seems to be a language-like structure to patterns of perception and interpretation so that conditions are never perceivable currently in the same way intended in the original description. Apparently educational administration will need to find its own directions, constantly updating and recodifying its knowledge base.

Administrators and Administrative Careers

Considerable information is available about those who serve as school administrators. A statistical profile can be drawn showing sex, age, training, experience, tenure, salary, attitudes, and problems encountered on the job. Yet principals and superintendents from urban, suburban, and rural areas have different characteristics. Administrators, with the exception of superintendents, do not usually move, either from type and size of school or district, or from one state to another. Futhermore, the number of women (except in middle schools) and minorities in administrative posts is declining: women comprise fewer than 20 percent of the elementary principals, fewer than 7 percent of the high school principals, and fewer than 2 percent of superintendents. The minorities fare even less well. However, each school and school district is different and a significant number of individuals do deviate from the norm. Therefore, in this section, we shall concentrate on career routes, opportunities for administrative careers and career planning for the individual, drawing a verbal rather than statistical picture.

Career Opportunities and Career Routes

The field of educational administration is varied and fluid. There are opportunities in every setting: in public and private schools, institutions of higher learning, education agencies, and foundations. An increasing number of career administrative posts for educational administrators is becoming available in business and industry, health service fields, churches, and the military. Often, individuals entering educational administration think only of public school administration in the school or district setting unless they already are in church or military service, are nurses or physicians or have engaged in some career study and planning.

One needs to undertake early study of opportunities and qualifications because preparation and experience are necessary for entrée to any particular career route, but they also close entrée to others. For example, the Department of Defense operates a large number of overseas schools for dependents (DoDDS). To be considered for employment in this system public school experience in this country is required. Certain United States Embassies support Cooperative Schools in which up to 50 percent of the enrollment must be from the host country. In a Cooperative School, experience in a U.S. school is not essential, but fluency in the language of the host country is required. The World Health Organization (WHO), the United Nations Educational Scientific, and Cultural Organization (UNESCO), the Institute for International Educational Planning in Paris, the World Bank, and other world agencies have administrative educational posts. United States embassies in countries to which this country supplies aid have education officers and human resource development officers among mission personnel. The list could go on; but the point is that those students of educational administration can deliberately consider options as they plan and manage their careers.

Van Maanen (1979) proposed examining careers in the context of the "career game" metaphor. In this game, there are winners and losers over the span of a career; the outcome is determined by certain rules of "play." "Rules" of the career "game" are created by personnel policies and practices, many being vague, implicit, or changing. Educational organizations within the game have career structures and attempt to manage careers in their interest. The individual "player" attempts to fulfill a career by "playing the game." Often the inability of the individual to construct realistic career plans, cope with family needs and personal conditions, "read" the organization, and prepare adequately for a career leads to confusion, frustration, and an ultimate sense of failure.

Personality variables and career orientations do make a difference. Matches and mismatches occur between personal predispositions and career choices, and between these and the career structures created by organizations. Some reject the criteria of success projected by organizations. Some feel a career is essentially a private concern, not to be examined with colleagues. Some, because of non job-related circumstances or by disposition, cannot play the career game. Some never recognize that their careers are a game to be played out with many implicit and few explicit rules. Some decide how they want their careers to develop, study the "rules" as best they can, and go about the career game quite deliberately. A career in educational administration is not as standardized and simplistic as might first be assumed.

Career Maps and Career Anchors

Career routes can be charted so that qualifications and opportunities for entry and exit along the route can be "mapped." We know that, in 1980, over 80 percent of all high school principals were appointed to their first principalship from the position of assistant principal. More than three-fourths of these appointments occurred between the ages of thirty-two and thirty-nine years. Ninety-nine percent had teaching experience, two-thirds in the district in which they received their appointment as assistant principal. Seventy-two percent had major preparation in educational administration beyond the master's degree (Byrne, Hines, and McCleary 1978). The mapping of a career route into or through the principalship would certainly require this minimal kind of information.

Certain constructs provide assistance in mapping careers. Roth (1963) suggested the idea of a timetable stretching into the future, divided into blocks of varying time lengths. An individual can measure progress through time blocks in terms of a reference group; that is, in terms of what is typical for administrators in a certain district or for administrators in general, as noted above. Rate of success and timing of moves can be judged with more assurance using Roth's construct. Graves, Dalton, and Thompson (1980) use the contract of career compartments. Here the concept of career is seen as sets of compartments, sequentially arranged. Entrance to or exit from each compartment requires specific qualifications and preparation, as well as "fit" in terms of organizational opportunities and interests.

Career mapping requires a knowledge of self, including an understanding of strengths and weaknesses, work values and attitudes, and self-perceived needs. Schein (1978) coined the term "career anchors" after studying career decisions of various groups. This career anchor is the set of driving or constraining forces in career decisions, serving to guide and stabilize the person and integrate the person's career. It is formed in real work experiences through encounters with superiors, peers, and through the work itself. Schein found such career anchors as: job security and need for long-term stability; autonomy and freedom from close supervision; service and self-fulfillment in helping others; technical-functional proficiency, and satisfaction of doing a good job; variety, and avoidance of routine; and the need for control and influence over others. The ability to recognize and accept career anchors is necessary to avoid self-deception and ultimate frustration.

Career Planning

Career anchors, career mapping, and career gaming may be of use to the individual in career planning. Mismatches of individual abilities, needs, and aspirations on the one hand and job opportunities or requirements, on the other, do occur in educational administration. When careers in education typically span periods of more than thirty years, it is tragic to discover how few give attention to or understand the rudiments of career planning. Lyons and McCleary (1980) applied the constructs noted here to study principals, using data from the United States, Great Britain, the Middle East, and Latin America. The similarities were remarkable. They found a large number who had prepared for careers in education and met requirements for licenses, but without any hope of placement. Of those who were principals, fewer than 20 percent had any semblance of a career map or plan. Most had acquired their first position and after a time, had begun to perceive that other opportunities might exist. Many were already locked in a career compartment which, for them, had no exit. The self-selecting nature of education requires that those who successfully pursue careers in it engage in career planning, locate mentors who can be helpful, and make realistic career choices. Opportunity is clearly present in the field of educational administration, but only for those who are prepared to grasp it when it appears.

References

Abbott, Max G. 1974. "Administrative Performance in the School Principalship: A Synthesis." In *Performance Objectives for School Principals*, edited by Jack Culbertson. Berkeley, Calif.: McCutchan.

American Association of School Administrators. 1981. *The Administrative Team Series.* Books 1, 2, 3, 4. Arlington, Va.: The Association.

Argyris, Chris. 1973. "Personality and Organizational Theory Revisited." *Administrative Science Quarterly* 18(2): 141-67.

Ausubel, David P. 1970. "The Use of Advanced Organizers in the Learning and Retention of Meaningful Verbal Material." *Journal of Educational Psychology* 51(5): 267-72.

Barnard, Chester I. 1938. *The Functions of the Executive.* Cambridge: Harvard University Press.

Berman, Paul, and Milbrey W. McLaughlin. 1975. *Federal Programs Supporting Educational Change.* Vol. 4. Santa Monica, Calif.: The Rand Corp.

Bloom, Benjamin S. 1976. *Human Characteristics and School Learning.* New York: McGraw-Hill.

Button, H. W. 1966. "Doctrines of Educational Administration." *Educational Administration Quarterly* 2 (Autumn): 216-24.

Byrne, David R., Susan A. Hines, and Lloyd E. McCleary. 1978. *The Senior High School Principalship.* Vol. 1: *The National Survey.* Reston, Va.: National Association of Secondary School Principals.

Corey, Stephen M. 1953. *Action Research to Improve School Practices.* New York: Teachers College of Columbia University.

Cronbach, Lee J. 1975. "Beyond the Two Disciplines of Scientific Psychology. *American Psychologist* 30 (February): 116-27.

Denton, David E. 1970. *The Language of Ordinary Experience.* New York: Philosophical Library.

Dewey, John. 1938. *Experience and Education.* New York: Macmillan.

Eisner, Elliot W. 1979. *The Educational Imagination: On the Design and Evaluation of School Programs.* New York: Macmillan.

Erickson, Kenneth A. 1977. *School Management Teams.* Arlington, Va.: Education Research Institute.

Fayol, Henri. [1916] 1949. *General and Industrial Management.* Trans. Constance Stores. London: Sir Isaac Pitman and Sons.

Fiedler, Fred E. 1967. *A Theory of Leader Effectiveness.* New York: McGraw-Hill.

Fiedler, Fred E., Martin M. Chemers, and **Linda Mahar.** 1976. *Improving Leadership Effectiveness.* New York: John Wiley and Sons.

Gage, N. L. 1964. "Theories of Learning," in *Theories of Learning and Instruction*, edited by E. R. Hilgard, 268–85. Chicago: National Society for the Study of Education.

Grant, H. L. 1919. *Organizing for Work.* New York: Harcourt, Brace and Rowe.

Goodlad, John. 1975. *Dynamics of Educational Change: Toward Responsive Schools.* New York: McGraw-Hill.

————. 1978. "Educational Leadership: Toward the Third Era." *Educational Leadership* 35 (January): 322–31.

Graves, Peter J., Gene W. Dalton, and **Paul H. Thompson.** 1980. "Career Stages in Organizations." In *Work, Family, and the Career*, edited by Brooklyn C. Derr. New York: Praeger.

Griffiths, Daniel E. 1958. "Administration as Decision-Making." In *Administrative Theory in Education*, edited by Andrew Halpin, 119–49. Chicago: Midwest Administration Center, The University of Chicago.

————. 1979. "Another Look at Research on the Behavior of Administrators." In *Problem-Finding in Educational Administration*, edited by Glenn L. Immegart and William Lowe Boyd. Lexington, Mass.: Lexington Books, D.C. Heath and Co.

Guba, Egon G., and **Yvonna S. Lincoln.** 1981. *Effective Evaluation.* San Francisco: Jossey-Bass.

Hage, Jerald. 1965. "An Axiomatic Theory of Organizations." *Administrative Science Quarterly* 10 (December): 289–320.

Hannaway, Jane, and **Lee S. Sproul.** 1979. "Who's Running the Show? Coordination and Control in Educational Organizations." *Administrator's Notebook* 27:9.

Havelock, Ronald F. 1973. *The Change Agent's Guide to Innovation in Education.* Englewood Cliffs, N.J.: Educational Technology Publications.

Herzberg, F. 1966. *Work and the Nature of Man.* Cleveland: World Publishing.

Joyce, Bruce, and **Marsha Weil.** 1972. *Models of Teaching.* Englewood Cliffs, N.J.: Prentice-Hall.

Kirst, Michael. 1970. *The Politics of Education.* Berkeley, Calif.: McCutchan.

Knowles, Malcolm S. 1978. *The Adult Learner: A Neglected Species.* Houston: Guld Publishing Co.

Lipham, James M., and **James A. Hoeh, Jr.** 1974. *The Principalship: Foundations and Functions.* New York: Harper and Row.

Litchfield, Edward H. 1956. "Notes on a General Theory of Administration." *Administrative Science Quarterly* 1 (June): 3-29.

Lortie, Dan. 1976. *Schoolteacher.* Chicago: University of Chicago Press.

Lyons, Geoffery, and **Lloyd McCleary.** 1980. "Careers in Teaching." In *World Yearbook of Education.* Edited by Eric Hoyle, Jacquetta Megarry, and Myron Atkin. London: Kogan Page; New York: Nichols Publishing.

McCleary, Lloyd E., and Scott D. Thomson. 1979. *The Senior High School Principalship*. Vol. 3: *The Summary Report*. Reston, Va.: National Association of Secondary School Principals.

McFarland, D. E. 1974. *Management: Functions and Practices*. New York: Macmillan.

McGregor, Douglas. 1960. *The Human Side of Enterprise*. New York: McGraw-Hill.

McNabb, Willis J., II. 1983. "Experts and Novices: A Framework for Understanding Information Processing." Unpublished Research Paper, The University of Utah.

March, James G. 1978. "American Public School Administration: A Short Analysis." *School Review* 86 (February): 243.

Maslow, H. H. 1954. *Motivation and Personality*. New York: Harper and Brothers.

Metcalf, Henry C., and L. Urwick, editors 1940. *Dynamic Administration: The Collected Papers of Mary Parker Follett*. New York: Harper and Brothers.

Meyer, John W., and Brian Rowan. 1977. "Formal Organizations as Myth and Ceremony." *American Journal of Sociology* 83 (September): 340–63.

Miles, Matthew B., ed. 1964. *Innovation in Education*. New York: Teachers College of Columbia University.

Moore, Hollis A. 1964. "The Ferment in School Administration." In *Behavioral Science and Educational Administration*. Chicago: National Society for the Study of Education.

Parsons, Talcott, and Gerald Pratt. 1975. *The American University*. Cambridge: Harvard University Press.

Roethlisberger, Fritz J., and William J. Dickson. 1939. *Management and the Worker*. Cambridge: Harvard University Press.

Roth, J. 1963. *Timetables: Structuring the Passage of Time in Careers*. Indianapolis: Bobbs-Merrill.

Schein, E. H. 1978. *Career Dynamics: Matching Individual and Organizational Needs*. Reading, Mass.: Addison-Wesley.

Schmuck, Richard A. 1977. *The Second Handbook of Organizational Development in Schools*. Palo Alto, Calif.: Mayfield Publishing.

Simon, Herbert A. [1945] 1965. *Administrative Behavior*. 2nd ed. New York: Free Press.

Stogdill, Ralph. 1963. *Manual for the Leader Behavior Description Questionnaire*. Columbus, Ohio: Bureau of Business Research.

Taylor, Frederick W. 1914. *The Principles of Scientific Management*. New York: Harper and Brothers.

Thompson, James. 1956. "Editorial." *Administrative Science Quarterly*. 1:1

Van Maanen, J. 1979. "The Self, the Situation, and the Rules of Interpersonal Relations." In *Essays in Interpersonal Dynamics*, edited by W. Bennis et al. Homewood, Ill.: Dorsey.

Verduin, John R., Jr. 1967. *Conceptual Models in Teacher Education*. Washington, D.C.: The American Association of Colleges for Teacher Education.

Weick, Karl. 1976. "Educational Organizations as Loosely Coupled Systems." *Administrative Science Quarterly* 21 (March): 1–19.

Whitehead, Alfred N. 1933. *Adventures of Ideas*. New York: Macmillan.

Wynn, Richard. 1976. *Theory and Practice of the Administrative Team*. Arlington, Va.: National Association of Elementary School Principals.

2

Politics and Education: Organization, Control, and Policy Making

Education and politics are inextricably related. Since the early colonial period, laws have been passed to encourage, control, and finance education. A variety of motives and interests has caused government, throughout the nation's history, to maintain a special interest in education and to provide a system of public schools. The term "system" of public schools is somewhat of a misnomer; for no single, unified organization exists. Nevertheless, formal education is a primary element promoting individual fulfillment and the well-being of society. This chapter discusses the politics involved in the organization, control, and policy making of the public schools, and, tangentially of the private schools and of higher education.

Organization for Educational Control and Policy Making

In the United States, control of education is exercised at three levels of government: national, state, and local with an intermediate unit in many states. Boards, agencies, and officials whose existence and activities are determined by law and practice at each level comprise formal structures for educational governance.

Federal Roles in Education

Federal influence in educational matters has always existed and will surely continue. It is part of the nation's tradition to engage in activities which tend to:

A. Equalize the disparities among states, particularly in their ability to finance education;
B. Improve conditions that have a national impact, such as assistance to vocational education and education of the handicapped;
C. Reform social conditions and solve problems through education, such as the protection of civil rights;
D. Promote what are perceived to be national goals and priorities; and
E. Provide assistance for problems that are felt to be too difficult or expensive at the state level.

The primary offices involved in policy making and administration at the national level are the President, the Congress, and agencies of the federal bureaucracy, particularly the Department of Education and the Office of Management and Budget. The courts also make policy. The federal government's active involvement in educational matters is of relatively recent origin.

The influence of the federal government upon education during the past two decades has been so powerful and pervasive as to be revolutionary. Basic shifts in political and legal philosophy occurred during this period on such issues as (a) whether education is the exclusive province of the state; (b) whether private schools can be supported in any way by public funds; (c) whether education is to be kept separate from direct involvement in the resolution of social problems and issues; (d) whether wealthy districts may provide for themselves the highest educational levels they are willing to support without concern for equal educational opportunity in less wealthy districts; and (e) whether education should become a primary instrument in attaining national purposes. Since 1965 a dramatic shift has occurred with reference to each item, with one exception. That exception is embodied in the National Defense Education Act (NDEA), which went into effect even earlier, in 1958. The NDEA provided for distribution of large sums by the federal government to support science, mathematics, and foreign language instruction. This aid was openly promoted as the means to counter a presumed threat by the Soviet Union due to deficiencies in scientific-technological, engineering, and language fields in this country.

The history of the U.S. Office of Education (USOE), now the Department of Education, reveals the rapid transformation in political philosophy and action at the national level. The Bureau of Education was established in 1867, and for almost ninety years functioned as an autonomous, low-key agency, first in the Department of the Interior, and, after 1939, in the Federal Security Agency. In 1953, through the efforts of the Hoover Commission, USOE became, under the changed title, a major branch of a new Department of Health, Education, and Welfare (HEW). At that time the Office of Education was staffed by just over three hundred people with a budget slightly in excess of $40 million. Its major responsibilities included collecting and disseminating information, coordinating education-related relief programs, promoting vocational education, welcoming foreign visitors, and supporting land-grant colleges. Although nine other bureaus and agencies conducted programs affecting education, such as the Department of Agriculture's "hot lunch" program and the National Science Foundation's research effort, these programs, like USOE's, did not serve to alter federal-state-local relationships. No influence was exercised regarding goals, programs, organizational patterns, or functions of the public schools.

With the exception of the 1958 National Defense Education Act, noted previously, no major changes seemed possible. President Kennedy's proposals for federal aid to education ended in disaster due to religious and racial issues and the political implications of federal involvement in education. In 1965, the enactment of the Elementary and Secondary Education Act (ESEA) changed all this when President Johnson made the improvement of education and the elimination of poverty the two central features of his "Great Society" program. The entire climate of national influence altered under the leadership of a series of able USOE Commissioners, the President, White House staff, and key members of Congress supported by a host of opinion leaders across the country.

ESEA was composed of five titles. Title I provided a formula for passing grants through states to local districts based upon indices related to the number of school-age children in families below the poverty level. Title II authorized grants for library resources, textbooks, and instructional materials allocated on the basis of the number of children enrolled in public and *private* elementary and secondary schools. Title III provided for supplementary educational services and centers. These could focus on a variety of activities: special courses, experimental teaching, remedial and vocational instruction, and guidance services. Participation was required from nonprofit private schools, libraries, and other community agencies. The significant factor, however, was that local districts submitted applications directly to the U.S. Office of Education. Title IV provided support for research, development, and dissemination of innovations. Title V provided funds for strengthening state education agencies. ESEA reached every school district directly through USOE, breached the church-state issues, avoided serious objections of the segregationists even as it aided children of minority groups, and smoothed conflicts with state agencies over state control of education.

ESEA, at one stroke, established USOE and the executive branch as a major center of power in determining educational policy throughout the country. It was a revolutionary piece of legislation marking a significant turn in Federal-state-local relationships. A former commissioner in a recent private conversation stated that even now another ten years of major political activity will be devoted to clarifying the limits of federal power and control initiated by ESEA. These efforts are likely to produce extended appraisal of revenue sharing, block, and general funding (as opposed to categorical funding), because wealth is a significant source of power in politics.

Experience gained at the federal level with the implementation of ESEA brought about a number of innovative mechanisms of control. First, Congress and the federal agencies began to use legislation for purposes of reform, as exemplified by Public Law 92-318 (Title IX) of 1972 which is aimed at ending sex discrimination in the schools and colleges. The act itself, on two printed pages, is quite general; however, the code of regulations is extensive, detailed, and prescriptive. Any regulation in the code, unless later specifically amended or overturned in the courts, has the force of law. Federal agencies prescribe policy in detail, and in the case of Title IX, legal provision was made to cover all educational institutions whether federal money was accepted or not. This latter tactic was employed partly because some universities and school districts were opting not to accept federal funding.

In addition to using legislation for reform purposes, federal law has successively introduced tighter requirements, including assurance of lay control of a specified kind. In the case of vocational programs, Public Law 94-482, Title II, Educational Amendments of 1976 prescribes a special state board for vocational education. The membership of this board is required to include one or more individuals from twenty specified categories. Appropriate representation of both sexes, racial and ethnic minorities, and the geographical sections of the state must be certified to the Secretary of Education. The board must not have more than 50 percent of its members from the professional ranks of teachers or administrators. The state board for vocational education has prescribed duties, one of which is to prepare a five-year plan with the active involvement of representatives to be chosen by groups with a specific interest in vocational education. The board must meet four times per year and the items to be considered by the board are prescribed. Detailed directions are given for an annual plan, evaluation, and publication of program evaluations as well as reporting of information to the National Center for Educational Statistics.

P.L. 94-142, enacted in 1975 with full compliance required by 1978, was even more detailed and prescriptive in terms of an individualized educational plan (IEP) for each handicapped child, opportunity for an independent educational evaluation, provision for an impartial due process hearing if requested by the parent or an agency, specific plans containing goals and descriptions of facilities, and personnel and services to meet specified handicapping conditions. As with vocational education, a state plan and state advisory panel are required; and states must conduct program audits of local districts and issue notices where noncompliance is found.

As indicated by this brief description, federal controls are exercised through laws and regulations. This form of control has been refined to include detailed prescription of school programs, services, record keeping, and reporting and use of nonschool specialists at district expense. Laws dealing with education require compliance whether or not federal funds are accepted. Funds made available in categorical grants, can be used only for specified purposes, and states and local districts must comply with highly detailed sets of requirements. In many cases districts must divert funds from other uses in order to administer and staff programs and to meet requirements fully. Thus, state and local discretion in education is sometimes reduced when federally funded programs are involved.

The enactment of prescriptive legislation, detailed regulation by agencies, and categorical funding are not the only means of federal control. Federal action also has created regional resource centers organized specifically to promote federal programs through a variety of services and training programs. Federal regulations contain specific requirements for pre-service and in-service education of teachers.

Note that no evaluation of programs is undertaken here. Whether these programs are meeting educational needs, whether they are effective and whether there are other needs of greater importance must be addressed elsewhere. This discussion describes the nature of federal-state-local relationships, the evolution of federal controls and their effects in education, and the nature of policy-making at the national level. Politics, as the exercise of power through policy-making and policy implementation, produces effects because of the substantial programs provided. However, programs also are used to initiate controls and alter power relationships between levels of government, as is the case in recent education policy-making at the national level.

State Government and Education

State decision-making structures are quite similar to those of the federal government. There are, however, fundamental differences in the manner in which they function relative to education. Although constitutional powers are different, a governor holds a position very much like that of the President. A governor usually can determine the principal legislation to be considered or can obtain a full hearing of counterproposals. A governor's influence over his own political party is probably greater than the President's over his, and a governor can exercise greater influence over members of the legislature than can the President over members of Congress. Unlike the Congress, state legislatures have, by constitutional authority with few limitations, plenary power to determine matters of basic educational policy. The execution of such policy is the responsibility of the governor.

States, with the exception of Hawaii, have chosen to operate schools through local districts governed by local boards of education, with a superintendent as chief executive officer. This arrangement, along with the establishment of state boards of education and state education agencies, provides a special and to some extent separate, governing structure for education as opposed to general state and local government. The education agency is unique among state agencies. First, its responsibility is exclusively that of education. Second, the agency includes a board or commission with delegated powers of its own and a chief executive (state superintendent, commissioner, or secretary) who is the administrative officer of the agency. Third, it is comprehensive in function, dealing with all aspects of education on a state-wide basis. Other state agencies, for example the planning and budgeting unit, the auditor's office, or the legislative analyst's office, have major governmental responsibilities with reference to education and often employ education specialists. Yet such agencies have the same general responsibilities for all government activities of the state as they have for education.

Though educational policy is in the hands of the legislature, the governor is central to the policy-making process. The chief state school officer is required to submit a budget proposal to the governor; but neither the governor nor the legislature is under any constraint to accept it. Programs and policy proposals developed by the education agency and approved by the state board for submission to the legislature are unlikely to be accepted without the governor's support. The governor is key to bargaining among advocates, for various organized interests. Moreover, except for the level of financial support, consideration of educational matters is likely to be undertaken quite separately from other issues. In most cases, policy decisions made at the state level have all the elements of political bargaining carried out among interest groups with established positions. The relative strengths of the interest groups and the positions of the political actors are relatively well-known, and the determination of policy issues is much more predictable than it is at the federal level.

The dynamics of interest groups and the power structures of a state in terms of policy-making for education differ considerably among the states. In a study for the Center for Applied Research in Education, Iannacone (1971) developed a typology for classifying power structures. These might best be referred to as the mechanisms through which political influence tends to be structured at the state level in order to bargain about educational issues. Iannacone identified four types: (a) statewide syndical, (b) statewide fragmented, (c) statewide monolithic, and (d) locally based, disparate. The *statewide syndical* structure is a statewide coalition usually organized formally to serve as a forum for debate and an open hearing of interest group proposals. The Illinois School Problems Commission is an example; here spokesmen of major groups with interests in education, key state legislators, and education specialists meet to study educational issues. The *statewide fragmented* type represents a situation in which competing groups either form coalitions or fight each other, depending upon issues and interests. Michigan has been identified as representing this type. *Statewide monolithic* structure represents a situation dominated by a tightly organized coalition or a single powerful group. Texas, New York, and New Jersey have been identified in various studies as being of this type. Finally, a *locally based, disparate* type exists in which fiercely independent local districts and interest groups join to achieve state political action, but only when faced with extremely pressing conditions. Utah, Vermont, and Massachusetts have been identified as representing this type.

Interest groups often join to create centers of influence to alter educational goals, determine levels of funding and funding formulas, or decide specific programs. Their proposals are made to various parts of the decision-making structure, depending on where they believe they will receive the most responsive support. In an early study Starkey (1966) examined in detail educational policy-making in Texas. He found a statewide monolithic structure in which leaders in the governor's office conferring with legislators and key agency heads determined the legislative program for education. When a degree of consensus was reached, certain members of the legislature introduced the measures agreed upon, and could get them passed. In this case very little public involvement was permitted, and education was cast as a nonpolitical, nonpartisan arena of state governmental activity.

Advocates of interest groups and centers of influence for education must deal with other centers of influence in a given state. These include business interests, farm groups, media, realtors, developers, coalitions, utilities, medical organizations, or union and trade groups. The astute observer can follow issues through the decision and obtain a reasonably accurate perception of how policy is made. Decisions at the state and local levels are achieved in terms of conflict-accommodation in win-lose strategies, bargaining and compromise, consensus building and adaptation, or by accident and drift.

The role of state government in education is receiving increased attention. States have become active in countering what is viewed by some as intrusion by the federal government. In this regard the concept of federalism appears to have been altered to what Campbell and his associates refer to as a national-federalism (Campbell et al. 1980, 22–24). A complex balance between local initiative and national influence is maintained—or sometimes not maintained—by the manner in which decisions are made at the state level (McCleary 1976).

Serious funding problems provide a primary reason for increased attention to education at the state level. In most states, education accounts for more than 50 percent of the state budget, and the costs of education have risen sharply in relation to general productivity. As a result, political figures have become very concerned lest education remain shielded from budget and other constraints that are imposed upon general state government. Other factors affect the political arena surrounding education. These include public concern for quality and a push for accountability, the increasing power of teacher organizations, and an increased activity of special interest groups. These conditions have heightened state level political activity concerning education.

Intermediate Units of Educational Governance

At this writing thirty-five states have some form of intermediate governing unit between state and local government. In the New England states, supervisory unions promote cooperative action of local districts. New York, a leader in shaping the intermediate unit into a service-centered organization, has created Boards of Cooperative Service Units (BOCSU). Minnesota and Wisconsin have well-established intermediate units of the New York type. In the Midwest, and to some extent in the West, a county office of education with a county superintendent serves primarily as an arm of the state agency and directly oversees schools in unincorporated and rural areas to provide mandated services. Large cities, such as Chicago, have subdistricts within the total system. In the South and in a few Western states, the county is the basic operating unit of school government.

Kansas has eliminated its intermediate units; other states have altered or are in the process of altering them substantially. Iowa created the Joint County School Systems, and Nebraska retained its county offices but created nineteen regional service units. Georgia, Florida, Virginia, Minnesota, and Texas have reorganized their intermediate structures within the past ten years as educational service centers. The intermediate unit is evolving to provide services which individual districts alone would find too costly or inefficient.

Local District and Local Governance of Education

Special constitutional and statutory provisions of each state establish unique local governance structures of public education, again excepting

Hawaii. Local districts are created with the power to tax (although some local districts are fiscally dependent upon the state), build schools, appoint teachers and administrators, institute programs of instruction, decide which pupils attend which schools, and take charge of other matters both mandatory and discretionary. Mandatory powers are those duties and responsibilities that boards are required to perform. Discretionary powers are those acts a board may choose to perform such as providing programs or services beyond the requirements prescribed by state statute.

Courts frequently have ruled on the limits of school board authority and generally have agreed that the powers of local boards are: (a) those expressly conferred by state statute; (b) those implied in the powers granted by state statute; and (c) those essential to the accomplishment of the objectives of the district corporation (Campbell et al. 1980, 189). Campbell and his associates point out that with powers go obligations. Boards have the power to employ teachers; but they are obliged to hire teachers certified by the state. They can build schools; but the buildings must meet safety codes, etc.

Schools are governed by their own locally elected, or appointed, representatives. Some schools are fiscally independent. Many have boundaries that are not coterminous with those of other units of local government. Consequently, education has its own political domain apart from the rest of local government. This point of uniqueness often creates problems of coexistence because education relates to the same group of citizens and competes with general government for tax dollars and special considerations.

The state-local relationship is unique, but this uniqueness is often not well understood. Even school administrators and board members are in the habit of pointing to the local district as having a relationship to the state that is analogous to the state's relationship with the federal government. If this were so, states could not abolish or alter the boundaries of local districts or remove local boards of education, as they rather frequently do. Many chartered cities are free of state control in the provision of services such as sanitation, police and fire protection, and building and maintaining streets. School districts do not have this freedom.

Administration of the school districts is vested in a superintendent who serves at the pleasure of the local board of education. The position is universally prescribed by state statute as both chief administrative officer of the school district and professional advisor to the board of education. (Chapter 3 gives the specific duties and responsibilities of the superintendent, and describes the evolution of the office.) However, the office is a changing one with the relationship of the superintendent to the board of education under constant examination and definition. The relationship is complicated by several conditions.

First, the superintendent is recognized as the representative of the profession and the key professional spokesman to the board and hence to the community. At the same time, the superintendent is required to serve the board in carrying out its wishes and mandates. Differences over program priorities, student treatment, educational services, and a host of other matters can easily place the superintendent in situations of appearing to compromise an important professional issue or of inadequately carrying out board policy.

Second, the superintendent as the administrative officer of the district may find the board of education prescribing administrative procedures or even taking administrative actions. The line between administrative prerogative and board responsibility is easily crossed and can lead to serious disruption of educational practices. Ideally, the board of education makes educational policy and the superintendent carries out board policy in terms of best professional practice. The ideal, however, is often difficult to achieve in a specific practice.

Third, the political character of policy-making often places the superintendent in the center of conflict either as the advocate of a particular course of action or as a mediator between contending factions. When a board becomes sharply divided over an issue, the superintendent can be placed in an untenable position. Many cases occur in which the superintendent's tenure in office becomes a matter of controversy within a board as a result of board division over policy.

The role of superintendent is critical to the stability of schools and to continuous improvement of education. Technical-managerial skills are important to sound administration, but professional leadership and policy-making skills are central to the superintendent's effectiveness.

The Court and Education

The judicial process is generally regarded as the last recourse in resolving conflicts and redressing injustices. In periods of rapid social change, groups and individuals who see themselves as being unfairly treated and unable to obtain redress through the political process have resorted to the courts. As the discussion of educational politics later in this chapter indicates those with strong feelings about educational issues may readily turn to the legal system when they are unable to achieve their ends more directly. Because of an increasing disposition to seek legal redress over educational matters, the courts, both state and federal, have become a significant and growing influence in education.

At both the state and federal levels, hierarchical systems of courts exist, and these systems may overlap. All states have courts of original jurisdiction, which conduct trials and hearings in which witnesses are called and evidence is collected. Most states have special courts of original jurisdiction as well, which deal with juveniles and probate matters. A second level, appellate courts, currently exists in only twenty-three states. These consider only cases appealed from lower courts. At the third level is a supreme court, or court of final appeal. Appellate courts only review the records of courts of original jurisdiction and usually restrict themselves only to points of appeal. Higher courts may uphold or reverse a lower court decision, or they may remand a case for further hearing by the lower court.

The federal courts have been called to deal with questions of segregation, unequal financing of schools, individual rights, and other matters arising in the schools. In carrying out their authority the courts have employed three concepts: *fundamental interest, strict scrutiny*, and *suspect classification*. (For a fuller explanation of these concepts see Chapters 8 and 9, pages (164-207.) The latter two concepts, in particular, have provided the courts the grounds to order busing, redraw school attendance boundaries, reinstate suspended students, remove boards of education, and directly involve the courts in the operation of schools. To gain an understanding of the conditions involved in a case and to ensure the enforcement of its findings, courts have gone well beyond normal court procedures of hearing pleas, taking evidence, and requesting testimony of expert witnesses. They have appointed advisory bodies, court experts as special consultants, and special masters. The latter serves as monitors of court orders by observing and supervising school operations.

Courts clearly have engaged in policy-making for education and have mandated specific plans for specific districts to carry out decisions made. The effect of court decisions and the legal actions which are likely to involve school administrators make school law a necessary branch of special study. Legal aspects of education are treated in subsequent chapters.

Politics and Policy Making in Education

Politics involves the activities and relationships of groups resulting in, or intended to result in, decisions of any governmental body. Politics also involves legal and quasi-legal influences directed at officials to effect policy changes or to affect the way in which policy is carried out. In making educational decisions, particularly policy decisions, groups external to the formal structure are always present attempting to achieve their goals through governmental action. Some of these groups are relatively permanent, as with parent-teacher associations, taxpayer associations, and teacher organizations. Some are less permanent, temporarily forming in terms of a condition such as a school closing or a single issue such as busing or sex education. In this light, politics can be defined as the formation and actions of coalitions (groups) whose aim is to influence which values (goals) will be implemented by government (structures).

Policy and Decision Making

Decisions relating to the governance of education have been studied through close observation of sequences of activities in reaching a particular decision, noting "actors", interactions, positions taken, and points of significant changes in proposals and outcomes. Generally in major policy situations, several governmental structures operate simultaneously, often partially or completely independent of each other. Interest groups are never equal in influence, because of differences in leadership, social status, or access to communications. Groups, therefore, tend to direct their appeals to the part of the structure most likely to be responsive to their needs. Furthermore, no goal is likely to have such overwhelming support that it can be realized in its original form. These three factors—variation in the governance structure, differentials in the influence of groups and coalitions, and the necessity to negotiate goals—characterize the political process as it applies to education.

Politics functions as a major sphere of decision-making in education. With the exception of certain judicial rulings, politics is the exclusive means of formulating and enforcing educational policy decisions.

Policy is the statement of an official decision that guides the making of other decisions. At the district level, school boards enact policy resolutions, for example, that teachers shall receive a formal evaluation based on classroom visitations by principals and district subject specialists. At the state level, the state school board, or the legislature, might enact a policy resolution requiring that the state superintendent establish audits of educational programs prescribed by state law and certify compliance to certain criteria. At the federal level, acts are written to guide officials in their implementation of policy.

Campbell (1960) proposed and expanded upon a Flow Chart of Policy-Making in Education which contains the following elements:

> I. Education policy results from. . . II. Basic social, economic, political and technological forces, often national and world-wide in scope, which produce . . . III. Political activity, extralegal in nature. Many groups debate and school leaders exert influence. These activities, usually interrelated at local, state and national levels, culminate in . . . IV. Formal, legal expression of policy which represents the value choices of influentials who participated in the process. (p. 73)

This four-part statement provides a first approximation of complex sets of processes, which differ considerably at each governmental level and often for each policy issue, but which do contain these general elements.

Organization and Control in Policy Formulation

Organization in formulating policy refers to the structure of interrelationships, including formal organizations at the three levels of government, which interact regarding any policy issue. National, state, and local levels of government are composed of a number of independent, semi-autonomous units, all related through a variety of linkages. Arrangements for interchange within these linkages are characterized by constantly shifting patterns of policy-making, resource allocation, and goals, often in a vertically-structured relationship. Local districts must relate to their state education agencies to obtain legal rulings, to clarify policies and guidelines, to communicate problems with state law and agency regulations, and to explore policy changes. State agencies relate to local districts for a variety of reasons, not the least of which is to muster support from superintendents to appear before legislative committees or to confer with aides of the governor on issues of educational policy. State agencies must also maintain linkages with the federal Department of Education and with certain other federal agencies.

On the other hand, sometimes the relationships have a horizontal structure. For example, the district superintendent or his representative, often with the board president, needs to confer with city and county officials. Zoning, health and safety, shared facilities, and financial planning are among the topics which require policy formulation. At the state level the three units most frequently involved in deliberations over educational policy matters are the state education agency, the governor's office, and the heads of key committees of the legislature. Also frequently included are the legislative analyst, state budget director, and the director of planning. However it may be structured, organization for educational policy-making is a loosely coupled, open system. The structure and the relative influence of any part change over time because the policy issues, the "actors" involved, and the opportunities and constraints which come into play also change.

Political Actors and the Exercise of Power

A number of positions exist at each level in the governmental organizations legally constituted to formulate public policy for education. At the district level are a superintendent and a school board; at the state level, a chief state school officer, a state board of education or commission, the governor and leaders in the state legislature; at the national level, the President, the Secretary of Education, and leaders in the Congress. With the exception of the local and state boards of education, each position represents an "office" with an attendant array of assistants and specialists.

A first distinction can be made between political positions (whose occupants are political decision makers in the fullest sense) and administrative positions (whose occupants ostensibly are administrative decision makers). The former office holders are dependent upon election to office, or their tenure depends upon the continuance in office of some elected official. The continuance in office of administrative decision makers usually depends upon the pleasure of an elected board or commission. There is evidence that considerable differences exist between these two groupings, differences which are geno-typical and which have important consequences for educational policy-making.

Dealing first with administrative decision makers at the district level, two predominant views exist concerning the role of the superintendent and, in turn, the role of the board of education in making policy. One view is that those who occupy the office of superintendent have dominated, even usurped, the policy-making function of the board of education and have reduced the board member to a role of "spokesman for the superintendent to the community" (Zeigler and Jennings 1974, 250). Zeigler and Jennings base their position on a study of more than eighty school boards. They even make the assertation from their findings that "school boards should govern or be abolished" (Zeigler and Jennings 1974, 17). In an earlier study, Kerr (1964) concluded that board members are socialized into their role by the superintendent and are thus ineffective in representing the true views of the community. Other studies indicate that the role of board members varies when districts are grouped in terms of type, size, and socio-economic status. In a review of political studies, Kirst (1970) found evidence that educational policy in urban and suburban communities was primarily the result of the influence of educational and other public officials. He also found evidence of strong, controlling boards in small towns and in stable, rural communities. While the number of districts studied and the methodologies used limits the scope of generalizations, evidence tends to support the view that the superintendent is highly influential in educational policy-making.

The second, opposing view is that the superintendent's role has been seriously eroded by a politicizing of education at the local level, by undue external influences and requirements of higher levels of government, and by the militancy of teacher organizations. McCarty and Ramsey (1971) refer to the superintendent as "engulfed" by pressures from all sides, caught in numerous conflicts not of his making, and forced into political coalitions to survive. The McCarty and Ramsey position is supported by a number of observations and pronouncements of superintendents themselves and by their professional association (Maeroff 1974). Often control of policy by the community comes about through replacing the superintendent. A study in California (Iannacone and Lutz 1970) documents how this process tends to occur. A change of any major kind produces conflict over school policies and an eventual change in the composition of the school board, usually with the defeat of one or two incumbent board members. When this or a later change precipitates a change in the control of the board, the superintendent soon departs or is dismissed.

From the limited studies available, one might use the two views as representing extremes, with some situations meeting the conditions of one extreme or the other, but with most situations falling somewhere between. The superintendent and key board members are clearly actors in the political process at the local level. The type and size of a community, the issues and the intensity of political conflict over them, the ability to "read" the community groups accurately, the influence of informal leaders, the degree of responsibility and imagination of the superintendent and key board members, are all important factors in the exercise of power for political decision-making.

At the state level the balance of power among key actors is more clearly evident, but the principles of political involvement remain much the same. Distinguishing between political and administrative decision makers, we see the governor's office functioning in terms of political decision-making, in contrast to the education agency and its chief officer functioning in terms of administrative decision-making. The governor attempts to place educational priorities in a total list including welfare, health, recreation, highways, and other interests backed by influential groups. The governor *tends* to function in terms of economic and social pressures, and programs are cast in those terms. On the other hand, the state chief school officer *tends* to develop educational plans based on expressed needs of local districts and various coalitions of lay and professional groups, some groups being branches of national organizations with attendant interests and support structures.

The political decision makers, including key legislators as well as the governor, base their programs on the legal right to direct public policy and their political support in the state. They work in terms of the economic resources that they can obtain for the programs they support. The administrative decision makers base their programs on an assessment of the needs and the support in their field of interest and the economic resources they can obtain from the legislature and the governor.

At the national level the executive has become the chief source of policy initiatives. The work of Congress is largely devoted to attending to the policy proposals of the President rather than initiating new

policy. The executive branch, through such units as the Department of Education, exercises program initiatives; and through agencies such as the Bureau of Management and Budget, develop recommendations for allocating resources. In the Congress, committee chairs exert considerable influence. Under this arrangement a relatively few members of Congress control specific arenas of policy, including education.

Formulation of policy proposals depends on a system of bargaining among key people within the executive and legislative branches. The bargaining process defines the limits within which action is feasible. Studies of voting patterns indicate that positions of Congressmen conform quite closely to positions of organized groups; these groups, in turn, tend to alter their positions in terms of how Congressmen perceive their constituents will receive proposals. Party influence, perception of the attitude of constituents, and individual conscience seem to be the key elements determining individual votes in Congress. However, individual members of Congress rarely can upset or significantly alter bargains arrived at during committee deliberations.

Those who provide the linkages between policy-making structures are key people. Most policy decisions involve more than one structure, and structures must be related both horizontally and vertically if policy decisions are to be enacted and successfully implemented. Those who provide this liaison represent important communication channels, and the clarity of their political perceptions is as important as the substance of their proposals. They are much more than communication channels, however, because they modify and test proposals as described earlier. Frequently they are the creators as well as the arbitrators in policy-making.

The activities and relationships of key actors make policy-making a difficult process to describe. For relationships of key actors are never static; new ones are constantly being established; older ones change in character. Relationships are particularistic, dependent upon personalities, specific problems and issues, and the particular times and settings. Nevertheless, activities and relationships are, to some extent observable. Activities and relationships take on patterns, such as frequency of contacts, content of communications, flow of influence, and even psychological characteristics of openness to closeness or hostility to freindliness. It is in relation to communication patterns and their characteristics that one can observe and predict the policy-making behavior of key actors.

Institutions as Instruments of Policy Decisions

Policy is intended to shape the nature of educational institutions by prescribing goals and functions, allocating human and fiscal resources, establishing expectations for output, and controlling treatments and activities. Policy has prescribed what subjects may and may not be taught; what programs may be offered; who is to be included and who may be excluded from schools; how educational treatments for special students are to be prescribed; what qualifications teachers and administrators must have; and a host of other matters. Practices in schools are expected to reflect the content and the intent of policies.

Several conditions characterizing public education determine how effectively a policy operates at the institutional level. To a large extent, the policy and the policy-making process are principal determinants of its execution. Policy may be judged in terms of the possibilities available to achieve its intended effects. Numerous examples are available of state legislatures passing statutes requiring such things as the teaching of the Constitution, the ill effects of drugs and alcohol, and the free enterprise system. Whether better citizenship, improved health or an appreciation and understanding of the economic system resulted from enactment of such legislation is debatable. Policy-making, by the processes used and structures employed, may create opposition resulting in conflict and resistance, which subvert intended results and may create undesirable or unintended results.

In addition to the soundness of a policy and the policy-making process, other determinants often enable effective policy implementation. First, schools and school districts are semi-autonomous organizations not subject to direct and immediate bureaucratic controls. The professionalization of the teacher and the school administrator and the advent of union-type bargaining units for teachers have placed further constraints upon intervention in local school and district operations. Conformity to and compliance with policy implementation are not a simple matter.

A second category of deterrents to effective policy implementation arises from certain myths that include "local control" of education; the "non-political" nature of education (as evidenced by the buffers created between general governmental structures and those erected to govern education); and the non-party-affiliation of elected and appointed officials. A final category of influences on effective policy implementation is the varying capability of schools and districts to respond to requirements imposed by policy. Districts differ greatly in size, resources, and demographic factors. A policy in recent federal legislation, for example, requires instruction in the learner's native tongue. Under this policy, a school in New York City provides materials in eight languages; and a school in Salt Lake City provides instruction in Farsi for three pupils.

Enlightened policy-making for education is complicated by the structures created to formulate policy and control its implementation, by the nature of the issues that educational policy addresses, and by the nature of the institutions whose task is to implement policy. When considerations of any of these three elements is ignored or misunderstood, serious consequences ensue. Those who attempt to influence educational policy need to be aware of the complexity and interrelatedness of controls affecting institutions. Rather than being targets of policy, schools should be treated as instruments of policy decisions and implementers of policy.

Policy Issues

Policy-making is geared to issues. Unless an issue is perceived by a large portion of a population as possible to resolve, there is little likelihood that the issue will be seriously considered as a policy proposal. A number of broad issues have no possibility of permanent resolution. The proper sharing of the financial burden of public education is one such issue. A funding formula with sufficient support for enactment will create perceptions of inequity that eventually lead to efforts for change. A state legislator commented to one of the authors that a major function of government was to adjust the burden of funding education upon the backs of those who would bear it until they could rise up and force it on some other segment of the population.

Another broad issue that continues to occupy state and national government is the balance of control in education. The political philosophy of *dual* federalism, during the 1960s and 1970s, shifted to a *national* federalism. The constitution provides a separation of powers between state and national government; but from the beginning, there has been disagreement about how this concept is to be worked out in practice. Other broad issues include educational equality, public involvement, limits of professional authority, the role of the judiciary, educational purpose and the breadth of educational offerings, the relationship of private education to government control, the nature of moral-citizenship education, and religious practices in public schools.

These large issues lead to more narrow ones that sometimes prevent a clarification of broader issues. The quest for equality, for example, brought about issues related to bilingual and multicultural education, school busing and "mainstreaming" of the handicapped. These become associated with other issues such as alternative schools, voucher plans, basic education, and competency testing. Each of these issues arose in large part because of the broader issue, equality, noted above. No complete cataloging or classifying of issues is possible or necessary here. The policy solutions to the many issues vary depending on the political climate of the time and the point(s) in the policy-making structures where a proposal is made. This situation partly accounts for what has been termed the episodic character of policy-making, wherein some issues and attendant policy proposals are raised under certain conditions in recurring or cyclical patterns. Furthermore, although policy is usually presented as a rational development, it rarely leads to long-term solutions. Issues in the domain of public policy more often than not have no single best solution. Rapidly changing political climates and coalitions force eventual reconsideration of the broader issues and the emergence of new policy proposals.

Educational issues now seem to be taken far more seriously and to involve a broader arena of conflict than in the past. An increased awareness has evolved that education is a powerful force for both individual welfare and social innovation. Many well-educated citizens think deeply and critically about schools and schooling. The media show a strong disposition to criticize social institutions and to apply rough and tumble tactics to education. A political polarization has arisen over social issues for which political solutions are hunted.

Politics of Policy Making

Tucker and Zeigler (1980), in a yearlong study of political activity relating to school policy, monitored communication between school officials and their constituents in eleven school districts. Their findings, which do not contradict the self-reporting and descriptive literature, confirm the position taken earlier in this chapter (p. 36) that the superintendent must function in a political relationship with reference to the board, and provide some useful conclusions. They found boards and professional administrators relatively unresponsive to their constituents largely because constituents failed to communicate their preferences effectively. They did not find local education professionals significantly threatened by school boards or the public. Although obviously such threatening pressure does occur in some districts, it is probably not the rule. Schools experience conflict, sometimes traumatic conflict. Yet Tucker and Zeigler found that school officials perceive the frequency and intensity of conflict erroneously. They attribute this misperception to three circumstances: (a) conflict is more memorable; (b) philosophically and institutionally, school professionals are unprepared to accept conflict as normal in school governance; and (c) school officials tend to misinterpret requests and preferences of constituents because of their own values and professionally socialized beliefs.

The separateness of educational government, the cloak of professionalism of school administrators, an emotional aura that surrounds educational issues, and the shunning of involvement in education by local party politicians have tended to create a closed political system for education. Under these circumstances, conflicts that erupt are difficult to resolve because they usually must be fought out before the school board in a confrontational type of struggle. Boards tend to hold administrators responsible for keeping conflict within bounds, and the professional administrator is forced to play a political role in a non-political guise. Under these circumstances, it is difficult to reach an accommodation in which all parties to a conflict are satisfied. School officials at the local level, tending to opt for the status quo, have been relatively unresponsive to their communities. Thus, local politics which should exemplify open, representative, and responsive government may not even approach this ideal.

Interest Groups and Education

Two theories describe how interest groups may arise in the political arena: (a) a resource mobilization or exchange model (McCarthy and Zald 1977); and (b) a catalytic or disturbance model (Turner and Killian 1972). Each is useful in explaining the dynamics of interest groups functioning in educational politics. In the exchange model, membership in a movement or support for a policy issue arises when individuals become aware of benefits they can achieve by their participation. Since leadership is required, the initial mobilization behind a policy issue usually comes from one or more individuals who see the possibilities and can link together potential supporters. If the movement can then be linked to a political elite, or to a policy-making structure such as a school board or a legislature, it has a good chance of bringing the issue to formal consideration. Membership in a group and/or support for an issue is the medium of exchange; and the characteristics of the political process provides the link to the issues. We shall use this model to describe interest groups which are "school-oriented."

The disturbance model assumes that changing conditions produce changes in the equilibrium among community groups or in the whole society. Specific events highlight the need for altered alliances, and one or more groups begin to see themselves at a disadvantage. Formation of a group to overcome the disadvantage is the catalyst or disturbance for a movement. When the group is sufficiently mobilized to take political action to achieve a remedy, it can force an issue into the political process. The phenomenon of single issue politics seems best explained by this model. What we term "other interest groups" as opposed to "school-oriented groups" can also be explained by the disturbance model.

In either model an issue must be brought to one or more political structures. This might be done with relative ease if the issue has "political currency" and appeals to those who control the "agenda," or if the issues and the supporting group are part of a normal policy-proposing structure such as mandated advisory boards, legally appointed task forces, or the bureaucratic governing structure. Those proposing a policy or policy change may resort to political action to elect board members, legislators, or executives who will support their proposal. They also, if unable to get support through established political structures, may resort to the courts. Or they may resort to extralegal means such as demonstrations, sit-ins, personal abuse, or public intimidation.

The resource mobilization or exchange model is highly effective in education. The uniqueness of educational politics is a major factor accounting for the widespread use of this model and government's allocating education, the largest percentage increase in share of gross national product of any sector during the past decade. We have referred to education's (a) separate governmental structures; (b) nonpolitical stance and non-alliance with political parties; (c) lack of buffers between the school board and the local community; and (d) involvement of the superintendent and other professionals in policy-making. The existence of these four conditions has worked to education's advantage. Education has a built-in professional-bureaucratic complex linked to its own governmental structure. Education also has a natural policy community made up of "school-oriented" interest groups.

Such school-oriented interest groups include the National Congress of Parents and Teachers, National School Boards Association, National Committee for Citizens in Education, National Committee for the Support of the Public Schools, National Association for Neighborhood Schools, and a host of locally-based groups in addition to local chapters and local groups affiliated with the national groups noted. These groups, although friends of education, are also critics. Among other goals, they work to increase public understanding of educational needs, increase resources, and provide instruction and assistance to parents to take advantage of education. They also monitor the performance of schools and foster community control of educational policy-making. With the educcational bureaucracy, they form an organized "in group" to work on behalf of education. They also work in coalition with major education associations to develop legislative programs that they can support cooperatively.

School-oriented groups are needed because a large membership, coalitions capable of political support, a network for information sharing, and an organization are essential to political influence. Threats to coalitions have occurred. Union-type organizations of teachers often have an agenda not compatible with school-oriented groups. Some school-oriented groups have split over financial issues, such as equal funding or pressures to reduce reliance upon the property tax. Some local and state groups have formed around single issues, thus drawing off support for established "general interest" groups.

Other interest groups do not have education as a primary interest. They support or oppose educational policies and practices according to the distribution of population within the interest group, and they can exert pressure from a broader power base than simply their own influence in educational affairs. Interest groups also exist whose ideology shapes their basic concern for education. The John Birch Society, Daughters of the American Revolution, and the American Legion are examples of national groups with a continued interest in education based on economic and/or political ideologies. Textbooks have been a popular battleground for these groups as have school practices relating to sex education, the United Nations, and the free enterprise system. Many groups with ideological interests have formed in states; examples are Texans for America, the Circuit Riders, and Pro America.

Racial and ethnic minorities have also formed groups with both a primary and a secondary interest in education. For Blacks the Urban League, the National Association for the Advancement of Colored People (NAACP), and the Southern Christian Leadership Conference (SCLC) have education as an important but not a dominant interest. The Reverend Jesse Jackson has organized People United to Save Humanity (PUSH), whose primary interest is education. Spanish-speaking and Native American ethnic groups are not organized into easily recognized national organizations as are Blacks, but do have organizations with local and national influence in education. Spanish-speaking Americans tend to organize by national origin (Mexican, Puerto Rican, and Cuban), whereas Native Americans are likely to organize by tribe. The agenda of these racial or ethnic organizations focuses often on their perceived need for equal educational access to achieve eventual equal social or economic access.

Varied feminist interest groups range from the National Organization for Women (NOW) to the Girl Scouts. The former takes political positions on major issues affecting women such as the Equal Rights Amendment (ERA), Title IX, or sex-neutral textbooks; the latter offers a social and educational program and seeks cooperative assistance from schools in promoting its program. The National Council of Jewish Women, American Association of University Women, and the National Federation of Business and Professional Women's Clubs have supported various programs for federal funding of education.

Finally, the Chamber of Commerce, the AFL-CIO, the National Association of Manufacturers, and the American Medical Association represent groups arising from business, labor, and professional interests. In all, only a very small number of organizations have been named that have expressed political policy-making agendas and have acted to support or oppose policy issues in education. Many of these "other interest groups" historically have supported policies that tend to increase the resources, broaden the programs, or improve the effectiveness of education. Others have operated primarily to oppose specific issues such as federal aid programs or efforts to shift or increase the tax burden. Still others have a special agenda to promote. Administrators must assure that issues and policy questions receive a fair hearing, and that the merit of a policy and its long-term importance to education receive primary attention amid the necessary political bargaining. We have indicated that the policy-making processes in education are vulnerable to political pressure and maneuver. In educational politics the school administrator, particularly the district superintendent, is required to assume a political role that is incompatible with a professional role and that is questionable in terms of good policy-making.

Other Influences in Educational Policy Making

One category of influence in educational policy-making arises from the nature of education itself. Real and potential influences derive from the involvement of the teacher as a professional, the learner as client, the college as the goal of many students, accrediting agencies as monitors of standards, and publishers as suppliers of the basic materials of instruction. The following discussion can only indicate their existence, something of their current status and their influence on policy-making.

The Teacher and Teacher Organizations

Just as there is no single unifying professional association for school administrators (see Chapter 1), there is also no single professional association for teachers. At the national level the National Educational Association (NEA) and the American Federation of Teachers, an affiliate of the AFL-CIO, have engaged in fierce competition for membership. There are also national organizations for Catholic, Lutheran, and Jewish teachers. However, the NEA-AFT rivalry has given immediate benefits to teachers priority over professional improvement of members. Neither organization has been able to exert consistently significant influence at the national level, although both have endorsed political candidates and taken an active, even militant, political stance. At state and local levels, however, the activities of the NEA and AFT have had considerable effect on the organization and control of schools.

At the local district level, either the NEA or the AFT is not only the teachers' professional association but also their bargaining agent for salaries, benefits, and working conditions. When an association has acquired authority to act as the bargaining unit, each school has a building representative. In such cases the building representative has a quasi-official status to enforce the bargaining agreement, file grievances, represent teachers at hearings and board meetings, develop reports on local working conditions, and participate in collective bargaining. At the state level a staff, headed by an executive secretary, conducts the business of the association. In most states the executive secretary is an active, vigorous leader with considerable political influence. With the assistance of the association staff and the linkages into at least the larger districts, the executive secretary is intimately acquainted with state political conditions and is ready to supply information to policy makers. The executive secretary and the staff monitor legislation, testify before committees and commissions of the legislature, appear at state board meetings, and draft legislative proposals for legislators and board members who desire such assistance. In short, at both state and local levels professional associations exercise considerable influence on policy-making.

Students as an Influence on Policy Making

Students have an influence on rules and policies merely by their presence in schools and their interactions with teachers and administrators. They represent the largest number of direct linkages that a school has into the community. Schools have formalized the participation of students through the creation of student government organizations, student newspapers, and participation on committees and study groups which prepare policy affecting the school. Many schools, under the auspices of the National Association of Secondary School Principals, participate in the National Association of Student Councils and in the preparation of an Annual School Improvement Plan that involves parents, teachers, administrators, and school board members.

Involvement of students on a formal basis in school and district policy-making varies widely from place to place. During the 1960s and 1970s student activism, violence and vandalism became widespread in the school districts of both large cities and suburban communities. Student unrest was generally interpreted as a reaction of youth to the traditional nature of schools in a changing society, and a resulting frustration due to alienation and lack of genuine involvement. The situation was considered so serious that a committee of the United States Senate, chaired by Senator Birch Bayh, made a lengthy investigation, reporting their findings in 1974 (U.S. Senate Committee on School Disorder 1974). A primary conclusion of the senate report, based on evidence from a number of other studies, was that student activism was largely motivated by a lack of participation in decisions. Students had discovered that violence and political protest command attention. Instead of dropping out or quietly acquiescing, students attacked the system and forced many changes in school policies. Most frequent were changes in dress codes, rules about smoking and conduct, freedom from editorial control of the student newspaper, choice of teachers and their evaluation by students, and content of the curriculum (Trump and Hunt 1969).

College Influences and Accreditation

Colleges and universities exert a variety of formal and informal influences on both public and private schools. Colleges prepare the teachers and administrators, develop the academic content on which instruction in the schools is largely based, and control admission requirements that must be met by schools who wish their students to go to college. They also exert a controlling influence in national testing, accreditation, foundations, and government agencies such as the National Science Foundation. Colleges and universities, well into this century, were the dominant influence on the secondary schools. This situation changed as school programs diversified and began to graduate large numbers of non-college-bound students. College criticisms of school programs, once quite influential, were sharply challenged by public school leaders and professional associations representing teachers. The retort to criticism was that college programs were inadequate; and measures were taken to wrest control of in-service preparation of teachers and to secure equal, if not dominant, representation on federal advisory boards and accreditation agency committees.

A group of colleges in 1900 formed the College Entrance Examination Board (CEEB) as a means to force some standardization and measure of quality preparation on the high schools. The use by member colleges of common examinations for admission controlled guidance and curricula of secondary school students. The aim, stated many times by CEEB presidents, is the exercise of control over the high school curriculum. The Scholastic Aptitude Test (SAT) Program is required by almost twenty-five hundred colleges today. Other tests are required by members of the American College Testing Program in addition to or instead of CEEB's Scholastic Aptitude Test. However, the national testing program, dominated by the SAT, is a powerful influence upon secondary schools. A decline in SAT test scores during the 1970s received major national attention and, in part, spawned requirements for state-wide competency testing in the schools.

Colleges are also influential in curriculum development for the schools. At the national level college scholars and scientists have obtained federal funding from the National Science Foundation and the National Endowment for the Humanities to develop curriculum programs in the schools.

Although colleges still influence accrediting agencies, those agencies represent a form of influence upon schools somewhat apart from others already noted. In 1885, the New England Association of Colleges and Secondary Schools was formed and today there are six regional accrediting agencies. The North Central Association of Colleges and Secondary Schools, established in 1895, is the largest, accrediting the schools of nineteen states and the Department of Defense overseas schools. Accreditation was first originated by colleges because students were coming from schools beyond the state and from in-state schools too numerous to visit. Colleges early recognized that variations in programs and quality of offering made the interpretation of high school records difficult. The larger universities established a high school visitor's office which, after World War II, rapidly changed to a high school-university relations office now largely used for recruitment and the communication of college programs and requirements. Accreditation is acknowledged today as important and graduates of nonaccredited high schools may be required to pass special examinations to be admitted to member colleges.

The control of accreditation agencies by colleges, and the resultant power over school programs became the source of a struggle primarily involving state education agencies who felt that they, not the colleges, had the authority to determine standards for a state's system of education. The result has been an accrediting procedure that has extensive participation of staff from the public schools and the state agencies. This procedure involves three phases: (a) a self-study by the school seeking accreditation; (b) a visitation by an evaluation team which checks the validity of the self study, conducts its own inspections, and reports its findings; and (c) a Board of Review which receives the self-study and the visitation report, and grants an accreditation status ranging from no accreditation to conditional, to full accreditation.

The self-study and the visitation report are usually taken seriously by boards of education and the school district administration. Evaluation criteria are detailed, beginning with a required statement of goals and philosophy and running through fourteen areas including teacher qualifications and assignments, program descriptions and learning resources, library and media support, administration, ancillary and support services, and physical facilities. Since 1974 the National Center for Accreditation Evaluation has standardized and refined the procedures and provides a complete set of materials to guide the data collection and report writing. Each association publishes a list of member schools and their accreditation status. Accreditation has been expanded to include the total program of the school and its institutional arrangements, not just its college preparatory program. The evaluation procedure is now being extended to both middle and elementary schools.

Publishers and Educational Materials

Beyond the influences on policy-making in the schools treated thus far is the large and significant area of educational materials, both print and non-print. Few schools have escaped the issues involving censorship of print materials, book and educational program adoption, copyright infringement, ethics of publishing school-produced materials, and relationships with publishing houses. Teaching materials are necessary for the educational process and their selection, processing and use is a major schools activity. They also constitute a substantial economic interest for those who market materials to the schools. This area of concern is complex, involving organization, controls and problems relating to policy-making. It is perhaps impossible, for example, to write a universally acceptable policy relating to the selection of texts or library books. Incidents are on record in which a publisher has excluded a chapter of a book through fear of losing sales; schools have withdrawn books due to public pressures; suits have contested the adoption of one reading program versus another, and a superintendent of a major school district had resigned because of a text selection procedure he initiated.

Policy-making for any aspect of instructional materials poses dilemmas. Teachers should have a major role in the selection of materials. Often, however, teachers feel vulnerable and tend to avoid any materials that might make them targets of attack. Dow and Weber (1975) document the problem in a case study involving *Man: A Course of Study*. The materials prepared by an eminent scientist with the support of the National Science Foundation were attacked largely on the grounds that it represented unwarranted government interference in curriculum making. Other key actors in the policy-making process also feel vulnerable; the school board of an affluent, suburban district spent most of one meeting discussing whether *Robin Hood* might be considered an encouragement of communistic thought. These somewhat extreme examples show the sensitivity of the problems encountered and illustrate that exercise of prudence and sound professional practice, although necessary, may not forestall problems in this area.

Issues relating to instructional materials have frequently been referred to the courts. In a recent decision, *Board of Education v. Pico*, the U.S. Supreme Court ruled 5-4 that students and parents can contest school board censorship of library books. Writing the majority opinion Justice Brennan stated that boards may not remove books from school libraries simply because they dislike the ideas contained in them. The case arose because the Island Trees, New York, Board of Education ordered removal of nine books from a school library. The court in this instance, and case law generally, does not condone the official suppression of ideas; but so far only the vague guidelines of "pervasively vulgar" and "lacking educational suitability" have been voiced in legal opinions to indicate what material may be removed. The final effect of Pico on the actions of boards of education remains to be seen.

It appears that cases involving controversial materials have dealt chiefly with the removal and only tangentially with the original selection of materials. Regular and unbiased procedures of selection and use are a protection before the courts; but again, sound practice alone will not forestall problems. Only sound policies and personnel with the strength to withstand controversy and pressure are likely to provide a solution for school administrators.

References

Campbell, Roald F. 1960. "Process of Policy Making Within Structures of Education Government." In *Government of Public Education for Adequate Policy Making*. Urbana, Ill.: Bureau of Educational Research, University of Illinois.

Campbell, Roald F., et al. 1980. *The Organization and Control of American Schools*. 4th ed. Columbus, Ohio: Charles E. Merrill.

Dow, Peter, and George Weber. 1975. "The Case For and Against Man: A Course of Study." *Phi Delta Kappan* 57 (October): 79-82.

Iannacone, Laurence. 1971. *State Politics and Education.* New York: Ballantine Books.

Iannacone, Laurence, and **Frank W. Lutz.** 1970. *Politics, Power, and Policy: The Governing of Local School District.* Columbus, Ohio: Charles E. Merrill.

Kerr, Norman D. 1964. "The School Board as an Agency of Legitimation." *Sociology of Education* 38 (Autumn): 34-59.

Kirst, Michael W., ed. 1970. *The Politics of Education at the Local, State and Federal Levels.* Berkeley, Calif.: McCutchan.

McCarthy, John D., and **Mayer N. Zald.** 1977. "Resource Mobilization and Social Movements: A Partial Theory." *American Journal of Sociology* 82 (May) 1212-41.

McCarty, Donald J., and **Charles E. Ramsey.** 1971. *The School Managers.* Westport, Conn.: Greenwood Publishing.

McCleary, Lloyd E. 1976. *Politics and Power in Education.* Morristown, N.J.: General Learning Press.

Maeroff, Gene I. 1974. "Harried School Leaders See Their Role Waning." *The New York Times* (March 5): 1.

Starkey, A. E. 1966. *State Level Education Decision Making in Texas.* Doctoral dis., University of Texas.

Trump, J. Lloyd, and **Jane Hunt.** 1969. "The Nature and Extent of Student Activism." *The Bulletin of the National Association of Secondary School Principals* 53 (May): 150-58.

Tucker, Harvey J., and **L. Harmon Zeigler.** 1980. *Professionals Versus the Public: Attitudes, Communication, and Response in School Districts.* New York: Longman.

Turner, R. N., and **L. Killian.** 1972. *Collective Behavior.* Englewood Cliffs, N.J.: Prentice-Hall.

U.S. Senate. 1974. *Report of the Senate Select Committee on School Disorder.* Washington, D.C.: Government Printing Office.

Zeigler, Harmon L., and **Kent M. Jennings.** 1974. *Governing American Schools*, No. 8. Scituate, Mass.: Duxbury Press.

3

A man gradually identifies himself with the form of his fate; a man is, in the long run, his own circumstances.

- Jorge Luis Borges

Administrative Roles and Responsibilities

Two positions in educational administration around which other positions became defined are the superintendent and principal. Each represents a key "line" position, of the school district and of the individual school, respectively. To understand the configuration of administrative and supervisory positions of a district central office, one can subdivide the responsibilities of the superintendent as required by the number, complexity and size of tasks into a range of positions occupied by specialists. This configuration of positions is referred to as the superintendency. In like fashion, the principal of a school together with special administrative and supervisory positions is referred to as the principalship. Teaching, the principalship, and the superintendency form a central trunk of positions with branches into many related educational organizations and agencies. Because of this we shall focus on the superintendency and the principalship, using theory and practice to examine legal, structural, functional, and human aspects of educational administration.

As pointed out in Chapter 1, educational administration is an evolving-emergent field, and as an applied field it has historical and legal antecedents largely shaped by practice and experience. It has also been subjected to investigation and analysis which have influenced practice. Finally, it is embedded in a cultural-societal setting that has provided, as shown in Chapter 2, a governance structure and mandates in the form of policies and organizational arrangements. A study of these elements provides evidence about how and why positions in educational administration were created, their current status, and influences from these sources indicating directions of change.

In addition to the term *administrative position*, a broader term is *administrative role*. In administration, as in teaching, it is not possible to describe all duties and responsibilities or the detailed manner in which they are to be performed. Standards of professional practice, range of interpersonal and agency relationships, latitude of discretionary authority, and individual administrative styles are partial determinants of how individuals perform in an administrative post. The concept of role is treated more precisely using role theory. The two terms are used throughout this chapter, with important distinctions between them.

Historical-Legal Antecedents

Educational administration evolved to its present condition from humble beginnings. A common view is that the principalship has no history; even today it has almost no legal recognition in statutes, although it was the first administrative position to appear. In Germany the *Gymnasium* and in England the Latin grammar school were secondary schools with a clearly defined administrative officer or head. From these schools the American Latin grammar schools derived their forms of organization and administration. The headmaster was the master teacher, who not only could teach each subject, but also could organize the classes, administer discipline, and oversee operation of the school.

Latin grammar schools were superceded by versions of Benjamin Franklin's academy and then by the forerunner of the modern high school, established in Boston in 1821. These three types of school overlapped in time periods, with the academy dominating the educational scene into the 1850s. The variations within the types, except in the curricula, were almost as great as between the types. Many of each type were boarding schools; many were supported primarily by fees. All were secondary schools accepting only students who could already read and write, usually comprising an age range from nine to fourteen years (Cremin 1980; Butts and Cremin 1953). Apparently the term *principal teacher* came into being with the advent of the high school. It was the high school that quickly developed into a public institution and became a direct continuation of the elementary school. The public nature of secondary schooling and the creation of a continuous educational ladder were unique American developments which gave status and the first noninstructional responsibilities to the high school principal.

The position of elementary principal evolved much more slowly than that of high school principal. Moehlman (1940, 526) reports that into the 1870s, few elementary schools had more than eight teachers and that most, if not all, elementary principalships evolved within well-developed school district structures in urban centers. The first superintendents of school districts were appointed to supervise elementary schools and were frequently the only nonteaching personnel in the district. The high schools were exempted from direct supervision and evaluation by district superintendents. However, high school principals usually did not attend school board meetings except when specifically invited (Moehlman, 184). Thus, a separate status evolved for the high school principal; but the role of the elementary principal well into this century was to be primarily a teacher, a building supervisor, and the general clerical-chore person for a school.

The advent of the position of superintendent of schools falls chronologically between that of the high school principal and that of the elementary school principal, assuming any semblance of an early administrative role for the elementary school principal. The cities of Buffalo and Louisville were the first to appoint superintendents in 1837. Boston, Cincinnati, Chicago, Detroit, Milwaukee, New York, and San Francisco were among those who appointed superintendents in the 1850s; by 1890 most school districts serving urban centers of over twenty-five thousand population had appointed superintendents. The creation of the position of superintendent arose during the rapid growth of cities in the industrial revolution.

The shift from the one-teacher village school to schools within a unified district organization was sporadic, even chaotic. States passed legislation to create school districts with power to levy taxes to support public schools, only to reverse themselves in subsequent sessions. Local communities often ignored state laws requiring public schools. To establish and support schools, a potpourri of devices was used, ranging from fees paid directly to teachers, to pledged subscriptions from parents and friends of pupils, to tithes collected by churches, to public and private endowments, to taxation of real property. Cremin writes of the movement to create public school systems during the 1840s and 1850s as "extending schooling where it had been sparse, regularizing schooling where it had been intermittent, systematizing schooling where it had been prevalent and shifting the support of schooling to the relatively certain foundation of tax funds." (Cremin 1980, 388). A group of able reformers within various states—Horace Mann in Massachusetts, Henry Barnard in Connecticut, John Pierce in Michigan, Samuel Lewis in Ohio, Caleb Mills in North Carolina to name only a few—conducted zealous campaigns combining astute political acumen with a combination of Christian moralism, Jeffersonian republicanism, and Emersonian idealism (Jones 1952, 91-107). The aim was to create a unified system of free universal education.

By 1860, a design had begun to appear. A majority of states had created publicly supported school systems, some including high schools. Elementary schools were widely available and various estimates calculated about half of all children were receiving some formal schooling. Children were examined and placed according to ability. English grammar, reading, penmanship, arithmetic, history, and geography were the common elementary subjects. Texts had appeared earlier, but *McGuffey's Eclectic Readers* and *Ray's Eclectic Arithmetic* introduced graded subject matter and provided exercises using an inductive logic. The new high schools maintained Greek and Latin and continued the basic elementary school subjects. However, French and sewing for girls, science and bookkeeping for boys, and elocution, physiology, drawing, and music for both sexes became recognized as necessary additions. The problems of grouping, discipline, pedagogy, and simply the deluge of numbers became almost overwhelming; in Chicago, in 1860, one hundred twenty-three teachers faced over fourteen thousand students, with perhaps that many more denied admission for lack of space.

The reformers had brought about a revolution in education largely without consideration for the organization and administration the system required to sustain an enormous educational effort. Local citizens' committees were the policy makers and the administrators, attending to every detail of business and management outside the classroom. High schools had part-time teaching principals, and overburdened boards, as indicated, began to employ a superintendent to look after the elementary schools. Initially, the superintendent was given responsibility over educational matters only; later the position of superintendent for business was created, with status equal to that of the general superintendents, to conduct business affairs for the board.

The first major court case involving the public schools came about because of the creation of the administrative office of superintendent. Boards of education had appointed superintendents and delegated responsibility to them without any specific statutory authority to do so. Considerable debate had arisen in many cities about spending public funds to employ a person to carry out the responsibilities of the school board. In 1874, the famous and precedent-setting Kalamazoo case was decided by the Michigan Supreme Court (*Stuart v. School District No. 1*, 30 Mich. 69 [1874]). The court held that local boards of education were given full control over the operation of public schools, and that their implied statutory authority was sufficient to permit them to appoint a superintendent and other administrative officers.

The superintendent was quite literally the superintendent of instruction. Boards of education jealously guarded their executive powers over employment of personnel, school buildings, finance, and other matters. The use of executive committees, dual administrators, and active control over all management matters by boards of education persisted as the norm well into this century. The superintendent was perceived as the assistant of the board and expected to do its bidding. Faced with overwhelming educational problems, superintendents turned to the development of a uniform, coherent, highly organized system of education; punctuality, order, system, morality, and industrious effort became the guiding concepts. The graded school with its "egg crate" architectural plan, uniform examinations, a textbook-based curriculum, "platooning" of pupils, and departmentalized teaching were all put into practice with many adaptations and combinations.

David Tyack (1974, 45) castigated the urban school model in a detailed historical analysis in which he coined the term, used as the title of his study, "the one best system." Tyack traced the development of the contemporary educational system from the 1850s, noting that by 1870 education had come "from no system to nothing but system." Callahan (1962) traced the development of educational administration from the turn of the century into the period following World War II, and labeled it the "cult of efficiency." Both document the changes in the superintendency as it became a strong, centralized authority in the administration of schools. Current proposals for changes, contemporary issues and ideologies, power struggles, and the nature of administration are often new forms of past efforts to resolve educational problems concerning which an historical perspective becomes important. The industrialization of the country had brought with it an obsession for organization and efficiency by those who exercised control.

The work ethic and the concept of the perfectibility of humankind gave a moral sanction to instilling order, obedience, and diligence in the young. Some educators, and a very few social reformers, saw the educational system as oppressive or discriminatory to minorities and women. But most school leaders often spoke of the schools as being impartial, based upon merit and equality of opportunity, and humane in preparing the young to meet the realities of life. John Dewey became the leading spokesperson of the first major effort to reform the schools. In a series of three lectures, instigated by criticism of the Laboratory School which he had founded, he placed the blame for conflicts over education squarely upon the industrialization of society. He argued that society educates and that schools had blindly followed. He proposed that schools become embryonic communities where pupils would actively participate in occupations and projects, and where teachers would inject the spirit of art, science, and history (Dewey 1899). The progressive movement, which became the label of reform, lasted in varied forms until World War II. The progressive education reforms heralded a continuing series of intense, organized efforts to change the nature of schooling and the institutions which provided it.

This and later reform movements are important for the administrator, because they exposed the school systems to the social, philosophical, and psychological conflicts inherent in education. There are a number of conflicting views of man and knowledge, of which humanism, idealism, realism, and experimentalism are dominant. Various schools of psychology, including behaviorism, connectionism, field psychology, social psychology, and psychoanalysis, offer contending views of mental development, adjustment, and learning. Numerous religious views of humankind and values are likely to surface in any controversy over education, including controversy over preferential treatment of a specific sect. Vastly increased organized bodies of knowledge claim a place in the school's curriculum. Contending economic and political ideologies confront schools and tend to view impartiality as unacceptable. The administrator cannot avoid conflict. Too frequently the educational administrator has tried to deal with the competing views as a social engineer rather than as an educational leader. A sobering task for all educational administrators is to meet the intellectual challenges of competing views and to assume leadership in resolving them. This is an increasingly necessary component of the educational administrator's role.

As indicated, a board of education holds primary statutory authority over a school district. As superintendents and principals have acquired a wide range of powers, they have been assigned an equally wide range of duties. However, administrators, with exceptions noted in the next paragraph, possess no statutory rights that they may exercise without prior authorization or subsequent ratification. Powers and duties vary greatly from state to state and district to district. Some states have comprehensive statutes, and state and local board policies and regulations describe the roles of each type of position created. Other states have few statutes or few state policies, although all states have a school code. Some local districts have carefully codified sets of board regulations; others, even large districts, have no single codified set of board policies and regulations. A first task of any school administrator is to obtain the school code for the state in question and to investigate the local school board policies and regulations. The National School Board Association has developed a system by which districts may bring together and codify policies and regulations. The NSBA also provides recommended policies for a number of important areas, including the roles of administrative officers.

Statutes invariably allow the exercise of independent administrative judgment in the day-to-day management of schools and in the routines and procedures appropriate to carry out board policy. However, any actions of significant consequence require board action. For example, although principals and superintendents may reprimand a teacher, suspend a pupil, and take similar action to maintain order, any severe punishment requires board approval or review. Superintendents, generally, have broader statutory power than do other administrative officers. In some states, they have certain powers exclusive of board action. In most, if not all states, superintendents have the statutory *duty* to report significant actions taken and submit recommendations to the board concerning policies being considered by the board as well as policies the administration feels the district should have.

The courts frequently have been called upon to resolve the question of whether the superintendent is a public official or merely an employee of the board. A body of case law exists that treats the superintendent clearly and unequivocally as an employee (Gee and Sperry 1978). Cases tend to be decided in terms of employee status, bearing in mind that superintendents serve according to the will of the board, whereas a public official acts independently on behalf of the public. However, the Supreme Courts of Montana and of Kansas have ruled that in some instances the superintendent must act as a public official, or at least a quasi-public official. Law has not resolved the issue of the superintendent's legal status. National associations representing principals, superintendents, and the school boards have sought statutes to define the various administrative roles, but the relationship between school boards and administrators remains unclear.

Even though the position of principal has evolved into one of considerable importance, the legal status of the principal is far from clear; historically, the principal has been accorded the same status as the teacher. Where principals have established tenure as teachers in a district or state, they retain their teacher tenure rights and legal status. The exception occurs when specific tenure laws exist for administrators, or in situations in which administrators voluntarily give up tenure acquired as a teacher when accepting an administrative post. In some states administrative officers serve completely at the pleasure of the board and their status and tenure is determined by individual contract. In some states and some districts, status and tenure are specified by general administrative statute or policy. Boards clearly have the authority to terminate administrators or to assign them classroom duties if they have retained tenure rights as a teacher. The position of principal, however, has become distinct from that of teacher. Their training and certification are different; their duties and responsibilities are different; and their recognized status as part of administration rather than faculty is clear.

At this writing only eight states have school codes which specifically define the role of school principal, establish the legal identity of the position, and provide separate legislation dealing with the principalship. Nine states legally provide the principal with teacher status. The remaining thirty-three states and the District of Columbia have school codes that mention the principal in relation to specific duties and responsibilities. Legally, the status of the principal remains largely a matter of historical precedent.

Roles Definition and Role Clarification

Descriptive Literature

The creation and development of a position leads to generalized perceptions about how that position is to serve to achieve its intended purpose. In education, this occurred very early as superintendents and principals wrote about their experiences, formed associations that held meetings and published journals, participated in efforts to establish licensing and training standards, and went about the business of developing a profession. The problems faced by education and the widely shared view of its importance gave considerable public support to efforts to define and clarify administrative roles. Chapter 1 reviewed literature descriptive of experience that provides evidence of "current best practice." Historical-legal sources of role definition have been presented that derive from this literature. Also in Chapter I was an overview of the scholarly literature. The present section describes the roles of superintendent, elementary principal, and secondary principal followed by an examination of several theoretical views of role derived research.

Role of the Superintendent

Several major problems were overcome in bringing the role of superintendent to its current status. Perhaps most important was the elevation of the position to that of chief executive officer of a school district. The organizational principle of "unity of command" was applied to provide one administrative head with one integrated staff. With this move came a general acceptance that a distinction should be made between policy-making and policy execution. The detailed direction of operations to which boards of education had held largely gave way to setting goals, making policy decisions, and reviewing results. Superintendents generally have also been provided with a staff of specialists and clerical assistants to fulfill the tasks of general supervision and leadership. Even where staff is not provided there is acknowledged need for it. Further, the continued rise in the level of preparation of superintendents and other administrative officers indicates an acceptance of the need for extended specialized preparation.

Some specific dimensions of the superintendent's role taken from the contemporary literature include the following:

1. The superintendent is responsible for the educational program of the district and for the leadership of its development and the supervision of its operation. The superintendent has the duty to provide regular reports to the board on all aspects of the educational program and the progress and welfare of pupils. The superintendent should also keep the board informed of educational needs of the

total community, educational innovations, and developments that show promise, and new programs that would benefit the community.

2. The superintendent is the chief executive officer of the board. The superintendent is to be present at all meetings of the board and any special committees which the board may create with the exception of consideration of the superintendent's reemployment.

3. The superintendent is to function as the consultant to the board by providing recommendations on all policy matters under consideration.

4. The superintendent is responsible for carrying out all policies and regulations established by board action. Where administrative action is required which is not covered by board policy, the superintendent should report actions taken at the first regular board meeting.

5. The superintendent shall submit an annual budget covering all school operations. Within the limits of an approved budget and the requirements of approval of major expenditures, the superintendent is responsible for all expenditures.

6. All employees of the school district are directly or indirectly responsible to the superintendent. The superintendent has authority to issue regulations and directions necessary to carry out board policies. Duties and the authority to carry them out may be delegated as the superintendent sees fit; however, actions of subordinates acting under such direction remain the responsibility of the superintendent.

7. All candidates for employment should be recommended to the board by the superintendent. The board has the right to reject candidates recommended, but candidates finally employed should have the positive recommendation of the superintendent.

8. Personnel policies relative to all personnel categories of the district should be based on the recommendations of the superintendent. Where special negotiating personnel are employed, the superintendent should be privy to all points of negotiation and make final recommendations to the board.

9. The superintendent is responsible for the maintenance and improvement of all district property and the personnel employed for that purpose. This responsibility includes a physical plant and custodial personnel policies and all recommendations for employment.

10. The superintendent is responsible for keeping the board informed of all vital matters pertaining to the district. This includes the preparation of an annual report of the district as well as special reports relative to projects and programs under development, planning, community involvement, and specific problems and issues.

The preceding list represents a set of critical *functions* that must be performed for a school district to operate effectively. Functions can be broken into specific tasks. A function, or a set of tasks inherent in a function, may be delegated to a specialist. In all large districts, for example, one will find a specialist in each of the areas of business affairs, personnel, curriculum, buildings and grounds, pupil personnel, and community relations. If the tasks for a given function are sufficiently complex and numerous, a complete division may be created with a staff of specialists and clerical support. Depending on the nature of the tasks delegated, the administration will be structured into levels with assistant superintendents in charge of one or more functions. Major tasks under the responsibility of an assistant superintendent may be assigned to directors. Although titles may differ, two- and three-level hierarachies of administrative specialists are not uncommon. In addition, some functions, such as curriculum and pupil personnel services, have responsibilities for tasks taking place in the schools. These tasks may be assigned to staff specialists with no direct administrative role in forming policy. Such positions are usually given the titles of "supervisor," "coordinator," or "consultant."

Tasks, then, represent a *functional* view of an administrative role. The nature of authority granted each position, including that of the superintendent by the board; the degree of autonomy to take action; the amount of discretion allowed to make decisions deviating from standard operating procedures: all figure in a consideration of role. Professional organizations require standardization of processes such as how certain types of decisions will be made and how activities are coordinated across functions. They also require uniformity in procedures such as requests from individual school buildings for equipment purchases, special or standard testing of students, etc. *Structure* follows function; and organizational design and analysis (Mintzberg 1979; McCleary et al. 1976) use what is called a "top-down" and a "bottom-up" procedure. In principle, the procedure is as follows: From general goals to be met, functions can be delineated and the major tasks of each function prescribed along with the necessary technology. The mapping of goals, functions, and tasks is a "top-down" procedure. Tasks are then grouped into positions. The degree of specialization, scope of authority, or experience and training desired can then be determined for each position. When an organizational structure is complete, a "bottom-up" procedure traces tasks back up the structure to determine lines of communication, extent of coordination required vertically and horizontally, and placement of authority to initiate or alter tasks.

Role of the Principal

The elementary, middle, and high school principals have many similarities in their roles relative to general functions and to the processes used to execute functions. Each role is heavily affected by person-to-person contacts and group meetings, often not of the principal's choice. In personal and group contacts, expectations are exchanged about the principal's role in relation to specific tasks. Expectations arise as well from formal policies, regulations, and standard practice. It is easy to see that expectations of teachers, central office, students, parents, and community groups are not likely to be in agreement, particularly about a controversial issue. Role ambiguity and role conflict are therefore inherent in the principalship. In dealing with the role of the principal, we shall first examine the similarities in general functions and processes and then turn to some of the major individual differences among the three types.

Information about the principal's role is available from national studies sponsored by the National Association of Elementary School Principals (Pharis and Zakariya 1979) and the National Association of Secondary School Principals (Valentine et al. 1981; McCleary and Thomson 1979). These studies, as well as case, ethnographic, and small sample research studies provide evidence of the nature and priority of work, perceptions of the job, problems pertaining to it, and working conditions. Tables 3-1 and 3-2 offer information from the national studies about principals' perceptions of time given each general function and time the principals would prefer to spend on the function.

TABLE 3-1 *Elementary Principals' Allocation of Time*
by Function: Actual and Desired *

Time Allocation as Estimated by Principals (%)	Rank Actual	Rank Desired
Supervision of Teachers (32)	1	1
Administrative Duties (28)	2	2
Clerical (14)	3	7
Curriculum Development (8)	4	3
Community/Parents (7)	5	5
Self-Improvement (6)	6	4
Teaching (4)**	7	6

*Note: Data supplied by NAESP staff; these data are not contained in the study report.

**Note: Data of principals who have regular teaching assignments are not included; this category represents demonstration, special, or substitute teaching.

Elementary principals perceived that they spent too much time with routine administrative duties, with clerical work of filing routine reports and record keeping, in meetings called by others, and in problems with personnel. They felt they had too little time for leadership of staff in program and school improvement, planning, curriculum development, and classroom supervision. With an estimated workweek approaching fifty hours counting school-related activities beyond school time, the allocation of time is a serious problem that elementary principals cannot control as they would like. The rankings in Table 3-1 lead to the conclusion that any significant changes in the role of an elementary school principal depend upon additional clerical assistance.

A different list for middle and high school principals appears in Table 3-2, showing the perceived time allocations, actual and desired. A national task force of principals identified nine areas of "primary responsibility" and identified specific tasks under each. These were then used in collecting information in the two national studies.

The general functions listed for middle and high school principal responses are slightly different than those used in the elementary school principal study.

In both "actual" and "desired" rankings of general functions, middle and high school principals gave remarkably similar ratings. Comparing the two in "actual" rankings, only "student activities" is different by more than one rank. In "desired" rankings, only "community relations" is different by more than one rank. In the changes each group would make in priority among functions, both groups of principals moved pro-

TABLE 3-2 *Middle and High School Principals' Allocation of Time by Function: Actual and Desired*

Time Allocation as Estimated by Principals	Rank, Middle School		Rank, High School	
	Actual	Desired	Actual	Desired
Management (routines, calendar, finance, plant)	1	3	1	3
Personnel (evaluation, advising, recruiting)	2	2	2	2
Student Behavior (attendance, discipline, meetings	3	8	4	7
Program Development (curriculum, instruction)	4	1	5	1
Student Activities (planning, government, etc.)	5	4	3	4
District Office (meetings, committees, reports)	6	9	6	9
Community Relations (advisory groups, parents, PTA)	7	6	8	8
Planning (weekly, annual, long range)	8	5	7	5
Professional Development (reading, conferences)	9	7	9	6

Source: Jerry Valentine, *The Middle Level Principalship*, vol. 1 (Reston, Va.: NASSP, 1981), 36; and Lloyd E. McCleary and Scott D. Thomson, *The Senior High School Principalship*, vol. 3 (Reston, Va.: NASSP, 1979), 17.

gram development to the rank of 1 and management to the rank of 3. In all other "desired" rankings the order of priority remains similar. Using a statistical treatment (Kendall's W-Correlation of Concordance), no significant differences were found in the rankings given to functions in their roles by the two groups. One of the present authors chaired the research team for the secondary school principal study reported here and was able to make comparisons of subsamples of the total gruop of high school principals. No significant differences were found between samples selected by school size, years of experience of the principal, geographical region, or independent ratings of principal effectiveness.

As with the elementary principal, middle and high school principals find expectations of others pushing upon their own priorities. These expectations arise from the daily demands of teachers, students, and parents; from the weekly cycle of events, activities, and special programs; from the monthly cycle of meetings and reports; from the yearly cycle of budgets, personnel, or school opening and closing. The principal, regardless of type of school, is far more involved with people of a wider range of maturity (learners, lay persons, professionals) and of needs than are most other types of administrators in business, church, or military.

Woolcott in an ethnographic study of one elementary principal found "an almost endless series of encounters . . . with almost 65% of the principal's day spent in face to face interaction . . ." (1973, 92). Blumberg and Greenfield conducted in-depth studies of four elementary and four secondary principals and produced eight case studies concluding that, "the principal's interpersonal competencies, particularly those relating to establishing and maintaining identities, both for the principal and for others . . . is probably pivotal in differentiating the more effective from the less effective principal" (1980, 198).

Time pressures, mediation of conflicting expectations, and the interruption of work by immediate demands and problems characterize the principal's role. Peterson in another observational study of urban elementary principals found that their day consists of short tasks, "sometimes several hundred separate activities . . . with a wide range of individuals . . . with differing cognitive demands" (1981, 2-6). This fragmentation of daily work activities makes for ambiguity in the role. Other sources of ambiguity are (1) lack of clarity of educational goals, (2) lack of understanding of the differing effects of educational technology, and (3) lack of identifiable cause-and-effect factors in the educational process (March 1978, 228). These three sources of role ambiguity (goals, technology, process causes and effects) would distinguish a school principal's role on logical grounds alone from that of a plant or department store manager, director of public health, or head of an engineering firm.

To some this ambiguity and intense interpersonal involvement is highly attractive.

Individual principals can and do exercise a great deal of discretion in their work, and even with the time pressures, have considerable choice in how that time is used. Morris et al. (1981) and the Blumberg and Greenfield study already cited, found that principals have a great deal of latitude in making decisions. Principals consistently rate their jobs high in independent thought and action, self-fulfillment, prestige, opportunity to help others, and job security (Byrne, Hines, and McCleary 1978, 23). Even though the general role functions are similar throughout types of schools, the principal enjoys a wide choice in performing the tasks making up each function. Effective principals tend to be great copers. (Morris et al. 1981, 217-20); they find a variety of ways to handle tasks (McCleary and Thomson 1979, 17); they use a variety of approaches for developing uniqueness in their roles (Salley et al. 1975, 96-97), and they exhibit different leadership styles (Kunz and Hoy 1976, 49-64).

Differences in the roles principals play in their professional lives appear to be more a matter of the principals' own choice than of environmental, organizational, or external professional controls. Although we are certain that influences upon the role derive from these three sources, the nature of the work itself, its diversity, fragmentation, ambiguity and diffuseness, permits freedoms and satisfactions not found in other types of middle management. School size does make a difference in the role; for principals of smaller schools become more involved with students while principals of larger schools more closely resemble managers. Socioeconomic status of student body and staff make a difference, and other differences derive from racial and ethnic mixes. These differences, however, do not control or condition the role so that the principal cannot shape it largely to his/her professional needs and interests.

To the studies already cited, we might add one from another country to raise the question of whether this diversity of role is not universal. After examining the effects of schooling in England, Rutter, et al. (1979) asserted: "The influence of the head teacher [principal] is very considerable. . . . Our observations indicated that no one style was associated with better outcomes. Indeed, it was noticeable that the heads of more successful schools took widely differing approaches" (203-4). Since interpersonal relations make up such a large part of the principal's work day, and since the expectations one has of others is an element in how one chooses to perform in a role, interpersonal skills become important. Lacey (1981) compared bank managers, government agency managers, mental health directors, directors of nursing, and school principals on nine interpersonal skills. Interestingly, principals were rated highest of all managers on "expresses warmth and concern," second on "manages conflict well," "considerate of others," "shares relevant feelings well," "expresses self well," and "assertiveness." Principals were rated lowest of all managers on "receives feedback well" (63). Research into the relative influence of role determinants and their effects in terms of characteristics of principals themselves is needed. Nevertheless, the studies cited give considerable insight into the role and are grounds for further inquiry as well as guidance to the principal.

Interrelationships of Positions and Roles

In describing the role of the superintendent, an explanation was given about the structuring of interrelated positions in the superintendency and how this is generally done. This section shows how administrative roles become organized into a coherent system, a role structure. General systems theory as well as role theory is of particular assistance here and will be referred to where appropriate. Chapter 1 presented administration as consisting of three identifiable arenas of activity: (1) policy formulation and external organizational responsibilities; (2) organization leadership or the translation of board policies into operational policies, programs, and procedures; and (3) technical-managerial operations to carry out policies, programs, and procedures in the daily activities of a school or school district. To achieve an effective administrative team effort, roles must be interrelated for each arena of activity both horizontally and vertically, from the board-superintendent level to the principal and teacher levels.

Using the general functions attributed to the roles of superintendent and principal, it is possible to provide a chart to show typical positions and key role responsibilities as they might be found in a medium-sized school district. Table 3-3 shows the recommended interrelationships of roles for developing operational policies to facilitate organizational leadership.

The superintendent as chief executive officer of the district bears the primary responsibility for seeing that board policy is made, and the ultimate responsibility for setting board policy in operation, as shown in Table 3-3. He also bears ultimate responsibility for the technical-managerial implementation of policies and procedures. The superintendent will have administrative officers to direct key divisions, and will designate to whom authority is delegated to develop operational policies and procedures. These officers, in turn, call upon technical-managerial staff to assist in that work. As shown in Table 3-3, coordination is required horizontally across divisions for most key functions. This coordination at the district level is also the superintendent's responsibility.

The principal, as head of an operating unit, has the responsibility for developing or shaping operational policies in keeping with board policies. Some uniform operational policies and procedures may be required throughout the district with little latitude for deviation. However, many operational policies are of such a nature that they must be developed at the school site. Different versions of what is termed site management, shared decision-making etc., systematize a degree of autonomy for the principal while protecting the ultimate responsibility which the superintendent cannot delegate. Whether at the district or the school level, participation and wide consultation are required to insure effective implementation and cooperative compliance. The expectations of others involved in carrying out policy is a major factor in shaping the administrator's role. Careful attention to current patterns and strong expectations to maintain and perpetuate them are required so administrators may determine how best to make changes. As noted in the research into the role of the principal, the principal's (and superintendent's) interpersonal competence, particularly in establishing and maintaining identi-

TABLE 3-3 *Suggested Interrelationships of Administrative Roles for Developing Operational Policy*

Legend:

1 Enact policy, approve operational policies
2 Recommend policy, coordinate, consult, direct
3 Major responsibility
4 Delegated responsibility
5 Advise on specific points
6 Exchange of views

Operational policies	Community/Agencies	Lay Advisory Councils	Mgr., Cafeteria, Bldgs & Grnds.	Dir., Adult Educ.	Dir., Student Act.	Dir., Libr. & Media Ctr.	Dir., Guidance & Counseling	Dept. Chr., team ldrs.	Asst. Principals	Middle/Sec. Principals	Elem. Sch. Principal	Dir. Transportation	Dir. Cafeterias	Dir. Bldgs. & Grnds.	Bus. Mgr.	Dir., Research	Coord., Adult Educ.	Coord., Guidance & Testing	Coord., Sec. Educ.	Coord., Elem. Educ.	Asst. Supt., Business Affairs	Asst. Supt., Pupil Personnel	Asst. Supt., Personnel	Asst. Supt., Curric./Instr.	Superintendent	Board of Education
1. Relations with local, state, federal agencies	6	6	5	5	5	5	5	5	4	3	3	5	5	5	5	5	4	4	4	4	3	3	3	3	2	1
2. Curriculum and instruction	6	6	6	4	4	4	5	4	4	3	3	5	5	5	5	4	4	4	4	4	5	4	4	3	2	1
3. Pupil personnel: services, activities	6	6	5	5	4	4	3	4	4	3	3	5	5	5	5	4	4	3	4	4	5	4	3	4	2	1
4. Staff personnel	6	6	6	5	6	5	5	4	5	3	3	6	6	6	5	5	4	5	3	3	4	4	4	4	2	1
5. Finance and business	6	6	5	5	6	6	6	5	5	4	4	4	4	4	3	5	5	5	4	4	3	5	5	4	2	1
6. Plant and facilities	6	6	4	4	5	5	6	6	4	3	3	6	6	3	4	5	5	5	4	4	3	4	5	5	2	1
7. Services: health, cafeteria, transportation	6	6	3	6	6	6	6	6	4	3	3	3	3	3	3	6	6	6	5	5	4	3	4	3	2	1
8. Community relations	6	6	4	4	4	5	4	4	4	3	3	6	6	6	6	6	3	5	4	4	3	3	4	3	2	1

ties for the administrator as well as for others, is pivotal to effectiveness.

The technical-managerial arena of administrative work could be charted as well. Here specific tasks under each major function can be identified and allocated to positions in terms of: (1) general supervision over the task, (2) direct supervision of the task, (3) work executed, (4) positions consulted, (5) positions to be notified of progress and point of referral for (6) decisions on matters in question. It is at the technical-managerial implementing of operational policy that administrative processes can be most clearly identified and explained although such processes are necessary in the other two arenas of administrative activity as well. These processes are: planning, decision-making, supervising, coordinating, motivating, directing, evaluating, and reporting. The formulation from which these processes were derived was presented in Chapter 1.

Names of the processes vary somewhat depending on the authorities' preferences, but they label sets of administrative acts for which technical tasks and skills have been specified. Processes such as planning, decision-making, motivating, and evaluating have a body of literature devoted to them. The standardization of practice for all processes and the need to apply the processes in every type of administration (business, government, military, education, etc.) first led to the belief that administration was fundamentally the same regardless of type. One might take a major task under any function and outline the necessary steps to set that task in operation. Systems analysis and attendant procedures are employed to do this.

Administration as it exists in formal organization is conducted through a system of interrelated roles based upon positions which are initially defined by function and process. Duties and responsibilities are assigned to positions and formal authority is delegated to those who occupy positions so that vertical and horizontal relationships form a coherent structure within which organizational tasks are carried out. In organizations composed of professional employees, such as school systems, professional preparation largely determines the nature and quality of performance. Also, administrative roles in education are relatively diffuse—not closely related spatially or by professional specialty. Especially at the level of principal, administration is broken into numerous diverse tasks. Each role must deal with varied functions in the line positions and with a wide range of clients (students, parents, professionals, and the public). The dynamics of roles and role systems as administrators carry out assigned duties and as roles and role systems interact to affect the organization will be the next topic.

Roles, Role Systems, and Role Behavior

Roles become dynamic as individuals assume them, occupying the positions upon which roles are based, interpreting and altering role expectations, bringing to a role special talents and performing it with unique styles. Likewise, roles change as role interrelationships develop that require mutual accommodations, coordination, and insights about possibilities and limitations. Role behavior is the resultant mix between formal definition, individual role perceptions, and contribution of individual effort or talent on the one hand and the effects of other roles in the system on the other. A role, such as superintendent or principal, has no meaning except in the context of a person assuming a prescribed position and fulfilling that role in relationship to other roles.

In an abstract sense the concept of role assumes that a system's requirements to provide some service to others causes the system to provide inducements for an individual to render a needed service. Inducements may be material, as in a salary that supplies physical and other needs, or psychological as in recognition, status, and other nonmaterial needs. Thus, *need-dispositions* of the individual are basic to inducing individual effort to take on responsibility and satisfy the *expectations* of the organization. An individual's need-dispositions and the organization's expectations are the major elements in the role behavior. Individuals perceive the expectations being placed upon themselves as incumbent on the role and they attempt to satisfy need-dispositions while meeting role expectations. The interplay of role expectations and need-dispositions is key to their satisfaction in fulfilling a role. Where role expectations coincide with need-dispositions, satisfaction with the role will be high.

Role expectations, as already noted, arise from the formal requirements of the job but also from the expectations of those occupying other roles who are also attempting to meet expectations, as they see them, while satisfying their own need-dispositions. Many roles in a school, for example, impinge on the role of the principal—teacher, student, parent, assistant principal, department head or team leader, central office roles such as superintendent, secretary, custodian, or community leader. Because of differences in these expectations, principals experience some role ambiguity and may sometimes have serious role conflict problems. Competence in dealing with role ambiguity and role conflict is basic to achieving satisfaction in the role as principal.

Role behavior results from the choices made in meeting expectations while trying to satisfy personal need-dispositions from the role. Superintendents and principals often cite the stimulation of problems and the satisfaction they receive in resolving conflicts, even those involving their own roles. One element of successful leadership in educational administration is the ability to change others' perceptions of their roles and to alter others' attitudes about their work and their colleagues.

The manner in which the administrator characteristically carries out the role is referred to as administrative style. No precise definition of style exists because it is difficult to identify all the factors that contribute to it. However, it is quite obvious that those in frequent contact with administrators have shared perceptions about how a particular administrator characteristically behaves in given situations. One useful approximation in judging administrative style is to observe the degree to which the administrator follows organizational expectations. One who "follows the book," "goes by the rules," and is relatively impersonal in the treatment of colleagues and staff can be said to have a *nomothetic* administrative style. One who is personable, has few fixed rules, and is relatively informal in treatment of colleagues and staff can be said to have an *ideographic* style. The terms *nomothetic* and *ideographic* derive from an early study on administrative relationships (Guba and Bidwell 1957). Role theory, then, provides useful concepts and generalizations to assist in understanding individual role and educational administration.

Some concepts of systems theory further explain role behavior. Just as positions comprise the formal structure of an organization, roles comprise a role system for an organization. The role system generates properties (variables) different from those of the formally prescribed position structure. Formal structure is static, capable of being described by an organizational chart, job descriptions, and procedures manuals. The role system is dynamic and reflects how an organization structures itself as work progresses. In professional organizations, such as schools and school districts, individuals discuss their work, reach agreements, and make accomodations in carrying out tasks. They also share concerns and ideas, develop opinions and understandings, and make decisions about their work. Natural leaders arise to serve informal group needs and serve as communication links. A group identity results, with shared feelings and understandings relating primarily to (1) the work activities, (2) the group itself, and (3) other outside groups and individuals. In this process the role system provides each organization with (a) role expectations and standards of performance, (b) attitudes and values, (c) traditions and customary ways of doing things, (d) status, (e) sets of informal controls, and (f) a communication system.

These six items are primary properties of an organization that grows out of the role systems. They are observable and measurable. They also produce secondary properties critical to organizational effectiveness. These secondary properties include organizational climate, member satisfaction, and productivity. Table 3-4 provides an overview of the properties of a social system that result from role behavior. Viewed logically, Table 3-4 might be summarized in the following statements: An organization is a dynamic system of roles that forms a social system. Role behavior factors result from human interactions, as organization members seek to meet role expectations and satisfy personal needs while carrying out work activities. Role system factors produce an organizational climate of measurable properties, which directly influences the achievement of organizational productivity and member satisfaction.

TABLE 3-4: *Properties of A Social System Produced by Role Behavior*

Organization	Role Behavior Produces:	Climate Factors	Outcomes
Goals	Role Expectations	Identity, Belonging	Productivity
Work Activities	Work Standards	Cohesiveness	Satisfaction
Work Processes	Values, Attitudes	Loyalty	
	Customs, Tradition	Support, Trust	
	Statuses	Risk Taking	
	Controls: Formal, Informal	Conflict Tolerance	
	Communications	Morale, Esprit	

feedback

The school administrator who understands the organization as a dynamic system of roles will be better able to monitor and influence climate factors and outcomes. General systems theory provides constructs which might assist in placing role theory into a total perspective. An organization conceived as a system has subsystems depending upon the arrangement of the work activity, but also upon the resultant role system. The system and its subsystems have boundaries, exist in time and space, have function and structure, and maintain vitality through exchanges of resources and information both internally and externally. In general systems theory, an organization is an entity which interacts with its environment by means of inputs from it and outputs to it. The processes between inputs and outputs are shown in Table 3-4. All human organizations such as schools and school districts are open systems having many linkages to their external environment. Conditions that affect a system, internally or externally, can be conceived of as factors (variables) that can be observed, measured, and, at least to some extent, controlled or altered. The measure of an administrator's success largely depends upon the knowledge of these factors and competence in changing them to achieve improved organizational productivity and member satisfaction.

References

Blumberg, Arthur, and **William Greenfield.** 1980. *The Effective Principal: Perspectives in School Leadership.* Boston: Allyn and Bacon.

Byrne, David R., Susan A. Hines, and **Lloyd E. McCleary.** 1978. *The Senior High School Principalship*, Vol. 1: *The National Survey.* Reston, Va.: National Association of Secondary School Principals.

Butts, R. Freeman, and **Lawrence A. Cremin.** 1953. *A History of Education in American Culture.* New York: Henry Holt.

Callahan, Raymond E. 1962. *The Cult of Efficiency.* Chicago: The University of Chicago Press.

Cremin, Lawrence A. 1980. *American Education: The National Experience, 1783-1876.* New York: Harper and Row.

Dewey, John. 1899. *The School and Society.* Chicago: University of Chicago Press.

Gee, Gordon, and **David Sperry.** 1978. *Educational Law and the Public Schools: A Compendium.* Boston: Allyn and Bacon.

Guba, E., and **B. Bidwell.** 1957. *Administrative Relationships.* Chicago: University of Chicago Press.

Jones, Howard Mumford. 1952. "Horace Mann's Crusade." In Daniel Aaron, ed., *America in Crisis*, edited by Daniel Aaron, 91-107. New York: Harper and Brothers.

Kunz, D. W., and **W. K. Hoy.** 1976. "Leadership Style of Principals." *Educational Administration Quarterly* 12 (Fall): 49-64.

Lacey, Miriam Y. 1981. *Behavioral Components of Interpersonal Competence and Their Perceived Importance by Managers in Different Fields.* Doctoral diss., University of Utah.

McCleary, Lloyd E., Donavan D. Peterson, and **Gene Lamb.** 1976. *Organizational Analysis and Change.* Salt Lake City, Utah: ILM Publishers.

McCleary, Lloyd E., and **Scott D. Thomson.** 1979. *The Senior High School Principalship.* Vol. 3: *The Summary Report.* Reston, Va.: National Association of Secondary School Principals.

March, James G. 1978. "American Public School Administration: A Short Analysis." *School Review* 86 (February): 217-50.

Mintzberg, Henry. 1979. *The Structuring of Organizations.* Englewood Cliffs, N.J.: Prentice-Hall.

Moehlman, Arthur B. 1940. *School Administration.* Boston: Houghton Mifflin.

Morris, V. C., R. Crowson, E. Hurwitz, and **C. Porter-Gehrie.** 1981. *The Urban Principal: Discretionary Decision Making.* Chicago: College of Education, University of Illinois at Chicago Circle.

Peterson, K. D. 1981. *Making Sense of the Principal's Work.* Paper presented to Division A of the American Educational Research Association, Los Angeles, 1981.

Pharis, William L. and **Sally Banks Zakariya.** 1979. *The Elementary School Principalship in 1978: A Research Study.* Arlington, Va.: National Association of Elementary School Principals.

Rutter, Michael, Barbara Maughan, Peter Mortimore, and **Janet Ouston.** 1979. *Fifteen Thousand Hours: Secondary Schools and Their Effects on Children.* London: Open Books.

Salley, Columbus, R. Bruce McPherson, and **Melany E. Baehr.** 1975. *National Occupational Analysis of the School Principalship.* Chicago: Industrial Relations Center, University of Chicago.

Stuart v. School District No. 1, 30 Michigan 69, 1874.

Tyack, David B. 1974. *The One Best System.* Cambridge: Harvard University Press, 1974.

Valentine, Jerry, Donald C. Clark, Neal C. Nickerson, Jr., and **James W. Keefe.** 1981. *The Middle Level Principalship.* Vol. 1. Reston, Va.: National Association of Secondary School Principals.

Woolcott, Harry F. 1973. *The Man in the Principal's Office.* New York: Holt, Rinehart and Winston.

4

The worst cliques are those which consist of one man.
- George Bernard Shaw

Staffing and Staff Development

Staffing and staff development practices are primary determinants of quality in educational programs of whatever type or level. Other determinants include the educational plan, the instructional materials, the technologies, and facilities. However, as substantiated by school effectiveness studies the competence of the instructional staff far outweighs these other elements. The human and humane character of schooling, as pointed out in Chapter 1, creates unique conditions for educational organizations that account for the centrality of the staffing function to educational productivity. Unfortunately, both public and higher education have tended to rely upon artificial criteria to define competence (credentials, resumes, degrees, course credits, etc.) and too frequently have not provided adequate opportunities for staff development. Many real constraints on staffing practices exist, but there is much that can be done to make staffing and staff development a dynamic element of educational quality and improvement.

The Staffing Challenge

Teaching, support, and administrative staff at the school level will be referred to as the *instructional staff*. Often personnel practices focus on the selection and placement of the teacher only. Certainly the teacher is the dominant element in instruction, particularly where the self-contained classroom is the primary instructional unit; however, schools no longer can provide adequate instruction without an integrated instructional staff concept. Teacher, teaching team leader, supervisor, counselor, special teacher, learning resource specialist, aide, or principal have varying degrees of influence over the learning process; each at times, is in a direct relationship with learners. Therefore, it is necessary to create conditions in which each staff member makes appropriate and coordinated contributions to the teaching-learning process. This can be done effectively only when a clear instructional plan is developed, when group and individual instructional needs are assessed and monitored, when instructional staff understand, and when staff can participate in a coordinated fashion. Flexible and adaptable staffing practices must be established for each segment of the instructional plan, and interventions must be made when teaching and learning conditions are inappropriate or inadequate.

The problems of educational quality and organizational stability present challenges to staffing and staff development practices in terms of the conditions noted above. Instructional staff members do not represent standardized parts. So personnel with proper credentials, grossly matched to job descriptions and placed in a school will not necessarily result in an efficient, effective instructional staff. Staff members need to be selected in terms of the conditions of a particular school, and every staff change should be considered in terms of opportunities for improving instruction. Specific competencies and talents should be identified; opportunities to re-vitalize, update, and alter programs should be assessed regularly. Quality and organizational stability require cooperative effort, and this requires participation of the instructional staff in program planning and development, and their involvement in specifying the competencies needed to deliver each educational service.

Involvement becomes a second major challenge to staffing and staff development practices. Quality and organizational stability are not static conditions. Definitions of quality change as the needs of learners change, the knowledge of teaching and learning improve, and the conditions faced within a particular school are altered by local circumstances. Organizational stability requires that staff members understand directions of development and have the skills and dispositions to alter practice in regular and consistent patterns. Staff development is the key to this process. Involvement of staff is the means to maintain a perspective which makes improvement a continuous effort. Staff development should provide involvement and the means to acquire the competencies needed to maintain stable, consistent organizational development.

Change is a third major challenge to staffing and staff development practices. Change, in the sense meant here, differs from development. The latter comes largely from within; the former is largely induced from without. Change in schools can be induced by only four types of intervention. First, programs can be revised or eliminated and new ones introduced. Second, technologies can be utilized so teaching and learning are substantially altered. Third, organizational patterns can be restructured so instructional practices and professional relationships are altered, as with team teaching or the use of instructional specialists. Finally, the competencies and attitudes of staff members themselves can be modified. Regardless of the basic strategy used to bring about change, staff attitudes and competencies must sooner or later receive attention. Change must be assimilated and institutionalized if the intended effects are to be realized. New staff members may be added; ineffective staff members may be transferred or terminated. Yet the challenge of change must be met through staffing and staff development practices.

Assumptions Relative to Staffing and Staff Development

Imbedded in the presentation thus far are a number of assumptions, both stated and implied. Some can be supported by theory and research; some are fairly widely accepted in practice; some are based on a logic derived from a knowledge of schooling and beliefs about the nature of formal education. This section will briefly identify key assumptions so the reader may better assess the remaining presentation of this chapter and more explicitly expose and examine his/her own assumptions. The rationale here is derived from school effectiveness studies, since the ultimate outcome of staffing and staff development practices is productive schools.

Four categories can be used within which variables associated with the effectiveness of schools may be identified. These include the following:

1. Intake variables: What learners are like as they enter a school; levels of achievement, talents, interests, aspirations; self-esteem, attitudes, and expectations about learning and knowledge of potentials.
2. Process variables: How the school carries out the development or alteration of the intake variables; expectations of instructional staff, time on learning tasks, home-work, use of library and other school-provided resources, access to instructional staff, and use of parental influences and support.
3. Ecological variables: What and how the school creates a learning environment; high standards, organized and individualized curriculum, positive and preventive versus punitive treatment, pleasant relationships, attractive physical surroundings.
4. Outcome variables: Effects of efforts relating to the above factors that produce levels of achievement, developed talents; personal characteristics and views of self, and knowledge of one's potentials and possibilities.

Research into school effectiveness (Madaus et al. 1980; Wynne 1980; and Rutter et al. 1979) tends to substantiate that significant improvements in measures of outcome variables requires conscious assessment of intake variables, and deliberate, planned actions relating to process and ecological variables. No single process or ecological variable is of greater importance than another; rather, the cumulative effects of efforts related to process and ecological variables produce changes in outcomes. Further, this line of research tends to show that effective schools having superior measures of outcome variables are present in every category of institution regardless of socioeconomic level of parents, location, or size.

From what is now known about effective schools, certain assumptions relative to staffing and staff development acquire a measure of validity grounded in logic and in research evidence. First is the centrality of the instructional staff, with the consequent need to develop an integrated staffing concept. Second is that instructional staff members need to be selected according to the needs of a specific school; therefore competencies required within the total instructional staff of a school need to be clearly specified. Third is that involvement of instructional staff is necessary to quality and organizational stability (defined as the alteration of practice in regular, consistent patterns to improve outcomes). Fourth is that change toward improved educational productivity requires flexibility and adaptability in staffing practice and that staff development is a key to achieving imaginative staffing practices and improved productivity.

Finally, any changes should include a careful assessment of the instructional staff's competence to effect the changes and institutionalize them into regular educational practice. When incompetence is present, a change in staffing or staff development practices should be insisted on to maintain and improve educational productivity.

A major assumption yet to be treated is that staffing and staff development in today's schools require an integrated instructional staff concept. This concept must be understood and applied from the top down, from district level to schools, if the complexities of staffing contemporary educational programs are to result in effective educational programs. As pointed out, many and diverse educational personnel are responsible for instruction of pupils. This condition requires careful coordination, mediation, and control or confusion can produce wasted effort, conflict, and deterioration of staff morale to the detriment of learning. There are six basic functions for which personnel are employed to provide instruction to pupils. These are teaching, guidance, support services, instructional supervision, management, and administration.

Teaching involves the direct instruction of learners. The teacher, learning resource specialist, special teacher, counselor, aide, and principal are obviously involved in a variety of ways: presenting information, advising, directing learning activities, tutoring, reinforcing learning, and a host of others. Guidance involves helping the learner (client) to solve individual, personal, and vocational problems and learn appropriate group behaviors. Support services, the most diverse in terms of personnel, are necessary to enhance the conditions of learning and to assist the leader to profit from instruction. They include: library, learning laboratory, health services, activities and recreation, food services, and transportation. The instructional supervision function involves activities supportive of improving instruction: curriculum and materials development, evaluation of programs and staff, instructional planning, and staff development. The management function includes materials preparation, audiovisual and book storage and distribution, and instructional equipment maintenance and delivery. The administrative function includes the decision-making, scheduling, controlling, coordinating, and allocating of resources as described in Chapter 1. Team leaders, department chairpersons, program directors, and principals have portions of time specifically devoted to this function. Others, including teachers, counselors, and supervisors participate in both management and administrative functions. Staffing these functions is not an easy task. Some of these functions can be carried out independently: a teacher delivering a lesson, or a school psychologist working with an emotionally disturbed student. Even here problems develop, as when the school psychologist needs to see the student during a scheduled class time. As the various functions become scheduled, several sets of coordination and control problems surface. We have already referred to the independent relationship in which individual staff provide service to learners. There is the condition in which staff members must jointly provide a service, as in team teaching or a teacher using the services of the learning resource specialist. Sometimes services compete for the same students, as when music, drama, and foreign language programs seek the same student(s) for activities occurring at the same time. On other occasions, different staff or students compete for the same service, as when several teachers request the same resource specialist, or when transportation is needed for field trips at the time a music festival requires that students be transported to other schools.

The combination of staff, students (clients), and service in a simple matrix reveals that six distinct sets of coordination problems are possible. The planning of functions by services to be provided exposes the staffing needs and the possible coordination problems. It also permits a rational identification of the staff competencies needed to fulfill the functions required for each service. The procedures for doing this are presented in the staff evaluation section of this chapter. The point to be made is that an integrated instructional staffing concept is required by contemporary education and that the implementation of this concept introduces staffing and staff coordination problems. The problems of staff coordination reveal the need for staff development activities to build mutual understanding, trust, and support while dealing with the substantive problems of planning and delivery of educational services. Finally, the coordination required in an integrated staffing concept necessitates staff leadership for each educational service. Obviously, this cannot always be provided by the principal. We have not extended the analysis at this point to show the staffing and staff development relationships between the school and the central office.

The Staff Personnel Function

The previous section of this chapter revealed assumptions basic to a view of staffing and staff development. These assumptions have not been fully embraced in practice although it is not likely that they would be opposed in principle. Traditional forms of schooling, control mechanisms, resource allocation, and resistance of educational institutions to innovative practice all have served to keep staffing confined largely to conventional tasks associated with recruitment, selection, placement, and review of staff performance. Principals are involved in these tasks, although this involvement is usually restricted to consultation with central office staff as substantiated by data from recent national studies of the principalship (Byrne et al. 1978, 24; Valentine et al. 1981, 40).

This section reviews traditions and innovations underlying current practice to give a perspective from which the management of personnel services is examined.

Traditions and Innovations

The graded structure of schools whose evolution was described in earlier chapters, resulted in the self-contained classroom at the elementary level, and a departmentalized teaching organization for the middle and high school levels. A separate subject curriculum taught using texts and workbooks gave a semblance of order and quality to instruction. The textbook largely defined the curriculum and provided a ready-made sequencing and articulation of content. Teaching competence was defined in terms of knowledge of the subject, methods of instruction appropriate to the subject, and the skills necessary to classroom management. Qualifications were evaluated by college training and experience; supervision was equated with inspection; and the quality of instruction could be monitored through standardized tests.

As enrollments diversified and school size increased, classrooms and teachers were added in incremental fashion, maintaining a standardized classroom unit. Problems attendant to ability levels and interests of learners brought about the addition of programs, such as vocational education and special education, ability grouping of classes within academic subjects, and the addition of specialists for certain categories of remedial and adjustment problems. College and state agency controls described in Chapter 2 (pp. 51–56; pp. 81–83), inhibited innovation in both curriculum and instructional organization, and the standard patterns remained. A circularity of preparation and licensing for narrow specialties reinforced fragmented educational services and programs conducted in rigid time schedules by departmentally organized specialists.

Efforts to individualize instruction, to integrate and interrelate subject matter, and to group teaching and support personnel in order to concentrate upon learning and learner needs have met with serious difficulties. Under the conditions noted above, a long history of educational innovation shows that attempts to achieve the broader outcomes of schooling, implied by our list of outcome variables associated with effective schools (p. 72), have been largely rejected. Dahl and Lindblom (1963) in an analysis of school organization and staffing practices, repeatedly illustrate the limited scope of school outcomes due to compartmentalized staffing and the inability to introduce innovation. Goodlad and Anderson (1962) and Trump (1969) criticized rigid instructional sequences, time allocations, and staffing practices as ineffective in achieving important outcomes. Mosteller (1975), and Aslin et al. (1976) point to the high rejection rate of innovation in the schools. These studies are representative of a large group of curriculum, evaluation, and administration specialists who have documented these conditions.

Although traditions have locked schools and schooling into rigid patterns, certain innovations have occurred and, moreover, have persisted because they "fit the established mode" and also because of leadership and dedicated staff. No attempt will be made to provide a comprehensive record or document the development of a particular innovation. A list follows, however, of innovations which are expected to persist and which have implications for staffing and staff development:

1. Individualization of instruction: Individual Education Plan (IEP) programmed instruction, peer and volunteer tutoring, work-study, self-paced learning.
2. Instructional technology: Computers and calculators, gaming, language laboratories and resource centers.
3. Instructional modes: Discovery learning, mastery learning, tutorials, independent study, non-graded grouping, teacher teams, learning-teaching styles.
4. Curriculum diversity: Alternative school and program, mainstreaming of the handicapped, bilingual education, advanced placement, questing, correlated and fused courses.
5. Guidance: Peer counseling, house plan organization of student body.

The list could be extended, but an impressive list of innovative practices can be produced which some schools have implemented in very effective ways.

The list of innovative practices results from several long-term influences. First is recognition of the need to individualize instruction and the firm psychological grounds for doing so. Second is the desire to provide an integrated curriculum because of the practical need to reduce redundancy and increase reinforcement across fragmented subjects; this integration, too, is strongly supported by established learning and curriculum theory. Third is the pressure to open the schools to encourage active parental involvement and to use community resources more fully. Fourth is the pressure to incorporate new technology and compete with the mass media. Fifth is the recognition of learning barriers created by noneducational influences, including physical handicaps, ethnic and language background, socioeconomic condition, or values orientation.

Both traditions and innovations in education have enormous implications for staffing and staff development practices. If traditional modes of formal education are to dominate, staffing practices will remain relatively routine, confined largely to the selection and placement of narrowly defined, specialized staff. On the other hand, if schools seriously undertake to achieve broader outcomes in effective ways, training, certification, selection and placement, performance evaluation, and staff development will need to be altered drastically. Several patterns of change are possible. They range from one projecting deterioration of the public schools to one projecting that schools will become coordinators of media and of experiences largely outside a formal school setting. A more realistic view may be based on the assumptions already presented. Schools show signs of effectively using the advanced technologies, of improving the use of community resources, and of integrating an increasingly diverse group of learners in substantive educational programs and services. The remainder of this chapter is based on what the authors view as this more realistic view of schooling and formal education.

Organization of Personnel Services

School districts have created organizational arrangements for dealing with the staffing function. This function is composed of a series of interrelated tasks usually administered, at the district level, through an office of personnel services. Headed by an assistant superintendent or director in the moderate-to-large size districts, this office deals with the three levels of administrative tasks as described in Chapter 1: (1) assistance with policy development and the oversight of board policy; (2) district leadership in policy implementation; and (3) technical management of personnel services.

Personnel Service Policy

Policies relating to personnel services are important not only to the effective conduct of the personnel function, but also because of the centrality of personnel services to the organizational health of the entire school system. In the following areas board policy is essential:

1. Organization and responsibilities of the personnel office including relationships to all administrative units, both instructional and non-instructional.
2. Specification of services to be provided and of the guidelines for procedures to be followed, including recruitment and employment of all personnel; placement and assignment; evaluation; separation; and personnel welfare.
3. Participation of the office in negotiations and staff development.
4. Communications with personnel and with the public, including employee relations, clarification of obligations, rights and privileges, and recognition of superior performance.
5. Cooperative involvement of staff in the development of personnel policies and assistance in maintaining high standards of performance and the conditions necessary to quality service.
6. Insuring the integrity of the district in all staff relationships through equality and fairness of treatment; active assistance in career enhancement; and prompt, accurate response to questions and problems.

The American Association of School Administrators, the National School Board Association, and the American Association of School Personnel Administrators regularly publish materials relating to needed policies and services. The AASPA periodically publishes a set of standards and a list of suggested practices. The last such publication listed more than one hundred eighty practices suitable for use as a check list, particularly for districts that do not maintain an office with trained personnel administrators (American Association of School Administrators 1978). The standards and practices could well serve as a guide in policy development and as a reference for students of educational administration.

Leadership in Policy Implementation
The leadership tasks in policy implementation are primarily those of planning, initiating, coordinating, directing, and monitoring personnel services. The size of the school district and the philosophy of the board of education and the superintendent will determine the nature and quality of personnel services. A highly centralized personnel office that focuses primarily on technical-managerial tasks and handling personnel services as routinized procedures, will not provide conditions to insure a high quality of instructional and support staff. Likewise, highly decentralized personnel responsibilities will lead to uncoordinated decisions and services. Even in small districts, where the superintendent or assistant superintendent serves as personnel officer, some specialized staff is needed to provide adequate support for personnel services.

Leadership to achieve a high quality of personnel services can be attained best when coordinated, collaborative relationships are created between school principals and administrative officers of non-instructional units. This requires a district personnel office that can offer a full array of services, headed (when size permits) by a trained personnel officer. Increasingly the writings in the fields of management, education, political science, and the military (Derr 1980; Meyer 1976; Harris et al. 1979) advocate that to optimize organizational systems, personnel directors should become human resource experts equipped to handle human problems. Pigors and Meyers (1973) offer a list of leadership tasks they feel to be essential in any modern organization. Applied to education a list derived from theirs would include:

1. Develop personnel policy that is part of a total system, focused on an integrated staffing concept to maximize performance and achieve satisfying careers at all levels.
2. Carry out manpower planning and forecasting within a district planning effort.
3. Offer working conditions and personnel services that recognize the changing nature of the work force and life styles, particularly with reference to minorities and women.
4. Provide services, such as personal counseling and career planning, which attend to the human problems found in all job classifications of a district.
5. Assist with the planning and conduct of staff evaluation and development.
6. Emphasize cooperative effort and support in promoting self-development within an integrated staffing concept.
7. Create new forms of compensation and rewards related to role performance and organizational effectiveness.

In providing leadership to the personnel function, neither the professional associations nor the authorities cited advocates that the personnel officer be a "line" officer. The personnel officer is seen as a coordinator, advisor, and developer of human resources. Line officers of units, principals of schools, and heads of noninstructional units need to staff the instructional and noninstructional services as described earlier in this chapter; the personnel officer and the personnel office provide services to them under the direction of the superintendent.

Technical Managerial Tasks

Associated with personnel services are the procedural, consultative, and informational technical-managerial tasks necessary to provide the services required by law and district policy.

Primary Personnel Services

These services are (1) Staff Needs Determination; (2) competency specification and job description; (3) recruitment and selection; (4) assignment, transfer, and separation; (5) evaluation and need assessment for staff development. The procedures and time lines for accomplishing each personnel service need to be specified and communicated to those who are to participate. Procedures should be prepared and coordinated at the district level so that principals and unit administrators can prepare compatible procedures and time lines to meet district schedules. Procedure specification permits checks to be made of legal requirements and district policy; then the necessary consultative and information requirements can be determined. (An illustration of a procedure plan is given in Table 4-1.)

TABLE 4-1: *Illustrative Procedures and Suggested Time Lines for Determining Staff Needs*

Procedure	Jan.	Feb.	Mar.	Apr.	May	June
Review annual plan progress	*					
Conduct staff evaluations		*		*		
Confer with District on			*			*
a. enrollment projections						
b. staffing formulas						
c. District planning						
Confer with instructional, support staff leaders on			*	*		
a. staff evaluations						
b. District information						
c. conduct of annual plan						
d. projected staff needs			*	*		
Conference with staff members on						
a. evaluations, b. career plans			*	*		
Determine staff retention				*	*	
Determine						
a. staff retention						
b. allowable positions				*	*	
Review						
a. annual plan goals						
b. competencies of retained staff				*		
Confer with District on special needs				*	*	
Determine						
a. positions needed						
b. competencies required to meet goals						
c. job descriptions						*
Check on any questionable retentions and evaluate procedures used						

Each of the primary personnel services named above is described and major considerations for each service are noted in this section. Policy and the nature of leadership at the school district level will vary considerably in practice although each service will exist in every school district. In the ideal arrangement, each personnel service is related to the others; and all staffing decisions are made in terms of the long range plans of district and school.

Staff Needs Determination

Each staff change presents an opportunity to improve the quality of educational service. Therefore a replacement or transfer should be made after careful assessment and specification of the competencies required to achieve improved practice. The logic of this position has already been presented, but too frequently school districts consider only a specific position as replacing one staff member with another, qualified by paper credentials to fill the position vacated. School-by-school planning with attention to the variables identified as determinants of effectiveness is essential. A school plan should include a needs assessment and projections of desired instructional and service goals. These cast against the current status of programs and results yield discrepancies, and an analysis of discrepancies can result in descriptions of staff competencies needed to move toward goals.

Many districts conduct long-range planning and require that schools prepare annual improvement plans based on need assessments and a discrepancy analysis. Whether or not this is an established district policy, principals of schools should develop the competencies to undertake such planning. Districts also establish staffing formulas based on "units of need" as determined by class size, special programs, services offered, and needs of specific schools. These latter factors determine the positions that are available. Known staff retentions subtracted from positions allowable produce the positions to be filled. A school plan should provide the goals and directions of development so that the needed competencies in available positions can be specified. Competencies of retained staff, determined by staff evaluation procedures, then provide the principal with information with which to balance the staff so that instructional and support services can be assigned to staff retained and needed positions can be specified.

Procedures for determining staffing needs are given in Table 4-1. As can be seen, it includes more than a simple determination of positions needed, and relates planning, competency specification, staff evaluation, and other administrative tasks to the determination of staff needs. Not shown is the need for regular consultation and feedback between the district level and the school staff. Often the superintendent, the personnel officer, and other specialists from the district office are heavily involved in each procedure. For example, central staff are likely to be conducting salary negotiations during a part of this period, district level planning will likely be going forward, and reviews of programs and staff will be under way.

Competency Specification and Job Descriptions

Competency specification in the personnel field is a common practice in business, industry, and the military. It has a brief history in education that has been linked to controversy over administration by objectives, accountability of teachers, and competency-based teacher training (Campbell et al. 1980, 374-76). However, both valid personnel evaluation and staff development depend on it. Unless one is able to specify what an individual must be able to do to perform effectively in a given role, there is little likelihood that performance can be assessed objectively, or that any pre-service or in-service education could be designed that could achieve intended results on the job. When arguments are set aside involving teacher union objections to evaluation and university fear of loss of control over teacher training, arguments involve (1) a reductio ad absurdum listing of numerous inconsequential skills which occurred in some training programs and (2) the technical capability to conduct personnel evaluation in any objective fashion. The former condition has largely fallen of its own weight, and the latter has to a considerable extent been overcome.

In the personnel field the specification of competencies needed in organizational staffing, in personnel evaluation, and in staff development are well-recognized (Harris et al. 1979, 111-43). Harris and his associates reviewed the research and development work pertaining to competency specification and applied it to the staffing problem. They advocated that each major segment of instructional and support services of a school be examined. Competencies that the best, professional opinion available deemed to be significant to successful service should be identified. The lack of this kind of competency specification leaves us with impressionistic judgments based upon unexamined criteria.

An illustration of a competency specification might serve to clarify how competencies are identified. When the position of elementary school teaching team leaders was being created in a school district, a small group of teachers, elementary principals, and district supervisory staff were asked to identify the competencies needed by a team leader. Twenty-six were identified, and several competency indicators were described for each. One competency was identified as follows:

The team leader will need to involve teacher teams in the development of lesson plans which will provide instructional specificity to district curriculum guides.

Technical indicator: The team leader will collect, prepare, and submit sample lesson plan formats for examination by the team.

Conceptual indicator: The team leader will present and explain several basic approaches to lesson planning as illustrated by specific examples.

Human indicator: The team leader will work with the team to select a format for lesson plans and develop a work schedule and work division with team members.

In the actual situation three to five statements were offered for each type of indicator. In this district, lesson planning had been haphazard or non-existent and was identified by the group as a serious deficiency. The role description was reviewed by the principal and a teacher group at each elementary school where situation specific competencies were added and the high priority items were identified for the school.

From the competency statements, job descriptions could be prepared in a more rational fashion than would otherwise be the case. Job descriptions should provide an accurate, yet not highly detailed, description of the position, the organization and working conditions, training and experience requirements, terms of employment, qualifications required and desired, and relevent information about the school district and community. The job description should provide sufficient information to attract a range of applicants yet not be so restrictive as to limit promising candidates or preclude job alteration after employment. As with competency specification, job descriptions require participation of a range of staff who will be expected to work with the person employed.

Recruitment and Selection

A rich pool of candidates is essential in getting competent staff for effective programs. Personnel officers, principals, and key staff should actively seek to interest individuals with a variety of backgrounds, interests, and talents in addition to their "paper" qualifications. Instructional personnel particularly need to be interesting people whose talents, outside interests, and diverse backgrounds enrich school life for staff and students. A small effort to recruit outstanding individuals can significantly improve the quality of the candidate pool. Too frequently, recruitment is conducted only through contacts with university placement offices and by published notices. Contacts should also be made with community leaders, professors, and government employment agencies. Many agencies such as Peace Corps, Teacher Corps, Vista, and the foreign agencies noted in Chapter 1 have highly qualified short-term employees who could be candidates. Recruiting minorities is sometimes difficult, but needed whether schools have substantial minority enrollment or not. Extreme care must be taken to comply with laws and policies that prohibit employment and promotion practices that constitute race, sex, or age bias. Schools and districts should be alert for staff members who are currently underutilized, who lack necessary qualifications but could obtain them, and who could be better employed if job assignments were rearranged.

Selection from the pool of candidates involves a first screening, checks, and follow-up for additional information, interviews and tests where appropriate, final screening, and decision. Studies universally point to the lack of validity or reliability of interviews, letters of recommendation, and even of candidate self-descriptions in response to relatively objective questions on application forms. A first screening should eliminate unqualified applicants and provide an initial priority rating of candidates. Validation of credentials and letters of the more highly rated candidates should be made before further follow-up. This can often be accomplished by telephone. Visits to the candidate's place of employment are used but should only be undertaken with the candidate's approval. Interviews can be conducted with individual candidates or in small groups. Panels of interviewers are frequently used, although this method usually is employed with individual candidates and often in combination with interviews by single interviewers.

As the selection process is undertaken, criteria should be established for data collection, interviewing, and making judgments. Careful notes and records of decisions should be made and kept confidential both by the individuals involved in the process and by the official in charge of selection. As noted in Chapter 3 the superintendent is ultimately responsible to make employment recommendations to the board. Therefore careful record keeping is important in addition to a mere record of decisions made. Many districts employ rating scales keyed to the criteria agreed upon and arranged for each element of the selection process. Important to the selection process is careful adherence to the provisions of the Equal Employment Opportunity Act of 1972 and subsequent revisions. This act specifies information that may not be collected; these items of information include a photograph, maiden name, marital or family status, spouse's first name and occupation, or religious preference.

A detailed chart of guidelines may be found in Beatty and Schneier (1977, 458-59).

A final important point often not deliberately conducted, is an assessment of the selection process itself. Such an assessment, in any formal way, is often omitted. Questions to be raised might include: Was sufficient information available about all candidates? Was certain information unnecessary or given too much weight? Were criteria for selection clear and properly applied? Is there evidence that better qualified people were not attracted to apply? Why? What weaknesses appeared at any stage of the process? Unless there is a conscientious assessment, the recruitment and selection process cannot be improved, and an unquestioned faith in the process might lead to systematic selection of weak candidates.

Assignment, Transfer, and Separation

Assignment, transfer, and separation of staff members should be based on a view of each school and of the district as a bank of human resources to be drawn upon to staff programs. Complex factors enter into decisions about the movement of personnel. First, there are the needs of the district and some aspects of determining staffing needs have been presented in a previous section. As staffing needs are identified, consideration should be given to whether a program or service is an effective one and should be maintained; whether it is weak and in need of strengthening by the addition of staff competencies not present; whether the program or service is to be fundamentally altered or eliminated in the foreseeable future; or whether a new program or service will soon require change in the established one. Declining enrollments, start-up of an area vocational center, addition of a new foreign language to the instructional programs, and implementation of peer counseling or work-study programs are examples that occurred in one secondary school in a two-year period.

A second set of factors involved in assignment, transfer, and separation applies to the overall staffing needs of a particular program or service. Characteristics such as age, ethnic or racial background, foreign language facility, computer expertise, or practical work experience may be of prime importance to staff balance and team effort. Transfers, when possible, can often balance an aging staff, include representatives of a minority group, or provide subject or other forms of competency.

A third set of factors involved in assignment, transfer, and separation is related to the needs of staff members. Challenge and career enhancement opportunities can benefit the individual and thereby the district. Job sharing, with part-time employment in business or industry, for example, has permitted many schools to retain staff who might have been lost. Even separation has been shown to be beneficial to some individuals when conducted under the proper conditions (Thomas and Sutherland 1982).

There are then, factors associated with basic competency needs, with specialized, even ancillary, competencies and characteristics, and with needs of staff members themselves. Such factors need to be identified well in advance. This identification requires persistent attention of the principal, supervisors, and key staff members at the school level and of district level personnel specialists. Properly conducted, this matching of staffing needs and opportunities with the human resources pool of schools is an effective approach to personnel planning. It provides opportunities both to increase educational productivity and to enlarge staff satisfaction.

We have not specifically treated topics such as induction of new staff, career counseling, or the range of concerns involved with separation. These topics receive more detailed attention in sections of this chapter dealing with staff development and due process.

Evaluation and Need Assessment

Personnel evaluation is a necessary but highly difficult administrative responsibility. This is so partly because of the dire consequences to individuals or to organizational morale and productivity from a poorly conducted evaluation or an unwarranted use of evaluation information. This danger is compounded by the complexity of factors that enter into any professional role and the difficulty of establishing performance criteria even when agreement upon factors to be evaluated has been reached. There are difficulties as well with the validity and reliability of instruments and procedures employed in evaluation. Finally, all evaluation requires that judgments be made both in collecting information about performance and in the interpretation and use of information after it is collected. Given these difficulties it becomes imperative that any evaluation process used be understood by those involved, and that the uses to which evaluations are put do not exceed the capabilities of the process used. Unless personnel evaluation is approached in a deliberate fashion it is likely to be haphazzard, subjective, and covert; it should be, however, objective, rationally judgmental, and overt.

The evaluation of instructional personnel is discussed in considerable detail in Chapter 6.

There remains in this section the question of the relationship of personnel evaluation to needs assessment for staff development purposes. Personnel evaluation should be based upon competencies needed to deliver instructional services effectively. Since educational productivity is dependent on variables that are highly situation-specific, and since competency specification depends on an integrated staffing concept, competencies need to be defined at the school level with a high degree of staff involvement. Further, if recruitment, selection and assignment activities are properly executed, the primary route to instructional improvement should be through staff development. Given these assumptions, the purpose of personnel evaluation is the identification of the discrepancies between personnel performance and desired educational outcomes. When personnel evaluation is undertaken in terms of competencies, the discrepancies identified indicate staffing skills which need to be obtained either by changes, by additions, or by developments.

Staff Development

Staff development practices are universally criticized as inadequate and misdirected (Neale, Bailey, and Ross 1981; Association for Supervision and Curriculum Development 1981; Lyons 1980). This criticism rests upon research evidence that no significant correlations are found between in-service education and measures of school improvement; upon complaints of teachers and school administrators that in-service programs are of poor quality and badly conducted; and upon the observations of authorities that most in-service programs are not targeted to needs or are insufficient. The citations given above document these criticisms. Yet where a careful need assessment has indicated staff deficiencies, a sound staff development program is a necessity.

Staff development should not be undertaken until needs have been identified. Criticisms of staff development practices typically do not include need assessment, possibly because an in-service program has usually been based upon what others *think* a given staff needs or wants. The lack of recognition of a school staff as being the most important element in educational productivity, and the propensity to expand resources on programs and services first, leaving little for staff development are principal reasons for providing an in-service educational program that only by hit and miss produces staff development. Identifying competency needs of *individual* staff members is the means by which a true staff development program can be designed.

The design of staff development programs involves: (1) specification of purposes based upon needs; (2) activities planned to achieve purposes; (3) the organizational arrangements to provide the activities; and (4) formative evaluation of individual staff competencies. The knowledge base, technologies, and materials exist to carry out each of these steps; schools, universities, state agencies, and professional associations have shown the capability to provide them. Four models for providing staff development exist that provide for the steps needed in program design and the participation of those agencies. These models are:

Organizational Development Model (OD). The OD model focuses on processes of communication, problem solving, decision-making, and change. External intervention is supplied over a long period to train the school staff in communication skills, develop norms and patterns for problem solving, and implement changes in practices and policies. Training in specific content is provided; but the long-term effort is directed toward building self-renewing schools (Schmuck et al. 1977).

Responsive Model of Educational Improvement. This approach is based upon the process elements of dialogue, decision-making, action, and evaluation (DDAE). As in the OD model, staff deal with concerns, issues, and problems of themsevelves and their school. An important element, however, is action research in which staff members individually or cooperatively undertake projects that ought to alter basic characteristics of the school. The final three elements of the process (decision-making, action, and evaluation) are strongly data-based so that all steps are monitored in terms of evidence. The primary outcome is the preparation of a staff to undertake self-renewal as a regular school activity according to a clear set of procedures (Goodlad 1975).

Change Agent Model. The Change Agent Model was proposed by the Rand Corporation following an extensive study of federal programs in local schools. The Change Agent Model, like the OD and Responsive Model, is based upon the school setting, particularly one with a strong leadership role on the part of the principal. Two other elements were needed: (1) a receptive school climate committed to staff development with such programs geared to individual and group needs; and (2) an effective strategy for producing organizational change. These, in turn, grew from four prerequisite conditions: adaptive planning, staff development tailored to local school personnel, on-site materials preparation, as well as mutual support and sharing. Adequate resource personnel must be present to achieve these four organizational conditions (Berman and McLaughlin 1975).

Linkage Model. Linkage models of several varieties exist. All view an organization such as a school as linked to its environment through individuals who transfer information, knowledge, and ideas from the outside and communicate conditions, problems and needs to supporting groups within and surrounding the organization. Havelock (1973) proposes three related activities beginning outside the organization and progressively moving inside the organization: (1) research, development, and diffusion; (2) social interaction or information exchange; and (3) problem solving within the organization. A need inside the organization creates a search for outside resources in ideas and assistance. Social interaction produces linkages that then permit solutions necessitating organizational and staff renewal.

Each of the four change models incorporates principles and supports assumptions made throughout this chapter. Movement toward improved educational effectiveness depends primarily on the quality of staff in each school. Adequate staffing practices are an essential beginning. Staff development carefully targeted to needed individual and group competencies is the only deliberate means by which schools can build permanent renewal strategies. Four tested models for achieving school renewal were noted, each depending on staff development to succeed. Need assessment, activities planned to achieve individual and group renewal, organizational arrangements to provide renewal activities and the organizational accomodation of them, and formative evaluation of staff performance are required steps to implement a staff development program.

Special Conditions of Personnel Administration

Three conditions are imposed on school staffing practices of which all administrators must be aware. They stem from external forces, legal and quasi-legal, and arise because of special concerns for personnel practices. They are (1) due process and other legal requirements; (2) treatment of women and minorities; and (3) conditions imposed by collective bargaining. Only brief treatments of these topics are offered here. Each should be given special attention by personnel officers and line administrators, and district legal counsel should be consulted when specific questions arise.

Both on the legislative side and the judicial side an increased interest in educational affairs is evident, as presented in Chapter 2. This is particularly true in personnel practices. Three areas in which a body of case law and legislation is developing are due process, open records, and employment testing. Procedural due process is particularly relevent to staffing in matters of termination for cause, suspension, and reprimand which endangers remuneration. Here timely notice of the action and reasons for it must be given, and the individual is entitled to a *hearing* in which his/her legal counsel is present. In procedural due process situations that have reached litigation, a legal principle upheld consistently is that a person must not be deprived of a right. Individuals must be properly informed of deficiencies, afforded the opportunity to remedy them, and be given access to all information upon which actions are based. One definition of a *right* is freedom from capricious and arbitrary action or deprivation of property; property rights include a legitimate claim to continued employment. Capricious denial of employment therefore becomes an invasion of rights. Details relevent to the many issues which may arise over due process must be reviewed periodically because state and federal law and judicial opinion in these matters are changing.

Types of information that may be requested and recorded have been treated in a previous section of this chapter. In addition, most states have legal requirements for open records (which only may be made public with special permission of the individual(s) about whom information exists) and records which may not be made public. Districts, whether in states with open records legislation or not, should provide board policy for the guidance and protection of administrators and staff. Such policy should include (1) how a request may be made; (2) conditions under which records are to be made available, including a list of records and specific information which can or cannot be made available; (3) the custodian of each type of record; and (4) procedures for resolving questions that may arise.

An additional set of legal questions, still largely unresolved, which can easily invite legal challenge, is that of testing personnel for employment, placement, or promotion. Court cases have resulted from tests that appear systematically to exclude minority groups, tests that have little relationship to the job in question, or in which criteria are not specially job-related. Even classification of individuals into groups for placement has been questioned, as in cases in which racial groups have been identified and given preferential treatment or the reverse. Extensive treatment of cases and their implications for personnel practices in education is provided in *Educational Law and the Public Schools: A Compendium* (Gee and Sperry 1978). This source is particularly useful to the practitioner, and it can be kept up to date through regularly issued supplements. Also, the federal Equal Employment Opportunity Commission (EEOC) publishes guidelines relative to a range of legal issues pertaining to personnel practices.

Some legal issues involving women and minority rights have been treated in this chapter and in Chapter 2. Title VI of the Civil Rights Act of 1964 prohibits discrimination by race, religion, or national origin on the part of institutions receiving federal funds. Title VII of the same act, amended by the Equal Employment Opportunity Act of 1972, prohibits discrimination in any and all conditions of employment on the basis of sex, race, color, religion, or national origin by any organization employ-ing fifteen or more persons. The amendment placed enforcement under the EEOC and specifies that complaints may be filed by any individual or organization on behalf of any employee or applicant. All conditions of employment in Title VII include, but are not restricted to recruitment, selection, transfer, assignment, dismissal, layoff and recall, pay, sick leave, retirement benefits, and medical and other benefits. Cases involving sick leave and medical benefits have been raised with reference to pregnancy of women employees and in reference to equal retirement benefits due to the separate classification of women in terms of life expectancy. In addition, the Equal Pay Act of 1963 provides that all individuals with the same skills and same job classifications must be equally paid. Execu-tive orders and state legislation have tended to specify and extend federal legislation and to add enforcement provisions.

Legal provisions, however, have not guaranteed equality of treat-ment. Evidence is available that women are paid less than men and are promoted less frequently. Furthermore, as noted in Chapter 2, women and minorities hold a declining percentage of positions in educational administration. Some, but not all, of the disparities arise from external conditions. Declining enrollments have harmed the minorities where re-duction-in-force policies are based upon a "last in, first out" principle. Consolidation of smaller districts and smaller schools also have eliminated many positions held by women, and in the South by Blacks, because these groups have tended to hold administrative positions in the smaller schools and districts (which in itself may represent a form of discrimina-tion). Under these conditions courts, acting under Title VII and related acts, have ordered "affirmative action" steps to remove discriminatory practices, redress employment balances, and end conditions, such as col-lection of non-job-related information, which might lead to discrimina-tory practices.

Complex, costly litigation is a good reason, but not the only one, for giving serious attention to the rights of women and minorities. Educa-tional institutions through their personnel practices need to make maxi-mum use of the professional competence available. To screen out sources of competent personnel, consciously or unconsciously, constitutes a serious deprivation to education that society can ill afford. Perhaps more important is the educational need for role models and for diverse perspec-tives for all students during the educational process. Those involved with personnel services need to examine the legal questions, quality of staff considerations, and the broader educational outcomes associated with the treatment of women and minority groups.

Collective bargaining is the last of the three special conditions af-fecting personnel services. Historians will likely report it to be the most pervasive influence upon education during the 1960s and 1970s. Dur-ing this period teachers gained the right to organize and bargain collec-tively for a long list of items related to salary, benefits, and working condi-tions. The right of representation to bargain may be specifically granted by a state legislature or it may be agreed upon by a board of education and the teachers of a given district whether or not a state statute exists. At this writing twenty states have attempted to restrict organizing and bargaining by passing right-to-work laws. Bargaining, where states have made it a statutory right or a mandate, includes the range of practices such as mediation, fact finding, and arbitration.

Bargaining results in an "agreement," which is a binding contract between the district's management and employees. The agreement covers all staffing and staff development practices brought into the bargaining process by either side. These include assignment, transfer, promotion, evaluation, and in-service education. The implications for personnel administration are clear. The agreement also may include items pertaining to curriculum, class size, extra activities and assignments, school calendar, and the administration. The underlying condition brought about by collective bargaining was the introduction of the adversarial relationship between teachers and school administrators. Collaboration has been made difficult by the hardening of the adversarial nature of relationships created by the bargaining process, and many constraints have been imposed upon administrators, particularly the school principal. The public school administrator, where bargaining exists, will need to examine the conditions imposed by the bargaining agreement in terms of competency needs. Imaginative leadership in use of staff, determination and communication of staffing needs, and targeted staff development will be required, with increasing constraints upon the administrators' discretionary powers.

References

American Association of School Administrators. 1978. *Standards for School Personnel Administration.* 3d ed. Seven Hills, Ohio: The Association.

Aslin, Neil, and **John W. DeArman.** 1976. "Adoption and Abandonment of Innovative Practices in High Schools." *Educational Leadership* 33:601–606.

Association for Supervision and Curriculum Development. 1981. *Staff Development/Organization Development.* Alexandria, Va.: The Association.

Berman, Paul, and **Milbrey W. McLaughlin.** 1975. *Federal Programs Supporting Educational Change.* Santa Monica, Calif.: The Rand Corp.

Byrne, David R., Susan A. Hines, and **Lloyd E. McCleary.** 1978. *The Senior High School Principalship.* Vol. 1: *The National Survey.* Reston, Va.: National Association of Secondary School Principals.

Campbell, Roald F., et al. 1980. *The Organization of American Schools.* 4th ed. Columbus, Ohio: Charles E. Merrill.

Dahl, Robert A., and **Charles E. Lindblom.** 1963. *Politics, Economics and Welfare.* New York: Harper and Row.

Derr, Brooklyn C., ed. 1980. *Work, Family and the Career: New Frontiers in Theory and Research.* New York; Praeger.

Gee, Gordon, and **David J. Sperry.** 1978. *Educational Law and the Public Schools: A Compendium.* Boston: Allyn and Bacon.

Goodlad, John I. 1975. *Dynamics of Educational Change: Toward Responsive Schools.* New York: McGraw-Hill.

Goodlad, John J., and **Robert N. Anderson.** 1962. *The Nongraded Elementary School.* New York: Harcourt, Brace and World.

Harris, Ben M., et al. 1979. *Personnel Administration in Education.* Boston: Allyn and Bacon.

Havelock, Ronald G. 1973. *The Change Agent's Guide to Innovation in Educa-tion.* Englewood Cliffs, N.J.: Educational Technology Publication.

Katz, E., M. Levin, and **H. Hamilton.** 1963. "Traditions of Research on the Diffusion of Innovations." *American Social Revolution* 28:2, 237-52.

Lyons, Geoffrey. 1980. *Teacher Careers and Career Perceptions.* Newark, N.J.: Slough.

Madaus, George F., Peter W. Airasian, and **Thomas Kellaghan.** 1980. *School Effectiveness.* New York: McGraw-Hill.

Meyer, H. E. 1976. "Personnel Directors Are the New Corporate Heroes." *Fortune* 93 (February): 84-88.

Mosteller, Frederick. 1975. "Effects of Field Experiments on Selected Promis-ing Innovations." In *Planned Variation in Education: Should We Give Up or Try Harder?* Edited by Alice M. Rivlin and Michael Timpane. Washing-ton, D.C.: The Brookings Institution.

Neale, Daniel C., William J. Bailey, and **Billy E. Ross.** 1981. *Strategies for School Improvement.* Boston: Allyn and Bacon.

Pigors, Paul, and **Charles L. Meyers.** 1973. *Personnel Management.* 7th ed. New York: McGraw-Hill.

Rutter, Michael, et al. 1979. *Fifteen Thousand Hours: Secondary Schools and Their Effects on Children.* London: Open Books.

Schmuck, Richard A., et al. 1977. *The Second Handbook of Organizational Development in Schools.* Palo Alto, Calif.: Mayfield.

Thomas, M. Donald, and **Maridell Sutherland.** 1982. "Human Development Works in Salt Lake City." *CCBC Notebook* 11 (July): 13-20.

Trump, J. Lloyd. 1969. *Images of the Future.* Washington, D.C.: National Education Association, Commission on Teacher Education and Profes-sional Standards.

Valentine, Jerry, et al. 1981. *The Middle Level Principalship.* Vol. 1. Reston Va.: National Association of Secondary School Principals.

Wynne, Edward A. 1980. *Looking at Schools: Good, Bad, and Indifferent.* Lexington, Mass.: D. C. Heath and Co.

PART II
Making Schools Effective

From the beginning of schools in this nation, the public has been occupied with expectations for each generation and the special role that schools assume in meeting these hopes. The schools of today are no different in this general regard but they are different in some of the specific concerns being expressed. It seems quite clear that today's schools have been elevated into a limelight that highlights the public view. And that view is being expressed in the media across the nation as one of public discontent. Though there are probably about as many objections as there are objectors, most concerns seem to focus on the schools not being as effective as the public wants them to be. And effectiveness is typically translated into achievement of pupils. Responsible educators have been expressing this same concern for years although the public and the educator may view the problem differently and may consider different criteria to be the basis on which schools are judged. There is, nevertheless, a strong enough movement afoot to include a discussion of the role of the administrator in promoting more effective schools. Whether the current public reaction has grown from real or imagined declines in pupil achievement, the reality is that the last decade and a half has seen increased research focusing on pupil achievement, teacher effectiveness, and the role of administrators in bringing about better schools. Part IV highlights this research and suggests administrative procedures that should improve the performance of the schools in developing curriculum, improving instruction, and evaluating the school's performance.

5

It is because modern education is so seldom inspired by great hope that it so seldom achieves a great result.

- Bertrand Russell

Effective Schools and the Role of Adminstrators

The general characteristics of administration have been described in the preceding chapters. The able administrator understands these characteristics and knows how to adapt and apply them appropriately in providing the leadership demanded by the complexities in schools. Administrative leadership also calls for attention to the specific and important features of schools. These include and indeed are dominated by the expectation that pupil performance should be at the highest possible level. Pupil learning is not only critically important as a factor in determining how well schools are performing; it is also at the center of the entire school enterprise. Many other responsibilities assumed by schools require attention, such as construction of facilities, maintenance of good school-community relations, proper utilization of personnel, and budgeting. But these responsibilities and most others are based primarily on facilitating instruction. Thus, pupil performance is the base around which most administrative activities pivot. The current designation of this concern for the performance of schools is "school effectiveness." The next section provides an overview to place this emphasis on school effectiveness in perspective.

School Purposes

One could return to almost any period of time during the last century to examine the school priorities and see the relationship between schools, society, and the special characteristics of that period. For example, in 1888 Charles W. Eliot, who was president of Harvard University, presented a paper at the convention of the National Education Association challenging the curriculum of the high schools. He argued for more efficient schooling and more rigorous standards focusing on academic preparation for college. His remarks led to the appointment by the NEA of the Committee of Ten on Secondary School Studies, which asked if school programs could be shortened and enriched. The Committee's 1893 report, after a year of deliberation, echoed Eliot's views. The report was one of the earliest successful efforts to exert national pressure on our decentralized system of schools (Eliot 1893).

Eventually the academically narrow and lock-step organization of schools advocated by the Committee of Ten gave way to the social pressures of a changing nation. Shortly after the turn of the century, social reform forced new roles on the schools. These reforms included the formation of unions to protect the rights of workers, the establishment of social agencies to help the downtrodden and unfortunate, the establishment of child labor laws and compulsory attendance requirements to rescue children from sweat shops and to place them in schools, the founding of agencies such as the American Civil Liberties Union, and movements for women's suffrage and mental health. At the same time, findings in the area of educational psychology by Alfred Binet, Edward Thorndike, G. Stanley Hall, and others altered the views of educators about how children should be educated and how schools should function. The impact of John Dewey began to dominate during the period shortly after 1900, and the idea prevailed that school was more than preparation for life, *was* life. These events are especially well described by Cremin in his book, *Transformation of the School* (Cremin 1961).

In response to these developments the NEA appointed a committee to re-examine the purposes of secondary schools. This committee, formed in 1913, was the Commission on Reorganization of Secondary Education. Their final report in 1918 recommended the *Cardinal Principles* for schools, which included concern for health, command of fundamental processes, worthy home membership, vocation, citizenship, worthy use of leisure, and ethical character (Commission 1918). Clearly these principles were more concerned with broader life skills than the more narrow academic position taken by the Committee of Ten. The social changes and the schools' response to them during the twenty-five intervening years between the two reports shows how closely the schools are tied to the society that supports them. Old positions do not disappear overnight, however, and new ones do not automatically sweep in with clarity and completely take over. Advocates of both the traditional and the progressive positions regarding the role of schools continued in their separate camps.

It was in this atmosphere of confrontation that the Progressive Education Association (PEA) was born in Washington, D.C. under the direction of Stanwood Cobb (Cremin 1961). The founding of the PEA gave a base on which those who favored a broader purpose for schools and a more experimental and instrumental approach to schooling could build their case. As the schools continued to grow throughout the third and fourth decades of this century, followers of these two positions were affected by a third development during the Great Depression, born partially of the depression itself. During the 1930s when people were unemployed, when the economy was a disaster, when suffering was everywhere, it was obvious that the society needed drastic change. Thus social reformers entered the arena of schools and found their voice through the writings of George S. Counts. Counts articulated his views in a 1932 pamphlet, "Dare the Schools Build a New Social Order?" (Counts 1932). The view of the social reconstructionists was that both schools and society needed drastic reform, and that by starting with the schools, they could educate a new generation of people to correct the ills of society.

As the country began to emerge from the depression and as World War II approached, the schools faced three different views of their mission: (1) academic preparation for college, (2) preparation for life, and (3) reform of society through reform of schools. Clearly when the question of effective schools was raised at that time, the answer was "Effective for what?" Obviously the point of view of those who answered determined whether the schools were "effective."

During the 1940s World War II and its aftermath placed the schools in the background, along with many other national concerns. After the war, as the 1950s approached, an increased concern for the schools and their purposes arose. One significant position during this period was started by Charles Prosser, who said in effect that 20 percent of the high school graduates plan to go to college, another 20 percent plan to enter the work force, and the remaining 60 percent don't know what they want to do (United States Office of Education 1951). He recommended that schools become more involved with helping students make wise choices through a "life adjustment" education that would combine the tenets of the progressive movement with guidance and counseling services. By the 1950s, the controversy over whether schools should be pupil centered, rather than academic centered, institutions flamed as they had half a century before. Opposed to the broader, life-adjustment role of schools were critics who wanted a back-to-basics curriculum with high academic standards. Attacks on the progressive bent of the schools included such publications as *Educational Wastelands* (Bestor 1953); *Restoration of Learning* (Bestor 1956); *Quackery in the Public Schools* (Lynd 1953); and *Education and Freedom* (Rickover 1959). During the 1950s the controversy was heated; the infighting that took place in educational literature and popular press is documented in the collection *Public Education Under Criticism* (Scott and Hill 1954).

When in October, 1957, the Russians launched Sputnik, those who favored more rigorous academic standards claimed that because United States schools had lagged seriously behind, Russia had won the space race. Others argued that Russian children's higher scores on mathematics and science tests did not mean United States schools were inferior. Defenders of United States schools said that we tried to educate everyone, and our purposes were different from the Russians'. Supporters also claimed our very best minds were being developed just as well as those of the best students elsewhere, and that if our government chose to draw on this talent, the United States could compete adequately with other nations in scientific research and development.

As these issues continued to be debated, an emerging movement known as "humanism" (primary regard for the individual) arose in the 1960s. The humanists expressed concern for the emotional, psychological, and social development of pupils. Humanism in education was encouraged by the civil rights movement. The Association for Supervision and Curriculum Development 1962 yearbook, *Becoming, Behaving, Perceiving*, provided an outlet for the views of Carl Rogers, Abraham Maslow, Arthur Coombs, and Earl Kelley, four well-known advocates of humanism in the schools (ASCD, 1962). The recommendations espoused in this book influenced the schools strongly throughout the decade of the 1960s. The humanists argued that people who felt good about themselves and were emotionally and psychologically secure were able to learn better and become more competent and strong individuals. Disagreeing with this convincing, persuasive position was heretical in some circles.

In due time concern was expressed about how teachers could become proficient in implementing the humanism of the day. School people, including teachers, started to ask how they were to acquire the skills, knowledge, and tolerance of psychologists, who seldom worked with large groups of twenty-five or thirty pupils. Another issue arose about whether the schools were trying to take over the responsibility of the home and of other agencies. Finally the question was raised about what part of the curriculum would be sacrificed to make room for humanism. As national test scores began to drop, as the school behavior of students seemed to show increasing violence and vandalism, and as teachers, burdened by their heavy loads expressed the strain known as "burnout," it became evident that schools needed to reconsider their purposes.

At the beginning of the 1970s the United States Office of Education's National Center for Educational Research and Development (NCERD), funded ten teacher-training institutions (later reduced to nine) to determine training programs that could serve as models to the nation. Directors of these models shared information as they began identifying approaches that would make teachers more effective. One evaluation report identified the common elements needed for teacher training: (1) individualize instruction; (2) model the teaching behavior students were expected to learn; (3) use systems analysis and computer technology; (4) utilize behavioral objectives to identify desired outcomes; (5) collaborate more with school districts; and (6) emphasize innovations within their programs (Shaftel 1969).

These recommendations were based on the assumption that schools made a difference in the learning of pupils and that teacher performance contributed substantially to this difference. As sound as these notions may seem, questions were being raised from other quarters about the actual impact of schools on learners.

Christopher Jencks' book, *Inequality* (1972) concluded that schools were marginal institutions in affecting the lives of adults. His findings were based on census data and an earlier report, *Equality of Educational Opportunity* (Coleman 1966), which reported that teacher experience and training, among other variables, had little impact on pupil success in schools. A more recent report, *A Nation at Risk* (Gardner 1983) acknowledged the importance of schools and listed factors that worked to the detriment of effective teaching, including low standards in teacher admission programs, noncompetitive salary incentives, too little time for in-service training, and failure to use qualified individuals such as recent graduates with degrees in mathematics and science to solve the immediate problems of shortages in these fields. All of these reports call attention to the issues the public perceives in schools and suggest ways to make schools more effective.

As a consequence of these diverse views, allies of schools were in the awkward position of praising the work of teachers and urging that more effective teacher training should be supported while these reports stated that teachers made little difference or lacked fundamental elements needed to bring about the outcomes sought by the schools. The National Center for Educational Research and Development was succeeded by the National Institute of Education (NIE), which began funding research activity in the early 1970s to determine the relationship between teacher performance and pupil learning. Their support, with earlier studies, formed the basis of recent research to determine the characteristics of effective schools. The next section reports the highlights of this research.

Background of Research on Teacher Effectiveness

In the early 1970s after he reviewed the completed research on teacher effectiveness to determine the relationships, if any, between teacher performance and pupil outcomes, Rosenshine wrote: "Most papers on teacher education contain the embarrassing recognition that the scientific basis for teaching and teacher education is primitive. That is, the number of studies which have looked at both teacher behavior and student outcomes is embarrassingly small. A diligent search will uncover less than a hundred studies. The quality of many of these studies is questionable. The results are most useful for suggesting future research; the results of these studies are *not* sufficiently strong or clear to direct teacher training practices or certification or evaluation of teachers." (Rosenshine 1974, 138)

After reporting on his earlier investigations, Rosenshine then listed nine teacher behaviors that were "most promising" for further research on the basis of his analysis of correlational studies. These nine variables were:

1. Clarity of teacher's presentation
2. Variety of teacher-initiated activities
3. Enthusiasm of teacher
4. Teacher emphasis on learning and achievement
5. Avoidance of extreme criticism
6. Positive responses to students
7. Student opportunity to learn criterion material
8. Use of structuring comments by teacher
9. Use of cognitive levels of questions or cognitive discourse. (Rosenshine 1974, 139)

In addition to these nine variables, he provided two other categories. One category included behaviors that had not shown any significant or consistent relationship to achievement, including non-verbal approval, teacher warmth, and teacher experience. He also listed twenty-one variables that had rarely been studied, including such teacher behaviors as establishing and maintaining rapport, pacing, giving homework, developing pupil's self-concept, and involving pupils in self-evaluation.

According to Rosenshine it was evident that the profession had no strong basis on which to recommend teacher training programs or evaluate teacher performance. It is important to remember that the lack of research evidence does not invalidate a teacher behavior; it simply means that evidence to support the behavior is lacking.

The American Association of Colleges for Teacher Education provided the leadership for a committee on Performance-Based Teacher Education (PBTE) and received support for their work from the USOE. After the publication of sixteen monographs on PBTE, they invited Donald M. Medley to review the process-product research on teacher competence and teacher effectiveness and consolidate his findings into a final monograph in the series. He was aided by a panel of ten people who were closely involved in the research on competence, and collectively they published *Teacher Competence and Teacher Effectiveness* (Medley 1977). His method was first to identify research studies and then to select those studies that were most useful by determining if they reported *original* research. From a list of 732 studies, only 289 survived this initial screening. He then applied four criteria to determine if a relationship should be reported in his study: (1) a generalizable relationship; (2) a strong and reliable relationship; (3) a defensible measure of teacher effectiveness; and (4) an interpretable measure of teacher behavior. The number of relationships that survived these criteria was 613; and all of these correlations came from just 14 of the 289 studies. The original document is too extensive to fully report here. However, Medley reported the following observations which have helped give direction to more recent research:

1. Teacher competence involves a knowledge component and a performance component.
2. Research in teacher effectiveness might split into two phases: the study of teacher behavior in relation to pupil behavior; and the study of pupil behavior in relation to pupil outcomes.
3. It would seem more productive if the focus of future research were on correlations between teacher behaviors and pupil behaviors (rather than pupil outcomes). (Medley 1977, 69-70)

The Medley study added more support to the earlier work of Rosenshine and directed the research along potentially productive lines.

The next section provides descriptions and findings of selected research conducted to determine the characteristics of effective teachers and the attributes of effective schools.

Research on Teacher and School Effectiveness

The Beginning Teacher Evaluation Study (BTES)

One of the first and most influential research studies conducted on effective schools was carried out under the direction of the California Commission for Teacher Preparation and Licensing. They received substantial support from the NIE and utilized personnel and resources from the Far West Regional Laboratory for Education Research and Development and the Educational Testing Service. Personnel from higher education, the public schools, and from related disciplines such as sociology, psychology, and anthropology also took part. This Beginning Teacher Evaluation Study (BTES) is summarized in *Time to Learn* (Denham 1980). The study, which required over eight years to complete, can be divided into time periods according to the following phases.

From 1970 and 1972 the researchers prepared and revised the research design. The original purposes were to identify generic teacher competencies and evaluate teacher education programs through follow-up of graduates. It became evident that any attempt to follow graduates and compare their undergraduate training to their teaching performance was an insurmountable task. As a consequence, the researchers revised their purposes to focus on identifying teaching skills and relating these skills to student outcomes. The original title of the study to look at beginning teachers remained, however, even though the teachers under study were no longer beginners.

From 1972 to 1973 the research plan developed, focusing on grades 2 and 5 and limiting the study to analysis of the teaching of mathematics and reading. The researchers devoted one year to observing experienced teachers to identify their skills. Researchers then observed additional experienced teachers to verify the list of skills acquired from the first observations. They also observed inexperienced teachers to determine differences between beginning and experienced teachers and to determine the entry skills of new teachers.

From 1973 to 1974 the ETS conducted initial field work and collected data on (1) student achievement and attitudes in reading and mathematics; (2) student background and characteristics; (3) teacher background and characteristics; (4) school background and characteristics; and (5) teacher behavior in the classroom. During this period they observed over ninety teachers from two to eight times each with two different observation systems, and videotaped their classes.

Between 1974 and 1976, two-hundred volunteer teachers taught two-week units and a subsample of forty teachers was identified who represented the ten most and least effective teachers at the second and fifth grade levels. Effectiveness was determined according to pupil achievement, allowing for entry level of pupils and regression analysis. As these studies went forward, the *use of instructional time* began to emerge as a dominant difference between effective and ineffective teachers.

Between 1976 and 1978 a final field study observed twenty-five teachers in grade 2 and twenty-five in grade 5 and measured six students from each classroom (300 pupils total) in respect to achievement and attitude in October, December, May, and in the following fall. The teachers maintained records on the use of time and the difficulty level of learning and reported their planning time in weekly interviews. Weekly observations focused on time allocation, student engagement on tasks, task difficulty, and teacher behaviors.

The major findings from the BTES research focuses on the following considerations:

1. The amount of time teachers allocate to instruction in a particular curriculum content area is positively associated with student learning in that content area.

2. The proportion of allocated time students are engaged is positively associated with learning.
3. The proportion of time reading or mathematics tasks are performed with *high success* is positively associated with student learning.
4. The proportion of time reading or mathematics tasks are performed with low success is negatively associated with student learning.
5. Increases in academic learning time are not associated with more negative attitudes toward mathematics, reading, or school.
6. The teacher's accuracy in diagnosing student skill levels is related to student achievement and academic learning time.
7. The teacher's prescription of appropriate tasks is related to student achievement and student success rate.
8. More substantive interaction between the student and an instructor is associated with higher levels of student engagement.
9. Academic feedback is positively associated with student learning.
10. Structuring the lesson and giving directions on task procedures were positively associated with high student success.
11. Explanation specifically in response to student need is negatively associated with high student success. (Effective teachers also focus on correcting underlying deficits, diagnosing *why* students don't understand.)
12. More frequent reprimands for inappropriate behavior are negatively associated with student learning.
13. The teacher's value system is related to academic learning time and to student achievement. Teacher emphasis on academic goals is positively associated with student learning.
14. A learning environment characterized by student responsibility for academic work and by cooperation on academic tasks is associated with higher achievement. (Denham 1980, 15-22)

The emphasis on allocation of time and the increasing of "time on task" clearly emerged as important factors in promoting pupil achievement.

One of the researchers in the BTES study has extended the notion of "time on task" into an analysis of more specific components of the use of time (Berliner 1982). This further breakdown begins with the time allocated for instruction in a particular course. A number of identifiable intrusions can reduce the effectiveness of allocated time. For example, the engaged time is less than the allocated time, since it takes some time for pupils to enter the room, get seated, receive instructions, sharpen pencils, and so forth. Furthermore, interruptions such as announcements on the public address system, noise from the halls or outside, or other events may detract from allocated time. Because peripheral and sometimes irrelevant activities occur in the classroom, even the engaged time is not always directly related to the intended outcomes; so the time spent in learning is still less than the time engaged in the content. After all these distractions are subtracted from the allocated time, the remaining portion should be time spent on tasks related to outcome. However, even this is not the entire picture, since not all students spend time related to outcome in an equally productive way. The difference among pupils here occurs in respect to high, medium, or low success rate. The student who devotes time to learning the intended outcomes but has a low success rate in understanding material is further diminishing the efficacy of the time spent on the content. The student who enjoys a high success rate while engaged in learning the materials is using the time more productively. This maximum time on task and high success rate are the goals that effective teachers achieve, states Berliner.

In another report one of the nation's leading analysts of classrooms and director of the Institute for Research on Teaching listed characteristics of well-managed classrooms and identified teacher behaviors contributing to effectiveness (Brophy 1983). Referring to the teacher as a manager of the classroom, Brophy asserts that effective managers (teachers):

1. Cut short problems before they can escalate into disruption.
2. Have learned to do more than one thing at a time if necessary.
3. Are well-prepared and thus able to move at a brisk pace.
4. Use presentation and questioning techniques designed to keep the group alert and accountable.
5. Have students often work independently rather than under the direct supervision of the teacher.
6. Maintain a continuous academic focus for student attention and engagement and avoid "down time" when students have nothing to do or are not sure about what they are supposed to do.
7. Hold students accountable for completing work on time.
8. Are clear about what they expect.
9. Are sensitive to student concerns and continuously monitor students for signs of confusion or inattention.
10. Expect prosocial outcomes when students from different groups are involved in cooperative activities that require active participation of all group members.
11. Increase desired behavior by praise and approval, modeling, token reinforcement programs, and establishment of clear rules.
12. Decrease undesired behavior by extinction, reinforcing incompatible behaviors, self-reprimands, relaxation, medication, self-instruction, and self-evaluation. (Brophy 1983, 267–73)

Brophy summarizes his remarks by stating:

> A comprehensive approach to classroom management must include the following: attention to relevent student characteristics and individual differences, preparation of the classroom as an effective learning environment, organization of instruction and support activities to maximize student engagement in productive tasks, development of a working set of housekeeping procedures and conduct rules, techniques of group management during active instruction, techniques of motivating and shaping desired behavior, techniques of resolving conflict and dealing with student's personal adjustment problems, and the combination of these elements into an internally effective system. (Brophy 1983, 282)

The Hersh Study

An excellent review of the division between *School* and *System-wide Characteristics* and the features in the area of *Curriculum and Instruction* was reported by Richard Hersh (1982, Part I). After a thorough analysis of the research on effective schools, Hersh identified the elements found to promote effectiveness in schools. In the following paragraphs each of these is described in detail.

Clear Academic Goals. These require an unambiguous, no-nonsense position that unequivocally asserts the importance of attaining the school's academic goals. Furthermore, these goals are shared among all principal parties—teachers, community, parents, and pupils. There is no doubt in the mind of those central to the operation that the dominant purpose of schools is promoting academic achievement. There is constant, but not nagging, emphasis on achieving high goals. This is reflected in the orientation of new faculty, in the agenda of the school board meetings, in releases to the press, in the selection of instructional materials, and in the allocation of resources and energies in the district.

Order and Discipline. Always listed as important, these can be lost between lip service given to the importance of discipline and development of a workable, uniform approach that is supported by all. The collective efforts of educators in the system to accept the rules of conduct and to share the responsibility for their enforcement seem to contribute to the effective observance of rules. Teachers, for example, who are willing to enforce rules of conduct even outside their own classrooms, strengthen the rules that have been adopted. Critical to the effectiveness of rules is the requirement that they be fair, enforceable, and necessary. Excessive rules, unfair rules, or oppressive rules will not establish an effective school climate. Spontaneity, individualism, creativity, and other expressions of personal characteristics should not be squelched by rules that prevent either teachers or pupils from being the growing and developing human beings they would like to be, and the school should encourage them to be. Extremism in either direction in establishing order militates against success.

High Expectations. Another way to express confidence in students is to say that the school has confidence in their ability to perform well. We can sense the difference between someone who expresses confidence in our ability, and is willing to assign challenging tasks for our completion, and one who lacks confidence, talks down, and asks for completion of simple, mundane, or even insulting tasks. The same tone, established in schools, is one of the distinguishing features that separates effective from ineffective schools.

Teacher efficacy. Related to high expectations for students but in this instance directed at teachers, is an acceptance that even very difficult teaching assignments can be undertaken successfully. The emphasis is shifted toward recognizing the schools' purpose to work with difficult learning problems and to give them our best professional effort. Contrast this attitude with one sometimes found in schools that certain students are "hopeless," or that there is nothing more to do. It is not the right of the teaching profession to give up trying to teach students any more than doctors have a right to give up trying to cure difficult health problems. The worthy intent is to do as much as possible. No profession wins all its battles; schools will never overcome all the learning problems of students. Yet effective schools accept the responsibility to teach as well as we know how and expect that teachers will be effective in meeting these learning needs. When students get the impression that school personnel want them to learn and expect them to be able to learn, and when teachers approach students with the expectation that both teachers and pupils will succeed, a dynamic and powerful "set" pays off with higher achievement.

Pervasive Caring. Care is recognizable by the effort put forth in attending to students and their work. In a school that "cares," the students will receive critical and helpful reactions to their tests and homework assignments. Extensive comments by teachers on student essays, careful supervision of students doing school work in the classrooms, inquiry into their thoughts, actions, and performance are all revealed through teacher and administrative behavior. One major distinction found between the caring and noncaring school is in the motivation and goals of the staff. In schools where a chief concern is how to get through the day or class period, assignments can be made and instruction provided whose purpose is to occupy time or energy and avoid problems. Some learning probably occurs under this approach. In a caring school the students are directed into activities because those activities will enable students to gain knowledge and skills called for in the content they are expected to learn. It is the difference between saying, "I care about getting through the school day," and saying, "I care about students meeting the objectives of the day's lesson." In the one instance teachers breathe a sigh of relief at day's end; in the other, they seek their satisfaction from student accomplishments and feel pleased when students learn. This difference is not only evident in the ways instructional staff and administrators behave. It is also felt in the students, who can perceive that staff and faculty want them to succeed in school.

Public reward and incentives. Provided throughout the school and the district, these give publicity to academic achievement in its various forms. Public recognition can be provided in classrooms by posting good papers; in academic areas, through selecting and acknowledging students whose performance exceeds expectations or who meet standards of performance that bring recognition for high academic effort. When realistic goals are set for students' achievement and pupils reach those goals, public acknowledgment gives credence and respectability to academic effort and generates a contagious climate of striving. A reward system places academic efforts in a positive context and gives students confidence that they can seek excellence in learning just as in other areas, particularly extracurricular athletics, and in some schools with music, theatre, and club accomplishments. In those few schools where students have won academic competition at the regional or national level, the schools often support their academic teams and enjoy the association with their achievements.

Community Support. To strengthen education's effectiveness through community support entails some difficulties, because it has become increasingly difficult to identify the community. First, the geographic boundaries of schools have been stretched and are often no longer contiguous with the school area. Furthermore, participation by community members in schools is often centered on discipline and truancy problems. The intent in developing community support is to promote parental cooperation and awareness of school goals and to create a cooperative and mutually active involvement that focuses on meeting the goals of the schools. Often this will require that the schools cultivate community interest by specifying actions that parents and others can take to help promote school effectiveness. It further requires that parent-initiated suggestions must be honored and encouraged. The intent in promoting community participation is to harness and direct the energies of the community to aid the school enterprise and to promote the inherent symbiotic relationship between schools and community.

Administrative Leadership. Actions that will support and encourage the elements outlined above give evidence of leadership by administrators. More discussion follows later in this chapter on the specific actions administrators can take to promote the characteristics identified here.

The list compiled by Hersh also includes five categories that focus on the instruction and curriculum of the schools (Hersh 1982, Part II). Before discussing these, however, a few comments are in order about the shared responsibility for pupil achievement. It is important and sometimes frustrating to recognize that administrators may be heavily committed to improving pupil learning, but cannot succeed without assistance from two layers of people who must also share in this commitment. One of these layers includes the classroom teachers; the other, the pupils. Of course, additional layers of supervisors, coordinators, and specialists exist in many school districts as well. Thus, the administrator who strives for high achievement must understand how to reach pupils through the efforts of others, rather than engaging directly in the instruction of pupils. Furthermore, it is the effort pupils put forth that really counts. Teachers can work hard, supervisors can provide direction, coordinators can emphasize achievement, but no one can learn for someone else. Thus, in all the efforts to improve curriculum and instruction, the most critical factor to examine is the performance of the pupil. Pupils may choose to respond differently to instruction than educators expect and this problem is at the heart of recommendations for improving school effectivenes. In all of the categories listed in the following discussion, the common element is the interaction that is required or implied. None of these categories contains single-level actions. None of them is limited to looking only at the performance of the teacher. All require that the work of the teacher be interpreted according to the response of the student. This will become more evident as each element is explained in greater detail. It is crucial to keep in mind that the joint efforts of students and others must

support the recommendations arising out of this list. This does not reduce the role of the teacher. It does emphasize that the professional responsibility of the teacher is to aim for targets that can be reached by pupils, not just expectations set forth outside of the pupils' world. This emphasis should not promote a reduction in standards; however, it should stress the importance of establishing realistic expectations that will be met, rather than impressive-sounding expectations that are filled with student failure. Hersh's categories follow, each accompanied by a discussion of the administrator's role in bringing about the desired characteristics.

High Academic Learning Time. During any school day the subjects to be taught are typically distributed according to a time schedule. This simply means that a school may designate forty-five minutes for reading instruction or thirty minutes for science or fifty minutes for social studies. These time periods help determine the school's priorities how much time can be allotted to learning the different content in curriculum. The previous discussion (p. 101) about engaged time and high success rate explains the concept of high academic learning time. The purpose of the administrator in promoting high academic learning time, then, is to look for "instructional time leaks" that can be avoided by identifying the areas in which high academic learning time is reduced. This can include classroom organizational procedures, ability to stay on the topic, selection of content that is appropriate to students, and avoidance of distracting discussions or other interferences. As these gaps are filled, the amount of time students engage in constructive learning activities is increased and higher academic learning time is achieved.

Frequent and Monitored Homework. Those teachers who assign homework commensurate with the pupil's time, ability, and opportunity to study outside of school are also emphasizing several characteristics about learning. They are saying that school is not the only place where learning can take place. They are emphasizing the continuing and individual nature of the learning process and indirectly stressing that responsibility for learning should be shared between the teacher and the pupil. They are also indicating that there is no more to learn than can be addressed in school. They may also be promoting the ideas of independence, responsibility, and autonomy as important qualities in going through school.

Teachers who monitor homework by emphasizing its importance and by supervising and evaluating its completion are also indicating their concern about whether or not pupils complete their assignments and whether or not they have reached the objectives intended in homework assignments. Their energy and interest communicate to pupils that the teacher is willing to put forth considerable effort and not just expect the student to do all the work. They are creating a further bond between themselves and their pupils by doing tasks together that will later become the arena in which they interact with one another. Schools that promote learning tend to respect the purposes listed above for assigning and monitoring homework. And they find that the assignment of homework makes unique contributions to the attainment of these expectations.

Ideally, homework should extend the lessons of the classroom and require that students do assignments that can best be completed outside school. They can complete such homework assignments best because they either need larger blocks of time than can be found in the school schedule or there are outside resources that are not available in school. For example, many writing assignments are done best outside the time constraints of the typical class period; or community resources become useful in out-of-class assignments to add another dimension to the structured learning provided in schools.

The monitoring of homework calls for considerable teacher effort in most instances; but teachers in effective schools do expend this energy. They convey to their students the high priority given to the efforts the students put forth in completing their assignments. They give the students an outlet to talk about or demonstrate the work they have completed. They also provide critical evaluations of student work and use these to help the students improve or gain more than would be acquired without the follow-up of the teacher. The teacher's monitoring is comparable to providing the student with an appreciative audience, but an audience that can provide both applause and constructive criticism. It conveys the notion that the teacher really cares about what the student is doing and what the student is learning.

Trivial homework or busy work, and teachers who provide no or little response to students' efforts, can be deflating and counterproductive. Helpful administrators can create guidelines and establish sound principles that will support the notion of monitored homework to allow students and teachers to take full advantage of out-of-school learning opportunities. Reasonableness must be employed and teachers must take into account the age of the pupils, the number of other classes in which homework is required, and events competing for the students' time.

Teachers who assign homework that conflicts with a major school event or who assign homework and ignore student products that are developed in completing homework invite low morale. Administrators can supervise teachers and set basic expectations to promote the positive effects and reduce or eliminate the abuse of homework assignments as a vehicle for learning.

Tightly Coupled Curriculum. In a tightly coupled curriculum the content to be learned, the methods of teaching content, and the evaluation of students are all highly synchronized. Furthermore, the curriculum in each subject is planned to support the curriculum in other subjects, and learning sequences have been structured to assure that vertical relationships throughout the school program are supportive. The material students learn is keyed to the objectives of the school and the district and specific care is taken to assure that materials, methods, and proportional emphasis on topics all reflect the objectives set forth in the school district. Cohesiveness, compatability, and consistency are all characteristic of the curriculum. Furthermore, teachers often prepare and use materials and experiences to modify commercial materials (textbooks, films, etc.) to adapt to the idiosyncrancies of the particular students and the criteria established in each school district. Such a school district challenges the student to achieve the standards and the objectives of the instructional program. Peripheral experiences will naturally occur, but teachers will hold these to a minimum and focus activities, homework assignments, materials, and learning activities on the school objectives. Furthermore, there is no "trickery" in which "everything not covered in class is covered in the exams." On the contrary, an honest, aboveboard disclosure between teachers and pupils creates a strong alliance and commitment to meet educational expectations. In this tightly-coupled curriculum the expectations at different grade levels and in different subjects are known throughout the school, and teachers and administrators depend on each person's living up to the standards. High trust among the professionals should produce more efficient transitions from class to class and from grade to grade by the pupils.

Variety of Teaching Strategies. A recommendation for variety in teaching methods can be found in methods texts and teacher preparation programs since the turn of the century. The reality is that variety calls for ingenuity and diversity on the part of the classroom teacher and support from the administration. When schools deny teachers the options provided through field trips, use of films, resource persons, technology, and a range of activities, then it is not possible for teachers to provide the variety they often may prefer. It is discouraging for teachers to create stimulating ideas that call for administrative support and then be denied the materials, time, or other resources to carry out their idea. Furthermore, when some teachers in a school use diverse teaching methods, the potential for a contagious climate to be created is present in which others may "catch on" and try different ways to instruct pupils.

Variety within a classroom also adds strength to the instructional program. Not all diversity requires elaborate planning or extensive time and energy. Variety may be had through demonstrations, presentations, learning centers, films, discussions, small group work, short- and long-term projects, individual projects, activities with different roles for pupils, encyclopedia or dictionary resources, simulations, programmed materials, or games. This diversity should contribute to the teacher's perceptions and enthusiasm, and provide some new approaches to avoid the rut that is easily found from doing things about the same way from year to year. More important than the teacher's motivation is the fact that not all pupils learn in the same way and not all content can be learned best through a single method. Simply consider the different approaches for students that would be required to learn physics, study poetry, write compositions, solve quadratic equations, or understand our heritage. Consider the different ways to learn concepts, rules, facts, principles, laws, values, and attitudes. Furthermore, consider the abilities of students to acquire knowledge that is concrete, representational, or abstract. Then add to this concern the difference between right- and left-hemispheric preferences and the inclinations of some students to use one to the exclusion of the other. Given this set of variables, it is little wonder that teachers who provide variety and diversity in their teaching win more success for all their students than those who rely on a single approach that may be appropriate for only a few students, a few subjects, a few topics, or a few of the different kinds of learning.

Administrators can function in three ways to promote such variety. One way is to encourage variety and approve diversity that seems reasonable and provide the administrative resources that prove support is available. A second way is to praise diversity and publicize the effectiveness of those teachers who succeed in using variety by calling their actions to the attention of the faculty and providing incentives to receive public recognition for successful innovative practices. The third approach is to bring ideas and materials to the faculty through systematic in-service programs and through faculty meetings, school bulletins, memos, and other techniques. This latter calls for the administrator to keep abreast of research and other information from the educational community that can be utilized in a particular school district.

Opportunities for Student Responsibility. This category applies to situations in the classroom and in the school. Making students responsible for their own learning is the flip side of giving students an opportunity to show what they can do. In the classroom, this takes the form of having students show their work, help determine learning activities, clarify assignments, explain information to classmates, tutor other students, and generally participate in classroom activities as an active rather than a passive learner. When student participation is encouraged, the teacher can determine whether students are learning correctly; whether they are acquiring knowledge, skills, and so forth; and whether they share in the ownership of the classroom and recognize their responsibility to themselves in the learning process.

As findings from research continue to be reported, it becomes evident that effective schools have certain characteristics in common. These common characteristics provide a set of expectations for schools, and also suggest that the performance of the total professional staff is required to promote effectiveness. Though much of the literature focuses on teacher performance, teachers cannot implement the recommendations without support and leadership from the administration. This point was well made by Schmuck when he said:

> Structures represent more than a summing of the individual teacher's thoughts about how the school is organized. They involve human networks of interdependencies, sequences of people-to-people interaction, and behavioral exchanges between people that constitute a larger social reality than any individual participant represents. . . .
>
> The school's norms, structures, and procedures taken together make up its formal social processes. . . . [The] myriad of informal social processes . . . are frequently referred to as the school's *climate*. . . . They include the feeling states created in interpersonal relationships and influenced by the group dynamics of the administrators, staff, teachers, and students. (Schmuck 1982, 95-96)

It is imperative that school administrators recognize the importance of the collaborative and leadership relationships they must assume to bring about the essential climate and consequences for effective schools. The next section recommends and describes the role, attitudes, and performances for administrators to lead schools into a more effective performance.

Administrator's Roles

As researchers spend more time in effective schools, certain behaviors and attitudes come to their attention as critical features of productive schools. One study examined teacher, administrator, and supervisor behaviors. The following behaviors and attitudes were identified as characteristics of effective schools.

1. Teachers talked about teaching practice as opposed to talk about teacher characteristics and failings the social lives of teachers, the foibles and failures of students and their families, and the unfortunate demands of society on their schools. Administrators who promote professional talk, as opposed to personal talk, promote the utility of collegial relationships in a professional direction.
2. Teachers and administrators observed teaching and provided each other with useful, candid, precise, and concrete talk about teaching.
3. In effective schools teachers and administrators plan, design, research, evaluate, and prepare teaching materials together.
4. Teachers and administrators teach each other the practice of teaching which enables the school to make maximum use of its own resources.

5. Principals identify the expectations for the schools and describe these expectations concretely for the entire school.
6. Administrators exhibit the behavior they expect of others including the evaluation of their own performance, seeking out teachers to talk about teaching, contributing to materials preparation, and giving time while asking for time. They also allocate time and resources consistent with the priorities that have been announced. (Little 1981, 1-2)

These six statements have a certain "no-nonsense" and "Let's-get-down-to-business" approach that is further emphasized by Tomlinson (1981). He recognizes that the level of generalization often reported in the research calls for more direct statements. He then says, in effect, that good schools simply leave little to chance; they *impose* the conditions that produce learning. That seems to be the discovery of effective schools research. Hard and efficient work improves learning. Hardly a miracle, but surely one of the most elusive common sense conclusions known to science. Among the specific findings he reports, the following typify Tomlinson's description of effective schools:

1. They reduce both the student's and the teacher's opportunities to engage in academically unproductive behavior.
2. They focus the student's attention and energy on the work of schooling by employing teacher's aides, by tighter management of the school and classroom.
3. They establish the legitimacy of schooling or introduce fear of failure (for example, by retention-in-grade) as a motive for students who do not bring with them a belief in the worth or desirability of schooling. (Tomlinson 1981, 506)

Tomlinson is saying that effective schools call for persistence, standards, organization, and an uncompromising demand that both pupils and teachers focus their energies on achievement. This approach assumes that pupils' emotional and psychological well-being is an outgrowth of becoming knowledgeable and successful in school. Those who express concern for the development of self-concepts and the promotion of self-actualization, as identified by the psychosocial humanists, would be told that the effective-schools approach is not inconsiderate of pupil needs. In fact, the effective school advocates would argue that it is an act of responsibility to pupils to set expectations commensurate with the demands of society, an act which prepares them to cope with life's realities. After all, successful people often struggle and work hard at their achievements; schools should provide a good foundation of hard work and excellence for pupils to launch successful adult lives.

One of the influential analysts of school effectiveness reported five factors under the direct responsibility of administrators that contribute to the pool of ideas which have been listed to support effective schools.

1. Strong administrative leadership by the school principal, especially in regard to instructional matters.
2. A school climate conducive to learning; that is, a safe and orderly school relatively free of discipline and vandalism problems.
3. Schoolwide emphasis on basic skills instruction (which entails acceptance among the professional staff that instruction in the basic skills is the primary goal of the school).

4. Teacher expectations that all students, regardless of family background, can reach appropriate levels of achievement.
5. A system for monitoring and assessing pupil performance which is tied to instructional objectives. (Edmonds 1979, 22)

These lists of attributes of effective schools provide some descriptions of the present state of knowledge. However, the current knowledge remains somewhat exhortative and lacks specific advice for action. Purkey and Smith have examined the current research on effectiveness, have identified the major problems in translating findings into practice, and have acknowledged the imperfections in the research samples, designs, instruments, and procedures. They state that "the existing reviews [of research] provide lists of ingredients, and rather divergent ones at that. What is missing and what we now turn to are suggestions on how to combine the ingredients. Unfortunately, we are not guided by systematic research on the development of effective schools. However, some research suggests alternative ways of approaching the problem and provides the missing directions" (Purkey and Smith 1983, 440). They continue by providing a portrait of an effective school, taking into account the information in this chapter and similar lists that have sprung up in abundance within the last few years. The following statements synthesize the research and findings as they relate to the mixture of teacher, administrator, and other personnel who interact to promote school effectiveness. The full description of these characteristics can be studied in the original source; this summary provides a reasonable overview from which the practicing administrator can take some important cues.

1. A number of studies indicate that the leadership and staff of a school need considerable autonomy in determining the exact means by which they address the problem of increasing academic performance.

2. Though we are suspicious of the "great principal" theory, it seems clear that leadership is necessary to initiate and maintain the improvement process. The principal is uniquely positioned to fill this role, and certainly his or her support is essential very early on. Nevertheless, groups of teachers or other administrators can provide leadership.

3. Once a school experiences success, keeping the staff together seems to maintain and promote further success. Frequent transfers are destructive and likely to retard, if not prevent, the growth of a coherent and ongoing school personality.

4. At the secondary school level, a planned, purposeful program of courses seems to be academically more beneficial than an approach that offers many electives and few requirements. If students are expected to learn science, math, and/or U.S. history, then they need to take those courses. If elementary school students are expected to acquire basic and complex

skills, the curriculum must focus on these skills, they must receive sufficient time for instruction in those skills, and those skills must be coordinated across grade levels and pervade the entire curriculum.

5. Essential change involves altering people's attitudes and behaviors as well as providing them with new skills and techniques. In order to influence an entire school, the staff development should be schoolwide rather than specific to individual teachers and should be closely related to the instructional program of the school. This effort is incremental and requires long-term support and reinforcement. It seems likely that staff development presented as a form of remediation for teachers deficient in certain skills or attributes will encounter resistance. More appropriately, staff development should be based on the expressed needs of teachers revealed as part of the process of collaborative planning and collegial relationships.

6. Though the evidence is more mixed here, it is reasonable to assume that parents need to be informed of school goals and student responsibilities, especially with regard to homework. A few studies find parental involvement and support to be a major factor in student achievement. Our feeling is that parent involvement is not sufficient, but that obtaining parental support is likely to influence student achievement positively.

7. Schoolwide recognition of academic success. A school's culture is partially reflected in its ceremonies, its symbols, and the accomplishments it chooses to recognize officially. Schools that make a point of publicly honoring academic achievement and stressing its importance through the appropriate use of symbols, ceremonies, and the like encourage students to adopt similar norms and values.

8. If schools choose to emphasize academics, then a greater portion of the school day would be devoted to academic subjects, students would spend more time during class periods in active learning activities, and class periods would be free from interruptions by the loudspeaker, messages from the counseling office, or disruptions from the hall or yard outside. Staff training might well be in the areas of classroom management and active teaching.

Fundamental change, building-level management, staff stability, and so on all depend on support from the district office. Few, if any, of the variables found to be significant are likely to be realized without district support. While specialized help in some areas such as reading or mainstreaming seems helpful, the role of the district office is probably best conceived as guiding and helping. (Purkey and Smith 1983, 443-44)

After listing these nine organization-structure variables, the authors identified four process variables that make a substantial contribution to creating a school climate conducive to effectiveness. These four process variables include:

1. Collaborative planning and collegial relationships. This variable comes from school effectiveness research and from implementation research that suggests that change attempts are more successful when teachers and administrators work together.

2. Sense of community. There is persuasive evidence that community feeling, the sense of being a recognizable member of a community that is supportive and clearly perceived, contributes to reduced alienation and increased achievement.

3. Clear goals and high expectations. Common sense, if nothing else, indicates that a clearly defined purpose is necessary for any endeavor hoping for success.

4. Order and discipline. The seriousness and purpose with which the school approaches its task are communicated by the order and discipline it maintains in its building. Furthermore some evidence exists indicating that clear, reasonable rules, fairly and consistently enforced, not only can reduce behavior problems that interfere with learning but also can promote feelings of pride and responsibility in the school community. (Purkey and Smith 1983, 445)

As we reflect on this chapter on school effectiveness, it seems quite clear that the emphasis is on shared obligations for the success of schools. Effectiveness requires that all do their part. It also requires that those in charge make it clear that others, whether pupils under the direction of teachers or teachers under the leadership of administrators, understand the goals the schools are setting out to meet and that the resources and procedures should be aimed at supporting the attainment of these goals. The literature also says that a more limited purpose for schools will increase the success of schools. The schools cannot be all things to all people and the fundamental responsibility to assure the transmission of systemic knowledge has been identified as the proper work of the schools. This point of view sounds more limited than it really is; the discussion of curriculum development in Chapter 7 will expand on this issue. Finally, at least from the perspective of school administration, leadership in promoting the essential features of effective schools must come from those in positions of authority if the necessary economic, policy, and other kinds of support are going to be put at the disposal of those who deliver instruction to pupils. Teachers will not optimize schools without help. It is this combination of collaborative and shared purpose that the research tells us will bring about the achievements schools are currently striving to reach.

References

Association for Supervision and Curriculum Development. 1962. *Perceiving, Behaving, Becoming.* Yearbook. Washington, D.C., The Association.

Beatty, R. W., and **C. E. Schneier.** 1977. *Personnel Administration: An Experimental Skill-Building Approach.* Reading, Mass.: Addison-Wesley.

Berliner, D. C. 1982. "Recognizing Instructional Variables." In *Introduction to Education,* edited by Donald E. Orlosky. Columbus, Ohio: Charles E. Merrill.

Bestor, A. 1953. *Educational Wastelands.* New York: Alfred A. Knopf.

_____ 1956. *The Restoration of Learning.* New York: Alfred A. Knopf.

Brophy, J. E. 1983. "Classroom Organization and Management." *The Elementary School Journal* 83 (March): 265-85.

Coleman, J. S. 1966. *Equality of Educational Opportunity.* Washington, D.C.: Office of Education, Department of Health, Education, and Welfare.

Commission on Reorganization of Secondary Education. 1918. *Cardinal Principles of Secondary Education.* Washington, D.C.: U. S. Government Printing Office.

Counts, G. S. 1932. *Dare the Schools Build a New Social Order?* New York: John Day.

Cremin, L. A. 1961. *The Transformation of the School.* New York: Alfred A. Knopf.

Denham, C., and **A. Lieberman,** 1980. *Time to Learn.* Washington, D.C.: National Institute of Education.

Edmonds, R. 1979. "Effective Schools for the Urban Poor." *Educational Leadership* 37 (October): 15-24

Eliot, C. W. 1893. "Can School Programs Be Shortened and Enriched?" *Proceedings* of the National Educational Association, 617-25.

Gardner, D. P. 1983. *A Nation at Risk.* Washington, D.C.: U.S. Government Printing Office.

Hersh, R. H. 1981 (Part I). "Clues to Good Education Shine Through." *Eugene* [Oreg.] *Register Guard,* 23 November 1981.

_____. 1981 (Part II). "Effective Teaching Counts More Than Money." *Eugene* [Oreg.] *Register Guard,* 24 November 1981.

Jencks, C. 1972. *Inequality.* New York: Basic Books.

Little, J. W. 1981. *Finding the Limits and Possibilities of Instructional Leadership: Some Possibilities for Practical and Collaborative Work with Principals.* Boulder, Colo.: Center for Action Research.

Lynd, A. 1953. *Quackery in the Public Schools.* Boston: Little, Brown.

Medley, D. M. 1977. *Teacher Competence and Teacher Effectiveness.* Washington, D.C.: American Association for Teacher Education.

Purkey, S. C., and **M. S. Smith.** 1983. "Effective Schools: A Review." *The Elementary School Journal* 83 (March): 427-52.

Rickover, H. G. 1959. *Education and Freedom*. New York: E. P. Dutton and Co.

Rosenshine, B. 1974. "Teacher Competency Research." In *Competency Assessment, Research, and Evaluation*. Washington, D.C.: American Association for Teacher Education.

Schmuck, R. A. 1982. "Seeing How Teachers Fit In." In *Introduction to Education*, edited by Donald E. Orlosky. Columbus, Ohio: Charles E. Merrill.

Scott, C. Winfield, and **Clyde M. Hill.** 1954. *Public Education Under Criticism*. Englewood Cliffs, N.J.: Prentice-Hall.

Shaftel, F. R. 1969. *The Stanford Evaluation of Nine Elementary Teacher Training Models*. Final Report. Washington, D.C.: U.S. Department of Health, Education, and Welfare, Project No. 081710.

Tomlinson, T. M. 1981. "Effective Schools for the Urban Poor." *Educational Leadership* (April-May): 49G-50G.

U. S. Office of Education. 1951. *Life Adjustment Education for Every Youth*. Bulletin No. 22. Washington, D.C.: U.S. Government Printing Office.

6

There are two ways of spreading light: to be the candle or the mirror that reflects it.

- Edith Wharton

School Administration and Evaluation of Instruction *

Chapter 5 identified characteristics of effective schools and emphasized the central role of classroom teachers in the development of productive schools. It also made emphatically clear that teachers cannot carry the entire responsibility for school effectiveness, and that leadership and support from the administration is crucial for school success. This chapter addresses the school administration's responsibility for teacher performance and focuses on evaluation of instruction and teacher competence. The ideal relationship between teacher and administrator in this important area is, of course, supportive and nonadversarial. However, there is an inherent tension in most evaluative activities, especially when they lead to criticism, irrespective of how constructive that criticism may be. The tension is even more pronounced in those cases where teacher dismissal is at stake. Even though many teachers receive positive and supportive comments from administrators, the potential conflict in this topic calls for special care and sensitivity to avoid weakening the positive contributions of a productive and well-implemented procedure of teacher evaluation.

This chapter provides recommendations for teacher evaluation based on the clinical evaluation model. The term *clinical* means direct observation of the teacher is involved; it also means the observations are objective, analytical, and detached from personal and emotional factors. Before this sounds too antiseptic, it is worth knowing that there is room in the clinical approach to include matters such as enthusiasm and

* Appreciation is expressed to Professor Donovan Peterson, University of South Florida, for his substantial contribution to this chapter.

responsible praise, criteria that have been shown to relate to teacher effectiveness. Evaluation also requires that the standards established be based on the teachers' impact on pupils. Although self-evident, it is sometimes forgotten that one attribute of any profession is that the criteria for acceptable performance are based strongly on protection of the client (student).

In addition to the evaluative procedures that are implemented, being aware of legal issues in the evaluation process is essential. Further concerns about evaluation include awareness of classroom teachers' rights to their academic freedom; the logistics of conducting effective evaluation; the time and scheduling issues that impinge on the time of the administration; and the consequences of capitalizing on the evaluative function to strengthen the instructional staff by a combination of improving instructional performance of existing staff, inducting new teachers to the profession, and reassigning or dismissing those whose competence is or becomes subminimal. These additional issues are either addressed directly or implicitly in the narrative of this chapter.

Clinical Evaluation

Briefly, the clinical model provides for screening observation(s); diagnosing to detect problems requiring remediation; conferencing with the teachers to communicate suggested/required change; providing time and assistance in making changes; and finally evaluating the teacher's ability and/or willingness to make change.

This process emphasizes improving teacher performance rather than rating minimum performance. The rating of minimum performance as a means of making decisions (summative evaluation) must be and is provided for in this approach. However, the process of identifying and remediating ineffective teacher behavior (formative evaluation) is the essence of this evaluation system. It is through this formative process that improvement in the quality of education is achieved. Carl Rogers (1961) conceptualized this process as a "helping relationship, one in which at least one of the parties has the intent of promoting the growth, development, maturity, improved functioning, and coping with life of another."

As evaluators of teacher performance engage in this process and use the approaches recommended in this chapter, a number of professional, legal, and ethical problems arise regarding both form and substance. This chapter lists problems and suggests a process in which many professional, legal, and ethical pitfalls can be avoided.

Professional Responsibilities and Issues

Evaluation of personnel is often threatening to them for it is exceedingly difficult to discard the negative connotations of the term. Nevertheless, every effort should be made to establish evaluation as an activity in which mutual gain of pupils, teachers, and the schools will take place.

Schools benefit from learning about their performance by correcting weaknesses and maintaining strengths. New knowledge from research and practice, the turnover of personnel, and ever-changing characteristics of the instructional staff all require monitoring and evaluation to maintain the best blend of resources to optimize effectiveness. Considerable professional growth potential is based on well-conducted evaluations of instructional personnel. New information about teaching, existing instructional practices, and the collective knowledge of the faculty and administration can all be assembled and effectively re-directed better when proper evaluations are conducted. The professional and objective approach to evaluation is critical to meeting these desirable goals. The administrative responsibility to create the neutral, objective, and helping approach calls for personal behavior and professional knowledge that is fundamental to successful evaluations. Some of these characteristics are described next to help set the tone for effective evaluation.

Adminstrators are typically charged with the responsibility to develop and implement evaluation procedures. These procedures should be developed jointly with those most affected by the evaluations. They should also be developed with a major role played by administrators. Administrative leadership in evaluation is an obligation that goes with administrative responsibility. Thus, one of the most important initial steps is to establish the procedures for developing evaluation procedures, to determine who is to be involved, and the relative responsibility of each party to the process. Care must be taken to include people whose knowledge of evaluation and whose respect and credibility with others in the district is high. Accuracy and fairness play a large hand in determining the acceptability of the procedures eventually developed. Consulting with teachers and their leadership, securing information from a cross section of supervisors and other key personnel, and openly discussing the issues with board members and other adminstrators are some of the essential steps in developing or revising evaluation procedures. Failure to account for these interests and viewpoints can undermine the evaluation procedure.

Administrators faced directly with implementing procedures must establish their credibility as persons who are *thorough*, *fair* and *objective*. These may sound like platitudinous words but they are also powerful considerations in the area of teacher evaluation. Each deserves a comment.

Thoroughness

Procedures that go beyond the brief visit or the rating of superficial features of classroom instruction are essential. Teachers' major criticism of classroom supervisors is that the visits are short, infrequent, fail to include follow-up conferences, and address relatively unimportant factors. Thoroughness demands a supervisor's time and requires knowledge about classroom instruction that recognizes the differences between important and shallow acts and between effective and ineffective teaching. It also requires the supervisor to be able to offer positive suggestions when needed, to recognize excellence, and to pinpoint its characteristics in a supportive way. Though it is difficult for administrators to engage in thorough supervision of this type along with the other duties of their positions, it is also unfair to the instructional staff to neglect the supervisory role and then make important decisions about retention, dismissal, or reassignment based on weak or flawed information. Some of the procedures for managing supervision and evaluation will be discussed later in the chapter. Here it is important to emphasize that evaluation of instructional staff is not an area that will ride along on its own with only an occasional glance. The expectations of those to whom the schools are accountable demand much more; and the instructional staff deserves well-qualified, supportive evaluation. Thoroughness in supervision requires knowledge, hard work, and comprehensive attention to important details of instruction.

Fairness

Such an obvious and unspoken tenet of proper assessment would seem to require little comment; but there is a drastic difference between claiming fairness, and performing fairly in supervising teachers. Some faculty relate better than others to administrators because of factors such as age, sex, personality, knowledge, or common interests. These personal relationships are natural developments between people; they help make the workday more pleasant by promoting enjoyable personal and collegial relationships. Regardless of the professional and personal relationships between the adults involved in these assessments, the critical factor in evaluation is the relationship between the teacher and his/her pupils. The wise supervisor or administrator separates personal relationships from the duties of evaluation and establishes trust among the entire faculty that fair evaluations will be conducted. This can be a narrow tightrope to walk but it is not an impossible task. One step in the right direction regarding fairness is the willingness to recognize both the importance of and the dangers inherent in the personal relationships and the evaluation responsibilities assumed by administration. Administrators must be careful with casual comments, especially in the presence of others on the staff, that might convey bias or preconceived notions about other teachers. A fair administrative performance of evaluation duties, over a period of time, will help establish a reputation for fairness warranting staff confidence. A failure to establish this credibility can undermine the potential of the administrator to be helpful and useful in the evaluation process.

Objectivity

Quite similar to fairness, objectivity nevertheless contains some additional elements. Objectivity calls for the quantification of as much of the teacher's performance as possible. It calls for the use of low-inference level (objective) factors when possible. It requires attention to evidence and factual data that will give uniformity and consistency to evaluation procedures. Evaluation of teaching is not limited solely to the purely objective; but there is considerable support for the objective measures described later in this chapter that will strengthen the hand of the evaluator. Certain facts cannot be ignored and should be consistently and uniformly obtained and analyzed for all teachers. For example, if one teacher requires five minutes at the beginning of class to engage pupils in learning and another requires only one minute, the objective evaluator will point out this information to each teacher and discuss its consequences. Even if the teacher who delays five minutes has filled the time interestingly and justified the delay as a "warm-up" period, the students have lost some valuable learning time and the evaluator is obligated to review this information with the teacher. The consistency of the evaluator in being objective contributes to the credibility and effectiveness of the evaluation procedure.

This underscores how important it is that administrators establish a high level of credibility through behavior and decisions that are thorough, fair, and objective. Through these actions the administrator can gain the confidence of the instructional staff so that even unpopular decisions about faculty will be built on a reputation for professionalism and therefore be more acceptable. Teachers know that administrators must at times make distasteful decisions; but if the confidence in the administrator has been established, acceptance of those decisions is more likely.

Another critical time for proper administrative behavior in the evaluation process occurs when new faculty are employed. During the interviews and before employing teachers it is the responsibility of the district to describe supervisory and evaluation procedures so new teachers can be informed about the district's policies and expectations concerning pupils, teacher performance, and standards. Such information can be supportive to beginning teachers whose work will be supervised and evaluated.

To summarize the professional role of the administrator in respect to evaluation, three factors have been identified. One is to establish an evaluation system in cooperation with other key personnel, especially classroom teachers, that is based on the best knowledge available and that is in keeping with the school district goals. A second important area is to establish credibility for those who evaluate, so as to increase their effectiveness and acceptability. Credibility can be established by practicing thoroughness, fairness, and objectivity in implementing evaluation procedures. The third factor is to brief new teachers to the system, beginning at the pre-hiring stage, about the supportive supervision and evaluation procedures to prepare them for evaluation activities, and to explain the expectations of the school district. These are essential professional activities for administrators. Next, the legal responsibilities for evaluation will be described.

Legal Issues in Evaluation

Violations of due process probably constitute the most frequently contested problem in teacher evaluation. Discussion follows of due process together with explanations of discrimination, validity, reliability, high/low inference variables, representative teacher behavior, research, kinds of instruments, observation approaches, context of evaluation, who should evaluate, and levels of evaluation.

Due Process

The Fourteenth Amendment to the United States Constitution states that no state shall "deprive any person of life, liberty, or property without due process of law. . . ." *Due process* means that established rules must be followed to protect individual rights.

Substantive due process includes the fundamental freedoms of speech, religion, association, and privacy. Procedural due process encompasses the procedure followed when administrators are engaged in summative evaluation, dismissal, or retention where decisions are made that directly effect teacher welfare (Deneen 1980).

Because contract wording varies from district to district, an administrator needs to study the district's contract for specifics of procedure. Accepted procedure for evaluating teachers typically includes:

1. Teacher awareness of the criteria and procedure used for purposes of evaluation
2. Direct observation of the teacher in the classroom or other teaching situations
3. Conferring with the teacher to negotiate and specify any area(s) in which the evaluator requires the teacher to make changes
4. Assisting the teacher with materials or in-service course work that addresses the area(s) in which the teacher needs to make changes
5. Providing time commensurate with the complexity of the change(s) that the teacher is required to make
6. Re-observation and evaluation to establish whether or not specified changes have been made

Violations of procedural due process become most evident:

1. When an evaluator recommends dismissal of a teacher without having directly observed the teacher
2. When evaluations are not properly documented
3. When directions for making change are not clear and not in writing
4. When there is inadequate time and or assistance provided the teacher to make improvements
5. When evaluators fail to check systematically to see the degrees to which the teacher has been able to change

The procedure must be legally and professionally intact by including as a minimum all the points stated above to comply with procedural due process.

Discrimination

The United States Constitution guarantees that citizens not be discriminated against for their beliefs, association, or personal characteristics. The criteria and procedure for evaluating teachers may not, therefore, in any way reflect factors that could be considered discriminatory.

Charges of bias and unfair discrimination normally protected under the Constitution were given additional muscle in Title VII of the Civil Rights Act of 1964; in the creation of the Equal Employment Opportunity Commission (EEOC), and in the Equal Employment Opportunity Act of 1972. In essence, it is unlawful to be influenced by race, color, religion, sex, national origin, or handicap; or to limit opportunity or segregate employees on any of these bases when evaluating for purposes of hiring, promoting, or discharging teachers (Deneen 1980).

Court cases have found instances where tests, interview techniques, and evaluation systems used for selection, promotion, or retention have been racially, culturally, sexually, or otherwise biased. Only when evaluation criteria are directly job-related may they legally be applied. For example, most teaching positions require teachers to speak English. Speaking English is directly related to their success as teachers. It is, therefore, legal to require applicants to speak English to be considered for employment. The key factor in determining whether or not a given criterion is illegally discriminatory is in its *job relatedness*. Since the main product of teaching is student learning, to be job-related, most criteria should focus on teacher behaviors whose connection with learning and student conduct has been proved by research.

Validity

Systems of evaluation must, as a principle of law, be job-related and, as a principle of measurement, measure the attribute(s) they purport to measure. The legal principle questions criteria such as appearance and grooming as being only questionably, if at all, related to the job of the teacher. Or, in the serious but gray area such as alcoholism or suspicion of drug abuse, if the teacher were clearly under the influence of drugs or alcohol while teaching, the established relationship would be evident. But if teachers are sober while in the classroom, unless their habit is of a scandalously public nature, dismissal on grounds of using drugs or alcohol would be questioned for its validity, i.e., its job relatedness (Deneen 1980).

At least two major concepts relate to validity as a principle of measurement—*predictive validity* and *content validity*. Predictive validity establishes the connection between what the teacher does behaviorally and how much students learn. Monitoring students while they do seat work to keep them on task and answering questions when they need help is one example of positive predictive validity (McDonald 1976; Rosenshine 1978). Basic research has shown in a number of studies that students learn more when teachers monitor seat work than if they disregard students by checking tests or doing something other than circulating and helping students.

Content validity refers to the extent to which knowledgeable people agree that the evaluation system contains items or categories that are clearly articulated and representative of the concepts that are to be measured (Mazur 1980). To determine content validity, an administrator selects concepts tested for productive validity, extracts definitions and examples from the original research(s) and engages a number of *knowledgeable* people who examine the definitions and examples for their clarity and representativeness. Consensus, rather than a statistical measure, constitutes content validity.

Systems of evaluation should be validated from a legal and measurement perspective prior to being used in teacher appraisal.

Reliability

Like validity, reliability has both legal and measurement implications. Legally, the courts are concerned that teachers not be dicharged by a district without documented evidence from qualified evaluators acting in good faith. Biased opinion, arbitrary ratings, capriciousness, or abuse of discretion are all causes for legal question (Deneen 1980).

To avoid legal problems associated with reliability, sound principles of measurement should be applied to the development and application of teacher evaluation systems. In the process of developing teacher evaluation systems, validity must first be established. As in the process of curriculum development, content is selected before method. In developing evaluation systems, first predictive and content validity are established, and then reliability, i.e., the method or process to be followed in applying the system (Mazur 1980).

Authors vary in their approaches to establishing instrument and observer reliability (Medley and Mitzel 1963). However, there are two major concerns that are best phrased in the form of questions:

1. To what degree can two or more persons observe the same teacher at the same time and independently draw the same conclusions?
2. To what degree can this be done in varying contexts over time?

Question number one addresses the concept of objectivity; question number two addresses the concepts of stability and generalizability. To measure objectivity, two or more persons learn the system being tested and observe a teacher teaching a class. What they record (what is recorded depends heavily on the items or categories in the system being tested) is then compared, usually using one or more statistical measures of variance, for similarities and differences. Once objectivity is reasonably established, multiple observations are then made in varying contexts (i.e., grade levels, subjects, etc.) over a period of time to establish stability and generalizability.

High/Low Inference Variables

Observation systems vary, depending upon the purpose(s) they serve, in both form and substance. An important substantive difference is whether high- or low-inference variables are to be observed. Whether a variable is of high- or low-inference is dependent upon the amount of *judgment* the observer must apply to determine the presence, absence, or quality of the variable. (Borich 1977).

Typical high-inference variables found in summative rating forms include warmth, enthusiasm, and effectiveness. These terms are general and subject to perceptual differences between observers. To rate the presence or absence of these variable qualities or to determine their intensity requires that the evaluator make highly inferential judgments. As the amount of judgment required to evaluate a variable increases, accuracy normally decreases. When this happens the system becomes subjective (i.e. judgmental) and may lack reliability—a potential legal problem for the school systems.

Remediation of this problem is dependent upon selecting low-inference variables that have, if possible, been validated. Low-inference variables are behaviors that can and must be defined, with examples, so that both the evaluator and the teacher being evaluated have a reasonably precise and similar understanding of the variable. The evaluator is thus looking for explicit behavior by the teacher, and judging that behavior by explicit standards. The notion of concepts and their behavioral indicators is critical to understand. Concepts are abstractions. Concept names are labels given to categories in which criteria enable us to specify the concept and also to classify behavior as representative of one concept or another. For example, the concept of *probing* as a teaching skill requires that:

1. A question be asked by the teacher.
2. A response be provided by a pupil.
3. The teacher pursue the pupil's response by asking additional information from the *same* pupil.
4. The student provide an additional response.

Thus, the concept of *probing* is differentiated from the concept of *questioning* because in *probing* the teacher and pupil interact beyond the initial question. The informed supervisor can recognize when a teacher utilizes *probing* in addition to *questioning* and also can determine the relative importance of probing according to the nature of the content under discussion, the characteristics of the pupils, and the nature of the probes employed by the teacher. The teacher and supervisor also can use the technical language of pedagogy, namely the distinction between probing and questioning, when they hold a conference about the classroom. Without the ability to conceptualize and to recognize the behavioral indicators of concepts in respect to teacher and pupil behavior, such evaluations and discussions will not occur.

An example of a low-inference verbal behavior is "specification of objectives." It is defined as, "Includes statement of aims or purposes usually given toward the beginning of the lesson to inform students of what they are expected to learn as a result of participating in that lesson." An example of a teacher specifying objectives is "After this discussion you should be able to state three of France's most important imports and three of her most important exports. Further, you will be able to list four countries that are dependent on France for markets or for goods" (Mazur and Peterson 1980). Items of this level together with their definitions and examples can be observed within acceptable levels of error by trained observers. They are low-inference variables.

Thus, on one end of the continuum, there are high-inference variables that are of a general nature and may lack the quality of reliability when included in teacher evaluation systems; on the other end of the continuum there are low-inference variables that are specific behaviors and can be recorded within acceptable ranges of reliability. The dilemma is that overly simplified systems of evaluation based on a limited number of low-inference variables probably do not distinguish between effective and ineffective teachers and do not assess a representative sample of the teacher's behavior.

An analogy that further illustrates this problem is found in the contrast between objective and subjective tests with which we are all quite familiar. Test items that are True-False can be consistently graded accurately by anyone who has the answer key and is careful to avoid clerical errors. Essay questions are inconsistently graded by experts in the field or even by the same person if time elapses from one grading to another. Furthermore, True-False test items, though they are low-inference items, are limited in the kinds of knowledge they can test. The more comprehensive knowledge that can be examined with subjective tests leaves room for argument between the student and the teacher and even among the experts. The combination of both approaches is probably best, especially where teacher performance is being evaluated; but the pitfalls found in testing procedures are similar to those found in teacher evaluation approaches.

Representative Observation of Teacher Performance

The fundamental purpose of teacher evaluation systems is to distinguish between effective and ineffective teaching and to identify practices that, if improved, would have a positive effect on student learning. To accomplish this purpose, the content of the instrument(s) must be valid and the procedure must be reliable and representative of teacher performance (Berliner 1977).

As mentioned previously, evaluation systems based on general concepts are probably not reliable; on the otherhand, systems based on specific concepts are probably not representative of what the teacher does and therefore are not valid. McDonald (1976) in the _Beginning Teacher Evaluation Study_ stated that "No single teaching behavior has been found that consistently accounts for significant measures of teacher effectiveness." When behaviors are grouped, however, _what_ the teacher does is the second most powerful predictor of student achievement. What students know prior to entering a given class is the most powerful predictor of how much they will learn, according to McDonald.

Summative evaluations, therefore, need to be comprehensive by including a wide range of validated variables that can be applied to a wide variety of contexts and levels to observe representative samples of teacher behavior. As such, groups of behaviors appropriate to the level and context can be applied to the evaluation of each particular teacher. Within the same system, however, instruments containing low-influence items must be used to focus on specific areas in which teachers can make improvement.

Research/Valued Variables

One of the first decisions in developing a teacher evaluation system is to select the variables (sometimes called items or categories) that are to be evaluated. In past practice, evaluation systems were generally constructed through the process of consensus. This process included accumulating lists of teacher traits and other variables that the contributers felt were important, i.e., items "valued" by the contributors.

Some items were selected because, in the opinion of the contributor, they seemed to work effectively in his or her teaching; other items such as appearance, friendliness, or hard work were frequently included because they represented a notion of community standards. Using valued items in an evaluation system frequently subjects the person being evaluated to little more than the personal judgment and value system of the rater, even though the items may have little to do with effective student learning.

The antithesis of developing evaluation systems around valued items is to develop the systems on the basis of researched items linking teacher behavior to student outcomes. Until recently, a paucity of research made this connection (Borich 1977). Present knowledge remains

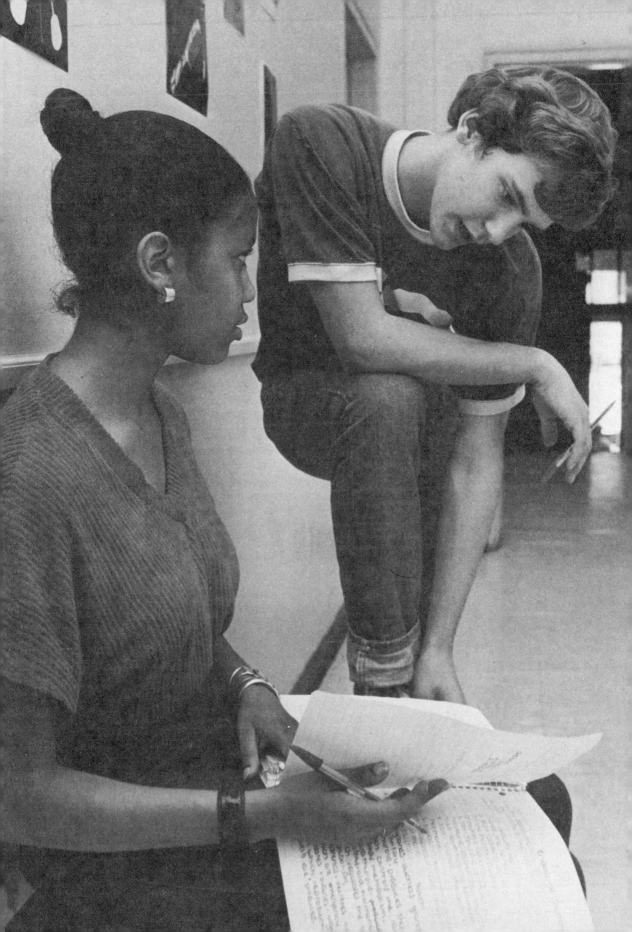

imperfect; but at last there are numerous studies identifying some teacher behaviors that link with student outcomes. Many of these behaviors were presented in Chapter 5. Furthermore, many studies are correlational rather than experimental; as such, they do not provide overriding evidence even when consistent correlations are found. For example, classroom organization as defined by several specific behavioral indicators consistently correlates with achievement whereas disorganization has a consistently negative correlation (Rosenshine 1970).

Development of the teacher evaluation approach described in this chapter is characterized by a movement away from highly judgmental "valued" items towards more specific researched teacher behaviors that are linked with student outcomes.

Number and Kinds of Instruments

Standard practice by school districts has been to adopt one instrument for purposes of teacher evaluation. Such instruments generally have included six to a dozen categories and have been used primarily for summative evaluations. However, a single instrument and one or two observations is probably an oversimplification. No single instrument of any degree of practicality could include all the potential behaviors worthy of observation and evaluation, particularly in formative evaluation. This being the case, instruments should be selected to fit the purpose or problem being evaluated.

Several methods can be used to develop observation instruments. They include naturalistic inquiry, sign systems, category systems, and rating scales. Naturalistic inquiry is almost a nonsystem, although varying degrees of structure may be introduced. Naturalistic inquiry is an observational procedure in which the observer enters the classroom without predetermined categories or behaviors in mind. Ideally, the observer will enter with a neutral attitude but armed with knowledge about classroom characteristics so not only the major events but also the subtleties in the classroom will be detected and remembered. The observer will report what is seen without using a predetermined vocabulary, although the descriptions of the classroom events must be articulate and technically accurate to be useful. It is a procedure that permits events that might not fit into a preplanned category or sign system to be recognized and included as part of the description of what has happened. The observer's behavior might be compared to that of a social scientist such as an anthropologist, who is viewing behavior and social interaction to learn about its characteristics and lets the events dictate the narrative that describes what is happening.

The advantage in naturalistic inquiry is that it frees the observer to record whatever he or she sees and it sets no parameters on what might be effective or ineffective teaching. The disadvantage is that although volumes of data can be accumulated using naturalistic observations, much of the data may be trivial. Examples of statements that could appear using naturalistic inquiry range from "teacher permitted a student to use the bathroom" to "teacher asked questions about the lesson and students responded."

Sign systems typically list a relatively large number of items identified out of research, theory, or from valued items that are listed on an instrument and checked once if they are observed. Some sign systems list positive and negative items that are then tabulated to determine the degree to which the teacher conforms to the research or theory. The Teacher Practices Observation Record (TPOR) is one such system (Brown 1970). It is based on Dewey's theory of "experimentalism." An example of a positive observation using the TPOR would be, "Teacher makes pupil center of attention." The corresponding negative observation would be, "Teacher occupies the center of attention." The Florida Climate and Control System is another example of a sign system format. In the Table 6-1, the sign system does include some categories but they are broad areas such as, "Teacher," "Pupil," and "Nature of Structure."

The advantage of sign systems is that they can include a fairly large number of items since the observer records each event only once regardless of how frequently it occurs. The disadvantage is that sign systems provide no information on sequence or frequency with which behavior occurs.

Category systems provide both sequence and frequency; but since observations are made on a timed basis (usually three to five seconds) the number of items (categories) that can be observed is limited. The classical example of a category system is the Flanders Model of Interaction Analysis (Flanders 1960). The Flanders system shown in Table 6-2 contains ten categories. Categories 1, 2, and 3 in Table 6-2 designate teachers' responses to students; category 4 is used to classify teacher questions; categories 5, 6, and 7 indicate teacher initiation statements; 8 and 9 signal student responses; and category 10 is used to indicate silence or confusion. In Flanders' system, as the teacher asks a question, the observer records one or more 4's depending upon the length of the question. If a student responds to the question, the number 8 is recorded — the category for student response to a question directed by the teacher.

Naturalistic inquiry, sign systems, and category systems are most appropriately used for formative evaluations where the purpose of the evaluation is to help the teacher improve. Rating scales are most frequently used for summative evaluations where quality judgments must be made. Frequently, the only instrument used for evaluating teachers is a summative rating scale.

The method of data collection recommended for the formative and summative instruments contained here is a combination of the category and sign systems, i.e., data are collected by category as in category and sign systems. Data are collected by frequency, however, which is unlike sign systems, but they are not collected on a timed basis such as they are in category systems. The rule of thumb followed in this system is that observations of specific behaviors are collected each time they occur, but they are not re-recorded until an intervening behavior is recorded.

Number and Length of Observations

In discussing previous issues, we reviewed the need to evaluate representative teacher performance established by research as having significant impact on student learning, and varieties of observation instruments used for purposes of teacher evaluation. It was pointed out that no single

TABLE 6-1 *Sample Sign System Schedule*

Florida Climate and Control System
Practice Form
By
Robert S. Soar, Ruth M. Soar, and Marjorie Ragosta

No.	Nature of Structure
S 1	Pupil as individual
S 2	Total group w/teacher
S 3	Small group w/teacher
S 4	Individual w/teacher
S 5	Structured group(s) w/o T
S 6	Free groups

Trainee's Name _____

Section _____ Episode _____

Score _____ of _____ correct.

No.	Teacher
1	Teacher central
2	Leads singing, games, storytime
3	Moves freely among pupils
4	Withdraws from class
5	Uses blackboard, A-V equip.
6	Ignores, refuses to attend P
7	Attends pupil briefly
8	Attends pupil closely
9	Attends P in succession
10	Attends simultan. activity

No.	Nonverbal Control
31	Tolerates deviant behav.
32	Positive redirection
33	Nods, smiles for control
34	Positive facial feedback
35	Uses "body English"
36	Gestures
37	Gives tangible reward
38	Touches, pats (gentle)
39	Holds, pushes, spanks (firm)
40	Takes equipment, book
41	Signals, raps
42	Shh! Shakes head
43	Glares, frowns

No.	Pupil (Cont.)
62	Engages in out-of-bounds behavior
63	Parallel work or play
64	Work with socialization
65	Collab. work or play
66	Works, plays competitive
67	Task related movement
68	Aimless wandering
69	Fantasy
70	Uses play object as itself
71	Seeks reassurance, support
72	Shows pride
73	Shows fear, shame, humiliation
74	Shows apathy

Verbal Control

No.	Verbal Control
11	Praises
12	Asks for status
13	Suggests, guides
14	Feedback, cites reason
15	Questions for reflective thought
16	Correct w/o criticism (SM)
17	Questions for control
18	Ques., states behav. rule
19	Directs with reason
20	Directs w/o reason
21	Uses time pressure
22	Calls child by name
23	Interrupts pupil, cuts off
24	Warns
25	Supv. P closely, immobilizes
26	Criticizes
27	Orders, commands
28	Scolds, punishes
29	Uses firm tone
30	Uses sharp tone

Pupil

No.	Pupil
44	Pupil central
45	Pupil—no choice
46	Pupil—limited choice
47	Pupil—free choice
48	(Seat work w/o teacher)
49	(Seat work with teacher)
50	(Works, plays w/much supervision)
51	(Works, plays with little supervision)
52	(Resists/disobeys direct.)
53	(Obeys directions)
54	Asks permission
55	Flws routine w/o reminder
56	Reports rule to another
57	Tattles
58	Gives information
59	Gives direction
60	Gives reason
61	Speaks aloud w/o permis.

Socialization

No.	Socialization
75	Almost never
76	Occasionally
77	Frequently

Materials

No.	Materials
78	Structure T behavior
79	Structure P behavior

Pupil Interest Attention

80	(Rank 1 low to 5 high)

TABLE 6-2 *Flanders' Categories*

Teacher Talk	Response	1. *Accepts feeling.* Accepts and clarifies an attitude or the feeling tone of a pupil in a nonthreatening manner. Feelings may be positive or negative. Predicting and recalling feelings are included.
		2. *Praises or encourages.* Praises or encourages pupil action or behavior. Jokes that release tension, but not at the expense of another individual; nodding head, or saying "Um hm?" or "go on" are included.
		3. *Accepts or use ideas of pupils.* Clarifying, guiding, or developing ideas suggested by a pupil. Teacher extensions of pupil ideas are included but as the teacher brings more of his own ideas into play, shift to category five.
		4. *Asks questions.* Asking a question about content or procedure, based on teacher ideas, with the intent that a pupil will answer.
	Initiation	5. *Lecturing.* Giving facts or opinions about content procedures; expressing *his own* ideas, giving *his own* explanation, or citing an authority other than a pupil.
		6. *Giving directions.* Directions, commands, or orders to which a pupil is expected to comply.
		7. *Critizing or justifying authority.* Statements intended to change pupil behavior from nonacceptable to acceptable pattern; bawling someone out; stating why the teacher is doing what he is doing; extreme self-reference.
Pupil Talk	Response	8. *Pupil-talk—response.* Talk by pupils in response to teacher. Teacher initiates the contact or solicits pupil statement or structures the situation. Freedom to express own ideas is limited.
		9. *Pupil-talk—initiation.* Talk by pupils which they initiate. Expressing own ideas; initiating a new topic; freedom to develop opinions and a line of thought, like asking thoughtful questions; going beyond the existing structure.
Silence		10. *Silence or confusion.* Pauses, short periods of silence and periods of confusion in which communications cannot be understood by the observer.

Note: Adapted from Ned Flanders, *Teacher Influence, Pupil Attitudes, and Achievement,* Final Report, Cooperative Research Project No. 397 (Minneapolis: University of Minnesota, November 30, 1960) instrument could include all potential teacher behaviors worthy of evaluation and that oversimplified observations and only a few observations are probably useless (McDonald 1980).

No firm guidelines exist to assist the practitioner in deciding how many appraisals should be made, or how long appraisal periods must be to base the summative evaluation on a representative sample of the teacher's behavior. At best, we can only offer the following considerations and examples to help with these decisions.

Research on teacher effectiveness suggests that appraisal periods have been as short as a single lesson or as long as a full year. Preferable practice, according to Borich (1977), is to arrange short appraisal periods that incorporate a series of interrelated lessons into a teaching unit.

It is important that all aspects of the teacher's handling of the class be observed and evaluated. This implies that observations include the teacher starting class, finishing class, and representative behaviors between those two points. It also implies that if the teacher uses a variety of organizational and operational modes of instruction, each mode must be sampled.

Examining interpretable lesson plans for instruction should help determine when a representative sample of teaching sequences can be observed, over what length of time, and how long each observation should be to accomplish the goal. DuBois (1980) stated in an *OSSC Bulletin* that Salem, Oregon, planned to observe first-year probationary teachers five times even though by law only two observations were required. Florida law requires a minimum of two summative and three formative evaluations of beginning teachers. This may also be a good practice when experienced teachers have new assignments or are found to need remediation.

Context of Evaluation

Teacher effectiveness varies by differences in context. Key factors that affect the context in which instruction is delivered include (1) teachers, (2) subjects, (3) students, and (4) classrooms.

Teachers vary in their knowledge of subject matter, in their pedagogical skill, and in their style of presentation. No two persons teach exactly alike. Their knowledge, skill, and style make them different. Competence in knowledge of subject matter and pedagogical skill are indicative of quality teaching, but differences in style have considerably less bearing on the quality of teaching. Two teachers with quite different delivery style can each be effective. Evaluation systems should measure knowledge of subject matter and pedagogy but should probably be neutral about style.

Subject matter affects the evaluation system because of its varying purposes. For example, mathematics requires that students learn a substantial number of facts, laws, and procedures, but social studies courses may stress values and attitudes. In mathematics, then, the teacher would probably lecture more often and be quite directive. In social studies, on the other hand, the teacher would be more likely to encourage extensive student participation. The evaluation system must be sensitive to these differences.

Students vary in their levels of intellect and style of learning. Some learn and retain knowledge quickly; others require extensive periods of time to learn the same material. Development of skills is of the same nature. The extent to which a teacher is assigned fast or slow learners, or the degree to which fast and slow learners are mixed in a teacher's class, affects what the teacher should do to be effective. Further, the same teacher behavior can have different effects on students. Praise is the classical example. Younger, less academically inclined students generally respond more favorably to praise than do older more academically inclined students. This dynamic quality of praise makes its use difficult to measure as a teaching technique in a standard evaluation system. The evaluation system should not be organized in any way that would limit the teacher's ability to structure behaviors—such as pacing, length of presentation, and repetition—to match differences in student characteristics.

Classrooms also vary in their effect on the learning environment. Consider the difference between a classroom in tranquil surroundings and one adjacent to a noisy lunch room. Extraneous noise, quality of lighting, chalkboard reflections, quantity and quality of instructional materials, and adequacy of furniture may all affect how much students learn. Evaluation systems should be sensitive to such differences and not negatively affect the evaluation if the teacher has no control over a problem.

Who Should Evaluate?

Past practice has shown that the main purpose of evaluation is to rate teacher performance, i.e., to do summative evaluation. These evaluations help make final distinctions between competent and incompetent teachers. Such evaluations are required by law. Although clinical evaluation recognizes the need for summative evaluation, it emphasizes the *improvement of teaching* (formative evaluation) as the main purpose of teacher evaluation.

This shift in purpose has a direct effect on who should evaluate. Assuming that the conditions described in the foregoing issues are reasonably met, i.e., the system of evaluation is primarily based on researched concepts of teacher behavior that have been defined, have had examples given, and have been satisfactorily validated, the evaluation system then becomes a teaching tool. Its primary purpose is to assist teachers to improve instruction.

Teachers should, therefore, know the content and mechanics of the entire system. Learning the system may in itself have a positive effect on their instruction. Such learning also enables formative self- and peer evaluation, as well as supervisory evaluation in the formative mode. The key to making this possible is that there is general structure that outlines both the teaching act (comprehensiveness) and the specific identification and definition of behavioral teaching concepts in a well-developed system of clinical evaluation.

Whoever evaluates must, of course, be adequately trained to do so. The amount of training required depends in part on the purpose of the evaluation. The only accurate way to determine "adequacy" is to compare purpose with tested results of trained users on site. However, a general notion of three levels is offered here as a starting point:

Level 1: *Teacher Self-Evaluation*

Simply learning the concepts and their definitions and examples as specified in the literature on effective teaching and practicing them should improve teaching. For instance, it is not uncommon for teachers to be aware that directive teaching reduces or eliminates the role of the pupil in participating or even feeling comfortable expressing his or her views in a classroom discussion. Directive teaching is described as behavior in which the teacher renders opinions and judges pupil comments in ways that might appear to be intimidating or insensitive to the student. When teachers are asked if they consider themselves to be directive teachers, many would say they are not because they feel they are sensitive to pupils and permit disagreement and discussion of diverse views. However, another characteristic of directive teaching is "domination of talk time." Once teachers learn that too much teacher talk has an effect similar to domineering behavior, since it denies others the right to participate, they can reduce the amount of teacher talk. Simply becoming aware of such concepts will not change behavior unless the teacher makes the connection with the new knowledge, and then only if the skills required to change are already a part of the repertoire of teacher behavior. A teacher will be unlikely to develop new skills merely by becoming aware of a deficiency, if to develop those skills the teacher requires new learning and practice.

Level 2: *Peer Evaluation*

A somewhat higher level of sophistication is required when one person observes another person's teaching and subsequently tells the person what has been observed. As in Level 1, the concepts, their definitions, and examples must be learned. The mechanics of the system of observation must then be learned and practiced. For the approach specified in this chapter, this includes learning the concepts, indicators, and definitions, studying examples of each and learning when they do and do not apply. It also includes learning and practicing the use of the formative instruments and how to use the data collected to improve teacher performance. It is assumed here that peer evaluations are informal, and they are unofficial evaluations done in a collegial relationship for formative purposes.

Level 3: *Supervisory Evaluation*

Official evaluations are usually done by supervisors. (Note that administrators are acting as instructional supervisors when they evaluate teachers.) Since supervisory evaluations are official whether they are formative or summative, the supervisors must be schooled in the evaluation system. This includes:

a. Learning the categories, definitions, and examples
b. Studying the background research for knowledge of sources, principles, and exceptions of each category (concept)
c. Learning and practicing the procedures for applying the system
d. Applying the system under controlled conditions where reliability can be measured.

Certified evaluators emerge from this procedure who are officially qualified observers. Who evaluates is then dependent on the purpose of the evaluation system. Optimum formative evaluation will most likely occur if all three levels of evaluation (teacher, peer, and supervisory) are encouraged. Training of supervisors, however, is the key to successful application of a well-designed evaluation system.

Levels of Evaluation

Adequate resources (i.e., time, qualified personnel, facilities, and money) are never available to implement the optimum evaluation system. Choices must therefore be made as to how available resources are to be spent and where to concentrate the evaluation effort.

The assumption here is that most experienced teachers do a good job and require little supervision. A small number of experienced teachers do, however, need assistance to improve their instruction. Because of inexperience and tenure laws, beginning teachers should be evaluated more frequently. Special attention should also be given to teachers in new assignments. A three-level evaluation system is suggested (Ward, Peterson 1980).

Level I

The first level applies to the majority of experienced teachers judged by qualified evaluators as generally doing well. These teachers should primarily be engaged in self- and peer evaluations for purposes of improving instruction.

The law in many states requires that each teacher must be evaluated at least once. This should include a conference with a department head or supervising administrator at which time past work is reviewed and future goals for improvement are set. Resources required to meet goals should be negotiated and planned, the plan recorded, filed, and used as a reference as needed throughout the year. It should also be used as a basis for the next annual evaluation. This kind of official evaluation is summative, but its purpose should also be formative.

Level II

Second-level evaluations are for beginning teachers, teachers who have new assignments, and those identified from a Level I evaluation as needing improvement. Identifying beginning teachers and teachers with new assignments is no problem. Identifying experienced teachers who need to improve is more difficult and sensitive.

Determining which tenured teachers should be included in the Level II evaluation can be done using several methods. One indication of experienced teachers who need Level II evaluating is frequent student and parent complaint about the teacher's performance and excessive discipline referrals. A second source is the Level I conference held each year for purposes of review and goal setting. The third source is comparative results of student gain scores often available through system-wide testing programs. Gain scores are difficult to work with, however, and assistance should be sought from someone with technical skill in measurement who knows how to control for the effects of variables other than teaching.

Each of these sources identifies teachers with *potential* difficulty. That the teacher needs improvement is not fully eatablished by these indicators, however. There should, therefore, be no stigma attached to being selected for a Level II review. Level II is a formative procedure during which decisions are made as to:

1. Whether the teacher has deficiencies needing improvement
2. What the specific problem(s) may be
3. What the teacher must do
4. How the supervisor will assist to remediate the problem(s)

Level II evaluations require several observations by trained observers using the formative instrument(s) selected to target and remedy a suspected instructional problem.

Level III

The third level of evaluation is summative in nature and is used when there is evidence that a teacher is judged to be incompetent. It is at this level that documentation becomes increasingly important and that more than one person independently judges the teacher. Due process must be followed, and documented evidence must be produced substantiating that the teacher either will not or is unable to change undesirable behavior. Summative evaluations lead to rating how competent the teacher is. The outcome of a negative summative evaluation is often dismissal or reassignment.

Summary

The discussion in this chapter should make it evident that teacher evaluation is a serious, humbling, and complex responsibility. The chief function of evaluation is to improve instruction, but other purposes sometimes include decisions about reassignment or teacher dismissal. Most teachers think they are doing a good job or at least feel that many others are doing no better. When they are singled out for needed improvement or compared unfavorably to a standard, the supervisor must have a wealth of resources to cope successfully with the issues that are likely to arise. This calls for the supervisor (administrator) to have full documentation of the teacher's performance, current and valid knowledge about the variables that have been used in the evaluation, and the attributes that engender confidence in the remarks that are made. All of these abilities call for supervisors who are knowledgeable, hard-working, and respected. These same qualities are required to work with effective teachers, either to lend support to existing performance or to make minor adjustments that will strengthen performance even more. The knowledge base of the administrator and the application of this knowledge through tactful and effective supervision can pay large dividends. The payoff in improved teacher performance not only makes their professional lives more effective and satisfying but also has a multiplier effect on students which increases the impact of the teacher. When the trade-offs between the amount of effort required to be an effective supervisor and the impact on students are compared, it should be apparent that the effort required is worth the consequences in the form of improved instruction and better pupil performance.

References

Berliner, David C. 1977. "Impediments to Measuring Teacher Effectiveness." In *The Appraisal of Teaching: Concepts and Practices*, edited by Gary Borich. Reading, Mass.: Addison-Wesley.

Borich, Gary D. 1977. *The Appraisal of Teaching: Concepts and Practices*. Reading, Mass.: Addison-Wesley.

Brown, Bob B. 1970. "Teacher Practices Observation Record (TPOR)." *Journal of Research and Development in Education* 4:14-22.

Deneen, James R. 1980. "Legal Dimensions of Teacher Evaluation." In *Due Process in Teacher Evaluation,* edited by Donovan Peterson and Annie Ward. Washington, D.C.: University Press of America.

DuBois, Donald W. 1980. "Teacher Evaluation: The Salem Public Schools Model." *Oregon School Study Council (OSCC) Bulletin*, vol. 24, no. 3.

Flanders, Ned A. 1970. *Analyzing Teacher Behavior*. Reading, Mass.: Addison-Wesley.

Flanders, Ned A., et al. 1974. *Interaction Analysis Handbook*. Berkeley, Calif.: Far West Regional Educational Laboratory.

McDonald, Frederick J. 1976. *Beginning Teacher Evaluation Study*. Princeton, N.J.: Educational Testing Service.

_____. 1980. "Principles and Procedures in Observing Classroom Instruction." In *Due Process in Teacher Evaluation*, edited by Donovan Peterson and Annie Ward. Washington, D.C.: University Press of America.

Mazur, Joseph L. "Issues Related to Measurement of Teaching Performance." In *Due Process in Teacher Evaluation*, edited by Donovan Peterson and Annie Ward. Washington, D.C.: University Press of America.

Mazur, Joseph L., and Donovan D. Peterson. *Lesson Organization: A System for Observing Related Teacher Behaviors*. College of Education, University of South Florida. Unpublished observation system.

Medley, D. M., and H. E. Mitzel. 1963. "Measuring Classroom Behavior by Systematic Observation." In *Handbook of Research on Teaching*, edited by N. L. Gage. Chicago: Rand McNally

Peterson, Donovan D., and Annie Ward. 1980. *Due Process in Teacher Evaluation*. Washington, D.C.: University Press of America.

Rogers, Carl R. 1961. *On Becoming a Person*. Boston: Houghton Mifflin.

Rosenshine, Barak V. 1978. *Academic Engaged Time, Content Covered and Direct Instruction*. Champaign, Ill.: University of Illinois Press.

_____. 1970. *Teaching Behavior and Student Achievement*. Stockholm: International Association for the Evaluation of Educational Achievement.

Scriven, Michael. 1973. "The Methodology of Evaluation." In *Educational Evaluation: Theory and Practice*, edited by Worthen and Sanders. Worthington, Ohio: Charles A. Jones Publishing Co.

Soar, R. S., R. M. Soar, and M. J. Ragosta. 1971. *Florida Climate and Control System: Observers' Manual*. Gainesville: Institute for Development of Human Resources, University of Florida.

7

There are no whole truths; all truths are half-truths. It is trying to treat them as whole truths that plays the devil.

- Alfred North Whitehead

School Administration in Curriculum Development

This chapter and the two previous chapters are close companions. Chapter 5 provided information about effective schools and their characteristics. The basis for determining when a school was effective depended primarily on pupil achievement. Chapter 6 addressed the importance of effective teaching in promoting pupil achievement. The basis for improving teacher performance was, in part, provision of effective supervision and evaluation that would strengthen instruction. After this discussion of effective schools and the promotion of effective teaching, a logical extension is to look at the school's curriculum. After all, it would be a mistake for schools to teach the wrong things—especially if they taught them very well. The distinctions between an improper and proper curriculum are not as clear-cut as we might like. However the criteria that enable us to make better distinctions and more functional decisions about curriculum are important. It is also important that the diverse influences that affect the curriculum and administrators working with the curriculum are addressed. Thus, the issues and basis for administrative behavior addressed in this chapter relate to the school's curriculum.

Strong administrative leadership in curriculum depends on a defensible rationale that guides critical decisions about school purposes and procedures to achieve these purposes. Without a clear and workable rationale, decisions will lack consistency and school practices will drift into confusing and often counterproductive directions. This chapter promotes a consistent and comprehensive approach to the analysis and implementation of an effective curriculum.

The School Curriculum

Schools serve three general purposes. These purposes include the custodial care of pupils, the promotion of knowledge and skills among pupils, and the development of personal characteristics among pupils such as interests, attitudes, and other behaviors often classified as affective learnings.

The Custodial Function

The custodial function is not as straightforward as it may first seem. It is apparent that when the schools provide a place for youth to spend a large portion of the day during the school year, they relieve parents of that responsibility. But there is more to this role than merely accommodating parents and their children. This nation considers schools an important contribution to the personal and social development of each generation. The compulsory attendance laws reflect this mandate, and the administration in schools is responsible for monitoring school attendance to assure that all pupils who are required by law to be there are in school. Over two and one-half million pupils are absent daily in the public schools of the country (Brimm, Fogarty, and Sadler 1978). These absences have a far-reaching impact on the effectiveness of the school curriculum. The absent students and the added complications to the teachers who accommodate irregular attendance burden both the administrative and instructional staffs in the schools. The task of the administrator in monitoring attendance is complicated further by the high mobility of the nation, the work schedules of itinerants, the revisions of compulsory age requirements, proper assignment of handicapped students, and the indifferent attitudes of some parents and pupils about school attendance. The school administrator must work constantly to establish rules and procedures that, on the one hand, make absenteeism unattractive while, on the other hand, promote attendance through incentives that help students overcome lethargic attitudes toward school.

Since the absentee rate ranges from over 50 percent in some schools to less than 10 percent in others, reasons other than illness are obviously behind these excessive absences. The reasons for unjustified absences include factors that are not under the direct control of school authorities. However, schools are still charged with the responsibility to enforce compulsory attendance laws. A primary contribution administrators can make in supporting the school curriculum is to do everything possible and reasonable to get and keep students in school. The administrator will find that, by working with teachers, guidance personnel, pupils, parents, school social workers, and law enforcement agencies, it is possible to promote school attendance.

Several examples illustrate procedures that have been successfully implemented to improve school attendance and also link attendance to improved academic performance. In a fourteen year longitudinal study, Hartford, Connecticut, utilized an integrated academic, cultural, and counseling effort with disadvantaged students (Nearine 1979). The clusters of students in this program averaged 94.7 percent attendance during 1977-1978, while the other school students averaged 81.4 percent. Ellison High School in Kileen, Texas, formulated clear attendance policies that focused on reporting methods to students and parents and an appeal process for students with excessive absences (Carruther 1980). They reported the best average daily attendance rate in the district after developing and enforcing a clear policy on attendance. A program that focused on parents' responsibilities for their children's attendance was instituted in Andover, Massachusetts, in 1975. Administrators reported an attendance increase from 89 to 93 percent among their 1500 students (DeLeonibus 1978). It appears that a combination of (1) clear and well-publicized attendance policies; (2) enforcement of the policy; (3) parent involvement; (4) and creation of positive support through counseling and program development improved school attendance.

When the achievement of students lags behind, it is wise to examine the absentee records and assess how much time students are missing school and any special patterns of school attendance. This effort is one way administrative support of the curriculum can be specific and the school's responsibility can be met.

Cognitive and Affective Learning

Three options are available to the administrator in respect to cognitive and affective learning in the curriculum. One possibility is to avoid direct involvement and rely on others to handle curriculum development and its implementation. This approach might be called benign neglect. Another possibility is to dominate the curriculum by controlling the entire program of studies and permitting no deviation from administrative demands. This approach is clearly dictatorial. A third approach is to share curriculum development and its implementation with others whose views and expertise are important and useful to strengthen school programs. This approach might be called the collegial approach.

The dictatorial approach is the least satisfactory of these three. It promotes low morale and assumes that one person has all the control and answers to curriculum problems and issues. Curriculum is too complex for any one person to be so powerful, to know about all content, to be aware of support materials in the various disciplines, and to be expert in implementing and evaluating the curriculum. Only the extremely arrogant or insecure administrator would attempt this dictatorial approach.

The second category of behavior, benign neglect, can be found in the schools. Such an administrator provides support for the curriculum through administrative decisions and allocation of resources, but avoids direct involvement and passes to others responsibility to make decisions about curriculum. Some administrators may find this approach an attractive alternative for several reasons. The work of administrators requires management of numerous details and problems. With so many other demands calling for attention, it is tempting to dodge curricular questions (unless there is a curriculum crisis) and trust that others will develop and maintain the program of studies. Furthermore, the requirements in the curriculum are often set forth by state and national agencies and interpreted locally by the school board. School administrators may feel they have little control over these decisions and that it would be a misuse of their time to deal with curriculum development. Also, the curriculum is implemented by classroom teachers as they refine and embellish it through the materials they use and their methods of instruction. Some administrators contend they are too far removed from the classroom, or lack the power to alter instruction by teachers. Because these are well-known realities, it is easy to see how an administrator might avoid direct involvement with the curriculum. Naturally there is a feeling of hopelessness and reluctance to try to develop or change something when others seem to have most of the control. In the case of the curriculum, however, administrative involvement is essential. Despite the common starting point established by state or even national levels, schools are not carbon copies of one another. Their reputations, problems, successes, and accomplishments vary greatly. And one of the most important factors that accounts for these differences is the personnel who attend and work in schools, especially the school administator. It was found by Blumberg and Greenfield (1980, 268) that "In a very real sense, by design or not, a principal develops the school in his/her own image." The role of the administrator at both the local school and district level is a strong element contributing substantially to the attributes and/or weaknesses in each school. It is not possible to assign a school administrator responsibility for hiring personnel, scheduling classes, administering the budget, assigning the use of facilities, supervising teachers (and more), and then claim that he or she has little control over the curriculum. The link between the curriculum and school administration is direct and obvious whether it is intentional or by default. Administrators should neither dominate the curriculum through dictatorial methods nor shirk their responsibilities through benign neglect, for they will make an imprint even under these circumstances. The active, collegial approach is best.

The days are gone when the administration was the ultimate and only authority in curriculum development. True, the administration does influence the curriculum; but curriculum is too pervasive to be determined by any single entity. However, responsibility for influencing and implementing curriculum must be met by the administration. A deliberate plan by administrators to create a process to engage in curriculum analysis and development is paramount in today's schools.

The degree of involvement by administrators in curriculum matters must be determined within the context of her or his total responsibilities. Administrators have many responsibilities; no single area, even curriculum, can be given exclusive attention to the neglect of others. One of the major concerns in this chapter is to identify essential elements that require administrative attention and to reduce the administrator's work in curriculum to a manageable size. No administrator can assume total responsibility for all curriculum elements, but a basic understanding of curriculum issues and an awareness of the structure and operating procedures for curriculum development can contribute substantially to administrative effectiveness in giving curriculum leadership.

What is Curriculum?

The school curriculum has been defined broadly by some to include all experiences encountered by youth under the direct and indirect control and influence of the schools (Caswell 1935). This definition, stated fifty years ago, has continued to dominate the thinking of many curriculum workers. Other definitions are so narrow that little more than the basic three R's are considered appropriate for schools to teach. The literature is replete with definitions and summaries of definitions of curriculum that would take us far afield if we elaborated on them here (McNeil 1981; Oliva 1982; Tanner 1980; Shepherd and Ragan 1982). You may want to review and study these various definitions in more detail; but for our purposes this opening discussion on curriculum will concentrate on the central issues in distinguishing between *schooling* and *education*.

Schooling contrasted with *education* addresses the division of responsibility among schools, family, and other institutions of society. Most individuals grow from birth to adulthood and acquire some degree of knowledge and ability to function in society. The total learned development of individuals is known as their education. However, no single institution supplies everything the individual learns. Those special responsibilities assumed by schools are separated from the responsibilities of other institutions according to the criteria in effect at a given time or under particular circumstances. For example, school responsibilities at the turn of the century were different from those now; or the expectations expressed by a small rural community are different from those found in most highly populated industrial and commercial cities. The time period and the location make a difference between what is considered schooling (responsibility of schools) and what is not. The function of the schools, family, and other institutions are not identical in respect to what they do or what they are expected to do. Some of the things they do are the same, some are different, some are contradictory, and some are mutually supportive. The most fundamental issue in curriculum development is to determine the responsibility for "schooling" and the responsibility for the "education" of youth. Another way to raise this point is to ask, "Where does the responsibility of the schools begin and end?" The answer to this question is critical; for it establishes the specific responsibilities of schools, and these, in turn, determine what the school is *expected* to do, what the school is *not allowed* to do, and what the school *may* do.

Three of the most highly publicized topics in which the "schooling" vs. "education" conflict arises are (1) censorship, (2) religion, and (3) sex education. In all of these areas almost any community will be divided over the precise line to draw between the role of the school and the role of nonschool agencies.

The separation between schooling and education is not easily established in these areas because the usual superior knowledge of the professional educator in discussions with laypersons is less evident here. A distinction between the typical professional relationship and the special nature of this relationship in the schooling versus education domain clarifies why this is so. One of the characteristics of a professional is that service to the client is the dominant criterion on which to make decisions. In those professions where the practitioner has knowledge obviously superior to that of the client, the professional can give information to the client, advise the client, and recommend the best course of action. There are many areas in schools where teachers and administrators possess this kind of knowledge and can serve students and parents well by recommending procedures. However, many of the decisions made in determining the rightful responsibility of schools occur in a different set of circumstances. This is so because the layperson may question school personnel in value-laden areas where the issue rests on what is "best" for the pupil. When decisions are made in schools about what is "best" for the students, the client (layperson or, often, parent) and the professional are often on equal footing. Discussion takes the form of the question, "Why is your opinion any better than my opinion on this issue?" When the schools or nonschool elements become the moral gatekeepers for the community, unresolved conflict and even hostility often result, partly because the community itself is divided on these issues. We might put this problem in the following, somewhat sardonic form. "The world is made up of the righteous and the unrighteous—and the righteous do the classifying."

Not all issues in delineating the proper work of schools focus on these controversial areas, although many do. Some delineations are based on the practical matter of how much time the school has to offer instruction, or the problem of not having enough facilities, enough personnel, or enough knowledge. (Can schools eliminate all the inferiority complexes of their students?). In making decisions about practical matters, the best answer may be obvious. Data help greatly in finding an appropriate answer. But in the controversial value-laden areas, where is the source of knowledge that guides decisions? One helpful approach for administrators is to clarify their source of final authority.

If administrators feel they have the final authority to make decisions about the programs and personnel under their direction then they will make autocratic and autonomous decisions, even in controversial areas. For example, an administrator who opposes censorship will fight for this viewpoint even when confronted with strong opposition from the community or other educators if she or he considers it the job of the administrator to be the decision maker in such matters. The administrator who considers the final authority to be the school board or some other "higher" source is functioning as a conduit, less likely to become directly *involved* in the decisions, but passing along the decisions made by others.

Separating personal views from educational policy is not easy when they conflict. Administrators will frequently face such conflicts in issues that involve the schooling vs. education issue. Policy statements that clarify this difference should ideally be provided through collective decisions acceptable to all. The curriculum of the schools is not packaged so neatly that clear lines are drawn between these two areas and administrators need a rationale that helps resolve conflicts.

One helpful way to look at the school curriculum is to determine its purpose or utility. If categories of utility can be identified, it helps classify the appropriate work of schools. One useful classification has been determined by Broudy (1974) in which he named four utilities of general education: (1) replicative, (2) associative, (3) applicative, and (4) interpretative. Because knowledge in these categories is useful in society, they seem reasonable at the macro level for screening the appropriate work of the schools. Replicative knowledge refers to learnings that become automatic in our daily lives. We know how to count, alphabetize, and read common words without stopping to think much about our actions.

For these frequently used learnings the school can provide supportive instruction. Associative knowledge is that collection of ideas, images, perceptions, and appreciations not used specifically but giving context to experiences. For example, when we view a movie about a historical period, we may not remember all the details about that period but prior knowledge nevertheless enables us to see the movie more meaningfully. Applicative knowledge enables us to solve problems and make decisions, such as how to invest our money, which political candidate to vote for, or which products to buy. Finally, interpretative knowledge is similar to applicative knowledge, but there can be interpretation without application. Further, interpretative knowledge helps us think through problems and information and distinguish between fact and opinion, propaganda and truth, and other kinds of information that require logical thought processes.

These four utilities of general education provide a framework within which decisions about the school's responsibility can be assessed. None of these is the exclusive responsibility of the schools but each is enhanced through schooling that aims specifically at providing cognitive knowledge in the areas.

Guidelines or criteria such as these help administrators make consistent decisions and, at the same time, serve responsibility in curriculum recommendations. Another set of elements many have found useful has been stated by Tyler (1949). In his recommendations Tyler emphasizes that consideration must be given to the data we obtain by (1) understanding pupils and their characteristics; (2) analyzing content; and (3) determining the priorities of the community the schools serve. After information has been organized from these data sources, some of the information can be screened out on the basis of practical realities (what the schools can accomplish) and philosophical realities. Philosophical reality is "what we believe in" in making curriculum decisions. Although this may be an imprecise element, it is honest in admitting that curriculum decisions in the long run are often based on the beliefs of those responsible for making the curriculum. The Tyler approach acknowledges and formalizes this reality and provides a systematic way to determine school objectives.

Whatever method is employed, eventually a tentative curriculum will be established. It is tentative because the forces that influence curriculum continue to function and at any time the established curriculum can and does undergo review and assessment. Thus, the never-ending search for the right curriculum continues and the constant responsibility for administrators to maintain contact and responsibility for this ongoing activity never quite stops. This is evident by listing some of the elements that have forced administrators to deal with developments in such areas as students' rights, Title IX requirements, desegregation, bilingual education, censorship, and religion. These are only some of the significant areas in which change is promoted through the schools. Since schools cannot be all things to all people, the distinction between schooling and education becomes essential to determine the proper work of schools. Moreover, it is necessary for survival, to avoid spreading school resources so thin that the system breaks apart.

How is Curriculum Determined?	To paraphrase the philosopher Reinhold Niebuhr, "Give me the serenity to implement the curriculum when I must, the courage to improve the curriculum where I can, and the wisdom to know one from the other." When it comes to determining the curriculum there clearly are some mandates administrators cannot change; other options administrators may strongly influence, however. This section describes how curriculum is formulated and distinguishes between the roles assumed by those who set curriculum requirements and the roles remaining for administrators who supplement or modify requirements set forth by others.

The National Level

Though the nation operates its schools as separate systems for each of the fifty states and territories, there are some national and universal requirements. Typically these requirements grow out of legislative or legal decisions rendered at the national level to protect the rights of individuals. Schools are subject to the laws of the land and compliance with these laws sometimes has implications for the school's curriculum. Legislative and court rulings usually do not tell the schools *exactly* how to operate. But, they do tell the schools when they are violating the rights of others and must change their practices. Some examples of rulings that have had implications for the curriculum include the prohibition of official school prayer, the sexual equality requirements of Title IX, the mandate to desegregate schools, and First Amendment protections of free speech for professional staff and students alike. It is the responsibility of school personnel to examine the implications of court and legislative decisions and to enforce the requirements established by these bodies. The discussion in later chapters about the legal aspects of schools provides more details about the role of the courts in determining school practice.

The State Level

Another level in which the curriculum is more specifically designated is in the various state legislatures and their state boards of education. Each legislature operates as a state "school board" and sets requirements and standards for the school curriculum. When they determine legal ages for school attendance, minimum competence performance levels for students, and stipulate high school graduation standards, they are setting curriculum requirements.

The Local Level

At the local level, policies are established by an elected or appointed school board, consistent with national and state requirements, but with the flavor of local interpretation and influence. Infrequently the local district may challenge national or state requirements. These challenges may create conflicts to be settled through the appeal process or enforced with the power of the state or national bodies. For the most part, the local school board will comply with higher regulations, but add policies to supplement requirements. These additional policies often have direct impact on the local curriculum.

Most of the decisions rendered at the national and state level are beyond the direct influence of local school administrators. However, over a period of time, individuals who make decisions are replaced, changes in society occur, and new policies are established at the national, state, and local level. As a consequence it becomes the responsibility of the school administrator to keep abreast of changes and the implications of these changes for the school curriculum. It is a further responsibility of the administrator to be active at the local level in curriculum issues to defend desirable portions of the curriculum and to promote changes that will strengthen the local curriculum. These specific activities of the conscientious administrator call for close contact with the programs and people under his or her leadership and an equally close contact with those administrators or policy makers who shape decisions that affect his or her responsibilities. Consequently, the administrator must exert a studious effort to obtain within the school district information that flows from the bottom up and from the top down. The administrator must also make a careful reading of the local newspaper for issues raised by the public; show sensitivity to events at school board meetings; and analyze budgets and other activities with the aim of gathering information. This is a tall order to fill and varies according to the administrative position held; but it is also an effort that will pay dividends in influencing curriculum policy, and developing credibility as a person whose views are respected.

Other Influences

Curriculum is also influenced by individuals and groups outside the official agencies at the national, state, and local level. The other groups include organizations such as the Chamber of Commerce, religious organizations, special interest groups, individual gatekeepers of the school curriculum, watchdogs of textbooks, and so on. The establishment of curriculum practices reflects the composite of pressures and interests as expressed through these organized groups and individuals. Though the official curriculum is determined by members of the profession and agencies charged with responsibility for determining policy for the schools, the efforts of vested interest, special, and pressure groups influences the curriculum. It is a wise educator who listens to the voice of the community and views the opinions of others with an open and responsive mind.

Thus, if we were to identify how the curriculum is determined, a large portion (but not all) of the curriculum is determined by national, state, and local legislative and legal actions and appointed officials charged with the responsibility to set requirements and standards. These individuals are influenced by the prior policies they inherit, the views they bring to their positions, and the influence of others (including educators). The official curriculum arises out of this set of negotiations and the local administrator usually has the primary obligation to be aware of and to enforce the requirements set forth.

In addition to the required curriculum there are some choices in the curriculum that are open for development. The next section provides a discussion of some of these options and how to utilize the position of the administrator to exercise them.

Options in Curriculum Development for Administrators

In this section the discussion about administrative options is reduced to two basic areas of concern. Both these areas are fundamental to establish directions for the curriculum and to provide a foundation on which many of the more specific options about curriculum can be selected. These two options relate (1) to the choices available to the administrator extending beyond requirements established by national, state, and local agencies; and (2) the relative emphasis on cognitive and affective learnings. Both areas can be influenced or even controlled by the administrator and both can make a critical difference in the nature and character of the curriculum taught.

After requirements have been specified for a school district, the remaining issues in curriculum require answers to such questions as: What electives should be offered and how will they be determined? Which teachers will be assigned to teach each subject and what factors (grade level, teaching styles, experience, and teacher preference) should be considered in making these assignments? Will subjects be taught through team teaching, in open-spaced classrooms, individualized classrooms, departmentalized organizations, or some other arrangement? How much time will be alloted to each subject? What time of the day will the courses be taught? There is considerable flexibility available for administrators to arrange the best fit of the resources at hand with the requirements of the curriculum. The practical aspect of simply arranging the parts must be influenced by the concern for effectiveness. There is an efficient way to plan schedules, assign professional duties, enroll students, and the other details that go into the organization of schools. There is also an educationally effective way to plan these components. Though considerable overlap may exist between the efficient and effective approaches, there is often room for choices that will make a difference in the work of the schools, the morale and effectiveness of the staff, and the consequent gains for pupils. Thus, one of the most direct ways for administrators to influence school effectiveness in the curriculum is to exercise appropriate options in utilizing human and other resources to bring about the best combination for school success. There is a similarity between the classroom teacher's efforts to individualize instruction to optimize learning and the administrator's efforts to individualize assignments to optimize teacher effectiveness. To provide this "best fit," the administrator must have a strong grasp of the total curriculum, the characteristics of pupils, the strengths and preferences of the faculty, and the sensitivity and insight to blend these elements into the best combination. Decisions made in these areas may have more impact on the curriculum than all the mandates and requirements handed down from national and state agencies. These options constitute one of the most powerful tools available to the schools and their abuse can be just as destructive as their proper use can be beneficial. Some of the questions the thoughtful administrator will ask in this area include the following: How can new teachers be assigned to assure the best induction into the school and also provide the best instruction for pupils? What balance between homogeneous and heterogeneous groupings of students will optimize learning and provide teachers with the best assignments? How will planning time be organized to enable teachers with common responsibilities to confer? What procedures will enable special teachers to work with certain students without disrupting the work of regular teachers? Can student assignments be scheduled to reduce the potential disruption between class periods, and thus increase the efficiency of supervision and the transitions from one class period to another? The questions continue ad infinitum. The wise administratior is sensitive to these problems and relies on the information from those most affected by the decisions. All administrators in the district can help one another by sharing procedures that have been helpful and identifying common problems that need attention. Good answers to these questions enhance the curriculum and instruction in the schools.

In addition to good organization and the enforcement of curriculum requirements there are also electives in most curricula. Development of these electives extends to the extracurricular (cocurricular, extraclass) as well. Electives should reflect local idiosyncracies and provide special opportunities to capitalize on the uniqueness of the district served, the interests of the pupils, the preferences of the community, and the special talents of personnel. It is in the elective program that special advanced courses can be offered, variety in the fundamental courses can be provided, community traditions can be maintained, and special vocational outlets can be recognized to accommodate local conditions.

Often the trends of society are not reflected by national, state, or other agencies so quickly as a local district may prefer. The technology of today, social change such as more working women, new roles for both men and women, increased divorces, and crises such as drug abuse, unwanted pregnancies, alcoholism, and economic recession are all areas in which the schools may choose to respond outside the programs that are established officially. The wise administrator is alert and analytically astute to devise a process to investigate and react to such trends. It is in this domain of the extended and extracurricular program that curriculum options are most available. The administrator should constantly assess these offerings and compare them with special interests that deserve attention in the school program. Some of the most creative alternatives in schools can be provided for pupils by exercising ingenuity with judgment in the development of these additions to the required school program.

Cognitive vs. Affective Emphasis

The comparative emphasis on cognitive learning in contrast to the emphasis on affective learning is a fundamental issue because the administrator's preference in this regard often swings decisions from one direction to another. It is important for administrators to arrive at a point of view that will provide a foundation on which consistent decisions can be made. As administrators address this concern, the fundamental orientation to the issue rests on the question of whether the major theme of the curriculum should be the acquisition of knowledge and skills or the psychological and social development of individuals. It is not necessary

to elect one option to the exclusion of the other; but the degree of emphasis given one over the other can lead to quite different curricula, methods, and school climate. The tactful administrator will try not to alienate proponents of either view; but in specific decisions, the administrator's preference may determine which point of view prevails.

The arguments posed by each side of this issue suggest the positions held by the proponents. Those who favor a more dominant emphasis on affective learnings argue that acquisition of knowledge alone is an insufficient and even secondary consideration in determining the role of the schools. It is evident that no amount of knowledge will be put to good use unless people have proper attitudes, motivations, or interests. The human characteristics of a civilized person emerge from building a good sense of self-worth and psychological well-being. In a learning situation, it is best to salvage the individual, even by some compromising with learning standards, if we are going to cultivate the lifelong characteristics that will form a basis on which people can become fully functioning adults. The writings of Carl Rogers, Abraham Maslow, Earl Kelly, and Arthur Coombs express the views of the humanists and provide a strong case for emphasis on affective learnings as the dominant concern of the schools. (ASCD 1962)

Those who favor a more cognitive responsibility for schools argue that the primary purpose of schools is to reduce ignorance. Schools are the only institutions established primarily for the purpose of perpetuating knowledge. Unless the schools serve their proper role, systematic knowledge will not be transmitted and each generation will be ill prepared to contribute to and strengthen the adult society. The public has invested in schools and has a right to expect a return in the form of the acquisition of basic, essential skills, knowledge, and the ability to think rationally. These are important learnings and unless there is an organized, disciplined effort on the part of schools to promote learning, it will not take place. The public has a right to expect students to acquire fundamental knowledge in basic subjects and to expect the potential of students to be developed whether they are college bound, headed into the professions, or will take their places in society at other levels of work. If the schools fail to provide the cognitive learning required for these purposes, then the schools will have failed in the one responsibility they are uniquely qualified to deliver.

Students of administration can add other arguments to these, assume the role of advocate for each view in turn, and see how each position holds up in professional reading and discussions with others. Beginning administrators can explore the issues that emerge from this analysis and examine its impact on themselves, colleagues, parents, students, and others. In this analysis it will be important to identify the strengths and weaknesses in being an advocate for each position and determine how decisions might be altered in respect to administrative responsibilities. For example, should an administrator employ teachers on the basis of different criteria because of the different points of view? Would an administrator recommend any changes in the grading system or report cards that are sent home? In the courses offered and the way sections are determined (homogeneous or heterogeneous grouping)? In other words, what are the implications for the position supporting a strong emphasis on cognitive development or that supporting affective emphasis as the proper focus of the schools?

Analysis of Curriculum

Thus far in the chapter we have recognized that curriculum is initially determined by agencies at the national, state, and local levels. We also identified the difficulties and the importance of distinguishing between the proper work of schools and the role of society in providing educational opportunities for youth. We listed some of the options available to the administration in making choices and influencing the curriculum and the extracurriculum in the local district and in individual schools. Then we provided a brief discussion of the relative emphasis that might be given to the cognitive and the affective learning of pupils. All these activities contribute to establishing the curriculum. However, once the curriculum is established, then evaluation and analysis of the curriculum remains as a continual and important activity. It is important to find out "how the curriculum is doing." Such analysis leads to the responsibility to strengthen weaknesses or to take action to modify the curriculum on the basis of the findings of the evaluation.

What Data on Curriculum Should be Obtained?

An educational leader must become informed about the schools' curriculum before she or he is likely to be helpful in promoting desirable or altering less effective curriculum activities. Thus one of the important elements of knowledge in a given school district is to learn about the curriculum that is offered. This may first seem like such an obvious requirement that taking time to discuss it seems unnecessary. Not so, however; for the illusion of simplicity in this request soon vanishes when a careful study of the existing curriculum is undertaken. Some of the major factors to consider in this study should reveal the directions such an analysis will require.

The overall expectations of the school district should become known to administrators at all levels and in all major aspects of school operation. This means that a well-informed administrator knows the expectations of the district. The informed leader also knows how these expectations are translated at the elementary, middle, junior high school, and high school levels. Such information benefits administrators as they deal with articulation from one grade level to another, share in making decisions about budget and materials, interpret information to the faculty of a given school, or provide information to the public and others who may wonder about the work of schools. Anyone who has worked in schools knows the respect and confidence gained by the knowledgeable administrator who is well informed about the curriculum and can articulate appropriate responses to questions from parents, teachers, pupils, and others with a stake in the schools. All administrators function as specialists in their private niche. The principal of the elementary school knows firsthand how young children look, behave, what their interests are, and how they learn. The characteristics and patterns of teaching used by teachers in elementary schools are known, and the rules for discipline, regulations for school management, and logistics of school operation are known uniquely by the specialists in school administration at the elementary school level. Similar information is known to the principal of the high school and the middle school administrator. The district superintendent, the school business manager, and the supervisors of major programs such as the secondary curriculum, federal programs, and subject areas all must be expert in their speciality.

This division of labor is important; for it strengthens the ability of the administrator to give appropriate direction to those dependent on the leadership he or she can provide. No level of schooling, however, can function well in isolation from others; and there is no part of the school operation more crucial for overall understanding than the program of studies, the content to be learned, or, if you will, the curriculum. The curriculum constitutes the payload. True, the curriculum often requires hours of meetings; decisions involving budget, staffing, building construction, and boundaries (as in the case of magnet schools); and the best collective thought that can be assembled. Yet that curricular effort can bring about a cohesiveness no other single aspect of the school operation is likely to produce.

Every administrator is obligated to possess a working knowledge of the basic offerings and goals that support those offerings at all levels of the school curriculum. Time spent in studying and analyzing the offerings of the entire school district is a good investment and provides a base from which discussion about schools often will spring. Those who are under the direct supervision of any administrator must trust that the administrator is capable of representing them in discussions and influencing decisions in which the work of the school's curriculum may be under discussion. It is vital to be forearmed with current, accurate information to participate effectively as a leader in the schools. Thus, one of the essential categories of knowledge required of all administrators is to be well informed about the curriculum throughout the school district. This knowledge constitutes the first-line information needed to develop other analysis of the curriculum.

Another major aspect to be analyzed relates to the impact of the curriculum on students. This impact can be analyzed in respect to (1) their achievement and (2) their attitudes and behavior. Neither of these alone is sufficient to commend or criticize the curriculum; but the collective impression made by these factors adds up to more than an "impression." They add up to a reasonable assessment of what is happening in the school program. In an oversimplified statement, one could say that a successful school is one in which students are high achievers, express enjoyment about being in school, and display, as do the faculty, a spirit of cooperation and high morale which permeates the schools. Conversely, one could describe an unsuccessful school as one in which achievement is low, and students are frequently absent and express dislike for school. Information about student achievement and student behavior becomes useful for curriculum analysis. A few comments about each will illustrate how an administrator might carry out this kind of analysis.

Student Achievement This is reported in a number of specific ways. Standardized scores on nationally normed tests provide some information about how well students are doing. Of course, the scores alone do not tell the entire story. The entry level of students and their potential must be taken into account. It is unreasonable to expect all of the achievement of students to be the responsibility of the teachers or the curriculum. The most appropriate curriculum and the best teachers may not promote the highest achievement among a group of students unless the prerequisite knowledge, potential to learn, and pupil application or effort are also present. Good teaching will promote student achievement but students must do their part and administrators must recognize which element is missing before trying to judge whether it is the teacher, pupil, or curriculum that requires improvement. Admittedly, it may be all three; but the ability of the administrator to properly diagnose problems in this arena is critical to apply efforts in the right direction.

Student achievement is measured by much more than results on standardized tests. The grades issued by teachers, the opinions of experienced teachers who can make comparisons with previous students, and follow-up information on students all add more information about student performance. The comments by students and the evidence they display in the form of academic interest and accomplishment provide a composite picture of student achievement. Academic interest may also be revealed through the courses selected by students. It is not necessarily the case that academic selections by students are appropriate for all; but it is important that each student strive for her or his greatest potential and not slide by with courses that demand less than the student could give, even though the same courses might be very demanding for another student. Through working with teachers, parents, and counselors the administrator can stimulate aspirations and promote selections and activities that will give students a strong foundation on which to build their future.

Student Attitudes and Behaviors. These help to distinguish between those schools where pupils' attitudes are poor and those where the attitudes are supportive. The responsibility for the climate that fosters positive student attitudes cannot rest exclusively on the shoulders of the students. The school and its social milieu must accept considerable responsibility for creating the atmosphere in which cooperation and support win over hostility and aggression. Though it is evident that students alone are, at times, responsible for disorderly behavior, it is equally evident that in those schools where antisocial conduct is the norm, the school must examine the environment it has established. A rather humorous solution to a complaint about speeding drivers makes an interesting point to consider about school rules. In a given neighborhood, residents complained that cars were violating the twenty-miles-an-hour speed limit and generally traveling about thirty miles an hour through the area. After reviewing the roads and the amount of activity, the police solved the problem. They changed the speed limit to thirty. The rules and regulations employed in schools constitute one part of the school environment, and overstrict or unnecessary rules should be reviewed.

When student behavior is characterized as nonattentive, off task, and disruptive, then this behavior serves as a clue that either the nature of the school or the nature of the student behavior (or both) needs to be adjusted. It would be well for administrators to heed the viewpoint about pupil behavior expressed by social psychologists, who recognize that:

> In general, the role of the student is to adhere to the organizational norms of the school and to apply himself to the accomplishment of the objectives defined for him by the school. A student must defer to the teacher as the initiator of activity and as the source of authority in the classroom. . . . When schools miseducate instead of educate, when schools operate against the self-interests of the students as individual human beings, then perhaps the most healthy response is for the students to refuse to meet their role requirements until the school makes some basic changes. (Johnson 1970, 75)

Some of the adjustment called for when student attention wanes may be an adjustment in the curriculum. Greater investigation into the curriculum and the extracurriculum may be called for to determine the students' desires and interests. It is eminently reasonable that students can have a voice in the determination of the curriculum and can identify the elements of the curriculum they find lacking as well as the parts of the curriculum that are satisfying.

Methods of Data Collection

Data collection brings together descriptive information about the curriculum and information about pupil and teacher performance. The descriptive information includes factual data about which courses are offered, number of students enrolled, electives selected, attendance records, and similar material. Inferences can be drawn from this information about student interest, facilities required, corrections to be made in scheduling, or trends in student interest. Conclusions drawn from such information are generally tentative and subject to validation through additional data collection.

Other data to collect include student ratings of courses and teachers, results of standardized tests, letter grades, and unobtrusive measures such as frequency of using the school library. Other helpful information includes reports from guidance counselors, feedback from students and parents, behavior in classrooms and at special events such as school assemblies and pep rallies, frequency of vandalism, and student response through comments in student newspapers.

An administrator armed with such information about the school and its curriculum and in tune with the behavior of teachers and pupils in respect to each other and the school program can be a walking data bank. These data collection procedures will enable the administrator to monitor school events and be sufficiently informed to anticipate strengths and weaknesses in school operation and make better judgments.

One of the most comprehensive approaches to data collection for curriculum is found in the self-study approach for regional accreditation. This process is lengthy, time-consuming, and comprehensive. The administration and faculty could not sustain this level of data collection on a regular basis without "burning out." Periodically, such a comprehensive analysis is an important part of the long-range operation of schools. At the other extreme would be the school that simply repeats the previous year and collects little or no data. What is recommended here is a middle ground between these two approaches. Each administrator must determine how extensive and frequently the data collection for curriculum analysis should occur. However, if a particular area of the school program requires a more intensive look, it should be more carefully examined. The administrator should map a sequence of priorities over a period of time to allow for each major area of the school program to undergo detailed scrutiny. A rotational basis might be developed in a five-year plan for example, in which each of the major academic and administrative areas could be examined in more detail. This is a good way to update the curriculum regularly without placing an undue burden on the administrative load or putting continual strain on other professionals to engage in constant intensive examination. It allows each study area breathing space from one review to the next and still provides a way to keep each area of the curriculum current.

Use of Data in Curriculum Decisions

The use of the data in making curriculum decisions should depend primarily on identifying areas of the curriculum in which there is a critical need for improvement. There is a common orientation to consider in making recommendations for change, and that orientation is to ask the questions, "What is the problem we are trying to fix?" or "What is the purpose of the change or improvement we are trying to make?" Changes in the curriculum should be solutions to problems. The information obtained about curriculum can serve the dual purpose of identifying problems to be solved and solutions to be tried. This is the proper use of curriculum data.

Formal, Taught, and Actual Curriculum

There are at least three curricula in the school. One is the formal curriculum, which consists of the publicly stated written and agreed-upon courses and learnings set forth as the intentions of the schools. One can read statements describing this curriculum and, if these statements are clearly written, interpret the schools' expectations for learners. Another curriculum is the one taught by the instructional staff. Individual teachers have different strengths and abilities; when they teach they will capitalize on their individual talents and emphasize different learnings. The third curriculum is the one that gets through to the students. Students can determine what they will pay attention to, what they will work at and what experiences they will seek. They select the content they will learn from the opportunities provided them by the teacher and the materials made available to them. The role of the administrator in working with teachers and what they choose to teach produces the most direct influence the administrator can have on the school program. Whether we are talking about the principal in a building, a supervisor in charge of a special program, or members of the central administration, their direct concern with the actions of the teacher constitutes a direct influential link with the curriculum that is taught.

If abilities of individual teachers are to be respected, then it is important that administrators tolerate different teaching approaches. Some teachers are excellent at lecturing, others lead discussions especially well, and still others may do best by individualizing their instruction. The trick for the administrator is to know when the variations in teaching methods or topic emphasis support the intended curriculum and when these different approaches stray too far or fail to meet curriculum requirements. Thus, one of the fundamental concerns of the administrator is how to distinguish between the formal, written, and official curriculum and the curriculum as implemented by teachers. That this linkage is sometimes indirect does not necessarily mean that teachers are trying to undermine the formal curriculum. Administrators should see their role as that of supervisors accepting the strengths of teachers who apply creative and effective interpretations to the curriculum. Just as the art of teaching becomes the basis for some teaching behavior, the art of supervising instruction becomes the basis for recognizing the different, but valid, approaches to providing instruction. Administrators do not need to enter classrooms like detectives looking for "crimes against the curriculum."

They can enter classrooms to learn from their observations to improve the curriculum. These are positive approaches to observing teacher performance and determining what is happening to the formal curriculum as it is translated into learning experiences for students. The focus of these comments is more on the curriculum as seen by teachers than on the effectiveness of the teachers' methodology. (The latter question was addressed in Chapter 6). However, quite apart from the methods employed is the more cogent curriculum issue of what the teachers presented. This latter question that can be answered by learning what the teachers actually present to students and the emphasis and special character of the content as perceived in their presentation. This kind of analysis helps administrators to specify and be aware of the curriculum that is being provided for students.

The Hidden Curriculum

The hidden curriculum has been viewed as unintended learnings that are beyond the control of school authorities; it has also been defined as intended and planned outcomes that usually concentrate on socialization of students. There is considerable truth in both statements. One of the best ways to define the hidden curriculum is to identify, first, the formal and actual curriculum planned and delivered by teachers, guidance personnel, or supervisors. These identified elements are then subtracted from everything that takes place in schools. The remaining portion can be called the hidden curriculum. The hidden curriculum includes the chance assignment of lockers that promotes certain friendships. It is the selection of cars for driver education that subliminally provide sales for the local car dealer who supplied the cars in the first place. It is the atmosphere established in the cafeteria or the hallways. It is the mood of the school during examination time, the facial expressions of students in elementary schools as they go to recess, and the social blundering and confusion of adolescents as they encounter each other in middle schools. The informal, unintended, concomitant learnings that each person individualizes constitute a significant force to shape and mold attitudes, feelings of self-worth, or a sense of inferiority. All of these elements are part of the school year and provide a portion of the hidden curriculum. The deliberate events planned in schools also produce consequences that can be classified as hidden. When schools elect homeroom representatives and form a student council, what is learned about democracy and participation in making decisions? What do the winners of class elections learn and what do the losers figure out? All this sorting and sifting of the "pecking order" and the development of priorities and criteria for selecting friends and learning about socialization constitute additional learnings that come from hidden curriculum.

Who determines the hidden curriculum? In some cases school authorities determine the atmosphere of the school and in other cases students take charge and set up the climate. In other cases, the hidden curriculum just seems to happen. For example, where does school spirit come from, where does school pride originate and what sustains it, why do certain cliques form among students though others do not? Whether the origin of these developments can be identified or whether the activities growing from these events can be controlled, the hidden curriculum makes a large impact on individual students. It is often in the hidden curriculum that students learn patience and tolerance. It is here they develop self-esteem through acceptance, or feelings of inferiority through rejection. It is the hidden curriculum that gives students release from pressure imposed by school authorities when, at school, they can escape into a world they may choose to create.

The role of administrators in schools is to promote an atmosphere for learning and achieving the goals of the school district. Yet it is also a responsibility of administrators to recognize the impact of compelling large numbers of students to be forced into close association with each other and with authorities who impose rules and roles on them requiring conformity to external standards. And it is also an obligation of administrators to at least acknowledge that students play a strong role in developing a collective behavior that will satisfy their personal choices and allow for the personal development which they, the students, consider important.

The sensitive administrator who acknowledges the existence of the hidden curriculum will ask different questions than will the administrator who is unaware of or chooses to ignore the customs, preferences, and behaviors of students. The administrator who is in tune with the hidden curriculum will be concerned about the prestige of the students and the resolution of conflicts in which students feel offended or rejected by the system. She or he will also be tolerant of behavior that may be minimally disruptive to the school but is exceedingly important to students. Tolerance for minor deviations may be a small price to pay to maintain the mutual respect that comes from the tolerance of one for another. Such an administrator will approach conflicts with students with an open mind and be willing to listen to their views. In no way do these suggestions mean that the students will take over the running of the schools or wrest authority and responsibility away from administrators. It does mean that there is a student society that administrators can recognize, where students learn from experience. There is no need for administrators to tramp on the personal and relatively nonthreatening interests students often cherish.

Curriculum Evaluation

In a classic article on curriculum evaluation one researcher (Cronbach 1963) organized evaluation around three types of decisions for which evaluation is used. He stated that evaluation is used to make decisions about (1) course improvement, (2) individuals, and (3) administrative regulation. These are useful areas in which to organize evaluation approaches.

Course improvement addresses questions about which materials and methods are acceptable and which need to be changed. The administrator can help in this area by alerting others to new materials and approaches that come through the research community and the research and development work of foundations, governmental agencies, and publishing houses. Materials that utilize the new technology may be especially appropriate. Frequently teachers or other professionals learn about new materials and it becomes the task of administrators to decide if the schools should venture into experimental or adopted use of such materials. These decisions require a combination of budgetary and instructional knowledge. On questions of instructional methods there are two areas of administrative responsibility. One is to use the talent within the district to promote interchange of ideas among teachers and others within the district. This can be accomplished by arranging for teachers to observe and confer with each other and to focus some of the school and department meetings on instructional methods. Another activity is to collaborate with the instructional staff to establish in-service training that will utilize knowledge from outside the district. These two approaches employ both the internal and external knowledge to maintain good methods and strengthen or replace weak ones. The specific details of observing teachers and promoting staff development was discussed in Chapter 6; but the application of the findings from such analysis of teacher performance can be implemented through the methods described here.

Decisions about individual pupils call for information about pupil needs, determining pupil characteristics for purposes of selection and grouping, and helping the pupil to be informed about his progress and weaknesses. The question of pupil needs can be answered by keeping abreast of occupational and educational requirements outside school and by also surveying in-school elements such as pupils, teachers, parents, and others who are aware of pupil interests and characteristics. A constant effort to match the utility of schooling to the characteristics of pupils is required to promote the proper curriculum effectively. When administrators are informed about the needs of pupils and society, decisions about the curriculum, the selection of courses, and the assignment of pupils to particular curricula can all be made with more confidence. Provisions to keep students informed about their progress should be promoted by encouraging teachers to communicate with students in respect to their work in school and their personal and educational plans. Realistic expectations and monitoring of student progress should be promoted. It is important to avoid the self-fulfilling prophecy drawbacks that come from labeling students too rigidly. However, justifiable feedback and encouragement by educators to pupils is an important responsibility assumed by schools. The work of specialists in this area, particular guidance counselors, should be harnessed to help students maintain accurate perceptions of themselves and their progress. It is extremely important that the concern for individuals remain central to the curriculum decisions for it maintains an emphasis on the fundamental work of the schools, providing services to pupils.

The third area of evaluation mentioned by Cronbach is to help in making administrative decisions that regulate the schools. These decisions require information about how good the school system is, how good individual teachers are, and how successful the organization and development of the school is in carrying out its responsibilities. The answers to questions in this category call for information about the basic operation of the school such as how smoothly the school day flows or whether procedures for carrying out the normal operation of the school are appropriate; and it also calls for external assessment of school success through follow-up studies and external evaluations. It is in this category that administrative "trouble shooting" may be required to improve the efficiency with which the school operates and to also be responsive to criticisms that may come from faculty, pupils, or outside elements. Both formal and informal evaluations should be carried out to obtain critical information. These informal data come from an administrator's close contact in the schools by circulating among pupils, teachers, and by paritcipating in key events of the district. An ostrich-like administrator will fail to obtain critical information that the active and participatory administrator will gather from these sources. The formal approach calls for systematic evaluations of teacher performance, organized follow-up of students, and deliberate, well-planned surveys.

All three areas described here in which administrative decisions are made relate directly to data collection and evaluation of key aspects of school operation with a direct or indirect impact on the school curriculum.

Summary

The work of administrators includes a range of responsibilities that limit the available time to spend on any single one. Some responsibilities demand attention because of their critical nature; others can slide because they seem less urgent. Curriculum planning and development seems to be one of these areas that can often be treated with benign neglect unless a crisis arises. For this reason, it is tempting to devote administrative time to other tasks. However, over a period of time, such a gradual removal from curriculum building and implementation will create a schism between the administrator and the instructional staff. Such a separation may lower morale, reduce administrative effectiveness, and, more importantly, deny the schools a program that benefits from strong and effective administrative leadership. Given this combination of neglect on the one hand and limited time on the other, the most realistic position for administrators in respect to curriculum is to learn how to monitor the school curriculum without neglecting the other duties of administering to the schools. To accomplish this balance, it is essential that the most fundamental matters in curriculum become a part of the knowledge and understanding of the school administrator. It is equally important that administrators apply their judgment skillfully to the curriculum as to which issues are most important to work on or which parts of the curriculum require their attention. They must also learn how to monitor progress and determine weaknesses in the curriculum. This chapter has focused on providing information and approaches to serve these purposes. These suggestions are summarized in the following paragraphs.

All administrators should know what the goals and objectives of the school district are, both in term of its overall plan and the specific plans for special components of the schools such as the elementary schools' purposes, special education programs, extracurricular offerings, and so forth.

It is critically important that administrators know the requirements mandated by federal, state, and local agencies to be able to conform to the statutes and court requirements for school operation. Schools are institutions supported by taxpayers or tuition-paying customers and therefore they are dependent on public expectations and support. Since schools deal with people instead of raw materials or manufactured objects, there are laws which must be followed to protect the rights of pupils. Administrators must know what these expectations are.

Though the curriculum is partly determined by legislative and legal mandates, part of the curriculum also remains for development according to local school district discretion. The able administrator knows the territory that is available for innovations and also knows how to capitalize on the collective wisdom of teachers, parents, pupils, and others to review and improve those aspects of the curriculum that can be developed. To provide leadership in these areas of flexibility, it is helpful to obtain information that can direct curriculum efforts. This information comes from pupil performance, both current and past, teachers, formal and informal measurements of the curriculum. This combination of data collection, collective wisdom, and implementation strategies all are the responsibility of the educational leader. The techniques for carrying out this process call for the administrator to use discretion to avoid tampering with parts of the curriculum that are working well and to know how to tamper with those parts that are not.

Undergirding all administrator's work in this domain are fundamental questions that must become part and parcel of the administrator's actions to provide consistent quality leadership. The most fundamental question, which all administrators should constantly ask and answer to determine where they stand, is where do the responsibilities of the schools begin and end?

References

Association for Supervision and Curriculum Development. 1962. *Perceiving, Behaving, Becoming.* Yearbook. Washington, D. C., The Association.

Blumberg, Arthur, and **William Greenfield.** 1980. *The Effective Principal: Perspectives on School Leadership.* Boston: Allyn and Bacon.

Brimm, Jack L., John Fogarty and **Kenneth Sadler.** 1978. "Student Absenteeism: A Survey Report." *NASSP Bulletin* 66 (February): 65-69.

Broudy, H. S. 1974. *General Education: The Search for a Rationale.* Bloomington, Ind.: Phi Delta Kappa Educational Foundation.

Caswell, H. L., and **D. S. Campbell.** 1935. *Curriculum Development.* New York: American Book Company.

Carruthers, R. L., and **J. Driver.** 1980. "An Attendance Policy Policy That Works." *NASSP Bulletin* 64 (December): 117-18

Cronbach, Lee J. 1963. "Evaluation for Course Improvements." *The Teachers College Record* 64 (May): 672-83.

DeLeonibus, N. 1978. "Absenteeism: The Perpetual Problem." *NASSP The Practitioner: A Newsletter for the On-Line Administrator,* vol. 5, no. 1.

Johnson, David W. 1970. *The Social Psychology of Education.* New York: Holt, Rinehart and Winston.

McNeil, John D. 1981. *Curriculum: A Comprehensive Introduction.* 2d ed. Boston: Little, Brown.

Nearine, R. J. 1979. *Higher Horizons 100, Hartford Moves Ahead: An Evaluative Report.* Hartford, Conn.: Hartford Public Schools.

Oliva, Peter F. 1982. *Developing the Curriculum.* Boston: Little, Brown.

Shepherd, G. D., and **W. B. Ragan.** 1982. *Modern Elementary Curriculum.* New York: Holt, Rinehart and Winston.

Tanner, Daniel, and **Laurel N. Tanner.** 1980. *Curriculum Development: Theory into Practice.* 2d ed. New York: Macmillan.

Tyler, R. W. 1949. *Basic Principles of Curriculum and Instruction.* Chicago: University of Chicago Press.

PART III
Legal and Financial Issues

Two of the most critical responsibilities of school administrators can be found in the areas of school finance and school law. It is in these two areas that precision, or the illusion of precision, often is sought. The questions to be answered in these two domains often call for precise answers. Specific information such as the exact millage allocated to the schools, the amount set aside for building maintenance, and legal rulings about who may have access to student records and what those records may contain are examples of the precision that is often expected. It is unreasonable to expect school administrators to be walking encyclopedias of legal and financial knowledge with ready answers to all the subtle questions that can be raised. However, this part addresses the areas of school law and school finance about which administrators may be reasonably expected to be knowledgeable. Included among these responsibilities is an awareness of the rationale and structure that undergird school law and school finance. It is important that administrators know landmark or significant cases but they should also understand the rationale behind court rulings and statutory requirements that protect school personnel. Legislation and court rulings determine allowable responses to individuals, as well as requirements in curriculum and instruction. They also have implications for the financial aspects of school operation. Part III describes the structure of the court systems and illustrates the relationships that exist at the federal, state, and local levels through specific cases and statutes. This part also explains the financial responsibilities and resources for schools and illustrates the changing face of school finance against the backdrop of the nation's social and economic changes. It is not possible or even necessary to provide a comprehensive treatment of the content in these two categories now. It is possible to provide essential information so the student of school administration may establish a foundation on which more detailed knowledge can be added. Part III provides this foundation.

8

The Legal Relationship of the Federal Government and Education: Guidelines and Implications for School Administrators

The authority for the establishment and the control of the public schools is well grounded in law. Within a framework of federal and state constitutional provisions and federal and state legislative enactments, guidelines for the operation of the schools have been established. In addition, regulations promulgated by various state and federal agencies dictate what schools may or may not do in their daily operations. The overlapping jurisdictions of state and federal constitutions, state and federal legislatures, state and federal courts, as well as the various governmental agencies, often confuse educational administrators. To provide some measure of clarification, this chapter presents a discussion of the various federal constitutional, legislative, and administrative guidelines that affect school administrators; a description of the federal court system and a discussion of its operation; and a discussion of the impact of federal enactments and federal courts on the practice of school administration. Chapter 9 provides similar descriptions and discussions relative to the legal role of state governments and agencies (including local school boards) and the state court system.

Federal Constitutional, Legislative, and Administrative Guidelines Affecting School Administration

The United States Constitution

The powers of the federal government are limited to those delegated by the Constitution and are specifically limited by the Tenth Amendment which provides that "The powers not delegated to the United States by the Constitution, nor prohibited by it to the States, are reserved to the States respectively, or to the people." Since education is not mentioned in the Constitution nor delegated to the federal government, it becomes one of those powers reserved to the states or to the people. However, although the courts have interpreted the Tenth Amendment as giving the states the power to control education, this does not mean that the federal Constitution does not affect the operation of the educational system or that the federal government has no jurisdiction over education.

The supremacy clause of the Constitution, article VI, states that "This Constitution, and the laws of the United States which shall be made in Pursuance thereof . . . shall be the supreme Law of the land; and the Judges in every State shall be bound thereby. . . ." In other words, state authority over education must be exercised in a manner consistent with federal constitutional guarantees. Those sections of the constitution that bear most intimately on the operation of the schools are article I, section 8; article I, section 10; and the First, Fourth, Fifth, Eighth, Ninth, and Fourteenth Amendments.

General Welfare Clause. Article I, section 8 gives Congress the power to "lay and collect Taxes, Duties, Imposts and Excises, to pay the Debts and provide for the common Defence and general Welfare of the United States. . . ." Since the time of its inception, the role of the federal government under the general welfare clause has been the subject of much debate and controversy. As a result of a long series of legislative acts and judicial decisions, it is now settled that Congress may tax and spend for a variety of general welfare purposes.[1] In fact, the Supreme Court has declared that the decision as to whether or not a given expenditure is for the general welfare is within the discretion of Congress and is not one that will be interfered with unless it is "clearly wrong, a display of arbitrary power, not an exercise of judgment."[2] However, as Thomas Jefferson first pointed out, the general welfare clause does not give Congress the authority "to do anything they please to provide for the general welfare, but only to lay taxes for that purpose."[3] In regard to education this means that Congress is authorized to levy taxes for the purpose of providing funds for education, but it is not authorized to legislate control of education. Nevertheless, if a state or school district decides voluntarily to participate in federal programs, when such participation is based upon compliance with certain regulations, then the federal government has the authority to enforce compliance.

Using the general welfare justification, Congress has over the years enacted massive legislation providing substantial federal support, research, and instructional programs in areas such as foreign languages (to facilitate international relations), mathematics and science (to improve technological and military standing), and career and vocational education (to meet specific needs of our highly industrialized, technological society). Also under its power to spend for the general welfare, Congress has provided for health care programs, the school lunch program, and services and programs to meet the special needs of specific students (e.g., special education, bilingual education, and compensatory education).

Obligation of Contracts Clause. Article I, section 10 of the Constitution reads in part: "No State shall . . . pass any Bill of Attainder, ex post facto Law, or Law impairing the Obligation of Contracts. . . ." This provision of the Constitution can be invoked when, for example, the legislature of a state seeks to change a teacher tenure or retirement law to the detriment of teachers who acquired a contractive status under the law. For example, in an Indiana teacher tenure case in which the Indiana legislature passed an act that repealed provisions of a 1927 law granting tenure to rural teachers, the Supreme Court directly applied article I, section 10 as a limitation on state legislative actions pertaining to public education and disapproved the legislation.[4]

The obligation of contracts clause protects teachers, administrators, and noncertificated personnel who have contractual agreements from arbitrary dismissals. It also protects the school board and those individuals and companies it contracts with from nonperformance. Courts are often called in to determine if a particular contract is valid (e.g., whether the school board has exceeded the scope of its legislatively delegated authority in negotiating certain points on the teacher's contract or whether it was a legally constituted board that issued the contract) or if one party has breached the terms of the contract.

First Amendent. The First Amendment protects several basic personal freedoms. It states:

Congress shall make no law respecting an establishment
of religion, or prohibiting the free exercise thereof; or
abridging the freedom of speech or of the press; or the
right of the people peaceably to assemble, and to petition
the Government for a redress of grievances.

Over the years, the first clause of the First Amendment, the religion clause, has been the focus of numerous suits affecting education. These school cases have generally been concerned with alleged attempts by schools to promote the establishment of religion and have fallen into two categories: those involving the use of public funds to provide aid to non-public schools or students (e.g., providing textbooks, instructional materials, diagnostic and remedial services, transportation, tuition tax credits, or tuition reimbursements; and those involving public school regulations or procedures that are objected to on religious grounds (e.g., mandatory flag salutes, prayers, released-time, shared-time, etc.). In contrast to the numerous cases dealing with the establishment aspect, relatively few have dealt with efforts on the part of school authorities to prohibit the free exercise of religion.

There have been, however, an increasing number of cases beginning with the landmark United States Supreme Court decision in *Tinker v. Des Moines Independent School District* (1969) that have been concerned with student First Amendment rights relative to freedom of speech and press.[5] Numerous cases have arisen involving students' rights to express themselves through the wearing of armbands, symbols, long hair, and a variety of other methods. Other cases have dealt with alleged abridgements of students' rights to freedom of the press as they have sought to publish and distribute student publications.[6] Teachers have concerned themselves with many of the same issues related to freedom of expression, as well as other issues that have arisen relative to academic freedom.

That part of the First Amendment that addresses the rights of citizens to assemble and petition has also received increased attention as employees seek to organize and engage in collective bargaining. Over the years the right to association under the First Amendment has been upheld by the Supreme Court and the rights of public school personnel to join employee unions and engage in collective bargaining have been established.

Fourth Amendment. The Fourth Amendment guarantees that "The right of the people to be secure in their persons, houses, papers, and effects, against unreasonable searches and seizures, shall not be violated, and no warrants shall issue but upon probable cause. . . ." The increasing problem of student possession of drugs and other contraband has resulted in an increased number of student searches and corresponding claims by students that they were subjected to unreasonable searches or that they are immune to search without a warrant. A few cases involving searches of teachers' personal belongings have also arisen. To date, most courts have refused to subject public school searches to the same strict Fourth Amendment standard that governs warrantless searches by the police. Since the Supreme Court has not issued a ruling on the issue of student searches, they must be handled on a case by case basis. In deciding whether the particular search was reasonable, the court will assess the age and maturity of the student, the seriousness of damage involved, and the necessity for search as protection of the health, safety, or discipline of the school. It has been held that the Fourth Amendment protects only a citizen from governmental action and is not intended as a protection against private persons. Thus, the decision as to whether a warrant is required will depend upon whether the court considers school officials to be acting *in loco parentis* (in place of the parent) as private persons or to be acting as officers of the state or involving police officials.

The Fifth Amendment. The Fifth Amendment provides, in part, that no person shall be "compelled in any criminal case to be a witness against himself, nor be deprived of life, liberty, or property, without due process of law; nor shall private property be taken for public use without just compensation." It has been held under the self-incrimination clause of the Fifth Amendment that persons may refuse to answer questions, the answers to which might be used against them or subject them to prosecution by the state. The courts have held, however, that teachers may not use the Fifth Amendment to avoid answering questions put to them by their superiors about their activities outside the classroom (e.g., membership in subversive organizations) which bear upon their qualifications or fitness to teach.[7]

The due process clause of the Fifth Amendment pertains to actions of the federal government and thus is not usually at issue in education cases. Due process litigation related to the schools is usually initiated under the Fourteenth Amendment, which pertains to state actions. The last clause of the Fifth Amendment is relevant in cases where the state or school board is attempting to acquire property for school building sites in the exercise of eminent domain.

Eighth Amendment. The Eighth Amendment provides, "Excessive bail shall not be required, nor excessive fines imposed, nor cruel and unusual punishments inflicted." The Eighth Amendment has been invoked in numerous cases where students claimed that corporal punishment in the schools was "cruel and unusual punishment." However, in the lead case in this area, *Ingraham* v. *Wright,* the United States Supreme Court held that disciplinary corporal punishment *per se* is not "cruel and unusual punishment" as covered by the Eighth Amendment.[8] This does not mean that corporal punishment cannot be prohibited by state statute or school board regulation, only that it does not violate the federal Constitution. The Court did say that if punishment has caused physical harm, the recourse for the parent is to file an assault and battery civil action.

The Ninth Amendment. The Ninth Amendment stipulates that the "enumeration in the Constitution of certain rights shall not be construed to deny or disparage others retained by the people." Using the Ninth Amendment as the basis, various unenumerated rights have been asserted in educational litigation. Among the unenumerated rights most commonly asserted in education cases are the right to personal privacy as it relates to teacher conduct outside the classroom and the rights of students and teachers relative to grooming.

The Fourteenth Amendment. The Fourteenth Amendment is the most widely used amendment in cases involving the schools because it pertains specifically to state actions. The Fourteenth Amendment provides, in part: ". . . nor shall any State deprive any person of life, liberty, or property without due process of law, nor deny to any person within its jurisdiction the equal protection of the laws." The due process clause of the Fourteenth Amendment has been invoked in numerous cases involving student rights and teacher rights. It is of obvious paramount importance to students who have been suspended or expelled, or to teachers who have been dismissed, that they be afforded due process. In 1975 in *Goss* v. *Lopez*[9] the United States Supreme Court settled the disagreements that existed in the lower courts relative to students' constitutional rights to due process and said that students do have a right to minimum due process before being suspended for even a short period of time. Precedent for the establishment of the procedural due process rights for teachers comes from two 1972 Supreme Court decisions in *Board of Regents* v. *Roth*[10] and *Perry* v. *Sinderman.*[11]

The equal protection clause of the Fourteenth Amendment requires that protection of the law be extended equally to all persons. Beginning with the 1954 *Brown* decision in which the United States Supreme Court interpreted this clause to mean that segregation of students in the public schools on the basis of race was unconstitutional, it has been used continually to deal with all types of discrimination.[12] Over the years the courts have made it clear that they will afford equal protection to all students regardless of state or school board enactments. In addition to the rights enumerated in the Fourteenth Amendment, it has been interpreted as extending all the rights and protection enumerated in the Bill of Rights to persons affected by state actions.

Federal Legislation

Despite the constitutional silence on education, the federal government has always shown a considerable interest in education and under the authority of the general welfare clause has established laws that reflect, in part, federal policymakers' opinions of how the general welfare might be enhanced by specific educational policies. A host of federal statutes directly affecting education have been enacted beginning with the Northwest Ordinances of 1785 and 1787, adopted by the Congress of the Confederation. Federal educational policy as expressed in the Ordinance of 1787 was that "Religion, morality, and knowledge being necessary to good government and the happiness of mankind, schools and the means of education shall be forever encouraged." Accordingly, lot number 16 of every township in the Northwest Territory was reserved for the maintenance of public schools. Beginning with the admission of Ohio into the Union in 1803, the granting of school sections became part of the system of admission for new states. When the Oregon Territory was established in 1848, Congress set aside two sections in every township for the public schools. This policy continued until 1896 when Utah was granted four sections in every township and continued with the admission of the other western states. In all, these land grants reached a total of over one hundred thousand square miles.

Land grants were made for the support of higher education by the first Morrill Act of 1862 which awarded 30,000 acres of government land for each member of Congress to which a state was entitled. This same grant of land was made available to states later admitted to the Union. A stated purpose of the act was to promote the teaching of agriculture, mechanical arts, and military science. A number of acts since 1862 (e.g., the Hatch Act of 1887, the second Morrill Act of 1890, Burkhead-Jones Act of 1935, and the Research and Marketing Act of 1946) have both increased the funds and expanded the activities of these land-grant institutions. Land-grant institutions now enroll about 20 percent of all college students and are the principal state universities in two-thirds of the states.

The first special-purpose grants to the public schools were initiated by the Smith-Hughes Act of 1917. This legislation together with such supplementary statutes as the George-Reed Act of 1929, the George-Ellzey Act of 1934, the George-Deen Act of 1936, the George-Barden Act of 1946, the Vocational Education Act of 1963, and its Amendments of 1976, supported the teaching of agriculture, home economics, and the mechanical arts and trades in elementary and secondary schools.

A number of the education statutes enacted by the federal government have been related to war or defense efforts. In addition to operating the various military academies, through the provisions of various statutes, the armed forces have worked with numerous educational institutions to provide specialized training or needed research. Public Laws 874 and 815 (the federal impact aid legislation) provide building construction and current operating aid to school districts who would otherwise have financial problems because of the location of federal tax-exempt property within the district. Various other statutes, most notably Public Law 346 (commonly called the G.I. Bill) have provided educational opportunities for veterans. In 1950 the National Science Foundation was established, providing loans, grants, fellowships, and institutes to promote research activities in the areas of mathematics, science, and engineering for the purposes of strengthening the national defense.

The year 1958 marked a turning point in the relationship of the federal government to education. Prior to this time federal participation in financing or in directing the course of education had been negligible. However, the launching of Sputnik by the Russians in 1957 caused great concern in the United States. There was a great fear that the Soviets were far surpassing the United States in mathematics, science, and engineering, and that our schools were producing inferior scholars. As a result, the National Defense Education Act of 1958 (NDEA) was passed, providing substantial financial assistance to institutions and students in the areas of mathematics, science, and foreign languages. Since the passage of the NDEA, federal interest and financial contributions have intensified and multiplied tremendously. Almost three-fourths of all school-related federal legislation has been passed since the passage of the NDEA.

The ever-increasing federal participation has not taken the form of general aid for education nor of direct attempts to control education. Rather, over the years the federal government's role has been one of specific support and indirect control of education. Through a series of categorical grants, Congress has fashioned educational policy and encouraged particular educational emphases to address certain perceived national interests. Federal policy in education has been described as being "instrumental."[13] That is, education is used as an instrument to achieve federal policies in areas such as poverty reduction, civil rights, and labor. For example, the Manpower Development and Training Act of 1962 and the Economic Opportunity Act of 1964, although education legislation, were part of the larger war on poverty. As a result of there being no definitive federal policy on education, a hodgepodge of legislation has been enacted. Through these laws billions of dollars in categorical grants have gone into schools, colleges, and universities for specific programs or targeted populations. The most comprehensive of these measures, the Elementary and Secondary Education Act of 1965 (ESEA), contains a broad program of categorical aids for compensatory education programs for economically disadvantaged students (Title I); libraries, textbooks, and audiovisual materials (Title II); supplementary education centers and services (Title III); educational research and training (Title IV) and; strengthening of state departments of education (Title V). The ESEA was the first piece of federal legislation to provide federal aid to private and parochial schools as well as public schools. Subsequent amendments to the ESEA, as well as legislation such as the Bilingual Education Act of 1968 and the Education for All Handicapped Children Act of 1975, have provided financial support for the education of special targeted students, such as the gifted, the non-English speaking, or the handicapped.

In addition to providing various kinds of support to public and private schools for the provision of education, the federal government operates a number of educational institutions. In addition to the various military academies and institutes, the Army Medical School, and the National War Colleges, elementary and secondary schools are operated overseas by the Department of Defense for dependents of military personnel and specific government workers. The Bureau of Indian Affairs also operates a number of schools both on and off reservations to aid in the education of Native American youth.

The 1980s have brought a new direction to federal involvement in education and a reversal of the trend toward ever-increasing numbers of categorical programs. The legislation of the "new federalism" of the Reagan administration is designed to reduce federal involvement in education through a program of reduced expenditures, deregulation, decentralization, and consolidation. The Education Consolidation and Improvement Act of 1981 (ECIA), which went into effect in 1982, contains two major sections or chapters. Chapter 1 provides federal funds for educationally disadvantaged children under a modified ESEA Title I-type program. Monies are allocated to states on the basis of census data relative to the proportion of the population classified as being in poverty. The state education agencies then make allocations to school districts for compensatory education programs. Chapter 2 of ECIA is the much-heralded (and much-criticized) education block grant. The purpose of Chapter 2 is to consolidate Titles II through VI, plus Titles VIII and IX of the ESEA, as amended, "into a single authorization of grants to states for the same purposes set forth in these titles, but to be used in accordance with the education needs and priorities of state and local educational agencies as determined by such agencies."[14] A major problem facing the states at this time is deciding exactly how these funds will be allocated within the state.

In addition to legislation that provides financial assistance to the schools, Congress has also enacted various pieces of civil rights legislation that have had considerable impact on educational programs, institutions, employees, and students. Among the more significant of these are the following: Title VI of the Civil Rights Act of 1964, which prohibits discrimination on the basis of race, color, or national origin in federally assisted programs or activities; Title VII of the Civil Rights Act of 1964, which prohibits employment discrimination on the basis of race, color, religion, national origin, or sex; the Equal Pay Act of 1963, which prohibits wage discrimination based on sex; Title IX of the Education Amendments of 1972, which prohibits sex discrimination in educational programs receiving federal funds; and section 504 of the Rehabilitation Act of 1973, which prohibits discrimination against qualified handicapped persons in all federally assisted programs or activities. Not only are federal funds not provided to fulfill the mandates of these acts, but noncomplying districts are subject to the loss of all federal funds.

A review of federal education legislation indicates that although the federal government has not attempted to dictate educational policies, programs, or content, no small measure of federal control has been attained through the enactment of guidelines that must be followed in order for school districts or states to receive grant funds under the various statutes. Court decisions have declared that where a state or school district has the option of accepting or rejecting federal funds for a particular program, the federal government has the authority to prescribe the guidelines under which the program will operate. Thus it is not only direct legislation enacted by Congress and the various constitutional provisions that provide the federal government's legal framework for education, but the rules and regulations promulgated by agencies pursuant to implementing the legislation.

Federal Administrative Agencies

Numerous federal administrative agencies have been created by Congress and authorized to regulate various activities that bear either directly or indirectly on education. For example, the National Science Foundation provides no direct aid to schools but administers various research projects whose purpose is the improvement of curriculum and of science and mathematics instruction in elementary and secondary schools; the Department of Agriculture administers the National School Lunch Act, designed to improve the nutrition of school children; the Department of the Interior, Bureau of Indian Affairs, administers numerous programs aimed at improving the education of Native Americans; the Equal Employment Opportunity Commission promulgates regulations specifying conditions of employment; the Department of Labor administers the Occupational Health and Safety Act, which requires employers, including school districts, to furnish a place of employment that is free of safety hazards; and the Office of Economic Opportunity was specifically created to administer and control the Job Corps.

By far the most important federal administrative agency dealing with education is the Department of Education, which was established in 1980 by an executive order that removed the Office of Education from the Department of Health, Education, and Welfare and elevated it to cabinet level status. The Department of Education is the only federal agency concerned with education at all levels and in all areas. In addition to sponsoring research and serving as a resource center and clearinghouse for information relevant to education, the department is responsible for the administration of the numerous grants-in-aid to school districts and the enforcement of legislation affecting education. Department staff review grant requests, determine applicant eligibility, disburse funds, and then monitor and audit programs. The large sums of money under the administration of the Department of Education and its predecessor, the Office of Education, have assured it an important role in public education. When categorical grants were the means by which federal aid was distributed, the department was instrumental in directing federal dollars toward perceived needs and weaknesses. However, with the cutback in federal aid, the consolidation into block grants, and the Reagan administration's stated antipathy toward the Department of Education, its intended impact has been somewhat diminished.

One important way federal agencies affect education is by carrying out their responsibilities for enforcing civil rights and nondiscrimination legislation. In this enforcement each of these agencies has promulgated rules and regulations which, so long as they do not conflict with constitutional provisions, statutes, or court decisions, have the full force of law. These regulations provide the guidelines that educational institutions are to follow to receive federal funds. Other regulations, such as those implementing Title IX, serve as guidelines for educational institutions as they develop employment practices. According to the provisions of certain of the civil rights and nondiscrimination legislation, such as Title VI of the Civil Rights Act of 1964 or Title IX of the Education Amendments of 1972, if a program is found to be in violation or noncompliance, the Department of Education is authorized to withhold funds. In addition, within the Department of Education, the Office for Civil Rights (OCR) has the responsibility for conducting compliance reviews, investigating complaints against schools, and monitoring implementation of rules and regulations. OCR staff engage in such activities as monitoring higher education desegregation, monitoring the implementation of bilingual education regulations, and conducting reviews of compliance with Title IX of the Education Amendments of 1972.

The Equal Employment Opportunity Commission (EEOC) is another agency charged with the enforcement of civil rights and nondiscrimination legislation with a major effect on education. As one example of its responsibilities, Title VII of the Civil Rights Act prohibits, in somewhat simple terms, employment discrimination on the basis of race, color, sex, religion, or national origin. It is the EEOC that has promulgated the implementing regulations that specify what the provisions of Title VII mean in terms of such things as disability benefits programs. Title VII charges the EEOC and the Department of Justice with its enforcement; and accordingly a number of cases and enforcement proceedings have been brought against schools to ensure compliance.

Organization and Operation of the Federal Court System

Function of the Courts

The courts have traditionally adhered to the concept of separation of powers with respect to cases involving education. That is to say, the courts take the position that they will not interfere with the actions or judgments of the legislative branch, of administrative bodies, or of legally constituted bodies such as school boards so long as they have not abused their authority nor acted in an unlawful manner.

The courts have also refused to intervene in a school-related controversy until all administrative appeals have been exhausted. For example, where statutes provide that decisions of school boards may be appealed to a higher jurisdiction, such as the state superintendent of education or the state board of education, these avenues of appeal must be exhausted before the courts will hear an appeal. The exception to this occurs when a case involves a federally protected right. In these cases, administrative remedies need not be exhausted before suit can be brought in federal court.

Courts do not act on their own initiative. They become involved only when controversies or legal matters are referred to them for decision. Whenever the courts do become involved in school cases, their function is threefold: (1) to settle controversies by applying principles of law to specific sets of facts; (2) to interpret the law within their jurisdiction; and (3) to determine the constitutionality of legislative or administrative enactments. In the first instance, applying principles of law to factual disputes, the principles of law governing the particular situation may be vague or virtually nonexistent. In such instances the judge must look to judicial precedent for guidance, and to the rule of *stare decisis*, "let the decision stand," which says that past decisions are binding on subsequent cases which have the same or substantially the same facts. The second function of the courts, that of interpreting statutes, is the most common litigation involving public school operation. It requires that the court determine, insofar as possible, what the intention of the legislature was when it enacted the law in question.[15]

In performing their third function, that of determining the constitutionality of legislative or administrative enactments, the courts have established guidelines they will follow. The courts presume the act to be constitutional; the one challenging the statute must bear the burden of proof. If the statute can be interpreted two ways, one by which it would be considered constitutional, the court will adopt the constitutional interpretation. The court will not anticipate a constitutional question in advance of the necessity for doing so, and will not rule on the constitutionality of legislation in a nonadversary proceeding. In addition, if the case can be decided on some other ground, the court will not rule on the constitutional question.

Organization of the Federal Court System

Article III, section 1 of the Constitution provides that "The judicial Power of the United States shall be vested in one supreme Court, and in such inferior Courts as the Congress may from time to time ordain and establish." Pursuant to this provision Congress has created a system that includes district courts, circuit courts of appeal, the United States Supreme Court, and special courts (Fig. 8-1).

Each state has at least one district court and some more populous states have as many as four. The district courts are given geographical names, for example, the Eastern District of Wisconsin (abbreviated *E. D. Wis.*), or the Northern District of California (*N. D. Cal.*). Federal district courts serve as the trial courts for federal cases, with a jury determining the facts and the judge determining points of law. Cases before district courts are usually presided over by one judge, although if an injunction against the enforcement of a state or federal statute is involved, a three-judge court is required.

At the second level of federal courts are twelve federal circuit courts, also known as Courts of Appeals, one for each of the twelve geographic *circuits* into which the United States is divided. The circuit courts are generally referred to by the number of the circuit, for example, the Second Circuit (abbreviated as *2d Cir.*). Each circuit court has from three to fifteen judges. Cases are usually heard by a three-judge panel, but under special circumstances all circuit judges will sit *en banc* and hear the case. The circuit court reviews the written records of the lower court decision and hears attorneys but does not hear witnesses. The geographic jurisdiction of the federal circuits is as follows:

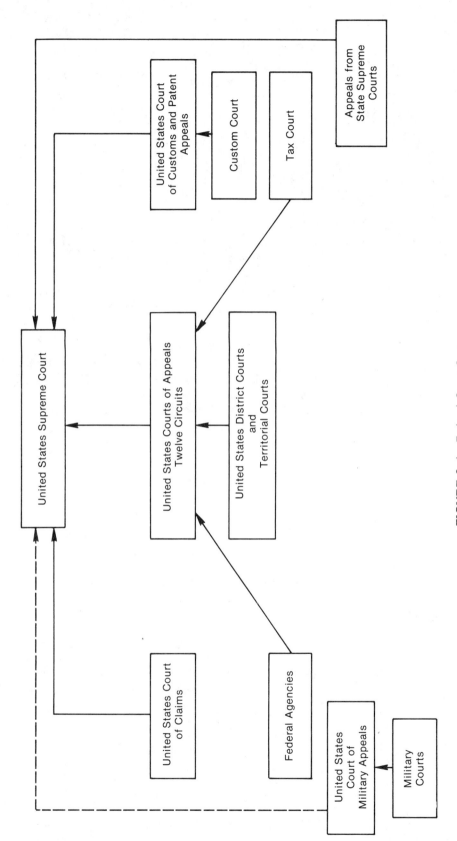

FIGURE 8-1 *Federal Court System*

First Circuit: Maine, New Hampshire, Massachusetts, Rhode Island, and Puerto Rico

Second Circuit: Vermont, New York, and Connecticut

Third Circuit: Pennsylvania, New Jersey, Delaware, and the Virgin Islands

Fourth Circuit: Maryland, Virginia, West Virginia, North Carolina, and South Carolina

Fifth Circuit: Mississippi, Louisiana, Texas, and the Canal Zone

Sixth Circuit: Michigan, Ohio, Kentucky, and Tennessee

Seventh Circuit: Indiana, Illinois, and Wisconsin

Eighth Circuit:	Minnesota, Iowa, Missouri, Arkansas, North Dakota, South Dakota, and Nebraska
Ninth Circuit:	Washington, Oregon, California, Nevada, Arizona, Idaho, Montana, Alaska, Hawaii, and Guam
Tenth Circuit:	Wyoming, Utah, Colorado, New Mexico, Kansas, and Oklahoma
Eleventh Circuit:	Georgia, Florida, and Alabama
D.C. Circuit:	Washington, D.C.

The United States Supreme Court is the highest court in the land, beyond which there is no appeal. The Supreme Court, the ultimate authority on interpretations of the federal constitution or federal law, is composed of nine justices. Cases may be brought before the Supreme Court through the original jurisdiction of the court, by appeal, or by a writ of *certiorari*. In practice, the latter two types of review are similar, in that in either situation the Supreme Court has the option of refusing review.

In addition to the three-tier structure of federal district courts, circuit courts, and Supreme Court, Congress has established a number of other federal courts to handle special problems or to cover special jurisdictions. These include the Court of Claims, the Tax Court, the Customs Court, the Court of Customs and Patent Appeals, the Court of Military Appeals, and the territorial courts. In addition there are the District of Columbia Courts, which include the Court of Appeals, the Superior Court, the Police Court, and the Municipal Court.

Jurisdictions and Appeals

With the exception of the Supreme Court, whose jurisdiction is specified in article III, section 2, clause 1 of the Constitution, Congress, through the enactment of statutes, determines the jurisdictions of the federal courts. Generally, federal courts may take only two type of cases: those involving citizens of different states, and those involving questions of federal statutes or the federal Constitution. If a case involves both federal and state law questions, the federal court can rule on the state questions but must do so according to the court rules of the respective states.

Since education is a function of the state, and schools and school districts operate under state law, which is principally a matter for the interpretation of state courts, most school law cases in federal courts would necessarily involve questions of alleged violations of constitutionally protected rights or violations of federal statutes, such as the civil rights statutes. If a case involves issues such that it could be filed in either state or federal court, but the litigant chooses to file in a federal court, the court in which the suit would properly be filed would be the federal district court. This is the trial court of original jurisdiction. Decisions of federal district courts may not be appealed to any state court (even a higher state court). But they may be appealed to the federal circuit court of appeals, and in some circumstances directly to the United States Supreme Court.

The federal circuit court does not retry the appealed case. The court usually accepts the facts of the case as determined by the trial court, unless it is clear that the evidence presented did not support the determination made. The court reviews only those questions raised on appeal, even though other questions not appealed may seem to be of greater importance. The court will not overturn the lower court decision unless there is a clear indication the district court erroneously applied the law. The court can affirm, reverse, or modify the decision of the lower court, or it can remand the case to the lower court for modification or retrial. The decision of a circuit court is binding upon all federal district courts within that particular jurisdiction but not upon state courts. (Nor do federal circuits hear appeals from state courts.) Since the decision of a particular circuit court is binding only upon the courts in its jurisdiction, it is possible in areas where the United States Supreme Court has not issued a ruling (as was the case with regulation of students' hair length) that a different standard may be in effect in different circuits. In many instances, however, the decision of one circuit court will influence other courts as they deal with similar issues. Decisions of federal circuit courts may be appealed to the United States Supreme Court.

As indicated before, the United States Supreme Court is the highest court in the land, from which there is no appeal. The Constitution specifies that the Supreme Court must hear (have original jurisdiction) all cases affecting ambassadors, other public ministers and consuls, and those in which a state is a party. Beyond these requirements, the Supreme Court exercises a great deal of discretion over which cases it will accept for review. It has appellate jurisdiction not only over cases originating in the lower federal courts, but also over cases on appeal from a state supreme court if the case involves questions of federal law. Review by the Supreme Court is obtained by a writ of *certiorari* if four of the nine justices agree. *Certiorari* (from the Latin, meaning "to be informed") is the name given to the appellate proceeding by which a case is taken from a lower court to a higher court for review. Thousands of petitions of *certiorari* are submitted to the Supreme Court each year. By the petition of *certiorari* the appellant tries to convince the court that the issues involved are of sufficient importance and magnitude to warrant the review of the court. Only a small percentage of those petitions submitted each year is granted. More often than not the court determines that the topic is inappropriate or of too limited significance to warrant review. However, the majority of school law cases do reach the Supreme Court by writs of *certiorari*.

Federal Case Law

Legislatures have the responsibility to enact laws. Courts, as previously mentioned, have the responsibility for making decisions regarding the application of the law, the interpretation of the law, and the constitutionality of the law. In the process of making these decisions the courts establish legal principles or rules of law that are referred to as judge-made law, common law, or case law. This case law is just as binding on school administrators as are constitutional provisions or legislative enactments. The case law thus promulgated can be changed only by a higher court or by the passage of constitutionally permissible legislation. One example of the latter occurred in 1976 when the United States Supreme Court interpreted Title VII as permitting the exclusion of pregnancy conditions from sick leave or disability coverage.[16] Congress reacted by amending the law to include pregnancy-related illness or disability, and thus indicated that the Court had misread congressional intent. It should be noted that this case involved the interpretation of a statute. If a case involves an interpretation of the Constitution, Congress cannot pass legislation that violates the Court's interpretation.

The Impact of Federal Court Decisions on the Practice of School Administration and the Direction of Education

The courts have traditionally been reluctant to become involved in school policy. For example, in 1948 in the well-known *McCollum* decision related to released time for religious instruction, Supreme Court Justice Jackson warned against the Supreme Court's becoming a "super board of education."[17] During the past three decades American education has been in a state of almost constant change. Much of this change has been a result of the postwar baby boom and a rapidly expanding technology. A large part of it, however, has been the result of an increase in the involvement of state and federal courts and a series of decisions which have altered the most fundamental operations of the schools. Not only have the local schools and school districts been affected by these decisions; but the very plenary power of state legislatures to formulate or enact educational policies has been limited by court decisions that have required conformance to the Constitution. A sampling of a few of the major federal court cases beginning with the landmark *Brown* decision should give some insight into the impact the federal courts have had on school administration and the role they have played in directing the future of education.

In 1954 the United States Supreme Court handed down perhaps its most important case related to education, *Brown v. Board of Education of Topeka (Brown I)*.[18] In its now famous opinion the court ruled that the doctrine of "separate but equal" has no place in the field of education and that separate educational facilities for blacks and whites are inherently unequal and in violation of the Fourteenth Amendment. In *Brown II*,[19] the next year, the court set forth general guidelines that were to guide the desegregation that was to take place "with all deliberate speed." The magnitude and complexity of the problems facing governing bodies and school practitioners as they faced the challenge of implementing the *Brown* decree can only be imagined by those who have not been in similar circumstances. Eliminating or amending hundreds or even thousands of statutes and regulations which in any way supported segregation was only the beginning. Setting the actual desegregation in operation was far more difficult. Unfortunately, for more than ten years little progress was made toward implementing the desegregation mandate of *Brown*. The freedom of choice plans which had been the most widely used attempt to end segregation did not work. In 1964 the Supreme Court ruled that "the time for mere 'deliberate speed' has run out,"[20] and in 1969 discarded the "all deliberate speed" criterion for evaluating school desegregation efforts and said that dual school systems must give way immediately to unified systems.[21] Whether this was to be accomplished by busing, rezoning, or other means did not concern the Court; it required only that it be done without further delay.

Since that time hundreds of lawsuits have been brought to seek integration of our nation's schools. The implementation of court decisions has changed the faces of many school systems. Neighborhood schools in many districts are a thing of the past, and "white flight" is a reality. Magnet alternative schools, paired schools, and clustered schools have been created as tools in desegregation plans. Alterations of attendance zones, reassignment of faculty, rejection of certain building sites in favor of others, and massive busing schemes have been required of other districts. In the midst of all this, administrators are being charged to implement in-service staff training and compensatory education programs to eliminate the vestiges of past discrimination.[22]

At the same time that the courts have frequently found constitutional violations in segregation cases and have ordered and monitored remedial measures, three decades of litigation have not fully clarified the obligations placed on school districts to achieve desegregation. As a result, numerous school districts remain involved in desegregation controversies. The problem for school administrators is enlarged by the cases in current litigation challenging various practices within schools as being racially discriminatory. The courts are now deciding cases related to ensuring that testing of students or assignment of students to special education classes or to lower instructional tracks be on a racially neutral basis.[23] In sum, the school segregation cases have dramatically affected school administration and the direction of education. Their impact on the larger society was possibly equally as great as on the schools. One Supreme Court commentator has observed that: "Except for waging and winning the Civil War and World Wars I and II, the decision in the *School Segregation Cases* was probably the most important American governmental act of any kind since the Emancipation Proclamation."[24]

At the same time that the litigation over racial assignment and classification of students was still continuing, numerous other school practices were undergoing the scrutiny of the courts. Beginning in 1969 with the historic *Tinker* decision, a series of decisions was handed down from federal courts which dramatically altered the relationships between educators and students. Pressures on educational systems intensified. One administrator in a major midwestern city complained that he felt he had administered his district from a federal courtroom because so many lawsuits had been filed against the district, and as the superintendent he was placed in the role of having to answer the complaints of the district's patrons.[25]

Tinker v. *Des Moines Independent School District*[26] dealt with a school regulation forbidding the wearing in school of black armbands signifying an objection to the Vietnam War and with the subsequent suspension of students who violated this regulation. The decision in this case has been referred to by some as the "Student Bill of Rights." In *Tinker* the Supreme Court held that neither teachers nor students "shed their constitutional rights . . . at the schoolhouse gate" and that restricting a student's right to freedom of expression is unconstitutional unless there are facts which would reasonably lead school authorities to predict the forbidden conduct would "materially and substantially" disrupt and interfere with school discipline and work. To justify a denial of a student's fundamental rights, school officials must have "more than a mere desire to avoid the discomfort and unpleasantness that always accompany an unpopular viewpoint."

In his dissenting opinion Mr. Justice Black forecast that the majority opinion would mark the "beginning of a new revolutionary era of permissiveness in this country fostered by the judiciary" and that students "turned loose with lawsuits and injunctions against their teachers" will "soon believe it is their right to control the schools rather than . . . the States." Many school personnel shared the same fears and misgivings as did Justice Black.

While the *Tinker* decision did not necessarily begin "a new revolutionary era" of permissiveness as Justice Black predicted, it did mark the beginning of increased activity by students seeking to establish their rights and initiation of lawsuits for damages and injunctions by students when they felt their rights had been violated. The opinion in *Tinker* foreshadowed a large volume of cases filed in federal courts related to the regulation of student behavior. These have included cases dealing with rules for student dress and hair styles, censorship of student publications, and disciplinary actions concerning student protestors who wore buttons, picketed, petitioned, sat in the halls, or otherwise demonstrated. The effect of *Tinker* was not only to encourage the filing of such suits, but to shift the emphasis of court action from the plaintiff having the burden of proof that the official actions were unreasonable or arbitrary to school officials having to show their actions were warranted.[27]

In spite of what might be considered misapprehension or misinterpretations by school personnel, the rulings in *Tinker* and subsequent cases have not eliminated the authority of educators to maintain discipline. Reasonable disciplinary regulations, even those infringing on students' fundamental rights, have been upheld if justified by "legitimate state interests" such as the protection of school property, preservation of the health and safety of those involved in the educational enterprise, or prevention of a material and substantial disruption of the normal operation of the school. While rules made by schools or school districts cannot conflict with constitutional or statutory provisions, school officials retain a great deal of latitude in establishing and enforcing conduct codes that are necessary for instructional activities to take place.[28] In the light of *Tinker*, school officials today are faced with the difficult task of trying to determine when or what form of student expression is sufficiently disruptive to merit prohibition. The challenge for administrators is to try to maintain a balance between their responsibilities to maintain an orderly school and to protect student rights; for the courts have made it obvious that if school officials do not safeguard the fundamental rights of students, the courts will.

Yet another of the many United States Supreme Court decisions that have in recent years had a significant impact on education and the operation of the schools is *Gross v. Lopez.*[29] In this 1975 case, Lopez and other students in Columbus, Ohio, who were suspended for up to ten days without a hearing claimed a violation of their rights to due process of law. In its five-to-four opinion, the Supreme Court ruled on a number of issues of importance to teachers, administrators, and students.

In *Goss*, the Court reiterated the holding in *Tinker* that students do not shed their constitutional rights at the schoolhouse door and the minimum due process must be provided before a student is suspended, even for a short period of time. At the very minimum, Mr. Justice White, speaking for the Court said, except in cases of emergency, when students are suspended they must be given: (1) oral or written notice(s) of the charges, and (2) opportunity to respond to them in some form of hearing. The majority expressed the opinion that a suspension of up to ten days is not so minor as to be imposed "in complete disregard of the Due Process Clause," and that it is a serious event for the suspended child. The Court also emphasized the potentially damaging effect the suspension can have if it is recorded on the student's permanent record where it might "interfere with later opportunities for higher education and employment."

What impact did the *Goss* ruling have on the operations of schools? The very strongly worded dissent of Mr. Justice Powell, who disagreed that suspension for a single day threatens any fundamental right, expressed concern that the majority decision would encourage numerous lawsuits related to every routine operation of the schools including grading, promotions, and classroom assignments.[30] Although the *Goss* decision did not substantially interfere with these operations, it did encourage school officials to be more protective of the due process rights of students; to maintain better records; and to exercise more care in explaining suspensions. Since the Court did suggest that its ruling applied to all short-term suspensions, but did not specify what due process procedures would be required in all circumstances, there have been some confusion and variations among school districts as to what policies are necessary. Some school boards instituted elaborate procedures even for very brief suspensions, whereas others were much more informal. One trend has been the substitution of "in-school suspensions" for the more traditional type of suspension. As with the *Tinker* decision, the challenge for school administrators in conforming to the *Goss* decision is to maintain that somewhat delicate, at times unclear, balance between the social interest inherent in conducting an effective and efficient school and the social interest inherent in protecting the rights of students as a means of teaching students the importance of such rights. While, according to some, the *Goss* holding "does not place any more burden on schools than fairminded educators have themselves accepted and practiced for many years before *Goss*,"[31] it has made school personnel more hesitant to take action to remove students.

Not all federal court cases that have had a profound impact on education have been United States Supreme Court decisions. The two cases that provided the legal impetus for increasing the rights of handicapped children came from two federal district courts, one in Pennsylvania and the other in Washington, D.C. The first case, *Pennsylvania Association of Retarded Children (PARC) v. Commonwealth,*[32] resulted in a consent agreement whereby the state of Pennsylvania was required to place each mentally retarded child in a free public program of education and training appropriate to the child's capacity. The agreement also stipulated that mentally retarded children could not be denied admission to the public schools or be expelled from the public school without procedural due process.

At the time of PARC many state statutes authorized teachers and administrators to exclude handicapped children from school. Even in the absence of statutes, it was frequently held that school boards had the authority to exclude handicapped children under the general grant of authority to administer schools[33] and under compulsory attendance statutes which required school attendance only of those children who could "reasonably be expected to benefit" from the educational experience. In Washington, D.C., the scene of the second case, as in many if not most school districts throughout the country, handicapped children were systematically excluded from the public schools. In *Mills v. Board of Education of the District of Columbia* the school district made admission that 12,340 physically, mentally, and emotionally handicapped children were not being served.[34] The district's defense was insufficient funds. The federal district court ruled that to deny these children an education was to deny them their due process and equal protection rights guaranteed by the Constitution. The court also held that the school district's financial difficulties were not sufficient reason for failure to provide the handicapped with an education and could not "bear more heavily on the 'exceptional' or handicapped child than on the normal child." The court also ordered school officials to adhere to strict due process procedures in pupil assignment and said that any change that would affect the student's instructional program for as little as two days required a hearing where parents were to participate.

Following the *Mills* decision, similar cases were litigated in numerous states, and in each case the basic right of the handicapped child to a public education has been upheld. Subsequent litigation went even further and affirmed the equal protection and due process rights of children and their parents in both the evaluation and the placement process. Perhaps primarily as a response to the decisions emanating from *Mills* and its progeny, numerous states have enacted legislation ensuring the rights of the handicapped child. In addition, Congress adopted the Rehabilitation Act of 1973, section 504 which prohibits discrimination by recipients of federal funds against an otherwise qualified handicapped person; and a broadly inclusive federal law, Public Law 94–142, also known as the Education for All Handicapped Children Act of 1975. This act requires that all states provide each handicapped child with a "free appropriate education." Exactly what this standard requires was for some time the subject of varying and contradictory interpretations by states and local school boards. However, the 1982 United States Supreme Court decision in *Rowley* has settled much of the confusion over what constitutes an appropriate education for the handicapped and the scope of school district responsibilities. According to the Court:

> The Act's requirement of a "free appropriate public
> education" is satisfied when the State provides per-

sonalized instruction with sufficient support services to permit the handicapped child to benefit educationally from that instruction. Such instruction and services must be provided at public expense, must meet the State's educational standards, must approximate grade levels used in the State's regular education, and must comport with the child's IEP, as formulated in accordance with the Act's requirements. If the child is being educated in regular classrooms, as here, the IEP should be reasonably calculated to enable the child to achieve passing marks and advance from grade to grade.[35]

The impact of all this litigation and legislation has been to alter the roles of public school personnel. The commitment of all educators is required if the spirit of the law is to be upheld. No longer are special educators held primarily responsible for the education provided exceptional children. More than ever before the responsibility for establishing educational goals for each handicapped child, and identifying reasonable means for attainment of the goals, has been placed on an inclusive set of public school personnel, including administrators, teachers, and psychologists.

In addition to its impact on handicapped students and education personnel, this litigation and legislation has also had a dramatic effect on state and local education budgets. Not only have states expanded the number of programs they support, but they have significantly increased the level of support for these programs. In spite of the significant federal revenues for education of the handicapped under Public Law 94-142, the state share of total federal-state expenditures for special education is 90 percent. Between fiscal year 1972 and fiscal year 1978, aggregate state special education revenue grew by an estimated 226 percent.[36] These increased expenditures have obviously necessitated increases in taxes. The emphasis on these special programs has also generated concern among many educators as well as among the public that perhaps special education is getting "too large a slice of the pie" relative to the regular program.

The federal and state legislation and court decisions on behalf of special education students have, far beyond these students and programs, potential impacts to all students and the total instructional program. For example, it has already been asserted that every child, not just the exceptional child, is entitled to an individualized educational program. And the procedural safeguards required to ensure the appropriate educational placement of the handicapped child may ultimately be sought to ensure the accuracy of all educational placements. Ultimately, Public Law 94-142, hailed as the Bill of Rights for the handicapped child, could affect the educational opportunities of all children.[37]

The Impact of Federal Court Decisions on State Court Decisions

For the most part, state and federal courts act independently of each other. State courts do not have jurisdiction over federal courts in the state; and federal courts in a state do not have jurisdiction over state courts.

The impact of federal court decisions, even United States Supreme Court Decisions, on state court decisions depends primarily on two factors: whether the issue is one involving federal law; and whether (and to what extent) the state courts choose to look to the federal courts for guidance. Although state courts can rule on questions of both state and federal law, as can federal courts, federal court determination of federal law take precedence over conflicting state court interpretations. Thus, if the matter before the state court is one involving a federal legal question, and a federal court with jurisdiction over that particular geographic area has ruled on the federal issue, the federal court decision is binding on the state court. Second, although it is not uncommon for the state courts to be persuaded or influenced by federal court rulings on similar issues, this is not always true. For example, it is possible for a federal court, ruling on an action under federal law, to say that something is unconstitutional, although at the same time, a state court, interpreting the issue from the perspective of state law, might reach the opposite conclusion.

This was what happened after the United States Supreme Court decision relative to school finance in *San Antonio Independent School District* v. *Rodriguez*.[38] In *Rodriguez* the United States Supreme Court held that the Texas system of financing education did not violate the equal protection clause of the federal Constitution; that education was not a fundamental right under the federal Constitution; and that district tax wealth was not a "suspect classification" that necessitated strict scrutiny of the financing plan by the court. In spite of this opinion by the Supreme Court, less than a month later the Supreme Court of New Jersey in *Robinson* v. *Cahill*[39] found the state financing system of New Jersey to be unconstitutional under the education clause of the state constitution which required the legislature to provide a "thorough and efficient" system of public education. Several other state courts including those of New Jersey, California, Washington, Connecticut, and Wyoming, have also ruled that their school finance laws violated either the equal protection clause of the state constitution or the state constitutional requirement relative to the provision for education. Yet others (e.g., Idaho, Arizona, Georgia, New York, and Colorado) adopted the rationale of the United States Supreme Court and upheld their financing systems. Thus, in assessing the impact of federal court decisions on state court decisions, it is perhaps most accurate to say that while they are always guiding, they are not always controlling.

Conclusions

The involvement of the federal courts in the years since *Brown* has prompted one commentator to say that court decisions have become more important determinants of educational policy than is the local school board.[40] This movement of the courts into the arena of decision-making relative to educational policy has had considerable impact on all spheres of education, from the daily classroom procedures of teachers through the exercise of authority by administrators and the fiscal decisions of school boards. Matters of school finance, student codes of conduct, disciplinary procedures, desegregation, student evaluation, and education of handicapped students are but a few of the areas in which the courts have set guidelines and established precedents. The general effort of court decisions has been to open the schools to judicial scrutiny and to decrease the schools' autonomy. In response to court decisions schools have worked to develop written policies and procedures that protect and expand the rights of teachers and students. As the courts continue to play an active role in reviewing school actions, educators are finding themselves increasingly in the role of implementing and anticipating court rulings.[41]

References

[1]*See e.g.,* 1 U.S.C. 229 (1792); 2 U.S.C. 257 (1806); United States v. Butler, 297 U.S. 1 (1936); Helvering v. Davis, 301 U.S. 619 (1937).

[2]Helvering v. Davis, 301 U.S. 619 (1937).

[3]Thomas Jefferson, *Writings of Thomas Jefferson*, Library Ed. (Washington, D.C.: Thomas Jefferson Memorial Assoc. of the United States, 1904), 147-49.

[4]Indiana *ex. rel.* Anderson v. Brand, 303 U.S. 95 (1938).

[5]393 U.S. 503 (1969).

[6]*See, e.g.,* Eisner v. Stanford Board of Education, 440 F.2d 803 (2d Cir. 1971); Board of School Commissioners v. Jacobs 490 F.2d 601 (7th Cir. 1973), *vacated as moot* 420 U.S. 128 (1975).

[7]*See, e.g.,* Adler v. Board of Education, 342 U.S. 485, (1952); Beilan v. Board of Education, 357 U.S. 399 (1958).

[8]430 U.S. 651 (1977).

[9]419 U.S. 565 (1975).

[10]408 U.S. 564 (1972).

[11]408 U.S. 593 (1972).

[12]Brown v. Board of Education, 347 U.S. 483 (1954).

[13]Jack H. Schuster, "Out of the Frying Pan: The Politics of Education in a New Era," *Phi Delta Kappan* 63 (May 1982): 584

[14]"Education Consolidation Approved by Congress Will Fold ESEA Programs Into Block Grants to States," *Education Times*, 13 July, 1981, 4.

[15]Kern Alexander, *School Law* (St. Paul, Minn.: West Publishing, 1980), 4-6.

[16]General Electric Company v. Gilbert, 429 U.S. 125 (1976).

[17]McCollum v. Board of Education, 333 U.S. 203 (1948).

[18]347 U.S. 483 (1954).

[19]Brown v. Board of Education of Topeka, 349 U.S. 294 (1955).

[20]Griffin v. County Board of Prince Edward County, 377 U.S. 218 (1964).

[21]Alexander v. Holmes County Board of Education, 396 U.S. 19 (1969).

[22]See. Milliken v. Bradley (Milliken II), 433 U.S. 267 (1977).

[23]Martha M. McCarthy and Nelda H. Cambron, *Public School Law, Teachers and Students' Rights* (Boston: Allyn and Bacon, Inc., 1981), 221.

[24]Louis H. Pollak, *The Constitution and the Supreme Court: A Documentary History, Vol. II,* (Cleveland: World Publishing Company, 1966), 266 as quoted in Alexander, *School Law*, 463.

[25]Richard Dobbs Strahan, *The Courts and the Schools* (Lincoln, Neb.: Professional Educators Publications, 1973), 63.

[26]393 U.S. 503 (1969).

[27]Raphael D. Nystrand and W. Frederick Staub, "The Courts as Educational

Policy Makers." In *The Courts and Education*, edited by Clifford P. Hooker. Seventy-seventh Yearbook of the National Society for the Study of Education (Chicago: National Society for the Study of Education, 1978), 35.

[28]McCarthy and Cambron, 284.

[29]Goss v. Lopez, 419 U.S. 565 (1975).

[30]Louis Fischer and David Schinmel, *The Rights of Students and Teachers* (New York: Harper & Row, 1982), 318.

[31]Fischer and Schinmel, 318-19.

[32]343 F. Supp. 279 (E.D. Pa. 1972).

[33]Leroy J. Peterson, Richard A. Rossmiller, and Marlin M. Volz, *The Law and Public School Operation*, 2d ed., (New York: Harper & Row, 1978), 294.

[34]348 F. Supp. 866 (D.D.C. 1972).

[35]Board of Education of the Hendrick Hudson School District v. Rowley, 50 U.S.L.W. 4925.

[36]Michael V. Hodge, "Improving Finance and Governance of Education for Special Populations." In *Perspectives in State School Support Programs*, edited by Forbis Jordan and Nelda H. Cambron-McCabe. Second Annual Yearbook of The American Education Finance Association. (Cambridge, Mass.: Ballinger Publishing Company, 1981), 14.

[37]McCarthy and Cambron, 241.

[38]411 U.S. 1 (1973).

[39]303 A.2d 273 (N.J. 1973).

[40]William R. Hazard, "Courts in the Saddle: School Boards Out," *Phi Delta Kappan* (December 1974): 261.

[41]Ronald J. Anson and Ray C. Rist, eds., *Education, Social Science, and the Judicial Process* (New York: Teachers College Press, Columbia University, 1977); ix.

9

The Legal Relationship of the State Government and Education: Guidelines and Implications for Schools

The previous chapter noted that education is not mentioned in the United States Constitution, and therefore under the Tenth Amendment the power to establish an educational system is a power "reserved to the States." The courts have been consistent in holding that a state's authority over education is a basic attribute of state sovereignty comparable to its authority to tax, to exercise police power, and to provide for the general welfare of its citizens. The state control of education is exercised within the framework of state constitutional provisions, state statutes, and the rules and regulations developed according to statute by state education agencies and local school boards. In addition to providing for a system of public schools, all states provide for a system of courts that become involved in the operation of the schools when disputes between litigants cannot be resolved through the administrative appeals procedures. This chapter contains a discussion of the type of state constitutional provisions and legislative and administrative agency enactments which affect the schools and serve as guidelines for their operation. This discussion is followed by a description of the organization and operation of state court systems and a discussion on the importance of state court decisions to the practice of school administration and the direction of education. The corollary issue of the role of school administrators in influencing court decisions and the direction of litigation is also treated.

State Constitutional, Legislative, and Administrative Agency Guidelines Affecting School Administrators

State Constitutions

Unlike the federal Constitution, which makes no mention of education, all state constitutions include a provision for education and all states except Connecticut expressly provide for the establishment of a system of public schools. These provisions range from very specific to general statements that the legislature shall provide funds for the support of a public school system. An analysis of these measures reveals that there is considerable similarity in their basic provisions. Virtually every one expressly states or implies that the legislature shall provide, from public funds, for the maintenance of a public school system. Many of the state constitutional provisions stipulate limitations as to how the mandate is applied, such as those related to age of pupils, minimum length of the school year, freedom from sectarian control, or nondiscrimination on the basis of sex, race, religion, or national origin. The constitutions of some southern states contain provisions that require segregated schools.[1] Of course, since the *Brown* decision in 1954, these provisions are meaningless.

The exact wording of the education clauses of the state constitutions has proved to be of great importance to the courts in evaluating the legislative enactments which have set the constitutional mandates in operation. For example, in a number of school finance cases, the courts have ruled that words such as "system" or "thorough and efficient system" as used in a state constitution indicate some degree of uniformity and equality of educational opportunity that must be provided in the legislatively designed school financing system.[2] In a few cases the courts have interpreted these provisions as creating a right to an education.[3] An acceptance by state courts that their state constitutions establish on behalf of every student a right to an education holds a wide range of implications for the schools and could become the basis for massive judicial involvement in shaping the educational policies of the states.[4] "At a minimum such a right provides the courts with a rationale for imposing negative limitations in many areas of school policy, if not also providing a premise for requiring affirmative action from the state and localities."[5]

Whatever the particular provisions related to education in a state constitution, a state constitution is not a grant of unlimited power to the legislature in providing for a system of public education. Rather it sets the parameters within which the legislature may operate. That is, the state legislature may not enact legislation which violates its state constitution or the federal Constitution, which is supreme over the state constitutions. State constitutions will often deal with the same matters as the federal Constitution. For example, many states have a state bill of rights that contains many of the same protections as the federal Bill of Rights. State constitutions may provide for more rights, but not fewer rights, than the federal Constitution. For example, as previously noted, education has been found to be a fundamental right under certain state constitutions, but has been declared by the United States Supreme Court not to be a fundamental right under the federal Constitution.[6]

189

State Legislation

Whereas a state constitution provides for the creation of a state public school system, the specific operation of that system is detailed in state education statutes. In enacting statutes dealing with education, a state legislature, unlike the United States Congress which has only those powers delegated to it, has plenary power and may enact any legislation that is not contrary to state or federal constitutional provisions. Literally hundreds of court decisions (usually arising out of some desire for self-control by local school boards) could be cited to sustain the point that the legislature has complete authority over the educational system and schools of the state. The following excerpt from the Indiana Supreme Court, which has been quoted by numerous courts and often cited in legal texts, concisely sets forth the legal principle that education is a function of the state and not an inherent function of the local government:

> Essentially and intrinsically, the schools . . . are matters of state, and not local jurisdiction. In such matters the state is a unit, and the legislature is a source of power. The authority over schools and school affairs is not necessarily a distributive one, to be exercised by local instrumentalities; but on the contrary, it is a central power, residing in the legislature of the state. It is for the law-making power to determine whether the authority shall be exercised by a state board of education, or distributed to county, township, or city organizations throughout the state. . . . The governing school boards derive all their authority from the statute, and can exercise no powers except they're expressly granted.[7]

Courts have held that the plenary power of the legislature includes the authority to:

> (1) direct or authorize the creation, modification, and abolition of school districts; (2) alter the structure and powers of school boards; (3) remove incumbent school board members, and abolish their offices; (4) prescribe school calendar, and curriculum; (5) determine the sources and procedures for raising school revenues and school spending; (6) fix the appointment term and qualifications of teachers; (7) require local schools to admit children of nontaxpayers; and (8) revoke charters of public schools for noncompliance with state regulations.[8]

Since the power of the legislature is plenary, the legislature can change the education statutes as often as it deems necessary or expedient. They may also be supplemented by subsequent legislation. However, every time a statute is enacted, revised, or supplemented it is subject to judicial review to determine its constitutionality or the legislative intent.

Most states compile their education statutes into a school code which serves as a reference for school administrators and others. The specificity of state education statutes varies from state to state and from subject to subject. For example, one state may only generally require that appropriate procedures be followed in budgeting and accounting for public funds; but another state may actually specify each line item of the budget and provide explicit procedures for accounting for these funds.[9]

In addition to providing for the funding of the schools and enacting statutes guiding their operations, state legislatures may, legally, actually operate the schools. However, they have not chosen to do this but have chosen to delegate the administration of the schools to other agencies. Since the state legislature is the constitutionally established legislative body for the state, it may delegate its administrative powers, but may not delegate its legislative authority to any other body. Because it is often difficult to distinguish between legislative and administrative powers, the courts are often called on to determine whether there has been an unlawful attempt to delegate legislative authority. As the operations of governments and their agencies have become more complex, the courts have become more liberal in interpreting the degree of delegation of legislative power permitted.[10] The legal test that is frequently used to determine the legality of the delegation is: Did the enabling legislation provide adquate standards so that the agency can interpret and implement the true legislative intent of the act?

State Education Agencies

Each state has created a central education agency, which has been given general control and responsibility for education at a level directly below the legislature. The functions of this education agency, like those of other public agencies, can be classified as: (1) legislative, (2) administrative or executive, and (3) judicial or quasi-judicial. The legislative functions of the education agency are usually performed by a state board of education. The executive functions are vested in chief state school officers and their staff, which is the state department of education. The judicial or quasi-judicial functions may be carried out by any combination of the above units, depending on the provisions of state statutes.

Legislative Functions: State Boards of Education. Almost all of the states have state boards of education. Selection of state board of education members varies from state to state, but the most common methods of selection are gubernatorial appointment and popular election. In a few instances the state board of education is made up of individuals who hold other state offices. The particular method of selection does not seem to bear on the legal powers of the board in that other appointing agencies do not exercise any veto powers over board actions.

The legislative functions of the state board of education include the promulgation of rules and regulations made pursuant to and within the scope of state statute. The state board may have very broad or very limited powers, depending on legislative authorization. Most state statutes tend to grant wide powers of general supervision and control to the state board. However, the generality of many statutes has resulted in numerous cases that seek to determine whether a particular power is within those legally conferred by statute. Generally the courts have upheld rules and regulations made by the state board unless they violate legislative or constitutional guidelines. Although the state board is normally given general responsibility for the operation of the state educational system, it has been held that the state board of education cannot exercise those functions which the legislature has specifically conferred upon local boards of education. An examination of state statutes shows the following to be the most common of the duties and functions assigned to state boards of education:

1. To adopt rules and regulations that have the force of law
2. To determine educational policies
3. To determine regulations governing the distribution of state funds
4. To regulate teacher certification
5. To regulate teacher education other than by certification
6. To prescribe minimum standards in specified areas
7. To adopt courses of study
8. To adopt textbooks
9. To determine the plan of organization for the state department of education
10. To prescribe the duties of the chief state school officer[11]

Administrative Functions: Chief State School Officer and State Department of Education. Once the state board of education acts and establishes its policies and regulations, a chief state school officer is charged with the responsibility of translating these policies into operational, day-to-day, workable rules and regulations. All states have a chief state school officer who is known variously as commissioner, superintendent, or secretary of public instruction or education. In the majority of states the chief state school officer is appointed by the state board of education and serves under its direction. In a number of states the person is elected, although there is a trend away from this method. There is also a trend away from appointment by the governor, although this method is still used in a very few states.

Generally speaking, the role of the chief state school officer is to provide the leadership for the state's educational system. However, the extent of authority and the areas of responsiblity vary from state to state. In some situations the chief state school officer is responsible only for elementary and secondary education; in others for elementary, secondary, and vocational education; and in yet other states for elementary, secondary, vocational, and junior college education. In a few states the chief officers are responsible for the entire educational program. In the past the functions of the chief state school officer were largely regulatory functions such as enforcement of laws, formulation of regulations and standards, supervision of schools, and accounting and distribution of state funds. More recently, however, research, planning, development, and the provision of leadership for the professional staff of the state have become significant functions of the office.[12]

The authority of the chief state school officer to make rules and regulations governing the operations of the schools has been interpreted broadly by the courts. In fact, it has been held by the courts that the chief state school officer has implied power to make rules and regulations for the operation of the schools even when such power has not been expressly granted by the legislature.[13] The chief state school officer may also have such legislative authority as might be conferred upon the office by the state legislature. Furthermore, as will be discussed in a following section, the chief state school officer is charged with exercising certain judicial functions as they relate to controversies within the system.

Each state has also established a state department of education that provides consultation and support services to the state board, the chief state school officer, and local school boards. The state department of education generally consists of a staff of professional specialists, supervisors, and administrators who perform numerous supervisory, regulatory, enforcement, research, and support activities. They carry out such tasks as certification of teachers, accreditation of schools, preparation of curriculum guides, adoption of textbooks, administration of special schools and programs, collection and compilation of statistical data, establishment of minimum educational standards, and distribution and administration of the state education funds. The necessary rules and regulations promulgated by the state department of education for the carrying out of these activities have the full force of law and constitute a significant portion of the legal framework under which the schools operate. As with the rules and regulations prescribed by the chief state school officer, often various rules and regulations of state departments of education have been challenged as an unlawful exercise of their authority or as an unlawful delegation of authority to them. Generally the courts will uphold the actions of state departments of education unless their actions constitute an abuse of discretion or violate constitutional or legislative mandates.

Judicial Functions. In most states the state education agency is vested with certain judicial functions. Acting in this capacity, state education agencies hand down many more decisions affecting individuals than do the courts. The decisions made by educational tribunals provide an important source of law under which the schools operate. This judicial authority can be vested in the state board of education, the chief state school officer, or both. In some states special tribunals have been established to handle certain kinds of disputes. The decisions of these tribunals are binding on all parties and serve to establish precedent for future disputes handled by the agency.[14]

In some states, statutes provide that the state board of education will be the final authority in all controversies and disputes within the educational system. In other states, the chief state school officer is vested with authority in appeals from local school districts. In states such as New York, where appeal is frequently made to the commissioner of education and where statutes specify that the decisions of the commissioner are "final and conclusive," and in New Jersey where the decisions of the commissioner are widely published, these decisions serve as important guidelines for the interpretation of the rules and regulations of the state board of education. In most states the state education agency is given broad jurisdiction to review educational matters and through this function exercises considerable influence upon the state educational system.

Local Education Agency

Like the state education agency, local education agencies, or school boards, are creations of the state, instituted for the express purpose of carrying out the constitutional mandate for the legislature to provide for a system of public schools. Also, like the state education agency, school boards do not possess any sovereign powers, but possess only such powers as have been conferred on them by the state constitution or state statutes or implied from those powers so conferred. As was true of the delegation of authority to the state education agency, the extent of the authority conferred on the local education agency varies among the states. In some states control of education is centralized, and local boards must operate within a limited framework. In other states rather broad powers are granted to the local board. In either circumstance, the courts have clearly established that boards of education may adopt and enforce such reasonable rules and regulations as are necessary to operate the schools, as long as they do not violate state or federal constitutional provisions or statutes. It is this large body of rules and regulations that most immediately affects teachers and students which is most often the source of judicial challenge.

Very often legal challenges relate to whether the school board has exceeded those powers conferred upon it. As was true of interpretations of the state education agency's powers, the courts are generally inclined to interpret the implied powers of school boards quite liberally. Other challenges to school board regulations contend that a particular rule or regulation is unreasonable. In ruling on the reasonableness of board rulings, the court will always presume the actions to be reasonable unless the evidence is to the contrary. The determination of the reasonableness of a particular rule or regulation is also considered to be a function of the particular circumstances of the case. For example, in *Burnside* v. *Byars* the court invalidated a regulation that prohibited the wearing of freedom buttons because in that particular school situation there was no evidence that any disruption was caused by the wearing of the buttons.[15] However, in *Blackwell* v. *Issaquena County Board of Education,* another regulation which also forbade the wearing of buttons was upheld because the particular circumstances involved indicated a disruption of the educational environment.[16]

Judicial Review of Agency Decisions

A party challenging the actions of state and local educational agencies must first exhaust available administrative remedies before the courts will accept an appeal. This requirement assures the courts that disputes have been properly dealt with at "lower levels, within the realm of administrative authority, thus preventing continuous involvement of the courts in educational disputes where legitimate legal controversy is not present."[17] The exception to this rule is a case that involves the interpretation of statutes or a constitutionally protected right. The interpretation of statutes and the determination of the constitutionality of actions are clearly functions of the courts. When an appeal is made to a court, the court will not evaluate the educational or other assumptions underlying a decision of the state agency or the widsom of such a decision. Instead, the posture is a refusal to substitute the court's judgment for that of the body to which the legislature has delegated the power to exercise judgment and discretion in matters affecting the operation of the schools unless such power was exercised in a manner that was clearly arbitrary or capricious, an abuse of discretion, a violation of the law, or beyond the legal authority of the agency. The presumption is made that the administrative agency acted properly and the burden of proof falls on the challenging party to prove that it did not.

An important issue in judicial review of administrative decisions is whether the decision being questioned is considered legislative or judicial. The courts consider legislative decisions to be educational decisions, and in those cases seem more reluctant to substitute their judgment for that of professional educators or the duly elected school board. However, if the decision in question involves interpretation of statutes, disputed facts of law, or fundamental rights, then it is considered judicial in nature and therefore more appropriate for review by the courts.

Organization and Operation of the State Court System

While cases involving education may be litigated in both the state and federal courts, since most education cases do not involve federal questions, the vast majority of such cases are decided by state courts. State courts are created by state constitutions and legislatures. Unlike federal courts, which have only those powers specified in the federal constitution, state courts can handle most types of controversies, unless restricted by state statutes.

In this section, before turning to a description and comparison of two state court systems, the general organization and operation of state court systems and the appeals process within the system will be discussed.

State Court Systems

Although the structure and name given to state courts varies from state to state, there are some commonalities. Generally, state court systems consist of: (1) lower courts of limited jurisdiction, (2) courts of special jurisdiction, (3) trial courts of general jurisdiction, and (4) appellate courts. Figure 9-1 depicts the general pattern of state court systems.

Courts of Limited Jurisdiction. Almost all states have courts of limited jurisdiction. These courts are authorized to handle cases involving a relatively small amount in controversy and usually simple issues. For example, the justice court, presided over by a justice of the peace, normally has authority to hear civil cases involving only a small amount of money and criminal cases involving only misdemeanors or petty crimes. Other examples of courts of limited jurisdiction are small claims courts (which in some states are classified as justice of the peace courts), traffic courts, police courts, and municipal or magistrate courts.

The names and authority of courts of limited jurisdiction will vary from state to state. The courts of limited jurisdiction are often organized by territorial courts. In California, for example, the courts of limited jurisdiction are the municipal courts and the justice courts and are organized into territorial units known as judicial districts. Each of these judicial districts consists of a county or a portion of a county. If the judicial district has a population of 40,000 or less, the court for the district is a justice court; if the population is above 40,000, the court is a municipal court. The civil subject-matter jurisdiction of the justice court is more limited

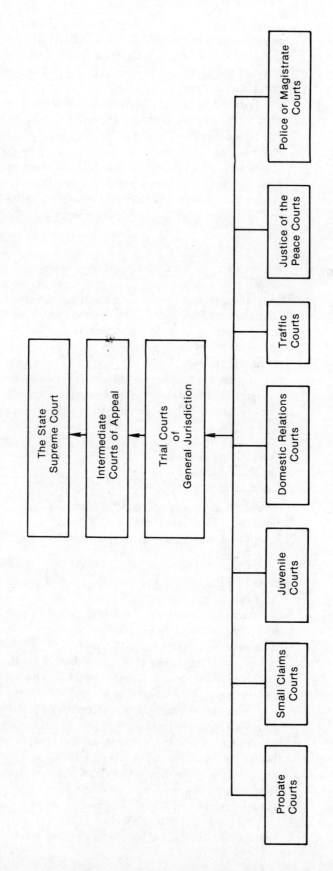

Figure 9-1 *State Court Systems*

than that of the municipal court.[18] Ordinarily, one judge hears cases in courts of limited jurisdiction. Decisions of courts of limited jurisdiction are not published and are not considered as binding on other courts.

Courts of Special Jurisdiction. Courts of special jurisdiction handle cases involving those special subject matters which have a large volume of cases. Among the courts of special jurisdiction are the juvenile courts, probate courts, and domestic relations courts. In some states these are actually separate courts staffed by separate judges. In many other states such terms as "probate court" and "domestic relations court" do not refer to separate courts but to specialized procedures applied to that particular type of case when it is in the court of special jurisdiction.[19]

Courts of General Jurisdiction. All states have courts of general jurisdiction that hear cases of all types, unlimited by subject matter or amount in controversy, that are not handled by the special courts. Courts of general jurisdiction are known as trial courts and as such hear witnesses, admit evidence, and conduct jury trials when appropriate. Hearing is by one judge. In some states the jurisdiction of the courts of general jurisdiction will be the same as that of the courts of special jurisdiction so the plantiff has a choice of court in which to file. In other states the maximum amount in controversy in the lower court is the minimum in the court of general jurisdiction. Courts of general jurisdiction are also known by different names among the states. Among these names are the district court, the county court, the circuit court, the court of common pleas, superior court, or (in New York) supreme court.

Appellate Courts. Appellate courts are found in all state court systems. In the less populous states there may be only one appellate court, the state supreme court, to handle the appeals from the courts of general jurisdiction. In the more populous states, because of the sheer volume of cases, intermediate appellate courts have been established. Their organization and name varies from state to state, but they are usually known as courts of appeals. The intermediate appellate courts are normally organized along geographic lines by groups of counties. The intermediate appellate courts usually have three or more judges who sit in panels of three when reviewing cases. In states that have intermediate appellate courts, appeal can then be made to the court of last resort, the state supreme court. This court also consists of several judges, the number varying from three to nine among the states, with the typical number being seven.

Appeals Process in State Court Systems

Most states do not permit appeals from the courts of limited jurisdiction to an appellate court. Appeals from courts of general jurisdiction and courts of special jurisdiction are appealed to the next possible level, be it the intermediate appellate court or the state supreme court. According to the statutes of some states, decisions of state agencies may also be appealed to the appellate courts. If an intermediate appellate court exists, normally appeal would be to that body, although in some states certain appeals such as felonious homicide, may be taken directly to the state supreme court. State law will dictate that certain appeals terminate at the intermediate appellate court, while others are appealable to the state supreme court. Review by the state supreme court, like that by the United States Supreme Court, is normally at the court's discretion and is normally obtained by a writ of *certiorari*.

The state appeals courts are the final authorities on questions of state law or the state constitution, unless a federal question is also involved. In cases involving federal questions, appeal may be made from the state supreme court to the United States Supreme Court.

A Comparison of Two State Court Systems: Illinois and Arizona

The following section compares two state court systems, Illinois and Arizona. These two states are illustrative of two broad classifications of state court systems: unified (Illinois) and more fragmented or complex (Arizona).

Illinois[20]

The Illinois court system has the distinction of being the first truly unified court system in the nation. It has the three-tiered system of general trial courts, called circuit courts, intermediate appellate courts, and a supreme court depicted in Figure 9-2

Illinois' highest court, the supreme court, is authorized by the state constitution and sits in the state capital. It is composed of seven mem-

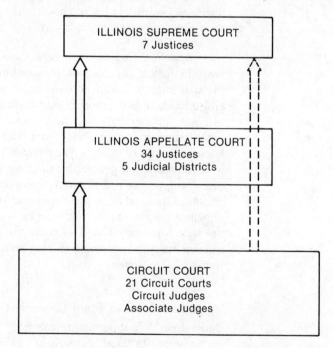

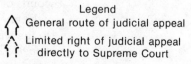

FIGURE 9-2   *The Illinois Court System*

bers: a chief justice and six associate justices. The jurisdiction of the supreme court extends to all civil and criminal appeals from the appellate courts. In cases where the death penalty has been imposed, there is a right of direct appeal from circuit courts to the supreme court. There is also a right of appeal from the appellate court to the supreme court if a question under either the Illinois or the United States constitutions is made an issue for the first time in and as a result of actions of the appellate court, or if the appellate court certifies a case as being of such importance that it should be decided by the supreme court.

The intermediate appellate courts constitute the primary courts of appeal within the state judicial system. There are five intermediate appellate courts, one in Cook county (Chicago) and four others with multi-county jurisdiction. Appeals to the appellate courts from the circuit courts are a matter of right, except those appealed directly from the circuit courts to the supreme court and except that after a trial on the merits in a criminal case, there can be no appeal of an acquittal.

The circuit courts are the major trial courts in the Illinois judicial system. There are twenty-one judicial circuits in Illinois. In multi-county circuits, court is held in each county. Circuit courts have original jurisdiction in all justiciable matters except when the supreme court has original or exclusive jurisdiction. Decisions of the circuit court may be appealed as a matter of right to the appellate court in the judicial district in which the circuit court is located, except in those previously mentioned instances where appeal is directly to the supreme court or where there has been an acquittal in a criminal case.

Arizona[21]

Unlike the very unified judicial system of Illinois, Arizona has the slightly more complex system shown in Figure 9-3. It consists of lower-level courts of limited jurisdiction, general trial courts, called superior courts, the court of appeals, and the state supreme court.

The Arizona Supreme Court, like the Illinois Supreme Court, is authorized by the state constitution, and sits in the state capital. It consists of five members: a chief justice, a vice chief justice, and three associate justices. The appellate jurisdiction of the supreme court includes all actions and proceedings except civil and criminal actions originating in the justice of the peace or municipal courts, and actions involving the validation of a tax, impost, assessment, toll, statute, or municipal ordinance.

The intermediate appellate court in Arizona is the court of appeals. It consists of two divisions: one, with nine judges, sits in Phoenix; the other, with three judges, sits in Tucson. The jurisdiction of each of the two divisions is multi-county, except that Division One has statewide responsibility for reviewing decisions of the Industrial Commission and unemployment compensation denials from the Department of Economic Security. The court of appeals has appellate jurisdiction over all matters appealed from the superior courts, except in criminal cases where the sentence has been life imprisonment or death, in which cases appeal is directly to the supreme court.

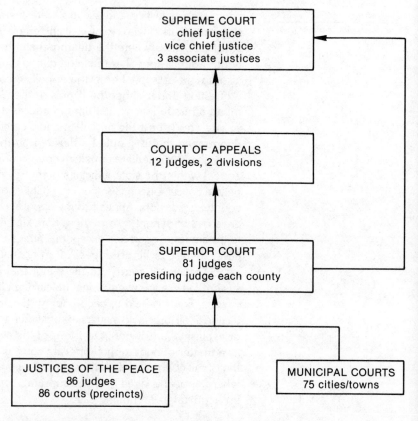

FIGURE 9-3   *The Arizona Court System*

The Arizona superior courts, like the Illinois circuit courts, are the trial courts of general jurisdiction. In 1983 the superior court consisted of eighty-one judges sitting in fourteen counties with a presiding judge in each county. The superior courts have original jurisdiction in cases of law and equity which involve the title to or possession of real property; in civil cases in which the amount in controversy amounts to $2,500 or more; in felony prosecutions and misdemeanors not otherwise provided by for law; in probate proceedings; and in cases involving divorce or annulment. The superior courts also have appellate jurisdiction in such cases arising from the justice of the peace or municipal courts as may be provided by the law. There are eighty-six justices of the peace in Arizona sitting in the same number of precincts. Justice of the Peace Courts hear minor misdemeanor cases. They may also conduct preliminary examinations on felony complaints. The Justice of the Peace Courts also have civil jurisdiction over lawsuits involving less than $2,500.

Municipal Courts are mandated by state law in each incorporated city or town in Arizona. As of 1982 there were seventy-five such courts. Like the justice of the peace courts, municipal courts have jurisdiction to hear minor misdemeanor cases. Municipal courts are also empowered to hear matters arising out of violations of city or town ordinances. Almost all traffic violations are filed in the justice of the peace or municipal courts.

State Case Law

As we noted in the previous chapter, case law is that body of law that emanates from the rulings of the courts and is variously referred to as judge-made law, common law, or case law. The legal principles that are established by the courts are just as binding upon those within the jurisdiction of the court issuing the ruling as are constitutional provisions or statutory law. Since education is a function of the state, and since most cases involving the schools are tried in state courts, the importance of state case law to the practice of school administration and the direction of education cannot be overstated. As one noted commentator has observed, "it seems likely that case law will define the substance, nature, and process of education with increased clarity."[22]

Impact of State Court Decisions on the Practice of School Administration and the Direction of Education

Although the decision of one state court is not binding on the courts of another state, much less the educators in another state, there have been numerous state court decisions that have indeed had a national impact and have altered the course of education. In fact, much of the shaping of education and our educational institutions has been as a result of state court decisions. The three state court decisions that are briefly discussed in the following pages are but a few of hundreds that could be mentioned. The 1959 *Molitor* case in Illinois was the landmark case in the abrogation of governmental immunity of school districts; the *Serrano* case was the undisputed catalyst for the entire school finance reform movement; and the *Peter W.* case is the seminal decision in the area of education malpractice.

Dissolution of Governmental Immunity. Governmental immunity or sovereign immunity is the common law doctrine that governmental agencies cannot be held liable for the negligent acts of their officers, agents, or employees. It originated in the English common law concept that the king can do no wrong. As the concept evolved in this country, it was translated into the principle that government agencies, including school districts, are not responsible for the negligent acts of the school district itself or its officers, agents, or employees. Various rationales are offered for applying governmental immunity to school districts, including the fact that state laws provide no funds for the payment of any damage that might be assessed the district and that to use tax dollars to pay a claim which could be considered a private or noneducation purpose would be an illegal expenditure of tax dollars.

Over the years certain exceptions have been made to the doctrine of immunity as applied in the various states. These include such exceptions as not allowing immunity if the district is maintaining a nuisance, or if the alleged negligence arose in connection with a proprietary activity as opposed to a governmental activity. In other states, "safe harmless" statutes that require districts to pay for negligence claims against teachers and "safe place" statutes that require the owners of public buildings to keep them in a safe condition for employees or users have been enacted. In spite of the partial erosion of the doctrine of governmental

immunity, there has been continued controversy as to whether this doctrine is viable and appropriate for today's complex government and society. The first complete rejection of the doctrine came in 1959 in a state supreme court decision in Illinois, *Molitor v. Kaneland Community Unit School District No. 302.*[23] In *Molitor* the court concluded that "the rule of school district tort immunity is unjust, unsupported by any valid reason, and has no rightful place in modern day society." To continue to support this antiquated doctrine, the court said, was to overlook the fact that the Revolutionary War was fought to abolish the "divine right of Kings" on which the theory was based. In fact, the court concluded:

> It is almost incredible that in this modern age of comparative sociological enlightenment, and in a republic, the medieval absolutism supposed to be implicit in the maxim, 'the King can do no wrong,' should exempt the various branches of the government from liability for their torts, and that the entire burden of damage resulting from the wrongful acts of the government should be imposed upon the single individual who suffers the injury.[24]

Since *Molitor,* there have been several other state supreme courts which have completely abrogated the doctrine of governmental immunity in their jurisdictions. In a number of states, the courts have continued to carve out judicial exceptions to the immunity doctrine. In still other states, the legislature has taken action to mitigate against the effects of governmental immunity. Although there has been no wide-scale abolition of governmental immunity since *Molitor*, it was the first case where the state supreme court actually abrogated the doctrine by judicial fiat and the decision did begin the trend toward moderation of the effects of the doctrine in the relationship between the state and its citizens.

School Finance Reform. Undoubtedly the state court case that has had the most impact on the direction of education in recent years in *Serrano v. Priest*.[25] In 1971 in *Serrano*, the California Supreme Court issued its landmark decision which held that the state's public school financing system was in violation of the equal protection clause of the Fourteenth Amendment to the United States Constitution in that it made the quality of a child's education a function of the wealth of the school district. This decision was the first major ruling against a state's school finance system on the basis of violation of equal protection for all public school pupils in the state and sent shock waves through the educational and legal communities.

The impact of the *Serrano* decision has been almost overwhelming in matters of school finance. Within five months after its announcement, courts in Minnesota, New Jersey, and Texas issued similar rulings; and in numerous other states the *Serrano* rationale was adopted as the basis for challenging the state's financing scheme. Even the United States Supreme Court decision in *San Antonio Independent School District v. Rodriguez*,[26] which held that education was not a fundamental right under the federal Constitution and that the Texas system of financing schools did not discriminate on the basis of wealth against any "suspect class" thus invoking the strict scrutiny of the court, did not slow the pace of the reform litigation. Instead, advocates of reform turned to state courts to challenge school finance systems on the basis of state constitutional provisions rather than the federal constitution. State after state "entertained" litigation and court decisions against the status quo. Most states undertook formal studies designed to modernize their school finance formulas. Such prompt action was considered necessary in the face of the apparent threat of nationwide school finance reform. State officials, fearing a possible court-ordered elimination or reduction of the property tax, undertook to correct formula inequities before court action became necessary. In sum, as a result of *Serrano* and its progeny, nearly all the states tried to provide greater equality in allocation procedures to insure the equal protection guaranteed by the Fourteenth Amendment to the federal Constitution or similar provisions of state constitutions. While not every reform effort becomes so concerted and so visible that it becomes classified as a "reform movement," the school finance reform which originated with *Serrano* can surely be so classified.[27]

Educational Malpractice. Perhaps the newest area of litigation in education is the area of educational malpractice. Educational malpractice is the alleged failure of a school district to educate adequately a student who has been compelled to attend school for approximately twelve years. These suits against educators are but one indication of societal dissatisfaction with the results of schooling. Although several lawsuits recently have arisen in state courts alleging educational malpractice, thus far there are no authoritative answers. To date, the courts have chosen not to recognize an educational malpractice cause of action. At a time when malpractice litigation is increasing in other professions, however, and considering the fact that the condition of the plaintiffs in the suits thus far is not unique, it is almost certain that litigation in this area will continue.

Peter W. v. _San Francisco Unified School District,_ commonly referred to as the "_Peter Doe_ case," was the first major case in the area of educational malpractice.[28] Thus far, the rationale and decision of the court in this case have been duplicated in those that have followed. In _Peter W._ the question before the court (in the words of the court) was "whether a person who claims to have been inadequately educated, while a student in a public school system, may state a cause of action in tort against the public authorities who operate and administer the system." The court held that the person may not. In reaching its decision in _Peter W._, the court considered such issues as whether the school district owed Peter W. the requisite legal duty to sustain a cause of action; how this duty might be measured; whether the alleged injury could be "comprehensible and answerable within the existing judicial framework"; and the difficulty of establishing the required causal relationship between the school's failure to educate and Peter W.'s illiteracy. Although these issues were not resolved in favor of Peter W., public policy considerations were, in fact, the major reasons the court reached the decision it did in _Peter W._ Recognizing that the public schools are under almost constant criticism, are held to be responsible for many of the social and moral problems of society, and are "beset by social and financial problems that have gone to major litigation," the court was not willing to subject them (or itself) to the "tort claims—real or imagined—of disaffected students in countless numbers." The ultimate consequences of doing so, "in terms of public time and money, would burden them—and society—beyond calculation."

The decision in _Peter W._, and the educational malpractice suits that have followed, indicate judicial hesitancy to enter another area of judicial review: the responsiblity educators owe their students. While there are some who see this as placing a judicially created immunity on educators in the discharge of their academic functions and reducing their accountability, the alternatives seem equally negative. Even one or two negative judgments against one school district can cause the overall quality of education to suffer. Spending large sums on judgments instead of ongoing programs would become self-defeating, given the thrust of educational malpractice allegations. Malpractice insurance for other professions is traditionally very expensive and presumably this would hold true for educators. To divert funds for this purpose (and the provision of such insurance would surely be a high priority item in teacher negotiations) would also direct dollars away from the instructional program. Teaching in the face of liability might discourage many qualified educators or it might cause them to focus their activities on the basic skills or "teaching to the test." Whether the gains to the successful plaintiff would outweigh the impact on the entire system remains unclear and perhaps for future courts to decide.

Impact of State Court Decisions on the Decisions of Other Courts

Under the American court system, the opinions of courts in one state are not binding on the courts of another state. This is not to say, however, that they are not considered "persuasive" on points that are similarly treated by other legislatures. Each time a judicial point of view is quoted with approval by another court, the weight of the holding is increased.[29] This was made apparent in each of the cases discussed in the previous section. Thus the experience and laws of one state often provide guidance to another state, and the development of legal trends or case law in one state may often influence lawmaking in other states.[30]

The Role of School Administrators in Influencing Court Decisions and the Direction of Litigation

The courts and the judges who sit on their benches do not operate in a vacuum. They tend to reflect the concerns of the larger society. Although judges often make decisions that are unpopular with politicians and the body politic, they cannot avoid the political dimensions of their decisions. Judges could not act for long without the support of the community, for they require enforcement of their decisions. At the same time that courts mirror the concerns of the larger society, they also respond to the interest groups and the attentive publics that use them. This is exemplified by the large volume of desegregation litigation.

The judicial and educational history of the past three decades indicates a judicial activism that has often, seemingly, placed the courts in the position of setting agendas, or initiating conflict, rather than resolving conflict. As has been discussed throughout this and the preceding chapter, the courts have become involved in every phase of the operation of the schools. However, in spite of the negative reception with which many educators view this involvement, educators have not been stripped of all authority and left in a position of helplessness. For one thing, although the law and the courts have indeed spoken to a broad range of school policies, the actual translation of legislation and case law allows school officials an equally broad range of legally acceptable school forms and responses.[31] Second, there exists a wide range of strategies educators can use so that they can become participants in judicial activity rather than feeling like victims of judicially sponsored change.

One of the most direct methods by which educators can affect the outcome of judicial decisions is by using their professional expertise. Judges must often seek information beyond their areas of expertise in order to deal wisely with the issues before them. For their part, educators can do research, develop the requisite skills, and generate well-thought-out positions about the issues being litigated. By so doing, they can serve as the fact finders and expert witnesses who are increasingly needed as cases deal with complex and specialized educational issues.[32]

In like manner educators, through the attorneys of a school district or professional association, can develop with the permission of the court amicus curiae briefs. An *amicus curiae* (friend of the court) brief is one submitted by someone who is not party to the suit. *Amicus curiae* briefs can be used to call the court's attention to certain issues, provide data or evidence relevant to the case, or advance a position for the consideration of the court. *Amicus curiae* briefs can be submitted on the initiation of an outside party, or in occasional instances on the initiation of the court. The latter procedure was followed after the United States Supreme Court decision in *Brown I*[33] that segregation by race was no longer permissible in public education, when the court postponed its enforcement decree for one year and invited the United States Attorney General and the attorneys general of all the states to submit *amicus curiae* briefs giving their views on the ruling and its implementation.

There are a number of other more indirect methods by which educators can attempt to influence the courts. One of these indirect methods is to write in the various technical publications and law review journals. This activity might not directly influence a particular case, but courts have been known to refer to these articles and such writings can thus have an eventual impact on a particular issue.

Yet another indirect practice that holds promise for being an important method of influencing the judiciary is the incorporation of law-related education in classrooms. Law-related education strives to expand the knowledge and understanding of legal concepts in the general community by recruiting, engaging, and energizing local members of the legal community, including judges, to engage directly in the education of young people. Judges in law-related programs teach students about the nature of the legal system through classroom activities and field trips. The involvement of judges in law-related education affects the judges' attitudes toward young people. While many members of the legal community are certainly expert in their area of the law, there is a need for training in communicating with young people. The more judges are actively involved in the community and its schools, the more likely they are to be sensitive to the needs of the community and to render decisions accordingly.

Certainly the most direct method by which educators can seek to influence court decisions and the direction of litigation is to bring suit as plaintiffs. The judicial remedy, used selectively, has the potential for bringing about the reform deemed necessary and proper by the education profession. For although the courts may play a role in social change, change must ultimately come from the people who initiate the litigation.

Conclusions

Despite legitimate concerns regarding judicial activism, the decade ahead will see a continuation of judicial involvement in the operations of the public schools. Developments in the law of public education in the future will be shaped, in part, by the seeds sown in the past. These seeds suggest that the areas of desegregation and civil rights will continue to be fertile areas of litigation. Within these areas new topics for litigation are likely to arise. We may well see "pattern and practice" litigation challenging disproportionate suspensions and expulsions of students of a particular race. The movement toward competency-based education and proficiency tests as a condition for graduation may also lead to litigation if disproportionate numbers of students of particular racial or ethnic groups do not pass the tests. Litigation involving exceptional children will also continue in the future as courts try to define the scope of services owed these students by school districts. In addition, the question of whether nonhandicapped students can assert a claim of denial of equal protection based on the fact that they do not have the individualized attention and instruction available to even slightly handicapped children is likely to be brought to the courts. In all areas of educational policy and practice, adjustments and refinements are likely to result from cases raising questions concerning the application of previous legislation and decisions in slightly different factual contexts. Overall, given our increasingly litigious society, there will be no shortage of attempts to promote change through the courts.[34]

References

[1]Edward C. Bolmeier, *The School in the Legal Structure,* 2d ed. (Cincinnati, Ohio: W. H. Anderson Company, 1973), 88.

[2]See, e.g.: Miller v. Childers, 238 P. 204; Miller v. Kouns, 140 N.E. 773; Robinson v. Cahill, 303 A.2d 273; Seattle School District No. 1 of King County Washington v. State of Washington, 585 P.2d. 71.

[3]See, e.g.: Serrano v. Priest, 487 P.2d 1241; Horton v. Meskill, 376 A.2d 359; Van Dusartz v. Hatfield, 334 F. Supp. 870 (D.C. Minn.); Washakie County School District No. 1 v. Herschler, 606 P.2d 310.

[4]Tyll van Geel, *Authority to Control the School Program* (Lexington, Mass.: D.C. Heath and Company, 1976), 97, 108-109.

[5]vanGeel, 109.

[6]*San Antonio Independent School District v. Rodriguez,* 411 U.S.1 (1973).

[7]State Ex Rel. Clark v. Haworth, 23 N.E. 946. (1890).

[8]William D. Valente, *Law in the Schools* (Columbus, Ohio: Charles E. Merrill, 1980), 20.

[9]Kern Alexander, *School Law* (St. Paul, Minn.: West Publishing, 1980), 3.

[10]For a discussion of delegation of lesiglative authority see: Leroy J. Peterson, Richard A. Rossmiller, and Marlin M. Volz, *The Law and Public School Operation* (New York: Harper and Row, 1978), 9-10.

[11]Bolmeier, 118.

[12]Peterson, Rossmiller, and Volz, 13.

[13]O'Conner v. Hendrick, 77 N.E. 612 (1906).

[14]Alexander, 106.

[15]363 F.2d 744 (5th Cir. 1966).

[16]363 F.2d 749 (5th Cir. 1966).

[17]Alexander, 109.

[18]David W. Louisell and Geoffrey C. Hazard, Jr., *Pleading and Procedure: State and Federal,* 3d ed. (Mineola, N.Y.: The Foundation Press, 1973), 15-16.

[19]Louisell and Hazard, 19.

[20]This section is based on David F. Rolewick, *A Short History of the Illinois Judicial Systems* (Springfield: Administrative Office of the Illinois Courts, 1976).

[21]This section is based on *Arizona Courts: 1981 Annual Judicial Report* (Phoenix: Arizona Supreme Court, 1982).

[22]William R. Hazard, "Courts in the Saddle: School Boards Out." *Phi Delta Kappan* (December 1974): 261.

[23]163 N.E.2d 89 (1959).

[24]163 N.E.2d 94. (1959).

[25]487 P.2d 1241 (1971).

[26]411 U.S.1 (1973).

[27]Percy E. Burrup and Vern Brimley, Jr., *Financing Education in a Climate of Change,* 3d ed. (Boston: Allyn and Bacon, 1982), 214-215, 221-223.

[28]131 Cal. Rptr. 854 (Cal. App. 1976).

[29]E. Edmund Reutter, Jr. and Robert R. Manilton, *The Law of Public Education* Second Edition (Mineola, New York: The Foundation Press, Inc., 1976), p. 11.

[30]Valente, p. 13.

[31]William R. Hazard and Victor G. Rosenblum, "Education, the Law, and Social Change," *Education and Urban Society,* 8 (May 1976): 259.

[32]Raphael D. Nystrand and W. Frederick Staub, "The Courts as Educational Policy Makers." In *The Courts and Education,* edited by Clifford P. Hooker. Seventy-Seventh Yearbook of the National Society for the Study of Education (Chicago: National Society for the Study of Education, 1978), p 45.

[33]Brown v. Board of Education, 347 U.S. 483 (1954).

[34]Ralph Stern, "The Law and Public Education: Projections for the 1980's," *Education and Urban Society,* 14 (February 1982): 229-234.

10

Experience is the name every one gives to their mistakes.

– Oscar Wilde

Financing the Schools

In the United States, education is big business. The cost of education, the largest item in the state-local government budget, is currently over $100 billion annually. One-fifth of the total population of the United States is involved in the education industry, either as students or as employees.

As with any enterprise, the financing of education consists of two dimensions: (1) the resource dimension, the sources of funds to support the enterprise; and (2) the allocation dimension, the ways in which funds are distributed among the various units of the enterprise. With respect to the resource dimension, a host of possibilities exists for generating revenue. In the businessworld, one enterprise might choose to generate all its revenue from sales; another from services; yet another from investments. The possibilities for financing education are also numerous. One state might choose to finance the entire cost of the educational program at the local level with the local property tax. Other states might pay the entire cost of supporting the schools at the state level with either a state income tax, a state sales tax, or a combination of taxes. In the same way that the sources of funds for business and education are varied, the range of allocation procedures is also varied and almost unlimited. States could allocate monies to local school districts, regardless of the wealth of the district or the type of student served, based on a flat grant per student in the district. Another of the possibilities for allocating funds would include the state's distribution of monies to a local school district based on the number of teachers in the district.

Consequently, there is a great diversity among the states in their school finance plans, with respect both to raising revenue and to allocation of it. Some states have no sales tax; others have no personal income tax; and still others have no corporate income tax or statewide property tax. Obviously, in each of these states the sources of funds for the support of education will be quite different. Even if two states were both using the same kinds of taxes, they might not be using them to the same extent. The sources of funds could also vary because of the level of support provided by either the local, state, or federal government. In a state where the responsibility for the support of education rests primarily on the local school district, the majority of the revenue supporting education would be generated by the property tax. In most states, this is the only tax the school district is allowed to levy. State allocation plans also vary, from full state funding to equalization formulas based on unweighted pupils, weighted pupils, teacher units, or other variables. State allocation formulas also vary from one legislative session to another as changes are made in the statutes.

Although the range of possible tax sources and allocation methods is in one sense unlimited, some proposals seem to be more realistic and equitable than others. For example, many states presently rely heavily on local support for the financing of the schools, in the form of a local property tax. However, any state plan that presumes significant increased reliance on the property tax is clearly being unrealistic in terms of public resistance to further property tax increases. Further, such a state would be making its financing system less equitable by a greater reliance on a tax that is generally considered the most inequitable of all major taxes. In this chapter the financing of education in terms of its two dimensions—the revenue dimension and the allocation dimension—with additional consideration given to the "school finance reform movement," and some future directions in school finance will be explored. The material presented should provide both prospective and present school administrators with the basic concepts and criteria necessary to discuss, compare, and evaluate state support programs.

The Federal-State-Local Partnership in Financing Education

The financial support for public schools comes from three major sources: federal, state, and local governments. For the most part, this partnership of federal, state, and local governments has worked well. As the data in Table 10-1 indicate, over the years there has been a shifting of responsibility for support of the schools from the local school district to what is now largely a state-local partnership. At the same time, the increasing inability of state and local governments to support certain recognized needy populations and needed programs has brought about increased federal support.

The Federal Role in Financing Education

As the data in Table 10-1 indicate, traditionally the federal government has played a limited role in the financing of education. The involvement of the federal government in education and the policy considerations related to that involvement beginning with the Northwest Ordinance and continuing through the Education Consolidation and Improvement Act of 1981 (ECIA) were discussed in Chapter 8.

The single largest increase in federal aid to education came with the passage of the Elementary and Secondary Education Act (ESEA)

TABLE 10-1 *Public Elementary and Secondary School Revenue by Government Source of Funds: Selected School Years 1919-20 to 1981-82*

School Year	Amount (millions)				Percentage Distribution			
	Total	Federal	State	Local	Total	Federal	State	Local
1919-20 . . .	$970.1	$2.4	$160.1	$807.6	100.0	0.3	16.5	83.2
1929-30 . . .	2,088.6	7.3	353.7	1,727.6	100.0	0.4	16.9	82.7
1933-34 . . .	1,810.7	21.5	423.2	1,365.9	100.0	1.2	23.4	75.4
1937-38 . . .	2,222.9	26.5	656.0	1,540.4	100.0	1.2	29.5	60.3
1941-42 . . .	2,416.6	34.3	760.0	1,622.3	100.0	1.4	31.5	67.1
1945-46 . . .	3,059.8	41.4	1,062.1	1,956.4	100.0	1.4	34.7	63.9
1949-50 . . .	5,437.0	155.8	2,165.7	3,115.5	100.0	2.9	39.8	57.3
1953-54 . . .	7,866.9	355.2	2,944.1	4,567.5	100.0	4.5	37.4	58.1
1955-56 . . .	9,686.7	441.4	3,828.9	5,416.4	100.0	4.6	39.5	55.9
1957-58 . . .	12,181.5	486.5	4,800.4	6,894.7	100.0	4.4	39.4	56.6
1959-60 . . .	14,746.6	651.6	5,768.0	8,326.9	100.0	4.4	39.1	56.5
1961-62 . . .	17,527.7	761.0	6,789.2	9,977.5	100.0	4.3	38.7	56.9
1963-64 . . .	20,420.0	865.8	8,113.9	11,440.3	100.0	4.2	39.3	56.3
1965-66 . . .	25,356.9	1,997.0	9,920.2	13,439.7	100.0	7.9	39.1	53.0
1967-68 . . .	31,903.1	2,806.5	12,275.5	16,821.1	100.0	8.8	38.5	52.7
1969-70 . . .	40,266.9	3,219.6	16.062.8	20,984.6	100.0	8.0	39.9	52.1
1971-72 . . .	50,003.7	4,468.0	19,133.3	26,402.4	100.0	8.9	38.3	52.8
1973-74 . . .	58,230.9	4,930.4	24,113.4	29,187.1	100.0	8.5	41.4	50.1
1975-76 . . .	71,206.1	6,318.3	31,776.1	33,111.6	100.0	8.9	44.6	46.5
1977-78 . . .	81,443.2	7,694.2	35,013.3	38,735.7	100.0	9.4	43.0	47.6
1978-79 . . .	88,057.0	8,643.0	40,245.9	39,168.1	100.0	9.8	45.7	44.5
1981-82 . . .	109,766.5	8,841.8	53,832.7	47,092.0	100.0	8.1	49.0	42.9

SOURCES: U.S. Department of Education, National Center for Education Statistics, *Digest of Educational Statistics, 1981;* and Education Commission of the States, using "Estimates of School Statistics, 1981-82," National Education Association.

in 1965. In 1964, federal funding for the support of elementary and secondary education was $897 million. In 1965-66, after passage of ESEA, it was almost $2 billion. Although the overall contribution of federal funds to the support of education may seem minor, in those states or districts with a high incidence of compensatory (Title I, ESEA) students or a heavy concentration of federal property (qualifying them for impact aid), a significant portion of the revenue comes from the federal government and federal aid is critical to the operation of the schools. The importance of federal aid to education is evidenced by the impact on states and school districts of the reduction in federal expenditures brought about by the Education Consolidation and Improvement Act of 1981 (ECIA).

Although many school districts experienced a real financial "pinch" as a result of the federal cut-back in spending, the actual nature of the federal involvement proposed by the ECIA is one which has been advanced by many educational organizations and school finance experts for years. That is, they have long advocated that federal aid should be in the form of general federal aid, or block grants, as provided for by chapter 2 of the ECIA, rather than the numerous categorical programs that have traditionally characterized federal aid and have been blamed for duplication of programs, a deluge of red tape, obstruction of state-local coordination, loss of local and state control, and distortion of educational emphasis. Many of these same experts who have supported the concept of general federal aid would not, however, support decreasing federal aid. In fact, pointing to the superior revenue-generating capacity of the federal government and its dependence on the income tax, which is considered the most progressive of the major taxes, experts suggest an even larger role for the federal government in the support of education. However, while no one can predict what the federal role will eventually become, limited and decreased federal aid seems to be the present reality.

The State-Local Role in Financing Education

Education is the responsibility of the state, but traditionally the states have relegated to the local school district the actual financing of education. Although state support for the public schools began in the early part of the nineteenth century, most states during that century exercised that responsibility primarily by authorizing local school districts to levy taxes for the support of the schools. The state funds were allocated on a school census basis, with little consideration for equalization or provision for a minimum program of education for all children. By 1890, 23.8 percent of total school support came from state revenues. During the period 1890 to 1930, this decreased to 17.3 percent. This decline in percentages was not due to decreasing state revenues but rather to large increases in local revenue, especially in the decade after World War I. This increase in local revenue was due largely to increasing public demand for universal secondary education.[1] The trends in state-local support since 1930 are shown in Table 10-1. As depicted here, until 1975-76 the local school districts supplied more than half of the revenues for the support of schools; and not until 1978-79 did the states supply a larger percentage of the revenue than the local school district. The developments in school financing theory that have led to the increased involvement by the states are discussed later in this chapter.

Tax Sources of School Revenues

The operation of the public schools relies primarily on revenues generated from taxation. In this section we will review the major tax sources used to support education, evaluate each of them on the basis of some of the most commonly accepted criteria of taxation, and discuss their potential in terms of generation of additional revenue for education.

Criteria for the Evaluation of Taxes

Several criteria have come to be generally accepted for evaluating tax structures. Most commonly mentioned as being most important by the National Education Finance Project are these criteria: (1) a tax should not cause economic distortions; (2) a tax should be equitable; (3) a tax should be collected easily and effectively; and (4) the revenue from a tax should be responsive to changing economic conditions.[2]

Economic Distortions. It is generally agreed that a tax should not bring about economic distortions by causing people to alter their economic behavior. This means, for example, that a tax should not distort consumer spending patterns in favor of one good or another; should not have a negative effect on the taxpayer's willingness to work; and should not affect decisions regarding the location of businesses or industries, or the choice of one means of production over the other. Any tax that causes persons to change their economic behavior to escape the tax will produce less revenue than otherwise could be obtained and will defeat the purpose of the tax.

Equity. The criterion that a tax should be equitable implies several things. First, it means that persons in relatively similar economic circumstances should be taxed equally. This is referred to as *equal treatment of equals*. Equity also implies that taxes should be based on the taxpayer's *ability to pay*. This means that the amount of tax paid by the taxpayer should be based on the taxpayer's income (salaries, wages, dividends, rental income, etc.), and that those with greater incomes should pay more tax dollars than those with lesser income. Equity also means, though this is perhaps less universally accepted, that the tax should be progressive relative to income, or at the very least proportional. A *progressive* tax is one in which both the amount of tax owed and the rate of the tax increase with income. Conversely, a *regressive* tax is one that takes a greater percentage of the income of low income taxpayers than of high income taxpayers. If the tax rate is the same percentage for all income groups, it is called *proportional.*

Ease and Effectiveness of Collection. A tax should be easily and effectively collected and not be easily avoided. This requires that the tax be collected with minimum costs to the taxpayer or the government. The percentage of the tax revenue that must be spent to collect the tax should be as small as possible. Ease and effectiveness of collection also implies that a tax should be both difficult to evade and without loopholes.

Responsiveness of Revenue. The criterion of responsiveness of revenue, sometimes referred to as revenue elasticity, implies that the revenue yield from a tax be responsive to changing economic conditions. That is, in periods of inflation, when government costs and expenditures are rising, the tax revenue by which activities are supported should also rise proportionately, preferably without raising tax rates.

These four criteria will now serve as the basis for our evaluation of the major tax sources which support education.

Property Tax

The property tax is the major source of revenue for the local school district and is thus the single most important tax supporting education. The property tax has a long history of usage in the United States, having been used since the early days of the Republic. However, whereas this form of taxation was well suited to a simple agricultural economy in which ownership of land was the major form of wealth, it can no longer adequately serve the complex needs of governments and the populations they serve. The property tax does rate well on the criterion of being a fairly stable tax in terms of predictability of revenue, although its revenue does not increase as rapidly as increases in the overall economy. It also is not an easy tax to evade and is the only tax that can be considered purely a "user charge" in that the revenue is generated locally and spent for local services. This is not true of sales tax or income tax revenue, where a particular locality may generate only one percent of total state revenue, but receive three percent of government services in terms of government dollars spent in or for the locality or its citizens. However, in spite of these few advantages, the property tax does suffer from some serious deficiencies that limit its potential to provide any increased revenue for the school.

First of all, the property tax creates economic distortions because it tends to discourage rehabilitation of deteriorating properties, especially in the central cities where renewal is most needed and property taxes are often higher. It can also cause economic distortion by affecting decisions by business and industries with regard to locations and plant sites. For example, in metropolitan areas that encompass numerous school districts and municipalities, property tax rates may be the key element in the decision of where to locate. The property tax is also distorting in that it does not bear equally on all businesses, but places a heavier burden per dollar of sales on those with disproportionate amounts of real property. For example, a fast food operation will normally require much less real estate to generate the same dollar of sales than will a warehouse.

The greatest failure of the property tax is on the criterion of equity. Because of differing assessment practices and lack of uniformity in evaluations, persons owning equivalent property may have different tax burdens; thus, there results unequal treatment of equals. The property tax is also judged inequitable because it does not distribute the tax burden according to ability to pay. Numerous studies have shown that ownership of property is not necessarily correlated with either income or wealth, the two best measures of taxpaying capacity or ability. This is exemplified by individuals whose retirement income may be half the preretirement income, but who, because they worked to pay off the mortgage for twenty or thirty years, have a house with the same or higher property tax bill after retirement as before retirement. This example also points out the regressiveness of the property tax. The property tax is considered to be a regressive tax because the poorer the household, the larger the share of its income is required to pay the tax. The reason for this is that poor people have to spend a larger portion of their income on housing than do wealthy people.

The property tax also does not rate well on the criterion of ease and effectiveness of collection. The variation in assessment practices previously mentioned is one problem. In addition, in many areas the tax collector is an elected official who may or may not have any knowledge or skill in the area. Too often the yield of the property tax will depend on the industriousness and integrity of the tax collector and/or assessor. Although many improvements in the administration of the property tax have taken place, such as computerization of assessments, poor and inequitable property tax administrative practices remain factors in the current opposition to the tax.

Sales Tax

The sales tax is the single most important tax for state governments. Since, as we have seen, states currently pay over one-half the cost of education, the state sales tax is the second most important tax supporting education. In 1982, forty-five states had statewide sales taxes with sales tax revenues constituting 31 percent of state tax revenues.[3] Many states exempt food from the sales tax base, and most exempt prescription drugs. Other states do not exempt items like food, but they do provide a credit against the state income tax liability for certain necessary items. A number of states also allow the use of the sales tax at the local level.

Measured against the four criteria for evaluating taxes, the sales tax rates fairly well. It does have the potential for causing economic distortions concerning the location of shopping centers and other large retail establishments. However, this potential is more of a factor with local sales taxes than with state sales taxes. In a state with a high sales tax, only shoppers living near the border and by a state with a low sales tax would find it worthwhile to make the interstate trip just to avoid a sales tax. Another potentially distorting effect of the sales tax comes when some goods are exempted from taxation, or when, as is customary, services such as dry cleaning, repairs, or hair care are tax exempt. In such cases consumers are encouraged to purchase the tax exempt goods or services. However, despite these effects, the distorting effects of the sales tax are minor compared to those of the property tax.

The extent to which the sales tax meets the criterion of equity depends primarily upon how the tax base is defined. If the tax is placed on all goods, it tends to place a disproportionate burden on the lowest income groups who must spend a large portion of their incomes on necessities. This tends to make the tax regressive and places the largest burden on those with the least ability to pay. If food is removed from the tax base, the sales tax becomes more nearly proportional. An alternative, allowing a credit against income tax liability for the sales tax paid on minimum necessary purchases, also removes much of the sales tax's regressive quality.

The sales tax is basically easier to administer and collect than the property tax, at least at the state level. It does not require any valuations, and is generally collected by the retailer according to actual sales figures, and then remitted to the government. In states where there are a number of exemptions, with fine lines of distinctions between taxable and exempt items (e.g., taxing all clothing except that for school-age children), the administration and collection are made more difficult. The primary difficulty in collection of the sales taxes arises with interstate sales, because a state cannot levy a tax on sales to be delivered outside the state. Often the state has difficulty collecting the tax on purchases made by its residents in another state. In many instances, it becomes almost impossible to enforce compliance.

The sales tax does have income elasticity in that the revenue derived from it does rise at about the same rate as does the rest of the economy. This elasticity becomes a defect during recessions, when sales tax revenues decrease as the economy slows down.

Income Taxes

As of 1982, the personal income tax was the second largest source of tax revenue for the state government (27 percent of state tax revenue), and the largest source of revenue for the federal government.[4] Only six states do not levy the personal income tax. However, the tax bases and the rate structures do vary widely among the states.

For all intents and purposes, a properly designed income tax at the state level should cause no economic distortions. The income tax also rates higher than any other tax on the criterion of equity. Income taxes are the only taxes directly related to the most generally accepted measure of taxpaying ability, the income of the taxpayer. The income tax is also the only major tax that can be considered to be progressive; not only do the actual tax dollars owed increase as income increases, but the percentage of income owed also increases. The income tax is also more equitable than other taxes because it can be adjusted through the use of credits and exemptions to take into account any special circumstances of the taxpayer such as number of dependents, illness, or moving expense.

The personal income tax is perhaps the easiest tax to collect as it is done through payroll deductions before the taxpayer gets the money. The use of computers has made tax evasion extremely difficult. State income taxes are relatively easy to administer because they rely heavily on federal Internal Revenue Service information and audit for control. Also, interstate collection of state income taxes does not present the same problem it does with the sales tax because the state of residence normally allows credit for the tax paid where the money is earned. Local income taxes do, however, present problems of interjurisdictional administration. Overall, the major problems related to the collection and administration of the income tax are the so-called loopholes that allow certain taxpayers opportunities for avoidance.

The personal income tax has a higher degree of revenue elasticity than any other tax. This can be considered both positive and negative. This allows the government to vary the rates from time to time to halt inflationary trends or to try to fight economic recessions. On the other hand, the elasticity of the income tax makes it a somewhat unstable source of revenue in periods of recession since the revenue derived from it declines at a faster rate than revenue from other tax sources.

In addition to levying a tax on personal incomes, both state and federal governments levy corporate income taxes. The corporate income tax is the second most productive tax for the federal government and the third most productive source (9.7 percent) of state revenue.[5] Forty-six states levy the corporate income tax. The rate structures vary from state to state. The state corporate income tax is primarily a means of guaranteeing that the state in which a business operates and which renders it services will receive some compensation.

In most respects an evaluation of the corporate income tax is comparable to that of the personal income tax. The corporate income tax is not likely to cause economic distortions unless the rate in one state is substantially higher than that of a neighboring state; even then, decisions about location are more likely to be influenced by factors related to sources of materials and labor than to a lower tax rate. The corporate tax structures are generally moderately progressive and can be equitably applied. Collection is fairly simple because, as in the case of the personal income tax, heavy reliance is made on federal returns and audits. Finally, although its revenue elasticity is not as high as that of the personal income tax, it is higher than for most other types of taxes.

Other Taxes

The only other taxes that contribute any significant amount of revenue to education are (1) excise taxes, (2) motor vehicle license taxes, (3) severance taxes on the output of minerals and oils, and (4) death and gift taxes. State excise taxes are primarily confined to motor fuel, liquor, and tobacco products (9.1 percent, 1.8 percent, and 2.7 percent of state tax revenues, respectively)[6] The tax on motor fuel, which is the third largest source of state tax revenue, is designated for highway construction and maintenance and cannot be used for financing education. Generally, excise taxes are not very equitable and are regressive. In addition they show very low revenue elasticity. However, excise taxes do have a certain amount of justification in that they are used to discourage the use of certain products (e.g., liquor and tobacco) or to regulate consumption of certain items (e.g., motor fuel). The other taxes—motor vehicle license, severance, and death and inheritance (3.6 percent, 3.0 percent, and 1.5 percent of state tax revenues, respectively)—together constitute a significant portion of state revenue, but have only limited potential for generating increased revenues for education.[7]

Potential for Additional Revenue

The discussion of the major taxes that support education made it clear that there are no major unused tax sources that can generate revenue for education. Though it is true that not all states are using every tax, for most states increased revenues must come from improving their existing tax structure rather than imposing new taxes. For example, the sales tax and the income tax structures could be improved so as to provide increased revenues. It has been suggested that all states could raise their sales tax rate to at least 5 percent, eliminate most exemptions, and include most services, and expand their auditing system, thereby increasing the yield of their sales tax significantly. Likewise, the state income tax structure could be improved if more progressive rates were imposed. However, there are limits to the potential revenue from the state income tax, given the already relatively high federal income tax.

Whereas the state tax and the income tax do offer some prospect for additional revenues, the same is not true for the property tax. As a means of increasing property tax revenue, there are proposals in several states to eliminate the property tax exemptions given churches, favored industries, and other institutions. Improved assessment practices could also improve the yield from the tax. At the same time that these efforts are underway, however, various measures which provide property tax relief are decreasing the yield from the tax. On balance, as was previously discussed, the property tax does not offer any promise for additional revenues to support education.

State Lotteries as a Revenue Source for Education

State lotteries are included in a discussion of revenue sources to support education because in many of the fifteen states where they currently exist or in the others when they have been proposed, increased revenues for education have been listed as one of their chief selling points. In fact, this was to be the major purpose of the New Hampshire lottery when it was introduced in 1964, the first modern lottery in the United States. Despite their billing, lotteries have done little to significantly increase revenues for education or to ease the overall tax burdens. In most states the lottery contributes less than two percent of the state's total revenue.[8] In addition, in some states where a certain percentage of lottery revenue was originally designated to go to education, this designation has been changed and education is no longer a major beneficiary of the lottery. In Arizona, for example, revenue from the lottery was originally scheduled to go into the state general fund which supports, among other things, education. However, after only six months the revenue from the lottery became earmarked for road construction.

Even if the lottery did produce significant revenues for education, a number of tax equity considerations would suggest that it not be used to generate increased revenues. Although there are those who would argue that the lottery revenues are not tax revenues, or at most constitute a "voluntary tax," the weight of expert opinion says that the revenue generated by the lottery is as much a tax as the excise tax on liquor or tobacco paid by those who "voluntarily" choose to drink or smoke. Numerous studies have shown the lottery to be a regressive source of revenue since each bet constitutes a larger proportion of the income of those with smaller incomes than those with larger incomes.[9] This situation is compounded by the fact that research also indicates that persons in higher income groups tend to play the lottery somewhat less, proportionately, than persons in other income groups, and that they are less likely to buy large numbers of tickets. In addition to its own regressive features, to suggest that the lottery be used to generate additional revenues for education is even "more objectionable in light of the fact that states appear to have adopted lotteries rather than implementing or expanding (progressive) income taxes."[10]

State Allocation Procedures

As previously mentioned, until the twentieth century the financing of education was considered an appropriate responsibility of the local district, with little or no assistance from the state. Beginning in the 1920s, school finance theorists began to draw attention to the inequities that existed within states as a result of such heavy reliance upon local wealth and local decision-making. Concepts such as a "foundation program" (under which the state guarantees a minimum educational program), a "percentage equalizing" approach (under which the state pays the local school district a larger percentage of locally determined expenditures in poorer districts than in wealthier districts), and "full state funding" were among the proposals advanced to provide greater equity in the funding of education. The intent of these early efforts was to provide state aid to local school districts in inverse relationship to local district wealth, so that poor districts would be compensated for their relative lack of property wealth. The dominant approach employed was the foundation plan.[11]

The development of the foundation program concept, which is generally considered the beginning of the modern approach to state equalization aid for education, is attributed to the work of George D. Strayer and Robert M. Haig. The Strayer-Haig model for "equalization of educational opportunity" included four provisions.

1. A local school tax in support of the satisfactory minimum offering would be levied in each district at a rate which would provide the necessary funds for that purpose in the richest district.

2. The richest district then might raise all of its school money by means of the local tax, assuming that a satisfactory tax, capable of being locally administered, could be devised.

3. Every other district could be permitted to levy a local tax at the same rate and apply the proceeds toward the cost of schools.

4. Since the rate is uniform, however, this tax would be sufficient to meet the costs only in the richest district, and the deficiencies would be made up by state subventions.[12]

Many states today base their state finance programs on the Strayer-Haig formula. The Strayer-Haig formula has three basic components: (1) a determination of how much money the school district would need to provide each student (weighted or unweighted) with the level of education guaranteed by the state foundation plan; (2) a determination of how much local revenue will be generated by a state-established uniform tax rate levied against the assessed valuation of property in the district; and (3) a determination of state aid obtained by finding the difference between the district's monetary need and the revenue generated by the required local tax. Initially, in many states a provision for local district add-on above the state guaranteed level, or "leeway" as it is sometimes called, was also a feature. However, this practice is becoming less common today because of its disequalizing features.

The work of Strayer and Haig in developing the foundation program concept of financing education was a major breakthrough in school finance theory and provided a way to remove some of the existing disparities in school district revenues and expenditures. Yet its rate of adoption was very slow.[13] Those states that did adopt some features of the model often compromised the strict application of its equalization objective. It proved difficult for states to overcome the longstanding tradition of flat grants, the desire of some districts to finance truly superior schools, and the reluctance of state officials to increase taxes to finance the program. In most states the foundation plan merely provided the poorest districts with a basic educational program that was well below that which many districts willingly or easily supported. The local leeway that allowed districts to supplement the foundation support level resulted in inequities as wealthy districts, with minimal effort, exceeded their poorer neighbors.[14] However, in spite of the common inequities in the tax rates, revenues, and expenditures, this situation prevailed until the school finance reform movement of the 1970s brought about the needed change.

Background for Reform

Analyzing the background of a reform often involves some consideration of cause. The identification of the precise time when a movement, including the school finance reform movement, began is virtually impossible. One appropriate place to begin might be with the 1954 and 1955 United States Supreme Court decisions in *Brown v. Board of Education.* As stated in previous chapters, *Brown* dealt with desegregation and initially had little direct bearing on school finance. Nevertheless, what *Brown* did that eventually influenced school finance policy was to increase national consciousness and concern regarding inequalities, in the schools in expenditures of available revenues, and in communities in terms of tax rates.[15] As an example of the inequalities that existed at the time of *Brown,* in one county in Iowa the local tax rate varied from slightly over 2 mills in the wealthiest district, to 154 mills in the poorest district.[16]

Shortly after *Brown* a number of authors and social scientists began to describe the inequities that existed in the nation's schools. In 1961 James Bryant Conant published his *Slums and Suburbs,* which described the inequalities that existed between the central city schools and the schools in suburbia.[17] In the same year, Patricia Sexton's *Education and Income* documented the intradistrict spending disparities in a large eastern city and the educational advantages these dollars represented.[18] Sexton found that the schools which served the children of higher income parents had such obvious educational advantages as lower pupil-teacher ratios, better facilities, and better trained teachers.

In 1967, the first suggestion that the courts might be the ones to bring about the needed reform by declaring state financing systems unconstitutional was made by Arthur Wise in his volume, *Rich Schools, Poor Schools.*[19] Wise contended that school finance systems which make the amount of money spent on the education of students primarily dependent upon the wealth of the area in which they live, do not form a constitutionally reasonable relationship to the state's purpose in providing education. Wise concluded that if the courts would review state finance systems using the standard that equality of opportunity exists when the child's education does not depend upon either parents' wealth or location within the state, many systems might be declared unconstitutional.

At the same time that Wise was publishing his potential legal remedies for the disparities that were characteristic of school financing, a group of lawyers (John E. Coons, William H. Clune III, and Stephen D. Sugarman) was reaching a similar conclusion regarding the use of courts to try to rectify a situation that legislatures seemed unwilling to tackle. In their *Private Wealth and Public Education,* Coons, Clune, and Sugarman suggest what became known as the principle of fiscal neutrality: the quality of public eduation may not be a function of wealth other than the total wealth of the state.[20] Although this statement is very similar to that proposed earlier by Wise, the authors extend their argument to the suggestion that the attack on school finance plans would be most successful if based on the grounds of a denial of equal protection.

The positive impact of the scholarly work of Wise, Coons, Clune, Sugarman, and the many others concerned with the state of school finance was soon evidenced by the court decision in *Serrano* v. *Priest* in 1971 and the host of similar decisions that followed in other states.[21]

School Finance Reform in the 1970s

At the time that *Serrano* was brought to court in California,

> educational expenditures per person in California ranged from $274 in one district to $1,710 in another, a ratio of 1 to 6.2. In the same year, two districts in the same county (Beverly Hills and Baldwin Park) expended $1,223 and $577 per pupil. This inequity was due to the difference in the assessed valuation of property per pupil to be educated ($50,885 in Beverly Hills and $3,706 in Baldwin Park—a ratio of nearly 14 to 1). The taxpayers in Baldwin Park paid a school tax of 54.8 mills ($5.48 per $100 of assessed valuation) while those in Beverly Hills paid school taxes of only 23.8 mills ($2.38 per $100 of assessed valuation). Thus, a tax effort in the poorer district of twice that in the wealthier district resulted in school expenditures of only 47 percent of that in the wealthier district.[22]

The situation in California was by no means an isolated example. The disparities that led to the suit in California could have been duplicated in nearly every state. In New York, for example, in 1969–70, 15,115 classrooms had expenditures per classroom of less than $12,000 while 37,442 classrooms had expenditures in excess of $24,000.[23]

In *Serrano* the California Supreme Court focused on questions related to whether education was a fundamental interest guaranteed by the Constitution, thus requiring the more stringent "strict scrutiny" standard of judicial review; whether the wealth of a school district, when it is a determinant of educational expenditures, is an impermissible "suspect classification"; and whether the state could show a compelling state interest to support the present financing system. In a six-to-one decision the court declared the state school financing system to be unconstitutional. The rationale of the court's decision was summarized by the court as follows:

The California public school financing system . . . since it
deals ultimately with education, obviously touches upon a
fundamental interest . . . this system conditions the full
entitlement to such interest on wealth, classifies its
recipients on the basis of their collective affluence and
makes the quality of a child's education depend upon the
resources of his school district and ultimately upon the
pocketbook of his parents. We find that such financing
systems as presently constituted is not necessary to the
attainment of any compelling state interest. Since it does
not withstand the requisite "strict scrutiny," it denies to
the plantiffs and others similarly situated the equal
protection of the laws.[24]

The 1971 *Serrano* decision was the result of a demurrer hearing
whereby the California Supreme Court reversed the decision of the lower
court in dismissing the case and sent the case back to the lower court
for trial. In 1974 the trial court found the California system of school
finance to be in violation of the equal protection of the California Constitution and ordered the state to provide a more equalized system by
August, 1980. On December 30, 1976, the California Supreme Court
affirmed the decision of the trial court.[25]

In the meantime, however, the original *Serrano* decision proved
to be one breakthrough for those advocating school finance reform. Only six weeks after *Serrano,* the state of Minnesota also had its financing
system declared unconstitutional on basically the same grounds and
against the same arguments as in *Serrano.* The court in *Van Dusartz* v.
Hatfield concluded that any "system of public school financing which
makes spending per pupil a function of the school district's wealth violates
the equal protection guarantee of the Fourteenth Amendment."[26]

In late 1971, Texas became the third state to have its system of
financing education declared unconstitutional. The federal district court
in *Rodriguez* went further than the courts in California and Minnesota
and said that "the state may adopt the financial scheme desired so long
as the variations in wealth among the governmentally chosen units do
not affect spending for the education of any child," but if the state legislature did not restructure its financing within two years, the court would
"take such further steps as may be necessary to implement both the purpose and spirit of this order."[27]

In January, 1972, the New Jersey Superior Court of Hudson County declared that state's school financing system to be unconstitutional.
And, in spite of the United States Supreme Court reversal of *Rodriguez*[28]
in March of 1972, the New Jersey Supreme Court in April, 1972, in
Robinson v. *Cahill* upheld the lower court decision and held that New
Jersey's school financing system violated that provision of the state
constitution which required the legislature to provide a "thorough and
efficient system of free public schools."[29] The court gave the legislature
until January, 1975, to approve a plan which would be less dependent
upon the local property tax. Finally, after three years of heated discussion, more litigation, and the unusual distinction of being the only state
in history to have its entire school system closed by the courts, the legis-

lature under duress passed the state's first income tax and thereby generated the revenue to finance a state support program acceptable to the court.

As discussed in chapter 9, the reversal of *Rodriguez* did not have the detrimental effect on the school finance reform movement that many originally feared. It did force school finance reform litigants out of the federal courts and back into the state courts and reinforced the traditional position that the state is preeminent in matters of education. In retrospect, *Rodriguez* may have served a very useful function by blocking a facile federal solution to a quite complex problem, the origins of which are to be found in state capitals.[30] The rationale of the *Rodriguez* decision was indeed adopted by the courts in states, such as Ohio, Oregon, and Idaho, when the constitutionality of the state school financing system was upheld. But in the majority of court decisions in the 1970s the *Serrano* ruling was the one that was followed.

Ultimately, however, the importance of all this litigation lies not in an account of the cases that were won or lost, but in the impact that this increased awareness of inequalities had upon the direction of school finance. The progress made in the courts served both to threaten and to inspire numerous other states to revise their school finance programs to incorporate the concepts declared in *Serrano* and its progeny. Whether inspired by court action or as the result of educational, social, economic, or political pressures, over half the states have now enacted reforms in their school financing systems designed to bring increased equity to the funding of the elementary and secondary schools of the state.

Post-Serrano School Finance Systems

According to the Education Commission of the States (ECS),[31] several major themes characterize the numerous and different school finance reforms enacted during the 1970s. Among those enumerated by the ECS are: (1) strengthened state general aid programs; (2) increased state aid; (3) increased equity; (4) increased attention to special student needs; (5) increased attention to special district needs; and (6) tax and spending limitations. These themes provide the framework for the discussion that follows and also provide a view of the current "state of the art" of school finance.

Strengthened State Aid Programs. Generally, throughout the states, state aid formulas have been broadened and strengthened to provide greater equalization. That is, formulas provide that poorer districts with low property wealth per pupil receive more state aid than richer districts with greater property wealth per pupil. According to the ECS, three types of formulas have been used in the efforts to increase equalization.[32] The most common has been what could be considered essentially a Strayer-Haig formula, but with a higher state support level. Under these plans, as with all Strayer-Haig formulas, the state guarantees a minimum level of revenue per pupil and the district may supplement that level. As a result of the school finance reform efforts, this operates differently than in the past in that the state support level often is now so high that the local school district is not required to supplement the program very much in order to meet the desired expenditure level. Another way in which present Strayer-Haig-type formulas operate differently from earlier models is that now most states limit the amount of leeway, or supplement, that can be added to the state support level. This reduces the opportunities for increasing expenditure disparities that existed with the previous formulas.

A second type of formula by which a number of states have approached the task of equalization is one designed to reward equal local effort with equal revenues per pupil. These plans have been entitled, variously, "district power equalization," "guaranteed tax base," "guaranteed yield resource equalizer," or "percentage equalizer." The most common of these types of formulas is district power equalization (DPE). The "power" that a district power equalizing formula equalizes is the financial power of a school district to generate revenues for the support of education, insofar as that power is expressed in the levying of a local school tax rate. "By definition, DPE refers to the principle that each local district mill levy should produce the same number of dollars of total school revenue per mill per weighted student in every district, and the last mill to be levied should produce the same total funds as the first one."[32] In most states DPE works as follows: (1) the state legislature establishes a schedule under which local tax rates are related to a set of expenditure levels per student; (2) the district chooses a particular level of expenditure per student for its schools; (3) associated with that level of expenditure is a required local tax rate; (4) the state provides the difference between the yield of the required local tax and the desired expenditure level. Unlike a Strayer-Haig formula, where the state sets the spending level and required tax rate, DPE programs are based on spending and taxing decisions made at the local level. The potential this creates for wide variations in spending is one of the major concerns with this type of formula.

A simplified example of how a power equalizing program might operate can be given based on the state schedule shown in Table 10-2. Suppose that three districts, A, B, and C, with assessed valuations of

TABLE 10-2   *Illustration of District Power Equalizing Schedule*

Local Tax Rate Required (per $100 of assessed valuation)	Expenditure Per Pupil
$	
3.00 (minimum)	$1000 (minimum)
3.50	1075
4.00	1150
4.50	1225
5.00	1300
5.50	1375
6.00	1450
6.50-----state "appropriate" level------------------	1525-----------------
7.00	1575
7.50	1625
8.00	1675
8.50	1725
9.00	1775

$10,000 per pupil, $20,000 per pupil, and $30,000 per pupil respectively, all choose the expenditure level of $1,300 per pupil. According to the schedule shown in Table 10-2, for an expenditure level of $1,300 the state requires that the local district levy a tax rate of $5.00 per $100 of assessed valuation. Multiplying the tax rate of $5.00 per $100 of assessed valuation by the assessed valuations of each of the districts indicates that District A would generate $500 in revenue per pupil, District B, $1,000, and District C, $1,500. Each of these districts would now receive equalization aid from the state that would represent the difference between the revenue generated locally and the chosen expenditure level of $1,300. Thus, District A receives $800 per pupil in state aid, District B receives $300 per pupil, and District C receives no state aid. In fact, according to some DPE proposals, the $200 per pupil difference between what District C generates and the $1,300 per pupil expenditure level would be "recaptured" by the state for redistribution to poorer districts.[33]

As shown in Table 10-2, DPE schedules normally have both a minimum school expenditure level and a minimum school tax rate. This insures that all students have at least a state-established adequate provision. It also insures that residents of very wealthy districts do not opt for very low tax rates for the public schools which are attended by the poorer residents of the district while their own children attend private schools. Upper limits of expenditures are also normally established for district power equalizing proposals. This insures that there will not be an excessive drain on the state treasury and that frivolous spending will not be encouraged. The schedule in Table 10-2 also indicates that there is a *kink* at a tax rate of $6.50 and an expenditure level of $1,525. Below this point every $0.50 increase in the tax rate increased expenditures per pupil by $75. Above this point every $0.50 increase in the tax rate increases expenditures by only $50. The state in effect has established $1,525 as an appropriate sum to provide a good education to the typical child in the typical district and is attempting to curb overspending.[34]

The third type of formula which the ECS refers to as being used to enhance equalization goals combines a higher level foundation program with a power equalizing component. The power equalizing component operates on top of the foundation program so that above the state support level districts are guaranteed similar revenues per pupil at similar tax rates.[35]

Increased State Aid. Throughout the 1970s, as a result of all these efforts to strengthen state general aid formulas, state funding consistently increased. As the data in Table 10-1 show, between 1969 and 1979 expenditure for elementary and secondary education more than doubled. However, there is increasing concern that education in the decade of the 1980s will not be able to match the fiscal gains in the 1970s. The nation's mood is one of decreasing government expenditures and taxes, not of supporting increases. In fact, estimates by the National Education Association indicate that revenues for public schools have actually decreased in real terms in the beginning of the 1980s. This is perhaps not surprising given cutbacks in government education spending, especially at the national level.[36]

Increased Equity. The school finance reforms of the 1970s have resulted in increased equity in state school finance structures. The concept of equity in school finance structures implies that there is fairness in the ways funds are allocated among school districts and students, as well as fairness in the tax structures which support education. As a result of the interaction between tax and expenditure limitation efforts and school finance reform efforts, increased equity has been achieved on both these fronts. The significant increases in educational expenditures previously mentioned have provided for significant expansion of the educational program for all children, especially the programs for special pupil populations. In addition, much progress has been made in reducing expenditure disparities within states and in breaking the link between educational opportunity and school district wealth. At the same time, tax reform efforts have brought about property tax relief and reform, and have resulted in more progressive state and local tax structures.[37]

Increased Attention to Special Student Needs. Educators have long accepted that certain children have needs requiring special instruction and that special programs normally cost more to operate than the typical elementary and secondary instructional programs. State aid programs traditionally have not compensated districts for the incidence of these "special" students, even though the incidence of such children is different among school districts and creates unusual expenditures for circumstances beyond the district's control. During the 1970s, however, states began to significantly expand their role in providing for these high cost programs by increasing the number of programs they support and the level of support for such programs. The program areas that seemed of the greatest concern and received the greatest attention were: (1) special education for handicapped children; (2) compensatory education for socioeconomically or educationally disadvantaged students, and (3) bilingual education for students with limited English language skills.

In addition to the significant federal aid provided by Public Law 94-142, the Education for All Handicapped Children Act, all states mandate service for handicapped children and all states provide funding for special education programs. One method commonly used in state allocation programs to provide for the varying costs of special education programs is the technique of "weighting" pupils, teachers, or classrooms. The weighting concept is based on the assumption that pupil-teacher ratios are smaller and that operating and capital outlay costs are higher for special education programs. Under the typical weighted pupil program, for example, the weight of 1.00 is assigned to regular elementary programs. Other weights are then expressed in relation to the cost of educating a child in a given program as compared to the cost of educating the regular elementary pupil. If it is found that the cost of educating an exceptional pupil in a given program is four times the cost per pupil in the regular elementary program, then the full-time students in the special program are given a weight of 4.00. Students in classes or programs that are not full time are prorated according to the time spent in various classes or programs and the weights assigned to each. Table 10-3 presents the weights used by the state of Florida in 1982-83 for allocation of state foundation program funds for special education and for K-12 vocational-technical education.

TABLE 10-3 *Weights Used By Florida's Department of Education in 1982-83 for Allocation of State Foundation Program Funds for Special and K-12 Vocational-Technical Education*

	Weighting Per Equivalent Full-Time Pupil
I. Special Education programs:	
1. Educable mentally retarded	2.149
2. Trainable mentally retarded	2.832
3. Physically handicapped	3.472
4. Physical and occupational therapy (part-time)	6.674
5. Speech and hearing therapy (part-time)	6.870
6. Deaf	3.835
7. Visually handicapped (part-time)	11.393
8. Visually handicapped	4.248
9. Emotionally disturbed (part-time)	5.094
10. Emotionally disturbed	3.242
11. Specific learning disability (part-time)	4.391
12. Specific learning disability	2.347
13. Hospital and homebound (part-time)	13.295
14. Profoundly handicapped	4.843
II. Vocational-Technical programs (K-12):	
1. Agriculture	1.991
2. Business and office	1.475
3. Distributive	1.414
4. Diversified	1.381
5. Health	1.967
6. Public service	1.975
7. Home economics	1.588
8. Technical, trade, industrial	2.013
9. Exploratory	1.390

A second category of special student need being increasingly addressed by state aid plans, particularly those of the states in northeast and central regions, as well as by the federal government, is the perceived need of low-income, neglected and delinquent, handicapped, and migrant students for compensatory educational programs. Through the use of weightings, flat grants, and project grants, states provide additional funds to districts on the basis of the number of low-income or educationally disadvantaged students. The state programs supplement the federal Education Consolidation and Improvement Act Chapter I program and generally channel funds to the same type of students and provide similar services as are provided in Chapter I programs.[38] Between 1970-71 and 1978-79, state aid for compensatory education grew by about 226 percent.[39]

The final category of special student need, which has increasingly become the concern of those seeking to improve the equity of school finance structures, is the need to provide for those students with limited English language ability. The growth of state bilingual education programs has occurred as a result of federal initiatives in this area. Court action, and specifically the United States Supreme Court decision in *Lau* v. *Nichols,* also spurred a number of states to enact legislation providing for bilingual education.[40] As of 1982, thirty states had enacted legislation either mandating or permitting bilingual education. Monies are allocated to school districts using a variety of methods including weights, flat grants, reimbursement for excess costs, and project grants.[41]

Other types of weightings are used in various other states. For example, some states weight secondary pupils more than elementary pupils on the assumption that at the secondary level there are more smaller classes, instructional materials and equipment are more expensive, and student activities and related programs create additional costs. However, the "validity of the assumption that secondary school pupils should have a weighting when compared with elementary pupils is seriously questioned."[42] And such a weighting is not widely advocated. A final area gaining increasing support is the weighting of vocational-technical programs. The rationale for these weightings is much the same as for those of special education. Pupil-teacher ratios must be smaller, and operating and capital outlay costs are higher. Increasingly states are adopting some form of vocational-technical weighting. Table 10-3 includes the 1982-83 vocational-technical weights used by the state of Florida.

Increased Attention to Special District Needs. In addition to the increased concern and attention given to special needs of students, attention is being given more recently to the special needs or characteristics of school districts that would warrant special consideration in state aid provisions. These special needs relate to several areas, including: (1) sparsity factors; (2) "municipal overburden" or density factors; (3) cost-of-living differentials; and (4) teacher experience and qualification considerations.

The excess costs associated with the operation of small schools have long been recognized and provided for by what have traditionally been rural dominated legislatures. The particular method used to accommodate the sparsity of pupils in rural areas may vary from state to state, but the results are much the same. "Typically, the process used involves weighting such pupils in the finance formula so as to require the state to pay its proportionate share of the higher cost involved in the education of pupils in small groups."[43] In Arizona, for example, in 1982-83 the per pupil support level weight for elementary districts of less than 100 students was 1.390; for districts with a student count of 101-499, the support level weight was 1.274; and for districts with a student count of 500 or above, the weight was 1.158. While this sort of manipulation may appear unnecessary to maintain equality, in a state with a number of small schools, it is "an important factor in maintaining harmony and goodwill among school boards and administrators who know the size and funding of their neighboring schools."[44]

While the sparsity factor has long been a part of state aid formulas, another kind of need related to size—that of density or "municipal overburden"—has gained only limited acceptance. Even most of the legislative reforms that have been enacted post-*Serrano* have failed to recognize the financial problems facing central city school systems which stem from higher costs for both education and for other public services. Large city school systems not only tend to have a high proportion of those types of students requiring more educational resources than the average (e.g., the handicapped, the educationally disadvantaged, and students with limited English language skills); also because of higher prices and higher wage rates they must spend more per pupil than rural or suburban districts to provide comparable education programs. At the same time, the schools must compete with such noneducation services as welfare and police protection for the dwindling of tax revenues brought about by the movement of families and businesses to the suburbs. The lower court decision in *Board of Education of Levittown* v. *Nyquist*,[45] which agreed with the municipal overburden argument of New York's large cities, attracted national attention and has served to advance the recognition of some urban or density factor in school aid formulas. Although this decision was overturned by the New York State Court of Appeals, there is no doubt that the fight for recognition of the municipal overburden problem will continue in other state courts and state legislatures.

As was pointed out by the large city districts in New York in the *Levittown* v. *Nyquist* case, the cost of living, or more directly, the cost of education, varies, in some cases rather dramatically, among school districts in a state. That is, while the cost of a given level of education may be one amount in the average school district in a state, in certain districts it may be considerably more and in others somewhat less. In the past few years there has been increasing interest in developing indices that could be used in state aid formulas to account for these cost differences. As of 1982, only the state of Florida uses a cost-of-living adjustment in the distribution of state aid to local school districts. A district in Florida can receive anywhere from 94 to 107 percent of its calculated basic support program depending on how much the district's cost of living has been found to be above or below the state average cost of living. Although Florida is the only state using a cost-of-living adjustment per se, those states which have adopted measures which attempt to address the concerns of urban districts have attacked at least a part of the same problem.

Although student populations are predicted to increase in the mid-1980s, the decline in student populations in the last decade has resulted in a reduced demand for new teachers. Concomitantly, the demand for increased quality in education has been translated in part to teachers with higher levels of training. The result of these two trends is a teaching force that is generally older, has more teaching experience, and has higher levels of educational attainment. Since most school district salary schedules are based on teacher experience and qualifications, this teaching force has become increasingly expensive. This is especially true for urban districts where teacher turnover rates are traditionally lower and where teachers generally have higher degrees.

A number of states do have provisions in their state aid programs for weighting or consideration of teacher experience or training, or both. This provision is often in the form of a teacher index that relates the average teacher experience or training level in each district to the state average, and gives additional funds to districts above the state average.

Tax and Spending Limitations. The final theme characterizing the school finance reform era has been the passage of state tax and/or spending limitations. The successful passage of California's Proposition 13 in June, 1978, heralded in an era of what has been called "tax revolt." After the passage of Proposition 13, tax or spending limitations were initiated in over half the states. The majority of these were similar to Proposition 13, seeking to limit the level of property taxation or the effects of property taxes. These actions ranged from homeowners' rebates to limited relief for the elderly, disabled, or economically disadvantaged. In numerous other states, such action reduced income taxes and sales taxes, either through rate reductions or through increased deductions or exemptions. In addition to these measures directed at limiting taxes, nine states passed spending limits for state and local governments. These efforts aimed at curtailing the growth of government expenditures by placing caps on state expenditure increases, or by limiting increases in state spending to increases in personal income.

The impact of these tax and spending limitations on the schools has been mixed. The reduction in the use of the local property tax has meant that the state's share of the financing of education has necessarily risen. Since state taxes are more progressive than the property tax this has made the overall tax structure which supports education more progressive. Greater reliance on state revenues has also enabled the state to bring about great equalization in per pupil expenditures. Both of these results of tax limitations can be considered positive in that they have brought greater equity to school financing systems. On the other hand, the limitations that have been placed on government spending have severely constrained government efforts to finance additional reform programs. It is anticipated that several states will experience severe fiscal pressures as a result of the passage of massive tax and/or expenditure limitations.

Determining the Best Finance Plan

Although determination of what would be the best school finance plan for any one state depends to a large degree on the values and goals of the citizenry, there have evolved over the years some principles which characterize good school finance systems. These include, but are not limited to, the following:

1. *Adequacy:* A school finance plan should provide for an adequate program of education for every public school student in the state.
2. *Fiscal neutrality:* School finance programs should be developed so that per pupil expenditures are not a function of school district wealth.
3. *Equality of educational opportunity:* The school finance plan should provide each child equal access to an instructional program suited to his or her own potential and such programs should be of similar quality. This does not mean equal expenditures per pupil or per program; it means only that the school finance program should not give preferential treatment to any group(s) of students.[46]
4. *Taxpayer equity:* The school finance program should be financed by an equitable tax system.

5. *Efficiency:* The state school finance program should promote efficiency in the operation of local educational programs.
6. *Cost variations:* The school finance program should provide for all justified cost variations resulting from special characteristics of students or districts.
7. *Simplicity:* The school finance formula should be as simple as possible so as to facilitate easy understanding and application.
8. *Local Control:* The school finance plan shall preserve local control of education and promote initiative for improvement, leadership, and responsibility at the local level.

Although some of these principles may seem incompatible with others, the development and implementation of any state school finance plan based on just one or two of these principles would ultimately lead to chaos. Instead, the state finance plan should be based on balanced judgment. Alexis de Tocqueville, the distinguished commentator on American democracy, although obsessed with the principle of equality, recognized the necessity of balancing many competing forces and principles in making decisions to resolve human problems. The same balance is necessary in designing programs for school finance.[47]

Public Funds and Nonpublic Schools

The question of whether public aid should be given to nonpublic schools is a matter of much debate. Such aid to nonpublic schools is not a new concept. The federal government provides a wide range of general and special financial aid to nonpublic schools ranging from school lunches to psychological services. Many of these services are provided under the Elementary and Secondary Education Act of 1965, as amended to date. Many states also provide some assistance to nonpublic schools in a variety of forms including the transportation of pupils, the provision of textbooks, and the provision of diagnostic, remedial, and therapeutic services.

The controversy surrounding public aid to nonpublic schools has generally not surrounded the provision of the above-mentioned services, but has focused on attempts to provide more direct financial aid to the parents of students who attend nonpublic schools. These attempts by states have primarily taken the form of tuition reimbursements, tax credits for tuition expenses, and, more recently, educational vouchers. The United States Supreme Court has consistently held tuition reimbursement plans unconstitutional. It has also held state tax credit and tax deduction proposals unconstitutional, except in those instances where the particular tax deduction was available to parents of public as well as nonpublic school children. For example, in the 1983 United States Supreme Court decision in *Muller* v. *Allen*[48] the high court held that by offering tax deductions for tuition, textbook, and transportation costs to parents of public school children as well as parents of private school children the state avoided what might otherwise be considered an unconstitutional promotion of religion. Attempts have also been made from time to time to get the federal government to provide for tax credits against the taxpayer's federal income tax liabilitiy. Although all such proposals have been defeated to date, they will undoubtedly continue to be introduced.

The arguments in support of public aid to nonpublic schools are numerous. One very real argument is that nonpublic schools save the taxpayers money. Approximately 11 percent of the total elementary and secondary school enrollment is enrolled in private schools.[49] If the private school system were to collapse, a significant financial burden would be placed on public educational systems. The financial impact would be greater in the central cities where private school enrollments are highest. Unfortunately, the districts of central cities are the ones already hardest hit by financial problems related to municipal overburden and eroding tax bases.

A second major argument by those who support public aid for nonpublic schools is that parents who send their children to such schools are paying double. That is, they are required to pay the taxes that support the public schools, and they pay tuition to the nonpublic schools.

The case against public aid to nonpublic schools also rests on at least two major arguments. The first of these is simply that such aid violates the First Amendment provision that "Congress shall make no law respecting an establishment of religion." The second argument is that nonpublic schools, because of their particular emphasis on religion, ethnicity, or socioeconomic status perpetuate a divisiveness that is the opposite of the cultural pluralism and values transmission that are goals of the public schools. A corollary to this argument is that nonpublic schools tend to discriminate on the basis of religion and/or race.

Voucher Proposals

There remains one other proposal by which nonpublic school supporters have attempted to gain public financial support: voucher proposals. Although numerous voucher proposals have been made over the past two decades, the most common is patterned after that advocated in 1955 by Professor Milton Friedman, the Nobel Prize-winning economist of the University of Chicago. Friedman and others who support voucher plans maintain that vouchers are the best way to provide parents with real choice in the education of their children, and at the same time promote efficiency by subjecting schools to the competition of the market place. Friedman's original voucher plan, which allowed parents to add to the voucher given by the school district to send their children to more expensive schools or to purchase additional educational services has not received acceptance from either school finance experts or the general public because it violates the principle of equity and makes the quality of a child's education even more dependent upon the wealth of the child's parents and neighbors.

By the mid-1960s, however, a number of "regulated vouchers" had been proposed that were intended to provide parents with greater choice in education while reducing the inequities of the original Friedman proposal.[50] One of the more highly publicized of these proposals is the "family power equalizing" (FPE) plan developed by John Coons and Stephen Sugarman of the University of California at Berkeley. Unlike the Friedman proposal, FPE does not allow any parental add-on. In addition, local taxation for schools would be abolished and the quality of education would thus no longer be a function of either parental wealth or district wealth. According to FPE, families select a school for their child from among schools of varying per-pupil expenditure levels.

Depending on the level of school chosen, the parent would pay a school tax. The amount of the tax would be progressive relative to income. For example, suppose parents have a taxable income of $20,000. If they decide to send their child to the lowest expenditure-category school, their school tax might be equal to, say, 2 percent of their taxable income ($400). If they choose the highest expenditure level, their tax might be at the rate of 4.5 percent or $900. If a second family has a taxable income of $50,000 and choose the lowest expenditure school, they may pay a school tax of three percent, or $1500. For the highest expenditure schools they would pay a tax of 7 percent ($3,500). In this sense family power equalizing works like district power equalizing where the district's share of expenditures per pupil was dependent upon the wealth of the district.

In 1979, Coons and Sugarman attempted to get an initiative on the 1980 ballot in California that would have amended the California constitution and transformed the entire state into a voucher system. "The complexity of the theoretical system" with its reversal of traditional philosophy of public school organization and administration made the proposal too radical for people to understand[51] or accept and resulted in a failure to gain the requisite number of signatures to be placed on the ballot. However, like tuition tax credit advocates, Coons and Sugarman plan to try their voucher proposal again in California; it will undoubtedly be raised in other states also.[52]

Future Directions in School Finance

The school finance reform efforts of recent years have brought significantly increased equity to the educational system of the United States. In fact, "the progress of school finance improvement has been little short of phenomenal."[53] Yet much remains to be done. Although a great number of states have enacted noteworthy school finance reforms, there remain state programs that have yet to embody the principles of current educational finance theory. Approximately one-third of the states still allocate some state aid on the basis of flat grants unrelated to district wealth or basic support programs. These and other allocation methods practiced among the states continue to discriminate against poor districts and fail to break the nexus between wealth and educational opportunity. Tax structures remain that generate insufficient revenue to fund an adequate program or which are inequitable.

The future of school finance at this time is somewhat uncertain. With the continued restrictions placed on the use of the property tax, and already high sales taxes and income taxes in some states, it is unclear what tax sources will be used to support education. It is also uncertain how or if states will make up for the loss in federal dollars at the same time they must replace local property tax dollars. What does seem to be clear, however, is that the gains of the 1970s will be jeopardized in the decades ahead if current trends in state and local spending for education continue. In the 1981–82 school year, the growth in state revenues for education was cut in half, while the growth in local tax revenues doubled. For example, during the six years preceding the 1981–82 school year, state revenues increased an average of 11 percent each year, and local revenues increased an average of 6 percent yearly. During the 1981–82 school year, these rates reversed: state revenues increased approximately 6 percent, and local revenues increased about 12 percent over the previous year. If this trend continues, the results could be a reduction of the equity gains of the school finance reform movement, and a reversal in the trend of property tax reductions.[54] It is also certain, regardless of the level or service of funding, that school finance reform will be an ongoing process.

References

[1]Roe L. Johns. "The Development of State Support for the Public Schools," in *Status and Impact of Educational Finance Programs,* edited by Roe L. Johns, Kern Alexander, and Dewey H. Stollar (Gainesville, Fla.: National Educational Finance Project, 1971), 1–2, 16.

[2]The discussion of the criteria used to evaluate taxes is based upon the work of John F. Due, "Alternative Tax Sources for Education," *Economic Factors Affecting the Financing of Education* edited by Roe L. Johns, Irving J. Goffman, Kern Alexander, and Dewey H. Stollar (Gainesville, Fla.: National Education Finance Project, 1970), 291–328.

[3]U.S. Department of Commerce, Bureau of the Census. Of 80. No. 3. *State Government Finances in 1980* (Washington, D.C.: U.S. Government Printing Office, 1981), Table 1.

[4]*Ibid.*

[5]*Ibid.*

[6]*Ibid.*

[7]*Ibid.*

[8]Russ Bellico, "On Lotteries," *Progressive* 41 (April 1977): 24; "Sure Thing for the States, for the Players—A Sucker's Bet," *Across the Board* 14 (November 1977): 90; J.R. Aronson, A. Weinsraub, and C. Walsh, "Revenue Potential of State and Local Lotteries," *Growth and Change* 3 (April 1972), 3–8.

[9]Studies which address the regressivity of the lottery include: Michael Spiro, "On the Tax Incidence of the Pennsylvania Lottery," *National Tax Journal* 27 (March 1974): 57–61; Jerome F. Heavy, "The Incidence of State Lottery Taxes," *Public Finance Quarterly* 6 (October 1978): 415–426; Roger E. Brinner and Charles T. Clotfelter, "An Economic Appraisal of State Lotteries," *National Tax Journal* 28 (December 1975): 395–97; Charles T. Clotfelter, "On the Regressivity of State-Operated Numbers Games," *National Tax Journal* 32 (December 1979): 543–47; Daniel B. Suits, "Gambling Taxes: Regressivity and Revenue Potential," *National Tax Journal* 30 (March 1977): 19–34; Kevin McLoughlin, "The Lotteries Tax," *Canadian Taxation* 1 (January 1979): 16, 18–19.

[10]Brinner and Clotfelter, 402.

[11]K. Forbis Jordan and Mary P. McKeown, "Equity in Financing Public Elementary and Secondary Schools," in *School Finance Policies and Practices. The 1980's: A Decade of Conflict,* edited by James W. Guthrie. First Annual Yearbook of the American Education Finance Association (Cambridge, Mass.: Ballinger Publishing Company, 1980), 79–80.

[12]George D. Strayer and Robert Murray Haig, *The Financing of Education in the State of New York.* Report of the Educational Finance Inquiry Commission. Vol. 1 (New York: Macmillan Company, 1923), 174–75.

[13]Percy E. Burrup and Vern Brimley, Jr., *Financing Education in a Climate of Change,* 3d ed. (Boston: Allyn and Bacon, 1982), 190.

[14]*State Aid to Local Government* (Washington, D.C.: Advisory Commission on Intergovernmental Relations, 1969), 39, as quoted in Burrup and Brimley, 139.

[15]James W. Guthrie, "United States School Finance Policy 1955-1980," in Guthrie, ed., 4, 6.

[16]*School District Organization* (Washington, D.C.: American Association of School Administrators, 1958), 84, as quoted in Burrup and Brimley, 183.

[17]James Bryant Conant, *Slums and Suburbs* (New York: McGraw-Hill, 1961).

[18]Patricia Cayo Sexton, *Education and Income: Inequalities of Opportunity in Our Public Schools* (New York: Viking, 1961).

[19]Arthur E. Wise, *Rich Schools, Poor Schools: A Promise of Equal Educational Opportunity* (Chicago: University of Chicago Press, 1968).

[20]John E. Coons, William H. Clune III, and Stephen D. Sugarman, *Private Wealth and Public Education* (Cambridge: Harvard University Press, 1970).

[21]Burrup and Brimley, 211.

[22]Burrup and Brimley, 211.

[23]Charles S. Benson, *Education Finance In the Coming Decade* (Bloomington, Ind: Phi Delta Kappa, Inc., 1975), 2.

[24]Serrano v. Priest, 487 P.2d 1241 (1971).

[25]Serrano v. Priest, 557 P.2d 929 (1976).

[26]Van Dusartz v. Hatfield, 334 F. Supp. 870 (1971).

[27]Rodriguez v. San Antonio Independent School District, 337 F. Supp. 288. (1971).

[28]San Antonio Independent School District v. Rodriguez, 411 U.S.1 (1978).

[29]Robinson v. Cahill, 303 A.2d 273 (1972).

[30]John Jennings, "School Finance Reform: The Challenge Facing Connecticut," *Journal of Education Finance* 4 (Spring 1979): 398 as quoted by Jordan and McKeown, 111.

[31]Allan Odden and John Augenblick, *School Finance Reform in the States 1981* (Denver: Education Commission of the States, 1981), 1-5.

[32]Odden and Augenblick, 1-2.

[33]Burrup and Brimley, 249.

[34]The description of DPE is based on Charles S. Benson, *The Economics of Public Education,* 3d ed. (Boston: Houghton Mifflin, 1978), 351-55.

[35]Odden and Augenblick, 2.

[36]Odden and Augenblick, 28-29.

[37]Allen Odden, Robert Berne, and Leanna Stiefel, *Equity in School Finance* (Denver: Education Commission of the States, 1979).

[38]C. Kent McGuire, *State and Federal Programs for Special Student Populations* (Denver: Education Commission of the States, 1982), vii-viii.

[39]Michael V. Hodge, "Improving Finance and Governance of Education for Special Populations," in *Perspectives in State School Support Programs,* edited by K. Forbis Jordan and Nelda H. Cambron-McCabe. Second Annual Yearbook of the American Education Finance Association (Cambridge, Mass.: Ballinger Publishing Company, 1981), 15.

[40]Lau v. Nichols, 414 U.S. 563 (1974).

[41]McGuire, viii-ix.

[42]Burrup and Brimley, 262.

[43]Burrup and Brimley, 259.

[44]Burrup and Brimley, 260.

[45]No. 8208/74 (Nassau County Supreme Court).

[46]Orlando F. Furno and Dexter A. Magers, "An Analysis of State School Support Programs," in Jordan and Cambron-McCabe, 177.

[47]Furno and Magers, 180.

[48]51 U.S.L.W. 3773 (April 26, 1983).

[49]National Center for Education Statistics, U.S. Department of Education, *The Condition of Education,* 1982 ed. (Washington, D.C.: U.S. Government Printing Office, 1982), Table 2-5.

[50]Benson, *The Economics of Public Education,* 168.

[51]Burrup and Brimley, 282.

[52]Guthrie, 33.

[53]Furno and Magers, 177.

[54]E. Kathleen Adams, *A Changing Federalism: The Condition of the States* (Denver: Education Commission of the States, 1982).

11

Fanatacism consists in redoubling your efforts when you have forgotten your aim.

- George Santayana

Fiscal Responsibilities of School Administrators

Fiscal resources (or their lack) govern the way an organization is managed and determine the relative success it has in meeting its goals. An educational activity may be encouraged by increasing its revenue, or it may be discouraged or impoverished by denying it financial support. The need for integrating school policy and planning with school finance is self-evident. Unless the financial planning process is integrated with the total program of educational experiences and support activities, the success of the educational program is jeopardized. For this reason alone school administrators cannot afford to be less than diligent in the financial management of the funds entrusted to them. Other very practical reasons for exercising competent stewardship are the legal and professional consequences of failing to do so. Many school officials become involved in legal difficulties each year because of poor fiscal management and because of involvement in civil rights and other legal disputes mentioned in preceding chapters.

This chapter discusses some of the fiscal responsibilities of school administrators. The school principal, the superintendent, and the business manager are the three key administrators involved in the fiscal management of the schools. As a result of the trend toward school-based management, the roles and responsibilities of the principal are increasing and thus will be given special attention. However, it would be impossible in one chapter to give even cursory treatment to all the areas of fiscal management, ranging from transportation to insurance; from facilities planning to custodial services; and from reducing vandalism to purchasing, supply management, and inventory control, which are the responsibility of school administrators at various levels. Thus, since the fiscal management of school administrators, including principals, centers around the administration of the adopted budget, discussion in this chapter will focus on the administrator's role in the budgetary process, philosophies of budgeting, and administration of the individual school budget.

The School Administrator's Role in the Budgetary Process

The school district budget has been defined as the planned educational program of the district expressed in dollars (Nelson and Purdy 1971, 77). So conceived, the budgetary process becomes more than a series of actions or operations leading to an approved document. Rather it is the fiscal expression through which the aspirations of local citizens are translated into programs and subsequently into observable results in a local school district's program. The results of the budget-making process should enable schools to (1) provide the quantity of resources needed to implement the educational program; (2) identify key elements in the management and allocation of funds, facilities, materials, and personnel; (3) give an account of financial stewardship; (4) facilitate the control of expenditures; (5) appraise the operation of school programs; and (6) provide information which will contribute to greater efficiency in subsequent budgetary planning.

The budget developed and adopted by the school board should not be viewed as a sterile, rigid document that places the school board in a financial straitjacket following its adoption. A budget is designed to be a servant to education and is not a master. On the other hand, the fiscal planning process of the local school district should not respond to every whim of the moment but should have the capability of being altered when unforeseen conditions emerge.

A school budget should not be used as a protective device so it can be said, "Sorry, but it's not in the budget, so the answer is 'No.' " Nor is it an accounting document dictated by bookkeeping activities (Nelson and Purdy 1971, 77). A school budget is only as good as the administrator who makes it; it is not a substitute for good administration; and the budget will improve as administration improves (Engelhardt and Engelhardt 1927, 553).

The budgetary process itself is cyclic and never-ending. By the time one budget is adopted, the planning phase for the next one has begun. While the current budget is being administered, it is also being reviewed and data are being collected for the preparation of the next year's budget. There are at a minimum four steps in the budgetary process: planning and preparation; presentation and adoption; administration; and appraisal and review. What is generally entailed in each of these steps is treated in the following sections.

Planning and Preparation

The most elementary rule in the budgetary process is that educational planning precedes financial planning. This is also the rule that is most frequently broken. Unfortunately, in far too many instances the budget is not the result of a deliberate study of the educational requirements of the schools, but reflects a continuation of previously existing programs. When faced with limited resources, decision makers may forego educational planning because of its abstractness or because of the necessity to deal with an immediate problem. Because money is a demonstrable reality and saving it is a universally admired act, starting with money seems far too often to be the trademark of the board's budgetary process. This appears to be more easily understood than attaching priorities to such intangibles as "better teachers," "more effective" instructional arrangements, or "expanded" curricular opportunities. Yet the effective administrator cannot start at this point, but must provide the leadership for such tasks as setting goals, determining priorities, identifying programs, computing costs, and balancing revenues and programs.

School district budgets should be based on prior-adopted, board-approved budget policies. The policies should not be abstract vagaries, but should be specific enough to have concrete meaning. For example, a policy might state the intended class size, and that when a class reaches a stipulated figure a new teacher shall be added if the extra pupils cannot be absorbed into existing classrooms. Other policies should cover such factors as responsibilities of principals in the budgetary process, supply allotments for various grades, use of buses for field trips, attitude of the district regarding self-supported food service programs versus subsidized programs, frequency of reconditioning typewriters or replacing roofs, and a host of other factors. Should it be found that adequate resources do not exist to support a budget based on policies, policies must be revised to meet the financial abilities of the district as opposed to just cutting the budget by some predetermined amount. If budget cuts are required, the administrator is then in the more advantageous position of defending policies related to class loads or per pupil allotments for supplies, rather than defending a certain dollar budget or tax rate. It also places the onus on those advocating expenditure cuts to state which policy should be changed and how, rather than just stating that expenditures in general be cut (Nelson and Purdy 1971, 81–82).

It is also critical in the planning and preparation stage of both the school district and the individual school budget that provision be made for maximum involvement of citizens and staff. Various approaches have been used to involve citizens. Some districts have used "unmet needs" conferences as a technique for identifying program areas in which the community believes the schools should take an active interest. Advisory groups may be formed to study either short-range or long-range problems. Budget hearings, another approach used to gain community input, also help keep citizens informed. Whatever approach is used, the key factor is that the local school district have some plan to involve citizens in budgetary policy determinations. However, it is also critically important that citizens' groups understand their roles in these situations. While their advice and counsel are to be respected and given serious consideration, the group must understand that they serve in advisory positions only and cannot usurp the board's legal power for final budget adoption. They do, nevertheless, have a right to know how their proposals have been received and what disposition has been made of them. Few things can be guaranteed to generate more ill will in the community than to have citizens agree to serve on committees or study groups and then have the board or administrator ignore their efforts.

While many of the same techniques of committees and hearings may be used to involve school district personnel, something more appears to be needed by and from those who actually operate the educational system. The actual extent of staff involvement in budget planning and preparation will depend largely on which of the budget philosophies discussed in the following section is operating in the particular district. The extent of staff involvement can range all the way from a situation where no staff help is asked for or desired to one where every staff member has a voice in how monies will be spent. Admittedly, a few districts are at either of these extremes. In most districts, teachers and support staff who are directly involved in final implementation of the budget are solicited to provide information on which budget decisions are based. Requests are normally submitted to the individual's immediate superior, who reviews, revises, and coordinates requisitions before forwarding them to the next level. This process continues until a coordinated budget package is prepared. As the link between the teachers and the central office, the principal has a critical role in this process.

One common practice in budget preparation and development that facilitates staff involvement is the use of a budget calendar such as that shown in Figure 11-1.

A budget calendar outlines, by dates, the data needed to construct the budget for the following year. Provision is made for input from all personnel and adequate time for continuing review and revisions. A well-organized budget calendar permits the budget development process to follow an orderly pattern and allows sufficient time to gather all needed information as completely and accurately as possible so that budget decisions can be based on information rather than expediency. In addition, and perhaps of equal importance, it provides sufficient time and opportunity for the ideas and aspirations of all staff members to be expressed and acted upon as appropriate (Jordon 1969, 122-23).

The preparation of the final budget document that is to be presented to the local board of education for review and adoption is generally the responsibility of central office personnel. It represents the most reliable estimation of expenditures and receipts that can be made, based on the information generated during the planning and data-gathering process. However, it is important that school administrators remember that budget estimates are just exactly that—estimates. It is folly to believe that any budget can be prepared with such accuracy and foreseeability that adjustments will not be necessary as the budget year progresses.

Presentation and Adoption

The school administrator should carefully prepare for the presentation of the proposed budget to the board of education or to any other groups. Months can be spent in making meticulous estimates, only to have them rejected because of a poor presentation. The budget may be presented in either a tentative or a definite form. In those districts where the board assumes a large share in discussion and review, or in the case of an individual school budget where the staff plays a similar role, the budget would initially be presented in a tentative form. In situations where budget development is an administrative function or prerogative, the presented budget may be in definite form. In any case, the form in which the budget

Date	Activity	Responsible Agent
Sept. 1	Approval of proposed budget calendar	Superintendent's Council
Sept. 15	Approval of proposed budget calendar	Board of Education
Sept. 30	Distribute capital budget request materials	Business Manager
Sept. 30	Distribute operational budget request materials	Principal
Sept. 30	Distribute general maintenance budget request materials	Principal
Nov. 1	All capital project requests and general maintenance requests returned to unit administrator	Department Heads
Nov. 5	Department furniture and equipment requests due in Unit Administrator's office	Department Head
Nov. 15	Submission of new program proposals to Director of Curriculum	Various
Nov. 20	Operational budget requests due in Unit Administrator's office	Department Head
Nov. 20	Review of proposed capital projects	Business Office Maintenace and Operations Supervisor
Nov. 30	Capital project requests to Maintenance and Operations Division for costing	Business Manager
Dec. 1	Vehicle, athletic, furniture and equipment requests due in Business Office	Director of Transportation Athletic Director Various
Dec. 20	Costed projects due in Business Office	Purchasing Division Maintenance and Operations Division
Jan. 15	Requests for additional staffing to be submitted to Personnel Director	Unit Principals Unit Administrators
Jan. 20	All certificated and classified staff requests to Business Office	Personnel Director
Jan. 20	Review of new program proposals	Superintendent's Council
Jan. 30	All operational budgets due in Business Office	Principals
Feb. 15	Preparation of operational budget	Business Office
Feb. 22	Review of operational budget with Superintendent's Council	Business Office
March 10	Board study, session and review of capital budget, transportation, and new program proposals	Board of Education
March 17	Board approval of partial budget relative to capital outlay and transportation	Board of Education
March 24	Board study session and review of operational budget	Board of Education
April 5	Board review study session of 1984-85 proposed budget	Board of Education
April 15	Deadline for personnel re-hiring	Personnel Director
May 2	Board meeting to sign proposed budget and notice of hearing	Board of Education
May 17	Advertise proposed budget and notice of hearing (must be no later than 15 days prior to the hearing)	Business Manager
May 27	Advertise second notice of hearing	Business Manager
June 3	Board meeting and public hearing to adopt budget	Board of Education

FIGURE 11-1 *Budget Calendar*

is presented is not as important as the spirit in which it is presented. Unfortunately, many administrators adopt a determined fighting spirit as they enter the annual "battle of the budget." This attitude is not necessary. The presentation of the budget gives the administrator an excellent chance to justify the estimates, not so much in terms of defending them as in terms of explaining them. The President of the United States prepares a "budget speech" in which he offers detailed explanations for increases and decreases in proposed expenditures and receipts. School administrators should do no less (DeYoung 1956, 159-61).

The presentation of the budget is logically and chronologically followed by the adoption of the budget. The length of time allocated between presentation of the budget and adoption in most districts is too short. In some districts the budget is actually adopted at the first meeting at which it is presented. Such action effectively prevents thoughtful discussion or consideration by interested parties and is not a recommended practice. Fortunately, this practice is not the usual one. In most cases the board will have reviewed the budget before it is presented for formal adoption. Most states have enacted legal requirements related to such items as the chronology of budget hearings, public notice, presentation, and adoption. In such states, these requirements will determine the process that must be followed and the time between steps in the process. It is critical that state mandates be closely followed lest the budget be declared illegal.

The actual adoption of the budget is obtained by a formal vote of the board of education. In some districts the budget must also be reviewed by either a city governing body, a county superintendent, or a county board of supervisors. After the budget has been accepted by the board of education and other reviewing bodies as might be required, and the calculation of the amount to be raised by local taxation determined, the board secretary or treasurer transmits to the proper official, usually the local or county tax assessor, information as to the tax levy. It is important to note that the school district does not actually levy the taxes or set the tax rate. The school district adopts a budget of a certain dollar amount; and the tax assessor, based on the assessed valuation of property in the district, determines and ultimately levies the tax at a rate necessary to support the district's share of the adopted budget.

In most school districts the formal adoption of the budget constitutes the authorization for expenditures. Large expenditure items are often referred back to the board, but the formal adoption of the budget is the signal for administrators to transfer the budgeted amounts to the designated accounts, and to administer the budget within the rules and regulations of the local board of education (DeYoung 1956, 164-65).

Administration

The preparation and adoption of the budget are preliminary to its administration or actual use in the school or school district. If the budget is to serve as a genuine guide or tool for administering the activities of the educational organization, budget estimates must be transferred to the various accounts, where they serve as guidelines for expenditures. As previously stated, this does not imply that the originally developed estimates should straitjacket the system as the day-to-day administration and ongoing review of the budget indicate that adjustments are needed. On the other hand, it would be questionable practice to exercise complete freedom in altering original estimates and designated expenditures. Since the original budget was developed with certain educational goals in mind, continual or major shifts in financial resources would undoubtedly influence the program which has been designed to move the school district toward the predetermined goals (Jordan 1969, 114, 135–36). In many states school districts are required to file legal notice of proposed changes in expenditures to prevent just such occurrences.

As has been stated, the budget as developed is based on certain decisions that have been made regarding direction of the education program for the budget period. The actual implementation of these decisions is essentially a matter delegated to those administrators responsible for the daily operation of the schools (Jordon 1969, 135). This administration involves a variety of activities that together should result in the sound management of all the areas that make up the budget. The budget indicates the essential activities that should take place; the administration of the budget assures that the maximum return is realized in each major area. This requires that there be sound purchasing of goods and materials, along with their proper distribution, care, use, and control. It also requires the employment of the best personnel available in terms of mix and composition, their proper assignment, the establishment of work loads and performance standards, and the provision of needed training and supervision (Nelson and Purdy 1971, 94). It involves, too, analyzing and evaluating the inputs and processes to determine if indeed the budget is serving as the tool it was envisioned to be for obtaining the desired educational objectives. Lastly, the school administrator must remember that since budgeting is a continuous process, while administration of the current budget is taking place, proper files must be maintained and data generated to expedite the preparation of the next year's budget.

Appraisal or Review

The last step in the budgetary process is appraisal or review. Placement of this step should not be interpreted, however, as implying that budgetary review takes place only after the budget has been administered. Appraisal, too, is a continuous process. From the very first day a new budget goes into operation, those affected by it begin to review it. Each experience with the budget constitutes a review step as assessments are made concerning the degree to which the budget facilitates or hinders the prime objective, the instruction of students. Data generated from these day-to-day experiences should be recorded and organized so the school administrator can capitalize upon these experiences in preparing the next budget (Jordan 1969, 114).

The continuing experiential type of budget appraisal is but one way of evaluating the budget. More formal methods include inside or outside audits, cost accounting recording and reporting, comparison with criteria established by professional organizations or central office, or school staff studies. In addition, it is important that periodic long-term evaluations be conducted, since certain efforts and concomitant results in the education of children are not immediately measurable (DeYoung 1956, 167). It can take a decade or more to measure the effectiveness of some programs. The fact that the annual budget has been administered in what might be judged to be a cost-efficient manner does not mean that the desired educational outcomes have taken place. For this reason, citizens and educators alike should be interested in long-term appraisal and review.

Philosophies of Budgeting

Over the years several philosophies of school budgeting have developed regarding the way the budget is to be developed and the way it is to be administered. These philosophies range from a very closed, authoritarian system to those that are very open, participatory, or decentralized. It is essential to the success, or indeed continued employment, of any administrator new to a system that he or she become aware of the operating philosophy of the board of education and the superintendent. Although these philosophies have no formal titles, in practice they can be classified as follows: (1) administrator-dominated; (2) centralized; (3) participatory; and (4) decentralized. Each of these is discussed in the sections that follow, with emphasis given to the emerging concept of decentralized, or site-based budgeting and administration.

Administration-Dominated Budgeting

The administrator-dominated philosophy views budgeting strictly as a responsibility of management. No help is asked for and no help is desired in constructing the budget. Teaching staff and principals are (or must appear to be) content with the allocations provided through this paternalistic decision-making process. The central office creates the impression that the budget process is beyond the understanding of ordinary professionals at the building level, and that in obtaining funds, the central staff is grappling with some mystic element which cannot be explained. Budgetary reporting is limited to the legal requirements and even then often is presented in such a complicated and ambiguous manner that parents and citizens are not inclined to ask questions. When the administrator-dominated budget is controlled by the board of education, it often becomes a straitjacket restricting the development of educational programs rather than a force for educational improvement. When the administrator-dominated budget is controlled by school administrators, it is invariably used as an administrative device. Teachers and staff find that their requests are denied although the administrators take those actions they themselves deem important (Nelson and Purdy 1971, 85). This philosophy of budgeting still operates in some districts, but it is not generally favored and does not appear to be an effective concept for the financial administration of today's schools.

Centralized Budgeting

Centralized budgeting operates from the philosophy that every school in the district should be treated the same. On the face of things this may appear to be a just and efficient way to budget; in operation it can be very unjust, in that it gives little recognition to the varying needs of schools or to the communities they serve. Allocation of resources to the schools is made on a per-pupil basis, with no consideration given to existing resources or to any backlog of requests. Decisions are made at the central office regarding pupil-teacher ratios, textbooks, supplies and materials, or curriculum. All schools are expected to conform. The centralized budget concept "tends to treat the entire system as a homogeneous unit, rather than recognize that even the smallest systems are mostly heterogeneous: made up of diverse people with unique needs, abilities, and capacities" (Candoli et al. 1978, 148). This practice, like that of administrator-dominated budgeting, is giving way to other forms that are more decentralized and participatory.

Participatory Budgeting

Participatory budgeting recognizes two basic principles. First, schools, as tax-supported institutions, must consult citizens in the planning process if they expect to gain their support. Second, the professional staff expected to implement the school program and use the equipment and facilities should be given an opportunity to suggest procedures and materials they believe will help do the best job. As the largest governmental budgetary unit in most communities, public education in the long run must convince people of the desirability of a particular educational program if continued support is to be provided. By the same token, teachers and staff members must believe in and understand the plan before they will be successful in implementing it (Candoli et al. 1978, 149).

The participatory budget process involves and provides for the interaction of school staff and the public in the various phases of budget development. A combination of formal and informal methods may be used to involve these people. Various committees may be formed on a district-wide basis to provide input for the budgetary process. Citizens can be involved as members of advisory committees and study groups. Teachers also may serve on such units as curriculum study committees, salary study committees, or budget advisory committees. Other alternatives involve holding staff hearings and in-service meetings on the budget. Public budget hearings also keep citizens informed and involved. The key factor in all these efforts is that the advice and counsel of these professional staff members and lay persons be respected and evidenced in the budget that is ultimately adopted.

Decentralized Budgeting

A number of school districts, especially larger, multischool districts, have recently moved toward a more nontraditional budgeting process referred to as decentralized or site-based budgeting. This movement is in part a reaction to what is perceived as the overcentralization of power within school districts. Decentralized budgeting is based on the philosophy that budget responsibility for the operation of an organization unit should be given to the managers of that unit. Under this concept, each school in the system establishes its own budget and educational priorities within the parameters of the total system's established priorities. Under a decentralized system, the school board continues to formulate and define the district's general policies and educational objectives. The role of the central office, however, is changed from dictating individual school actions to facilitating those actions (Lindelow 1981, 94).

Under the more traditional concept of budgeting, the central office dictates the resources the school principal and staff must use to achieve educational outcomes. Under a decentralized budgetary process, once a dollar amount for a school center is calculated, the principal and staff of the school determine how most appropriately to carry out their responsibilities for the educational program. The budgeting process at the school level includes determining what administrators, teachers, paraprofessionals, custodians, secretaries, supplies, equipment, or utilities, are appropriate to provide the most viable educational setting. "Where once the principal was merely the administrator of a staff, the size of which was centrally determined, he and his staff now determine the size and kind of staff at the site, with the only limitation being a total dollar amount" (Longstreth 1977, 14, 16).

Under a decentralized budgeting system school principals become the key persons responsible for education in the district. Principals are confronted with educational decisions that were never before a principal's prerogative. Under the budgeting systems previously discussed, central office officials were the ones who worried about enrollment fluctuations, utility costs, and the budget in general instead of each building principal. The intended benefits of this shifting of responsibilities are that resources will be used more efficiently and that there will be increased awareness on the part of the school site personnel of the cost of educational decisions. Because of their involvement in preparing the budget, staff members should better understand the importance of turning off lights, maintaining and caring for equipment properly, and ordering supplies economically. In essence, expenses are controlled by giving those involved a sense of responsibility and a motivation for controlling them.

The principal is also the person who has major responsibility for determining and meeting local needs. Decentralized budgeting, by its very nature, forces wider participation in educational planning and budgeting. Since the concept stresses the individuality of each school, principals, teachers, and citizens are brought more closely together in designing a custom-made program for each school based on the community it serves. A citizen advisory council or some similar vehicle for community input is normally established at each school to advise the principal regarding local needs and expectations so that the educational program options selected will reflect community desires. The more the public becomes involved in school decision-making, and the more the schools become responsible to community and student needs, the greater will be the sense of community ownership of the schools.

Budgeting Methods

Within the framework of the particular budget philosophy operating in the district, alternative budgeting methods may be applied. Traditionally, local school district budgets have been organized on a line-item basis. In fact, a 1982 survey by the American Association of School Administrators showed that 78 percent of the responding districts used line-item budgets (Hymes 1982). Several alternative budgeting methods have gained popularity in recent years, however, as the weaknesses of this approach and public demands for accountability have grown. In the following sections the traditional line-item budgeting method is described as well as two of the most common of the newly developed alternatives: program budgeting and zero based budgeting.

Line-Item Budgeting

A line-item budget, or object budget as it is also called, is one where expenditures are broken down "by object" or general categories such as instruction, administration, salaries, or maintenance. This method of budgeting emphasizes the allocation of expenditures into categories of "inputs." Because these categories summarize expenditures in gross terms, however, it is often difficult to determine what these figures mean in terms of actual programs or classroom teaching. In addition, an expenditure category in one school district will often not include cost data that are reported in the same expenditure category in another district, making it difficult to compare expenditures among districts. A typical section of a line-item budget is shown in Table 11-1.

TABLE 11-1 *Typical Line-Item Budget*

Category	Description	Budget Amount
2000	Instruction	
2100	Supervision	$ 18,880
2200	Principals	190,197
2300	Teachers	2,347,485
2400	Textbooks	53,920
2500	Library	34,691
2600	Audiovisual	31,240
2700	Guidance	70,501
	TOTAL INSTRUCTION	2,746,914

Program Budgeting

As opposed to the input orientation of the traditional line-item budgeting, program budgeting allocates monies, not by line items, but by programs. It is, most simply put, a spending plan tied to programs. Program budgeting does not operate in isolation. It is a segment of an overall system, be it PPBS (Planning, Programming, Budgeting System) or some other system that involves, minimally, the following items: (1) grouping of all district efforts and activities into programs (Transportation, Food Services, Language Arts, Physical Education, etc.); (2) establishing the major goals of each program; (3) determining specific objectives, that, if achieved, will insure the accomplishment of the larger goals; (4) establishing alternatives for achieving program goals; (5) comparing costs and effectiveness of alternatives; (6) establishing evaluation criteria to measure the success of each program; and (7) allocating resources necessary for each program to accomplish its goals.

If the budget section shown in Table 11-1 were presented as a program budget, it might appear as in Table 11-2.

TABLE 11-2 *Typical Program Budget Entry*

Program	Equipment	Supplies	Textbooks	Contracted Services	Certificated Employees	Classified Employees	Total Cost by Program
Instruction							
Language Arts	$2,474	$16,460	$6,460	$1,672	$632,240	$15,500	$674,806
Science	7,782	15,345	2,232	695	388,300	6,200	420,554
Mathematics	6,150	11,494	4,300	100	360,420	6,200	388,664
Social Studies	1,676	13,621	5,104	1,435	526,471	9,300	557,607

Zero-Based Budgeting

Zero-based budgeting is presented as an alternative to prevent the incremental growth or "budget creep" of the traditional budget. When zero-based budgeting is employed, each program, function, or activity must "justify its existence." Each year program managers are required to construct a budget from a zero base by providing new objectives, evaluation criteria, and justifications. A decision package is prepared for each activity which provides information relative to goals, desired outcomes, methods of attainment, costs, alternatives at various levels of fulfillment, and the consequences of any reductions. After review and analysis of each decision package, an activity or program may be funded at the optimum level of operation, a reduced level of operation, a minimal level of operation, or may be terminated. No expenditures are guaranteed for any program. Under a zero-based budgeting system, teachers and administrators must be able to identify, and justify, and state the cost of what they need for each program. It is intended that application of zero-based budgeting will eliminate nonessential services and programs, duplication, and misappropriation.

Administration of the Individual School Budget

Whatever philosophy of budgeting may be operating in a particular district, the school principal will be responsible for a variety of financial activities. These activities can range all the way from accounting to auditors, custodians to cafeterias, budgeting to busing, and contracts to computers.

The trend toward decentralization of school business administration has made it even more important that school-building administrators possess some expertise in each of these areas if they are to perform their roles effectively and efficiently. The following section covers the two areas that cut across all other areas of fiscal responsibility: budgeting and accounting.

Developing the School Budget*

Developing an individual school budget, like developing the school district budget previously described, involves a number of steps or activities. In a district where budgeting responsibilities are decentralized or where individual school staff members are expected to play a major role in budget development, the kinds and number of activities expected of the principal increase. The first step in developing a school budget is to determine the size of the pupil population to be served. In many districts this calculation is done by the central office staff. If this is not the case, a variety of projection techniques is available for this purpose. One of the most accurate, and also the most simple, is a cohort-survival-ratio technique based on past records comparing birthrates to eventual enrollment figures in kindergarten and successive grades.

Once the size of the school population has been estimated, the next step, perhaps the most important budgetary decision, involves determining the number of personnel required. District policies regarding pupil-teacher ratio, grouping, and staff loads must be applied. Employee collective bargaining agreements may also specify guidelines that must be considered. Computing the dollar cost attached to the required personnel should be based on the district salary schedule and fringe benefit package. If new personnel are needed, one technique used to estimate the cost of these unknown personnel is to budget for them based on the third or fourth step of the beginning teacher scale. This provides for the hiring of experienced personnel and counterbalances the economic attractiveness of hiring only recent college graduates.

The next major step is budgeting for supplies and equipment. If a decentralized budgeting concept is being employed by the district and the school is given a "lump sum" budget figure, determining expenditures for supplies and equipment within the school may be based solely on the needs established by staff and advisory groups. In other situations, requests may be made to the central office who decide what program areas will receive what items and services and how allocations will be made.

The most common approach to budgeting for supplies and equipment (and one that has been used in each of the budgeting approaches that have been discussed) is a per capita basis. One technique is to simulate the needs for a typical pupil in a particular set of circumstances. For example, for the typical third grade student it may be reasonable to assume a need for a set number of books and workbooks, certain art supplies (crayons, water colors, paper, modelling clay, rulers), as well

---

*Information in this section related to the development of the school-building budget is based on that presented in John Greenhalgh, *Practitioner's Guide to School Business Management* (Boston: Allyn and Bacon, 1978). This source could also serve as a reference for administration of many of the day-to-day business-related activities of the school principal.

as other materials and purchased services. Standards recommended by various professional groups indicate suitable equipment and supply quantities for libraries and the different instructional areas; even though these may need to be modified for local needs and resources, they serve as useful guides in arriving at a per capita simulation. Once the needs have been determined, a price can be affixed to each item by consulting the district "standards list" or some other pricing guide. (A "standards list" is a list of frequently used items, developed by the district, providing desired specifications and current prices.) This same sort of simulation can be employed for each category of supplies within a school planning unit, whether it be program, course, or grade, until a total budget estimate for supplies and equipment can be made.

Not all supply items lend themselves to per capita analyses. Office, first aid, library, and custodial supplies require a projection of anticipated needs and costs based on previous consumption. For these items, unit analysis projects the number of gallons of floor finish needed, dozens of light bulbs to be replaced, reams of office stationary to be consumed, or number of library books that will require processing or repairs. Based on recent known consumption, a year's quantity can be estimated and a reasonable budget plan generated.

Many other school recurring expenditures can vary in cost from year to year, and so must be estimated based on current market conditions. These include such items as fuel, electricity, telephone, postage, printing, and service contracts. The rates for these items are subject to increases at any time. The school administrator must keep abreast of information relative to proposed or approved rate increases by the postal service, public utilities, telephone company, or other needed services so that reliable expenditure estimates can be made.

After assembling information related to personnel, supplies, equipment, and other recurring costs, and preparing on the basis of this information the budget for a particular school, the school principal has the task of getting the budget approved by the next budgetary review body. The document presented must be based on realistic data, conform to district policies, staff program plans, community desires, and must be designed to serve student needs best. To enhance the "sellability" of the budget there should be adequate support data, including complete justification for equipment or materials requests and comparable statistics from other schools or districts. The latter might include such statistics as per capita costs, staff ratios, costs of subjects offered or extracurricular activities provided, or percentages of the budget assigned to functions, programs, or objects.

Accounting

The budget that is ultimately accepted or adjusted becomes the spending plan for the school. The accounting function can be viewed as the instructional support system that is designed to see that spending is done according to the plan. Accounting has been defined as the act of recording, classifying, summarizing, reporting, and interpreting the results of financial activities of an organization. The use of standard accounting and terminology in school will aid in proper initial recording of information, provide for orderly record keeping, supply information for action determinations, facilitate comparisons, provide internal control, protect individuals responsible for handling money, and serve as a base for writing reports (Greenhalgh 1978, 16). Overall, the data and information available from the accounting function provide the information upon which to base better decisions and school operating plans.

Because of the legal restrictions placed on the schools' sources of revenue and on the purposes for which funds may be expended, accounting for school funds differs from accounting for business and industry. The accounting procedure known as "fund accounting" is used to account for school finances. A fund has been defined by the Association of School Business Officials as "an independent fiscal and accounting entity with a self-balancing set of accounts. These accounts record cash and/or other resources together with all liabilities, obligations, reserves, and equities that are segregated for the purpose of carrying on specific activities or attaining certain objectives in accordance with special regulations, restrictions, or limitations" (quoted in Tidwell 1974, 5, 8).

Each school will have a number of funds. Although some schools, primarily those operating in decentralized systems, have direct access to the funds for such items as books, materials and supplies, repairs and replacement of equipment and miscellaneous expenses, normally the responsibility for control and accounting for these funds rests with the central office. The school funds that are normally the accounting responsibility of the school principal are those that arise from, or may be generated within, the educational program by means other than taxation. These would include such monies as the student activity funds; nonstudent funds collected and expended by nonstudent groups and organizations such as the P.T.A. or the booster club; discretionary funds from staff contributions, gifts, special parent or student fund-raising ventures, or earned interest, (often used for such items as special awards, cards, flowers, or aid so low income students can participate in otherwise unaffordable school activities); and school lunch funds. In view of the large amounts received and expended for these activities, the proper handling and accounting for these funds by the principal is essential. Because of the significance of school activity funds, and because they are so often neglected and poorly managed, special consideration will be given to the management of these funds following a brief discussion of the basic accounting practice involved in managing all such school funds.

The actual accounting procedures required or needed for the management of these non-tax revenue funds will vary with the size and needs of the school or school district. Some districts have a centralized accounting procedure with a computer terminal in each school. The school transmits via the terminal the details of each transaction; the central office computer records all these transactions, updates the account balances, and provides financial statements. Other school systems employ an activity fund manager who does the accounting for all such funds in all the schools of the district. In most districts, however, the accounting for these funds is the prerogative and responsibility of the building principal. Although very detailed and elaborate accounting procedures may be installed or required, at the very least an accounting system for school building funds should involve the following activities: (1) journalizing transactions; (2) reporting; (3) auditing.

Journalizing transactions. Every financial transaction, whether it is an expenditure or receipt, cash or noncash, must be originally recorded as a debit or credit into either a cash receipts journal, or cash disbursements journal, or a general journal. These are books of original entry where records of all financial transactions of the school are recorded in chronological order. Cash receipts journals record just exactly that—cash receipts. All cash receipts are recorded in detail and should ultimately be reflected in deposits. Distribution of the credits provides an accounting by funds of all sources of cash. Cash disbursements journals record all checks paid out. They should balance with bank statements. The distribution of charges provides a record of expenditures by accounts and funds.

The general journal can be used to record all transactions, cash or noncash; or, if a school uses a cash receipts and cash disbursements journal the general journal would be used to record only noncash transactions. The general journal entries include the date, account identification, explanation, the post reference that indicates the account number in the general ledger where the account will be posted, and debits and credits of all accounts affected by the transaction. Whenever an entry in an accounting ledger constitutes an increase in funds or assets, it is entered on the left side of the ledger and is called a debit. Whenever an entry in the ledger is an expenditure or reduction in funds or assets, a subtraction is made from the right hand side of the accounting ledger and is known as a credit. A single financial transaction might have two or more debits or two or more credits. However, the total amount of debits must equal the total amount of credits. Such a system of bookkeeping whereby the accounts are self-balancing through equal entry of both debits and credits is known as double-entry bookkeeping.

The accounts which show the various debit and credit entries are known as "T" accounts. The left side of the "T" account is the debit side; the right is the credit side. Table 11-3 illustrates a simple "T" account for a school activity.

TABLE 11-3 *School Activity "T" Account (Band)*

Date	Explanation	Debit Amount	Date	Explanation	Credit Amount
9/01	Previous Balance	$1,889.00			
9/13	Booster Club gift for trip	20.00	9/30	Flyers for Concert	$ 7.28
			10/03	Moore's Chevron (bus fuel)	48.00
9/21	Sale of Booster buttons	16.00			
			10/07	M. A. Taylor (bus driver)	60.00
10/01	Deposits for trip	63.00	10/10	Hunt Photos	8.25

Reporting. A major function of accounting is the periodic preparation of financial reports. With the current public pressure for accountability, the preparation of complete and accurate reports has become increasingly important. The exact number and format of reports that must be prepared is often specified in state or school district policies. Under any circumstances, sound accounting practices would call for, at the very least, monthly and annual financial reports for each fund. Monthly reports for each fund or activity should include (1) the opening balance at the first of the month, (2) all receipts during the month, (3) all expenditures during the month, and (4) the closing balance on the last day of the month. The sum totals must be reconciled with deposit slips and bank statements at the end of each month. Any discrepancies should be reconciled while transactions and participants are still current. The annual report would contain the same information as the monthly report, except that it would cover the budget year. Exception reports may also be included if there are exceptions which deviate more than some specified percentage from the monthly expenditure estimates submitted with the budget.

Auditing. To verify the accuracy and completeness of the school or school district accounting system it is essential that periodic audits be performed. Auditing may be internal or external in nature. That is, the audit may be conducted by a school district employee or by private auditors engaged for a fee. The extent of internal auditing will depend primarily on the nature and size of the school district, with larger districts finding it more feasible to conduct such audits. Whenever possible internal auditing should be done by a separate department so that it can truly serve as an independent appraisal (Trine 1981, 17-18).

The purpose of an audit, whether internal or external, is not to uncover mismanagement or embezzlement of funds. Although an evaluation of the stewardship of those responsible for funds is a consideration, the major purposes of the audit are (1) to determine whether the financial statements made by the school district, the school, or the activity are accurate and are the result of the application of generally accepted accounting principles; (2) to determine whether procedures used comply with statutory provisions and are in accordance with administrative policies and procedures; and (3) to identify any operational problems and to suggest to school officials improved methods and procedures. In recent years there has been an increase in state-mandated audits. In addition, although student activity funds do not come from public tax dollars, there is a growing tendency on the part of states to include these funds among those subject to audit. Whether initiated by the state or local school district, an audit should not make school administrators feel threatened. Audits are an important tool in maintaining accountability and credibility.

Student Activity Funds

Student activity funds include monies derived from such activities as athletic contests, concession sales at student activities operated by a student association, operation of a school store, concerts, plays or other special programs, student publications, salvage drives, various kinds of fund-raisers, or earned interest. Even in a small school, revenue from these sources can amount to many thousands of dollars each year; in large school systems the money easily reaches six digits and beyond (Roe and Drake 1974, 219). It is essential that school activity accounts be managed as thoroughly and efficiently as other district accounts. Districts should establish policies for managing school activity accounts in accordance with sound business practices.

The following general guidelines are suggested to ensure the proper management of student activity funds.

1. All money received should be acknowledged by issuing prenumbered receipts or prenumbered tickets to the person from whom the money is received.
2. Deposits should be made daily if possible. Cash should never be left in the school over the weekend or holidays.
3. Receipts should be issued to the person making the deposit. Deposit slips should be retained by both the depositor and the school accountant or bookkeeper.
4. Purchase orders or requisitions should be initiated by the person in charge of the activity fund.
5. Payments should be made by check, prepared and mailed from the business office to the payee.
6. The principal should designate two or more persons in addition to himself or herself who will be authorized to sign checks. Two of the three authorized signatures should also be required for all withdrawals.
7. No payment should be made unless supported by a written purchase order and by a signed invoice certifying receipt of merchandise and accuracy of prices.
8. Student activity funds should not be used for any purpose which represents a loan or accommodation to any school district employee or other nonstudent. Emergency loans may be made to students for lunches, carfare, and the like on written permission of the principal. Individuals may not make purchases through the student body in order to take advantage of better prices.
9. Student bodies may enter into contracts for the purchase of supplies, equipment, and services from an approved vendor provided the term of the contract is within the tenure of the students of the school (usually three years).
10. The student body should operate on a budget reflecting past experience and future plans; like the school and school district budget, the student budget should serve as a guide to the year's financing activities.
11. Student activity books and financial procedures should be subjected to periodic internal and external audits. An annual examination by outside, independent accountants is also recommended.
12. Regular reports (monthly and annual) should be prepared and submitted to the principal, business office, or any others responsible for the supervision of student activity funds. (Association of School Business Officials 1977; Roe and Drake 1974, 210-221)

Summary

The development and administration of the school district and school budget are critical tasks of the school administrator. Perhaps the most important functions of the administrator in these areas are the establishment of the necessary processes and procedures to ensure that responsibilities are clearly fixed, that maximum citizen and staff input is provided for, that the necessary information is collected, and that a plan for continuous review and appraisal be established. It is also important that a proper and efficient system be developed and implemented to account for school funds. If these budgeting and accounting areas are operating smoothly, the administrator will have the credibility necessary to be effective in other areas.

References

Association of School Business Officials of the United States and Canada. 1977. *Guidelines to Student Activity Fund Accounting.* Research Bulletin No. 17. Chicago: Research Corporation, Association of School Business Officials of the U.S. and Canada.

Candoli, I. Carl, et al. 1978. *School Business Administration: A Planning Approach.* 3d ed. Boston: Allyn and Bacon.

DeYoung, Chris A. 1956. "The School Budget," in *School Business Administration*, edited by Henry H. Linn. New York: The Ronald Press.

Engelhardt, N. L., and Fred Engelhardt. 1927. *Public School Business Administration.* New York: Bureau of Publications, Teachers College, Columbia University.

Greenhalgh, John. 1978. *Practitioner's Guide to School Business Management.* Boston: Allyn and Bacon.

Hymes, Donald L. 1982. *School Budgeting: Problems and Solutions.* AASA Critical Issues Report. Sacramento, Calif.: Education News Service for American Association of School Administrators.

Jordan, K. Forbis. 1969. *School Business Administration.* New York: The Ronald Press.

Lindelow, John. 1981. "School-Based Management." In *School Leadership: Handbook for Survival*, edited by Stuart C. Smith, Jo Ann Mazzarella, and Philip K. Piele. Eugene, Ore.: ERIC Clearinghouse on Educational Management, University of Oregon.

Longstreth, James W. 1977. "School Site Budgeting—A Superintendent's View." *Educational Economics* 2 (February): 14, 16.

Nelson, D. Lloyd, and William M. Purdy. 1971. *School Business Administration.* Lexington, Mass.: Heath Lexington Books.

Roe, William H., and Thelbert L. Drake. 1974. *The Principalship.* New York: Macmillan.

Tidwell, Sam B. 1974. *Financial and Managerial Accounting for Elementary and Secondary School Systems.* Chicago: The Research Corporation, Association of School Business Officials of the U.S. and Canada.

Trine, C. Lewis. 1981. "School District Internal and External Audits." *School Accounting, Budgeting, and Finance Challenges.* Chicago: Research Corporation, Association of School Business Officials of the U.S. and Canada.

PART IV

Leadership in the Real World

As Part IV begins, it is important to recall the previous sections of this text. These have provided information and context in the major areas of work of school administrators, establishing a good sense of the work of school administrators. This background is important; in fact, it is essential if an administrator is to serve well and confidently in a leadership position in the schools. However, this knowledge can be wasted or misdirected unless it is appropriately aligned with the realities of the schools. These realities include the special role of the schools as professional bureaucracies, their relationship to the communities they serve, the controversies and issues that often arise, and the techniques that allow a school to be responsive to and responsible for change. The challenge to the administrator to convert knowledge into action without creating disruption and chaos is found in the topics presented in Part IV. Successful administration calls for a well-thought out philosophy with sound policies and consistent decisions that are sensitive to the critical issues. Challenges can also be met successfully by anticipating events and being prepared to act rather than just re-act. Responsibilities are further met successfully by being sensitive to the rights and responsibilities of others to participate in administrative decisions. The discussions in Part IV are aimed at providing experience in thinking through the realities of administration. This process occurs best by blending the information presented earlier in the text with the realities of schools and applying this combination to the complex school issues that emerge. Part IV was planned and written to help in this process.

12

In a relatively small number of years, all human enterprise has gradually changed its complexion.

- Edward C. Schleh

Schools as Professional Bureaucracies

Organizations Before Bureaucracy: Why Was It Conceived?

Just as life in the 1850s differed substantially from the present (kitchens, pace of living, technology), so organizations of that time differed fundamentally from those of today. First, they were much smaller, most being family affairs, such as farms and cottage-type small industry. Second, for the most part they lacked today's bureaucratic features. Indeed, their inefficiency and unfairness spurred Max Weber, a late nineteenth and early twentieth century German sociologist, to devise structures and procedures to remedy what he and many others considered the gross favoritism and incompetence abounding in organizations of the day (Weber 1946).

The alternative he articulated from systems developing in Germany at the time, the bureaucracy, has taken the planet by storm. In fact, most people accept the model so completely that they have difficulty conceiving of other forms of organizing complex organizations.

Elements of Design: Weber's Five Characteristics

Division of Labor

Weber proposed to reform organizations by using five elements to redesign them. First, he suggested that organizations utilize a division of labor to deal with tasks that were becoming too complex to be performed by one person or that required more expertise to be done well than the individual could provide. Division of labor allows people to become more expert at their tasks because they can specialize by focusing on one specific job, task, or even subtask. As a consequence, this device can increase competence and efficiency considerably. For example, in schools we have specialists based on level, such as kindergarten and high school teachers, as well as other specialists based on subject, such as mathematics, industrial arts, and reading. In administration we have increasingly developed specialists in finance, curriculum development, and personnel administration (who negotiate with teacher associations and unions); and in supervision we have subject matter specialists whose expertise is focused on a subject such as social studies or music. With the increasingly accelerated growth of knowledge (Schwab 1960) this trend toward specialization appears nearly unstoppable; for the specialist has trouble keeping up even in his or her own field.

Division of labor, however, produces negative side results discussed in the next section; it also has implications for power and control in professional organizations that will be explored later in this chapter.

Impersonal Orientation

Second, Weber propounded an impersonal orientation, arguing that the official should work with ". . . a spirit of formalistic impersonality, *'sine ira et studio,'* without hatred or passion, and hence without affection or enthusiasm" (Weber 1946, 341). This was to replace the practice of making decisions based on the socioeconomic status and importance of the individual, or on whom he knew, or on the official's feelings. Decisions were to be based on the facts of the issues; equality of treatment and a rational approach were expected. Impersonalism produced a more universalistic approach with everyone treated relatively the same, contrasting with the then-prevalent particularistic approach to administrative practice. In contemporary education the growth of teacher associations and unions has led to greater emphasis on universalistic practice and a move away from the former paternalistic practices of considering requests for exceptions to policies one by one or on the basis of who made the request. All cases of requests for such items as leaves of absence are now to be considered on the basis of the provisions of the contract (where one exists). The same applies to sick leave, pay for coaching, etc. They are settled by an established scale negotiated in group contracts. The individual can no longer negotiate these alone, and an administrator's flexibility of operation is virtually eliminated in areas covered by contracts.

Hierarchy of Authority

Hierarchy of authority was another device included by Weber. In it "each lower office is under the control and supervision of a higher one" (Weber 1946, 331). Thus, each is responsible to one and only one superior. For example, with a clear line of authority employees know they are responsible to the supervisor, who is also responsible to the person ranked next above in the organization. The concept of chain of command developed, because subordinates were linked to superiors in terms of authority and command, in hierarchical relationships which were characterized by clearly understood lines of communication and authority. Coordination was made far more achievable. Organizational charts best illustrate the hierarchy of authority characteristic of bureaucracy. Figure 12-1 deals with a small district of 5,000 to 8,000 students; Figure 12-2 is appropriate to a much larger district.

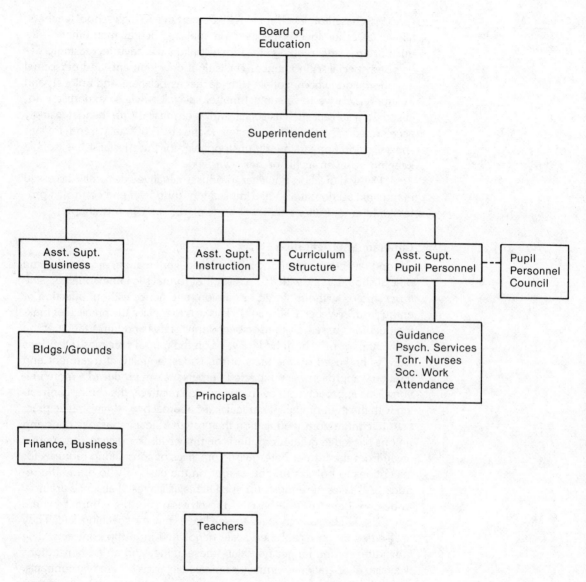

FIGURE 12-1 *Hierarchy of Authority in a Small School System*

Rules and Regulations

Another widespread flaw in Weber's day lay in the absence of rules and regulations, both in the smaller organizations that Weber observed and in those of the large landowners. People made decisions based on whim, impulse, or socioeconomic status of each individual, so that administrators' behavior was capricious and unpredictable. Weber suggested rules and regulations as Campbell notes, because they meant "reliability and predictability in the bureaucratic behavior," (Campbell 1978). Employees, subordinates, and clients then could predict more effectively how various situations would be handled in light of established rules. Weber noted; the "administration of law is held to consist in the application of these rules to particular cases," (Weber 1946, 330). Indeed, Weber wanted

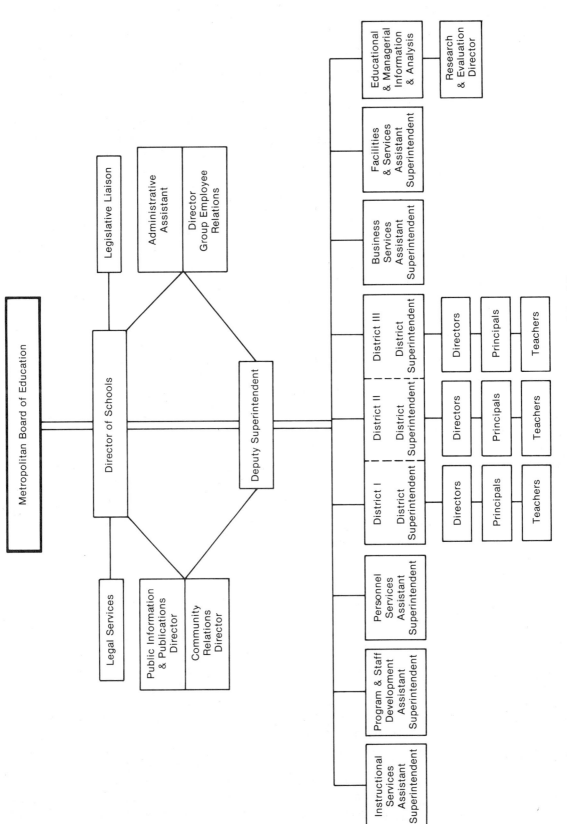

FIGURE 12-2 *Hierarchy of Authority in a Large School System*

rules and regulations published to increase predictability and accountability, words in high repute today in education. For several decades,
individual consultants, private organizations, and even state and national administrative associations have developed model systems and sample policies for districts to systematize or organize their board regulations
and policies. Workshops have been held all over the country to help districts cope in predictable, accountable ways with the intricacies of delicate and sensitive issues such as police on campus, policies on students
involved with drugs; and student publications and freedom of speech.

Career Orientation

The last major device conceived by Weber was Career Orientation,
whereby the members of organizations, it was hoped, would make a
career out of their work (Weber 1946, 334). Weber perceived this as
valuable because in time the bureaucrats would become more proficient
and expert in their work, adding to the competence and efficiency of
the organization. In education this has meant that from a field in which
the public once believed that anyone could teach, we now have grown
to have entrance requirements and certification. In California these have
increased to a five-year college program before one can teach. Teaching and administering are clearly perceived as careers, and increasingly
teachers have poured into the universities of the land to be certified for
administration and to acquire advanced degrees.

Functional and Dysfunctional Results

As with many ideas and innovations, the results Weber anticipated did
occur, but unforeseen consequences also developed, all of which are
familiar to modern eyes. Efficiency increased. Division of labor did produce specialization and bureaucrats did become expert, making careers
out of their work. Employees did become more impersonal. Hierarchies
became a tool to organize enterprises by clarifying responsibilities and
relationships; rules and regulations became operating principles to provide reliability, continuity, and predictability.

Division of Labor: Unintended Consequences

Dysfunctional results developed, producing problems and difficulties that
plague us as we make our way through the plethora of organizations
that constitute the milieu of contemporary life. Division of labor, of course,
produced specialization. Unfortunately, this often led to increasing nar-
rowness of perception, to a lack of vision, to development of rigid com-
partmentalization as departments placed their priorities ahead of those
of the organization and of the client. Such goal displacement was widespread and may be considered almost normal as organizations increase
in size and complexity. Subordinates' and superiors' thinking is often compartmentalized, focused on their function only. Mannheim called this
"functional rationality," where the individual knows only how to put the
nut on the bolt, being unable to tell where the bolt fits into the scheme
of things (Mannheim 1936). He coined the term, "substantial rationality"
to describe the individual who perceives the total picture and the way

264

his or her contribution fits into it. One of the present authors recalls that during a schoolwide curriculum development process, the foreign language department's main goal was to "save the department." Their strategy to accomplish this task was to stand pat, literally to do nothing. Since most of the other departments began thinking of developing curricular offerings that might be focused on students' interests and needs, some interesting proposals surfaced, moved through the curriculum structure, and were offered. Foreign language enrollment took a precipitous drop as a consequence. The department was then in the beleaguered position in a public high school of trying to defend total enrollments of 60-70 students per day per teacher.

Division of labor also leads to repetition of task and to boredom. Indeed, considerable literature has developed on employees' sometimes inventive efforts to make their work more interesting or more varied. Such boredom can lead to lowered productivity, exactly opposite of the result intended by specialization. Charlie Chaplin's *Modern Times* characterized the results of mechanization for the industrial worker. Oddly, a great many teachers and some administrators and supervisors have recently begun to express similar feelings that their jobs are dull, routine-bound, and unstimulating. The phenomenon of career burnout, one of the hottest topics in the professions, is related to the sense of specialized repetition. Indeed, a whole new terminology has developed, focusing on career changes for those in the professions and administration, including "mid-career shift" and "mid-life crisis." The question, of course, is how to retain, in a specialized teaching or administrative position, a sense of professional self and growth rather than to become entropic in nature and, like the physical universe, lose energy and drive, and run downhill?

The Hierarchy and Effectiveness

As hierarchies grew even larger, problems began to develop inhibiting their effectiveness. It became harder to communicate upward through the various levels or layers of command. Few administrators like to hear bad news or criticism, so subordinates learn not to pass negative information to their supervisors. Consequently, communication tends to flow downward much more easily than accurate information and perceptions flow upward. Subordinates find it safer to avoid sending information up through the channels because they are not sure how it will be perceived. Dry humor in organizations recalls that Greek kings killed messengers bearing bad news. Usually, however, administrators feel perfectly safe in communicating their orders and policies downward. In addition to being blocked at each level, communication can be distorted and filtered as people try to make themselves look good to superiors or as they color and shape information to make it more acceptable.

Mintzberg (1979) points to five basic flows in any organization. Communication is one of them. Barnard (1938) points to communication as one of three indispensable elements in an organization. But communication, as the game of "telephone" graphically displays, is totally dependent on personnel doing their best to convey data, feelings, ideas, and information accurately. Words are so subject to shifts, changes, and alteration by each sender that even under the best circumstances, with people in the same profession and socioeconomic class, communication of meaning is not easy (Whorf 1947, 1956). Under these conditions, it is a wonder that much is communicated at all. One of the best informal methods reported to the authors for finding out what was going on in a school system was the case of a superintendent who had eight children, virtually one in each grade. The nightly dinner chit-chat, always a casual conversation about the day's events, tended to be quite "informative," although we don't necessarily recommend this approach to all would-be superintendents.

Last, a hierarchy, as Campbell notes, "provides some subordinates with more potential power than they are capable of exercising, hence organizations must find ways of mediating the influence of some formal offices" (Campbell 1978). Almost everyone is familiar with the power wielded by an executive secretary, a superintendent, a president, or a principal. In some districts, the second most powerful person is the secretary who controls what persons see the superintendent, and often even controls who reaches the executive by telephone.

Goal displacement (p. 264) is further compounded by self-protective behavior in which people are careful to shield themselves or their operation. Writing memos to "cover oneself" has become almost reflexive behavior in bureaucracies. Protecting the subunit or accomplishing the subunit's mission regardless of whether it contributes to the goals of the total organization is also commonplace in contemporary organizations. A previous incident mentions a department that was self-destructive by its emphasis on self-protection. Yet protective strategies tend to produce conservative efforts to recognize and solve problems. The mind-set is that if people protect themselves or their department with a paper cover, that is enough. Forgotten is the reason for establishing the organization or the department in the first place—to get a certain job done.

Indeed, the bureaucracy generates another mind-set toward efficient use of resources. As a result, secretarial and other subordinate levels focus on utilizing resources as efficiently as possible, often to the detriment of accomplishing the organization's goals (Barnard's effectiveness). Reams of needless work have often been generated in the name of efficiency (Barnard 1938). The hallmark of efficiency is order: resources are utilized well. The hallmark of effectiveness is vigor: the job gets done, the goals are accomplished. Goal displacement, the confusion of means and ends, becomes operative when the goal of order becomes the first order.

In the case of the foreign language department, (p. 265) the goal of serving children and doing an effective job became supplanted by one of saving the department. Other departments operated with more vigor and produced interesting programs, with an inevitable result.

Impersonalism and Rules and Regulations: Their Effects

The emphasis on impersonalism and on developing rules and regulations to establish policies and procedures has led to a good deal of organizational and operational rigidity, and furthers the tendency to turn means into ends. Often rules are followed to the letter regardless of consequences. Frequently, regulations are enforced whether they accomplish the broad goals of the organization or not. People protect themselves by "following the book." Actually, some people derive a good deal of satisfaction from defining their jobs as enforcing rules and regulations. Following the "regs" is easier for some officials, who perceive themselves as implementing the rules rather than interpreting them and using judgment in their jobs.

Herrmann's research on left brain–right brain points to such phenomena (Herrmann 1981). People who are primarily or solely left-brained in their behavior may tend to operate "by the book" and avoid the more complicated process of solving problems or trying to develop satisfactory solutions toward meeting needs within the regulations. Indeed, many left-brained people seem to be drawn to such jobs, and do not seem to consider using available options or altering rules to meet problems. A certain degree of creativity appears to be needed to perform this latter task. For some it appears much easier to apply the regulations than to try to interpret them.

The revealing, if perhaps apocryphal, story is told about a German war plant that was totally destroyed, leveled to the ground in World War II. The bureaucracy was still happily generating paper six months later as if nothing had happened.

Excessive reliance on rules and regulations has led some principals to treat their own policies as set in concrete. Many of us have had administrators who talked about the Teacher's Handbook as "The Bible." Oddly, when a new principal enters, often the first thing jettisoned is "The Bible," which one and all perceive as a series of shackles limiting everyone, including the administration. Few people seem to miss the junked tome, and rarely, if ever, is it referred to.

Older organizations with a stable environment, which have had some time to develop their policies, may develop organizational rigor mortis and an abundance of red tape. Yet they seem to shuck off the policies when new and vigorous leadership takes over the reins, as if people want to start afresh.

Other dysfunctions are often seen in the use of rules to avoid work, in actually using the rules to "beat the system," and in people becoming legalistic. This use of the rules to immobilize rather than to solve problems has been immortalized in Gian Carlo Menotti's opera, *The Consul*.

Bureaucratic organization runs into operating problems in school because one of its basic assumptions is that the superior has more technical expertise than the subordinate. Clearly, teachers and supervisors often know much more about their subject than do principals. Division of labor and specialization produce this. This is a major reason why many male elementary principals stay away from supervising curricular matters in the primary grades. Because few have any personal experience with young children, they tend to avoid trying to supervise teachers who do have that experience. The principals sense their obvious lack of expertise.

Dynamics of Professional Bureaucracies

The bureaucratic characteristics produce additional problems. As social and physical distance increases with layer upon layer in the hierarchy, as this hierarchy places more people between those at the top and those at the bottom, distrust can also grow. We tend to be cautious of those whom we do not know. As a matter of fact, trust is built slowly and by personal contact. Usually, it is earned. But how can it be built when people at the top layers are usually faceless and even nameless to those on the lower levels? One of the authors, employed as a consultant, once found it necessary to introduce department chairpersons in a very large, but decentralized, high school to each other. The school was so large that they had never met, although they were fellow employees. In a larger bureaucracy it is not possible for most people even to know of each other's existence, let alone to know each other. How, then, can people build trust and then support each other? Barnard (1938) noted that a second indispensable element of administration is cooperation. But how can we cooperate with those we don't trust?

Loyalty, a key ingredient in any organization, can suffer as people become more remote from each other. Loyalty cuts both ways: employee loyalty to the organization, and organization loyalty to the employee. Many administrators tend to forget that to generate loyalty they have to be loyal to subordinates. In addition, American organizations have been criticized as looking for short-term accomplishments often to enhance the image of an administrator rather than looking for solid accomplishment over the long haul. Subordinates pick up such self-centeredness and lose interest in performing well or, at best, play interesting "games" to affect the top administrator's image and performance. Others grow discouraged and perform as little as they can (minimal compliance).

Last, too much competitiveness can arise and become a destructive force as units vie with each other. Barnard's previously cited view that cooperation is indispensable has much merit. Americans tend to focus on competitiveness and glorify that aspect of life. In truth, competitiveness in an organization can be ruinous if people try to outdo each other because they want more prestige, or if they're jealous of one another's accomplishments or status. Terms and organizational effectiveness have been destroyed when service to clients becomes secondary to personal aggrandizement or conflict.

Contemporary Dysfunctions or Career Orientation

Career orientation has had unintended results also. This phenomenon often locks people into professions or jobs they dislike or even detest, jobs they may not feel able to leave because of high salary or eventual pensions or loss of status. As has been noted, career burnout has become an example of this kind of situation. Numerous educators talk of "waiting for retirement," indicating thereby not only disenchantment but often decreasing productivity and effectiveness. It is startling to hear people at the height of their professional lives in their mid- and late forties talking with conviction of retiring in seven or eight years. The waste of talent and energy suggested by such statements is enormous.

Professional Bureaucracies and the Schools

When Weber articulated the bureaucratic concept for the organizations of his day, schools and other professional organizations were generally small, scattered, and only just beginning to respond to the concepts of professionalism and of themselves as "professional." Indeed, Flexner

didn't make his watershed analysis of the nature of professions until 1910 (Flexner 1910). Utilizing the bureaucratic model in today's highly developed and increasingly professional organizations produces a host of even more complex problems.

As the first order of business it is useful to investigate the differences between business and industry and the professions. Increasingly widespread technical knowledge and expertise form the basis for decision making by the professional. Nurses and physicians in an emergency room, teachers with an upset child disrupting class, administrators building a schedule, all must include an enormous and highly complex variety of considerations in their decision making.

A second major difference lies in the norms of the professions that differ from those in business. Providing specialized service to clients is the key of any profession. Ideally, such service is offered objectively, impersonally, and impartially, regardless of the person's situation, socioeconomic status, or other factors. Because professionals have difficulty maintaining such emotional neutrality with family and close relatives, they do not generally accept them as clients.

Professions are also characterized by colleague-oriented reference groups. Boards of colleagues examine prospective professionals, admit them to the field, and in certain circumstances may censure and even expel them. Licensing in business is considerably more perfunctory, if it exists at all, and certainly it doesn't depend on fellow business associates permitting entry into the field. Nor are there any sanctions exercised, as is possible in the professions.

Professionals are expected to evaluate situations and problems and then make autonomous decisions, reserving the right to consult with even more specialized specialists. Autonomy, thus, is of fundamental importance to the soul, to the core of the practicing professional.

Professions also have self-imposed control structures based on expertise and professional standards. In education in recent years, competency-based certification has begun being considered for entrance into teaching; in some states, accreditation of education programs in the colleges may be removed if a designated proportion of the program's graduates fail the competency tests. Although expulsion in education is uncommon, it can happen if some major state rule or law has been violated.

Different norms and standards distinguish professions from other forms of human enterprise, among which are the development of a specialized language. Education, indeed, has certainly developed this criterion. (Critics assert that this criterion has over-developed in education.) The term "pedaguese" has been coined to poke dry humor at excessively specialized and obscure terminology, which nonprofessionals cannot understand.

Last, although professions provide a living to practitioners, economic profit is not perceived as the basis of success and failure, nor of prestige.

Professions and Bureaucracies: Settings for Conflict

In the development both of schools as organizations and of teaching and administration as professions the seeds for organizational conflict are sown.

In recent years, starting with Lewin, Lippitt, and White's (1939) experiments with ten-year-old boys' groups, a good deal has been learned about organizational climate (Halpin and Croft 1963). As Halpin and Croft note, climate is to the organization as personality is to the individual. That is to say the climate of the educational organization comprises the social, psychological, and human relationships atmosphere of the schools. Although no direct cause and effect relationships may be determined yet respecting teaching and learning, we have discovered in research on the brain that threat can significantly reduce learning (Hart 1975). Heavy conflicts in schools between administrators and teachers, such as strikes and administrator-union strife, surely pose problems for youngsters and adolescents in need of positive, mature role models and in need of a stable supportive environment. Most people need a stable and peaceful setting for optimal learning.

Consequently, some of the malfunctions and dysfunctions of professional bureaucracies should be investigated to avoid a severe effect on both clients and staff and to find alternatives that may serve professional teachers, administrators, and clients better.

It is obvious from the earlier discussion that bureaucratic organizations have well-developed chains of authority or hierarchy and clear expectations about who uses authority, when and where and how. Administrative positions are perceived to have authority delegated to them. A principal may decide when, where, and how to hold the required fire drills. Calling fire drills is in the zone of authority granted principals (Barnard 1938). Even this most stable area may be changing as Lynam notes (1979) in his study of teacher reactions to perceptions of attendance pressure by the principal.

Complexity has increased because of the great growth of knowledge in recent years (Schwab 1960). This enormous growth, which time and again has doubled our knowledge in less than a decade, has caused increasing specialization, leading supervisors and teachers to know considerably more in their areas than most principals.

Additionally, the development of numerous instructional and supervisory delivery systems, and of large numbers of alternative curricula for each subject, has led many teachers and supervisors to be far more knowledgeable than their supervisors, the principals. This has led to increasing demands by teachers and supervisors for more respect for their increased expertise and professionalism. It has inevitably caused greater insecurity among principals as they realized that their subordinates (both teachers and supervisors) know more than they. This is particularly true because so many male principals have come out of physical education and coaching, and often lack both broad academic background and elementary experience.

Consequently, we see in education increased valuation of the importance of knowledge and decreased valuation of the authority of position. Added to this is the general erosion of the authority of position since the end of World War II, exacerbating the problem even further. Recent developments in professionalism, therefore, have produced conflicts between authority of position and authority of knowledge. The old dynamic of paternalism is being changed, producing conflict and stress.

Between older male principals and the increasingly large number of modern and assertive women, still another source of conflict has emerged. The large trends discussed in Chapter 15 have arrived with a vengeance, and none of us is immune to their effects. Added to this is the development of the Women's Movement, an aspect of the general movement toward human rights taking place in western society. Because most administrators are men, and the majority of teachers are women, the rise of women's consciousness and of new, different identities creates new dynamics for conflict and/or accommodation.

At the same time expertise is increasing, teacher associations, and unions and militancy are growing, too. The professional negotiations being carried out in almost three-quarters of the states are a struggle for higher salaries, to be sure. But it is also an intense struggle over increasing teacher participation in decision making. In short, it is a struggle over power.

The struggle has strengthened the polarization between teachers on one side and principals and other administrators on the other. Many strikes, when they have occurred, have ripped relationships in the school system apart, in many cases altering them negatively for years or even permanently (Shapiro and Nicaud 1980). As we noted in the section on dysfunctions of bureaucracy, as both physical and social distance develops, the organization can encourage the growth of distrust; or with wise administration it can also produce trust, stability, and cooperation in achieving mutually agreed upon goals. But this takes time, effort, thought, and action. As with any good relationship, it grows with attention and care—and involvement.

Structures, Models, Procedures to Cope with Bureaucracy

While the preceding constitutes an overview of the problems of bureaucracies in professional settings, what possibilities have our best thinkers developed to avoid some of these results?

Decentralization

One structural change widely used in urban settings, large counties, and large schools has been to decentralize into smaller units and develop flat rather than hierarchical organizations. Decentralized high schools or junior high schools have smaller entities called "houses" or "halls." Total districts have areas or regions with area superintendents heading them. Even smaller districts have moved toward school-based management in which many budgetary decisions are made in the local school. General Motors historically organized by making each major division (Buick, Pontiac, Chevrolet) autonomous and responsible for its operations. In the late 1960s a brief movement, the Great High Schools, flourished and then rapidly faded. We began to realize that schools of 2,000 or more, even on elementary levels, provided problems that were difficult to manage because of size. Decentralization for such large schools, and even smaller ones, is virtually a necessity (Leggett et al. 1979). Figure 12-3 illustrates a decentralized organization within a school. A major problem with this plan lies in communicating effectively across divisions. Often such units may become independent duchies operating in isolation because the head administrator may have his own needs for power.

The Ombudsman

The Swedish-derived "ombudsman" is a very highly respected official appointed at the very top of the organization, be it a university or a government, whose function is to right grievous wrongs by the established bureaucracy. Although having no authority or power, the ombudsman can investigate problems and make subsequent recommendations which carry considerable weight or influence. A number of universities (The University of Chicago and others), school systems, and governments have adopted this interesting idea. It is another device for balancing power between adversaries by intervention of a neutral force, because a subordinate has a legitimate right to appeal, and retaliation is considered improper.

Japanese Management

The Japanese-perfected "quality circle" is a participatory management approach based on trusting both workers and management (Franklin 1981). It involves workers in the range of actions and decisions, on issues that affect them and the product. The quality circle consists of groups of workers organized to study and discuss improving the product. Behind this lies the realization that the people doing the actual work know a great deal about the product and how it is being produced, and that this knowledge is essential to improve the operation (Bonner 1981).

"Consensus-based decision making," a commitment both to long range results and to the organization's goals, as well as a commitment

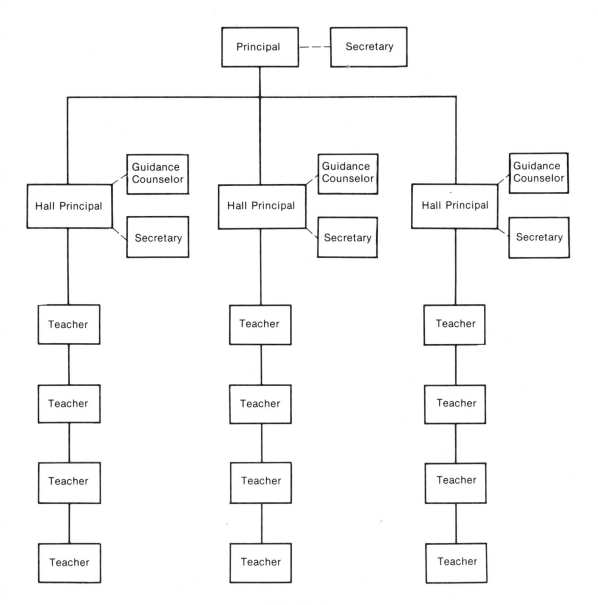

FIGURE 12-3 *A Model of a Decentralized School Organization*

by the organization to the workers, are basic characteristics of this philosophy. Another key is a lifetime commitment to the worker by the organization. The results in Japanese products, particularly autos, steel, and electronic products, point to the success of this approach. Some American and British firms—for example the Harmon Kardon Company in Bolivar, Tennessee—have used this approach, but such examples are unusual. These efforts also take work, commitment by management, and faith (Ouchi and Jaeger 1977).

American organizations with their proclivity for short-term results to make administrators "look good" and with their distrust of the operating cores of workers (or teachers) and lower level administrators (Mintzburg 1979) are not easily able to adopt this institutional structure.

Organizational Development

Organizational Development (OD) that focuses on solving organizational problems with personnel is one way to ameliorate bureaucratic as well as other problems (Golembiewski 1979; Pfeiffer and Jones 1971–1983). As with all of the above approaches, commitment by top management to implementing the idea is essential to any success. In OD approaches, people's relationships with each other are a major focus, particularly if the relationships are interfering in setting or accomplishing the organization's goals and objectives. Overly aggressive behavior by employees toward one another, hostility that interferes with the operation, attempts to dominate and control, passivity in function, all by individuals or groups are the focus of those who can use OD approaches to help improve relationships (French and Bell 1979).

OD also involves helping people have experiences in groups and in the organization with struggles for power or prestige and their impact on all group members. In short, OD approaches focus on helping people understand themselves, and others, and how organizations operate; it helps people understand how they can function better in groups. (Schmuck 1977; Fullan, Miles, and Taylor 1980).

Another approach attempts to vary jobs by job enrichment, or organizing along team lines so that a product is produced by a team or a function is performed by a team. In both these strategies the individual becomes responsible for a variety of roles rather than for only a single, narrowly defined function. People have to think to function, so that some managers become anxious at the thought of these approaches.

The Arena

Last, the concept of the "arena" as an alternative to the bureaucracy has been proposed (Strauss 1964; Martin 1975). Martin notes that if one treats schools as professional models and looks for interactions among personnel, then rather than using the organizational chart as the focus, the "arenas" in which interaction occurs become the focus. In short, arenas are "the repetitive focal situations in which the life of the institution proceeds," such as administrative staff, academic departments, teaching teams, or committees (Bucher 1970).

Included in these repetitive focal situations are informal associations and groups, thereby encompassing the range of interpersonal interaction occurring in organizations. Martin notes that "this approach entails researching questions of how the occupants of the different formal positions in the schools interact; how decisions are made concerning what is to be done, when and by whom; and how social boundaries are established among and between teachers, administrators, and pupils." Figure 12–4 illustrates arenas.

The figure points to the social system (any two or more persons engaged in meaningful interaction) as the keys in which people interact in organizations, gives an idea how decisions are made, and points to the informal process as providing the arenas for people to interact and carry on the organization's life processes.

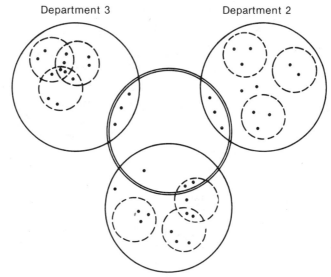

Department 3   Department 2

Department 1

=== Interdepartmental arenas (committees, teacher-administrator overlap. etc.)

—— Departments

— — — Interdepartmental arenas (teaching teams, committees, etc.)
• Personnel

FIGURE 12-4 *Arenas in the School*

SOURCE: Martin, Wilfred B.W., "The School Organization:
Arenas and Social Power." *Administrator's Notebook* 23, no.
5 (1975): 2. Reprinted by permission of the Midwest Administration Center, The University of Chicago.

Summary

While bureaucracy has provided enormous advantages, its two-edged
blade cuts us to the quick all too often. It slices even more deeply with
professional bureaucracies by setting up, among other problems, conflict between the authority of position and authority of knowledge or
expertise.

Several alternatives have been developed to deal with these problems. Among them are decentralizing organizations, the ombudsman,
quality circles and staff involvement, Organizational Development approaches, job enrichment, and enlarged job responsibility through team
operations, and the organizational alternative of the "arena."

References

Barnard, C.I. 1938. *The Functions of the Executive.* Cambridge: Harvard University Press.

Blau, P. M. 1955. *Bureaucracy in Modern Society.* New York: Random House.

Bonner, J. S. 1981. "Applying Japanese Management Strategies to Educational
Management." *Michigan School Board Journal* (December): 21-23.

Bucher, R. 1970. "Social Process and Power in a Medical School," in *Power
in Organizations,* edited by Mayer N. Zold, 97-143. Nashville, Tenn.:
Vanderbilt University Press.

Campbell, R. F. 1978. "A History of Administrative Thought." *Administrator's Notebook,* vol. 26, no. 4.

Flexner, A. 1910. *Medical Education in the United States and Canada.* New York: Carnegie Foundation for the Advancement of Teaching.

Franklin, Jr., W. H. 1981. "What Japanese Managers Know That American Managers Don't." *Administrative Management* (September): 36-51.

French, W. L., and L. H. Bell. 1978. *Organization Development.* 2d ed. Englewood Cliffs, N.J.: Prentice-Hall.

Fullan, M., M. B. Miles, and G. Taylor. 1980. "Organization Development in the Schools. *Review of Educational Research* 50 (Spring): 121-83.

Golembiewski, R. T. 1979. *Approaches to Planned Change.* New York: M. Dekker.

Halpin, A., and D. Croft. 1963. "The Organizational Climate of Schools." *Administrator's Notebook,* vol. 11, no. 7.

Hart, L. A. 1975. *How the Brain Works.* New York: Basic Books.

Herrman, N. 1981. "The Creative Brain." *Training and Development Journal* (October): 11-16.

Leggett, S., C. W. Brubaker, A. Cohodes, and A. S. Shapiro. 1979. *Planning Flexible Learning Places.* New York: McGraw-Hill.

Lewin, K., R. Lippitt, and R. K. White. 1939. "Patterns of Aggressive Behavior in Experimentally Created 'Social Climates.'" *Social Psychology* 10:271-99.

Lynam, R. 1979. *An Exploratory Investigation of the Relationships Between Teacher Morale, Attendance Pressure, and Absenteeism.* Unpublished doctoral diss. Nashville, Tenn.: George Peabody College.

Mannheim, K. 1936. *Ideology and Utopia.* London: K. Paul, Trench, Trubner and Co.

Martin, W. B. 1975. "The School Organization: Arenas and Social Power." *Administrator's Notebook,* vol. 23, no. 5.

Mintzburg, H. 1979. The Structuring of Organizations. Englewood Cliffs, N.J.: Prentice-Hall.

Ouchi, W. G., and A. M. Jaeger. 1977. "Type Z Organization." *Stanford University Alumni Bulletin* (Fall): 13-31.

Pfeiffer, J. W., and J. E. Jones. 1971-83. *Annual Handbook for Group Facilitators.* La Jolla, Calif.: University Associates.

Schwab, J. J. 1960. "Inquiry, The Science Teacher, and The Educator." Speech to Association for Education of Teachers of Science." Kansas City, Mo., March, 1960.

Schmuck, R. A., et al. 1977. *The Second Handbook of Organization Development in the Schools.* Palo Alto, Calif.: Mayfield Publishing.

Shapiro, A., and R. Nicaud. 1980. "The Four Phases of a Teacher Strike." *American School Board Journal* 167 (July). 28-29.

Strauss, A. 1964. *Psychiatric Ideologies and Illustrations.* New York: Free Press.

Weber, Max. 1946. *From Max Weber: Essays in Sociology,* edited by H. H. Gerth and C. W. Mills. New York: Oxford University Press.

Whorf, B. L. 1947. "Science and Linguistics." In *Readings in Social Psychology,* edited by T. M. Newcomb and E. L. Hartley. New York: Henry Holt and Co.

_____. 1956. *Language, Thought, and Reality. Selected Writings of Benjamin Lee Whorf,* edited by John B. Carroll. Cambridge, Mass.: Technology Press; New York: Wiley.

13

If the people around you are spiteful and callous and will not hear you, fall down before them and beg their forgiveness, for in truth you are to blame for their not wanting to hear you.

- Fyodor Dostoyevski

School-Community Relationships

The School: Integral in the Community

Through the 1950s and 1960s of this century most Americans viewed "their" schools as controlled by the community. From the beginning of the colonies schools were local in nature, established, operated, and controlled locally. In recent decades observers have noticed a change, from local to state or national control. This change has elicited much criticism.

Although landmark decisions occurred earlier, starting with the Brown decision of 1954, the federal courts have increasingly functioned as a quasi-national school board, setting policy on a host of fundamental issues that some communities and school boards refused to face and that others found difficult to handle. Matters of desegregation, women's, students', and teachers' rights, equality of educational funding and opportunity, and rights for the handicapped are examples of basic issues and policies federal courts have faced and acted upon since the 1950s. Although a number of Americans still do not like some of these decisions, in these issues and others increasing numbers of American citizens were accorded the civil liberties and rights and the benefits of democracy as they applied to education as interpreted by the federal courts.

Almost immediately, state courts followed suit in these and other areas, making great changes in educational policy and practices on state and local levels. Equality of educational opportunity, programs for the handicapped, and desegregation were examples of state court focus. Next, the administrative and legislative branches of federal and state governments moved into these and other arenas. On the federal level special grants and programs were developed in education such as National Defense Education Act (NDEA) of 1958, designed at first to improve science and mathematics education, making education a matter of national policy related to our defense; Title I of ESEA (1965), for schools with a high percentage of students with poverty level incomes; Title III, for innovative and exemplary programs; regional educational laboratories to support state, local, and regional thrusts, and the Teacher Corps. On the state level both special and general program support in these and other areas emerged, such as funds for busing and desegregation, funds to improve educating the poverty-stricken and the handicapped and in some states, programs for the gifted.

As a consequence of these efforts, many have interpreted some of the federal action as eroding local control, although state initiatives centralizing control on the state level have been generally overlooked by the public and by educational critics.

Nevertheless, in addition to the state and federal initiatives described above, and also quite unnoted by advocates of local control, a quiet revolution began that consisted of extralegal developments on a national scale. This revolution also significantly affects local control (Campbell 1963). The major changes of national scope include the Scholastic Aptitude Test (SAT) and the National Merit Scholarship Program. While these are private and not governmental in nature on either federal or state levels, they have affected local schools and communities across the nation so far that many persons evaluate both public and private schools by the number of National Merit Scholars graduated, or the number of graduates going to "good" colleges. Most high school guidance departments for years have prepared fact sheets pointing out the average SAT scores of graduating seniors.

Furthermore, the major curriculum reform movements that have been both governmentally and privately funded have had major impact on the world of education. These have ranged across the fields of education from physics (Physical Science Study Committee—PSSC), chemistry, and mathematics, to the social sciences (Anthropology Curriculum Study Project), to industrial arts. Physical education has had its curriculum reform thrusts with Movement Education; and music has had the Suzuki, Orff, and Kodaly movements. The list of major curriculum changes and programs in the social sciences alone exceeded one hundred by the early 1970s (Taylor and Groom, 1971).

As a consequence, the Weberian ideal-type model of the schools held by Americans as purely operated and locally controlled has increasingly become more mythical than real. Interestingly, even before the beginning of the nation, education was supported nationally (the Northwest Ordinance of 1787), and states regularly established floors and minimum standards for schools even in the last century.

To summarize, Tucker and Ziegler (1980) pointed to three major eras or stages of school control:

1. To 1900: local lay control of education.
2. 1900–1954: local professional control by educational administrators. This trend actually was started with Horace Mann's recommendation in 1843 that schools be supervised by a professional superintendent, and led to a "cult of efficiency."
3. 1954–present: nationalization of education. Strong emergence of state

and federal controls on education with strong impact by the "imperial judiciary."

While many others bemoaned the loss of local control, another interpretation may be suggested. Many of the new state and federal policies and thrusts may be interpreted as bringing democratic rights and liberties to various groups and minorities, such as teachers, students, women, black citizens, non-English speaking, handicapped, religious, and racial minorities, etc. In our colonial days voting, too, was restricted to white male property holders. These restrictions have been lifted to include the total population. So, too, in education various inequities are being addressed, so that equality of opportunity for all Americans (and even illegal migrants) to achieve a good education is increasingly a realistic goal of the country.

Relating to the Community: A Rationale

Several relatively basic reasons support the need for administrators and teachers to make special efforts to establish close, positive working ties with their school communities. Without knowing the community, educators cannot begin to understand the parents and students coming to the schools. They need to understand the hopes and aspirations, the needs, and character of the community to design and build programs suited to its children and youth. And this means not merely knowing the most influential publics but rather relating to minority groups also, to publics that often are not involved with the schools, such as the disadvantaged, or racial and religious minorities. Having close relationships with and understanding these groups are necessary to develop appropriate programs and to build support and commitment to the schools.

A legitimate criticism of any school may be made if the needs of a large percentage of its student body are not being met by programs designed for them. A high school with college-bound upper middle class students should have programs suitable for them. If the school has working class youth whose parents want vocational and commercial programs, these should also be provided. This holds true even if the educators do not sympathize with the ideas of those groups. Their children are in the schools, and have the right to have their needs professionally considered.

Another major reason to know the community, aside from the need for developing appropriate policies, programs, and practices, is to build support and commitment for them. In crisis, whether it be financial, legal, or critical, community support is a joy to defenders of the ramparts. Consequently, we must look for support from the very people we try to serve. People support those whom they perceive to support them. Support is like bread cast upon the waters: it can reappear at the most difficult times to sustain the board, the administration, the teachers, and the schools; but it has to be a major daily consideration in the minds of the administration and teachers as they work with the community and students (Campbell and Ramseyer 1955). A later section will address various means of communicating as well as vehicles to garner support and commitment.

The Local Community—Its Past, Present, and Future: A Perspective

The beginnings of any enterprise affect its later development and its beliefs, its rationale for existing and its operation, its selective memory of the past (its myths), and its procedures. When schools were first developed in this country, the colonies were thinly populated, the towns were tiny; communication was at best slow and primitive if it even functioned; and transportation was, by today's standards, a horror. As a consequence of the rural nature of the colonies, schools were developed that fit a rural society. They were small, local, focused on rudimentary skills, and usually run by local people. Indeed, lay control can actually be traced to 1647 when the Massachusetts Bay Colony established legislation for schools and gave responsibility to local officials (Cubberly 1948). Thus the local aspect was built into the very fabric of education as an institution. Although the colonies passed legislation relating to education in the seventeenth century, it was only later, in the eighteenth century, that most state governments began to establish even minimum floors below which local schools could not fall. Even this legislation was sporadic.

Yet in the more than two centuries since the founding of this republic, the very fabric, the very nature and essence of the nation have changed. They have changed so enormously, so radically, that the educational system that received its local and parochial imprint three centuries ago has been altered dramatically in recent decades. A visitor from outer space who visited this continent at the founding of this republic and who returned today would find a society that had:

1. Expanded from three million to over two-hundred-fifty million people
2. Developed cities, indeed, megalopoli
3. Developed suburbs
4. Become multicultural
5. Begun to accord all citizens (even children) their political and civil rights and so had developed
   a Black Movement
   a Women's Rights Movement
   a youth protest movement (now deceased)
6. Become a continental state
7. Become a major international power
8. Become organized bureaucratically
9. Developed a technology that could communicate across the nation in milliseconds, but also become highly impersonal
10. Found that knowledge was doubling every decade and now even more frequently than that
11. Developed a huge industrial complex
12. Developed socioeconomic class and regional subcultures transcending local communities (e.g. the suburb, the South, Appalachia)
13. Doubled and tripled people's life span
14. Achieved a rate of change that has become exponential
15. Begun to explore space
16. Begun use of solar power
17. Moved into DNA and genetic engineering
18. Developed the atomic and hydrogen ages
19. Become specialized—specialized—specialized

In the last two decades other major developments have occurred that have enormous impact on education:

1. Greater perceived difficulty in influencing governmental decisions, causing feelings of powerlessness for many publics
2. A serious decline in school-age population
3. An enormous growth of single-parent families
4. A great growth of working women, exceeding over 50 percent of adult females
5. The entrance of women and Black citizens into the professions
6. A considerable decline of the authority and prestige of the schools and in public respect for teachers
7. A greater willingness to litigate educational matters
8. Desegregation, which among other consequences, has influenced school attendance areas greatly
9. Collective bargaining in almost three-fourths of the states which has resulted in major struggles over power and decision making and has alienated teachers at times from their great support, the public
10. School readiness and preparation greatly enhanced by TV and by special children's programs such as Sesame Street and The Electric Company
11. Educating the handicapped as a national priority
12. An enormous increase of foreign language minorities, particularly Spanish-speaking
13. Arrival of the information revolution with data processing
14. Major shifts in the economy, with manufacturing declining precipitously, but service and high technical industries expanding

The impact of these and numerous other major developments in education has been phenomenal:

1. Education has become a multibillion dollar industry.
2. Desegregation is now national in scope although major problems persist.
3. The number of minority children completing high school and attending college has increased prodigiously.
4. A new paradigm is in order, the Learning Society, in which, to make a living, people must learn all their lives.
5. A growing consciousness of multicultural as well as bilingual education is developing.
6. Formerly simple roles (teacher, principal) have multiplied, much as in medicine.
7. School closings and the phenomena of decline occupying educators' minds except in parts of the Sunbelt.
8. Legal issues and procedures at center stage.
9. Suburban parents have developed high expectations for high quality programs.
10. Redrawn individual school districts have produced attendance areas miles from the school resulting in distance and isolation from the community.
11. Single parent families and those with both parents working have complicated communications, involvement, and support.

12. Day care is becoming more important for the working mother, despite a reduced federal role in the social sector adversely affecting development of this service.

13. Adequate nutrition and the latchkey child are now widespread problems.

14. Working parents find less opportunity to share the child's educational experiences—increasing distance between parents and children; declining communication and understanding.

15. Decreasing contact with parents reduces the school's capacity to detect and treat early warning signs.

Notwithstanding, the schools remain in the community, belong to the community and must develop and nurture support and commitment by the community to survive and flourish. Note the formation of the National Coalition for Parent Involvement in Education in 1981 for just these goals (Rosenau 1981).

Role of the Board of Education in School-Community Relationships

The Board of Education is traditionally the repository of local responsibility for educating the young of the community. Responsible to the citizenry, it ensures local input, and within the limitations partly described previously, also a degree of local control.

Boards, therefore, have major responsibility to relate to the community and to communicate with the various publics. "There is probably no enterprise in America which depends so much upon the winning of consent from so many groups simply to be able to do a good job—parents, taxpayers, teachers, custodians, politicians, businessmen. A school district never functions well unless it has the understanding and enthusiastic support of all these groups." (Olds 1965).

Communication also implies a two-way process. The board has to inform the community; it also is obliged to listen to the community and to interpret its needs and wants to the administrators and teachers. (New York State School Boards Association 1973). This means often that special vehicles have to be established to assure communication with all the publics, with all segments of the community. On the other hand, this does not mean that the board of education literally runs the schools; obviously, it cannot. Rather, its function is to set policy. Merrill Phillips (1963), a widely respected school board member, noted that "Experience over the years and in various localities indicates conclusively that school boards function best when they concern themselves with legislation and policy-making and delegate executive and administrative functions to the superintendent and his staff." (For more of Phillips' comments, see p. 305.) In a companion article, John Miller (1963), a former long-time superintendent of the Great Neck, N.Y. schools, stated, "The school board is a policy-making, evaluative body. It delegates to the superintendent of schools responsibility for administration." A range of means useful to communicate with school publics will be discussed in a later section (pp. 283-294, 306).

The board also has to establish and maintain its relationships to the power structure of the community to assure its continued support and involvement (Hunter 1950). Unless its power base is secure, the board and administration will be unable to count on the support of the key decision-making segments in the community.

Role of the Administration in Communicating to the Board and the Community

It is the obligation of the administration to recognize and support the board's role and to recommend to the board professionally appropriate ways to accomplish close and effective communication with all segments of the community. It is imperative that the administration also understand its own obligation to communicate with various publics in the community. Last, administrators and board should avoid what Olds calls the "Swamp of Underestimation." "We underestimate the amount of effort to be made. We underestimate the scope of the public relations task. We underestimate the standards of competency which must be met if we are to communicate effectively. We underestimate the hard thinking and the thoughtful planning which must underlie a public relations program which gets results" (Olds 1965, 6).

Interestingly, Olds focuses on setting clear and realistic district objectives as the basis for an effective school-community relations program. This, of course, is one of the foremost responsibilities of the administration, facilitating establishing realistic goals that point to believable and achievable results. The objectives, thus, can be used to evaluate progress made in accomplishing what we are trying to do and in further setting our sights on how we can do it better.

Olds (p. 7) notes that a school-community-relations program driven by top management commitment to three questions will avoid the pitfalls that render so many programs ineffective. These questions are:

What are we trying to do?
How well are we doing?
How can we do better?

However, communication is a two-way process. The administration wants to make sure that its message is carried to the relevant publics and will be heard by them; similarly, it has to *hear* those publics (Becker and Epstein 1981). In addition, administrators have to realize that they must communicate equally effectively with the staff and students as well (Kaye 1981). Barnard noted that one of the three *indispensable* elements of any organization is communication (1938). The administration has to signal its own intentions, hopes, aspirations, and implementing behavior to its publics, including not only the school board, but also the community, staff, *and* students. How else can the community and staff support their board and administration in their efforts to develop and implement quality programs in the schools?

Vehicles

Communication at School Board Meetings. Of course, at every board meeting a great deal of communication can and does occur. Special arrangements can be devised by boards and administrators who perceive the necessity of communicating more effectively about the schools with the range of various publics. For example, one board meeting per month could be devoted to discussing a major curricular program or a single school's program and presenting it to the community. The new junior high school reorganization can be a focus, as could the business education program or the social studies program. When the board deals with such areas as gifted students, mathematics, and reading programs, it can expect some fire; but questions by the public should be encouraged, both to persuade the board to look into problems, and to develop stronger support by the community.

Of course, participation by the teachers ought to be a part of board meetings as well as in the district program and in each school for more effective communication. Who else knows the program, school, children, and youth as well as the teacher? And who has the greater confidence of the public?

Citizens' Advisory Councils. It is good to have positive intentions, but as administrators have learned, they have to design and use vehicles or organizational structures to accomplish various purposes. As a consequence, administrators are alert for structures and other organizational devices to help them accomplish their goals. A number of vehicles have been devised to establish two-way communication, one of which includes Citizens' Advisory Councils (CAC) (National Schools Public Relations Association 1973). A Citizens' Advisory Council generally is established to include leading community members who provide advice and data on one or more major issues. An important value of such committees or councils is that they are useful to organize the public and interest groups in a proactive manner *before* controversy begins and people become aroused over an issue. A positive approach is recommended to avoid community groups having to organize on their own as a "Concerned Citizens' " group, with the administration placed in a reactive, defensive position. An administration and board who perceive a problem needing community assistance and who then organize to solicit that aid are being proactive. Citizens' Advisory Councils are useful in encouraging the community's views and in developing options to recommend to the administration and/or board to deal with major issues and problems raised, such as bond issues, remodeling needs, reorganization needs, rate increases, or new curriculum (Else, 1983).

The National School Public Relations Association (1973, 6) notes that Citizens' Advisory Councils are most effectively used to focus on major challenges such as:

1. Agreeing on educational philosophy for the district
2. Long-range planning
3. Significant curriculum revision
4. Instituting major organizational changes.

It further adds, "When a school board becomes involved in opening up a new activity (e.g. open education, the twelve-month school year, or career education for the lower grades) the Citizens' Council is a proper medium for helping the board get new insights, facts, or concepts" (NSPRA 1973, 6). Other functions include:

1. Building programs, including site selection
2. Vocational education
3. Adult education
4. Student behavior (including student rights, discipline, dress code, smoking)
5. Sex education and drug programs

6. Curriculum and other instructional matters (including report cards, guidance, gifted students . . ., new programs)
7. Boundaries . . .
8. Integration
9. Transportation and lunch programs
10. Federal programs
11. Purchase of equipment and uniforms
12. Special education
13. Use of school facilities
14. Human relations . . .
15. Improving public relations . . .
16. Needs assessment recommendations . . . (NSPRA 1973).

Interestingly, in some cases school boards have asked citizens advisory groups to do far more than provide advice. Such groups have published newsletters for the district, policed streets against older youths bullying youngsters going to school or returning to their homes, provided scholarships, acted as grievance panels, and performed a host of other functions. As the list indicates, the former relatively clear advising function has opened up into Citizens' Advisory Councils actually providing services and performing selected operations (NSPRA, 1973).

What is clear is that boards and schools have at their fingertips an abundance of willing, able talent that can be harnessed and focused to resolve problems and issues. When one has a useful tool there are often temptations to use it for other purposes. As NSPRA notes, when administration and boards begin to have problems, they can misperceive the basic functions of Citizens' Advisory Councils and try to get them to rubber stamp an unsound idea or policy. Or they can misuse the committees as shock absorbers to cushion the negative feedback the board or administration is receiving. Another misuse is to ask CACs to propagandize or function as a promotor of an idea. Still another misuse is to ask a CAC to rescue a board or administration in trouble. None of these is wise; none will work to accomplish these tasks.

To be sure, such councils should be informed at the outset of their life span, when they are charged with their mission by the official responsible for their formation, that they are *advisory* in nature. Many an administrator and board who have forgotten this item have regretted their forgetfulness in the aftermath of bruised feelings and anger raised when the council, thinking it was a decision maker, found its advice not fully taken or not binding.

Another issue to be considered is the life span of such a structure or committee. A number of administrators in recent years have opted for such advisory committees and councils to focus on a specific task to be performed within a specified time. In these circumstances the council will end its existence with the completion of its task and will not hang around looking for something to do, possibly getting in the way. Other top administrators favor a continuing council, although this then appears more as an advisory board and would seem to have a wider function, such as ongoing budgetary studies.

Other keys to successful action include a specific purpose for the council, and representation of all significant interest groups and publics, regardless of the administrators' personal views and feelings about them. A citizens' group, to consider issues and problems fairly, has to speak for all views. An administrator who chooses to ignore one or more publics only buys long-term problems. Interest groups, once ignored, can wreak havoc if they become sufficiently aroused. Moreoever, a greater divergence of ideas and thinking generally yields a better outcome.

The chairperson is crucial in setting agendas, selecting committee members, and lining up support among key publics and power groups. The chairperson may be selected or elected. If the former, then administrators or boards should pick a person known to be fair and well-regarded in the community, with the influence to command the attention and respect necessary to do the job. The same criterion applies to the other members. Their prestige within their interest groups must be high, or their recommendations will not be respected even by their own constituents. Consequently, selection of members is crucial; yet a myriad of methods of selection abound, used singly or in combination. They include appointment by the board, self-selection or volunteering, election or nomination by a group, or appointment by the professional staff.

As for size, councils can vary from six to several hundred; the most frequent and successful usually range from fifteen to forty-five members; work groups coming from within the CAC may be smaller.

In recent years Citizens' Advisory Councils have begun to develop at the school building level. There the CAC may, indeed, function in an advisory capacity. A survey by *Education USA* as early as 1973 found an increasing number of school buildings are employing CACs to provide such direct services as cafeteria and playground supervision in addition to advice.

As with any complex human enterprise, to function effectively council members need to understand their roles and responsibilities. Consequently, CACs may need in-service training. As the range of CACs increases and as federal guidelines mandate members chosen from a variety of socioeconomic levels, in-service orientation becomes a clearer need for effectiveness.

Some CACs encounter opposition from professional educators, or express antagonism toward the professional staff. Recognition of common interests can help resolve this trap, as can mutual respect.

Volunteers and Paid Aides. Volunteer and paid aides programs, although designed with other purposes in mind, are also vehicles to communicate with the public. Many volunteers are available and willing to help with a great range of tasks needed by the teachers and pupils. The list of tasks in the previous section on advisory councils can be greatly augmented. For example, volunteers can work with a single student in tutorials or with small groups. Specialists can come in to talk on special topics of great interest, or they can present unusual collections or displays. Business persons and professionals can add variety and enrichment to the school program.

Communities typically encompass an enormous wealth of talent and resources, usually available to the schools at the slightest show of interest. Volunteers for schools can include people from business and industry; senior citizens who want to use their skills with children and

and paid aides in the schools can communicate persuasively because they youth; students and professors from universities; physicians; accountants; and other personnel who can enrich the program. Besides enriching the program, such talents, when used constructively and appropriately, can develop considerable goodwill toward the schools. Moreover, volunteers are eyewitness observers with high credibility. They can be highly useful and effective to the schools, if appropriately organized.

Because of this, volunteers and aides should be selected very carefully, however. People who are considered punitive to children or who might be unstable should be shifted to other jobs or even to agencies that require less personal contact with children. One screening method is to have all the human service agencies cooperate in establishing a volunteer bureau that takes community applications and utilizes professional personnel to process them. Communities employing such a device have found it worth the effort. Problems have been avoided without hard feelings because people who would not do well with children have been assigned tasks in settings where they can be successful. An organized volunteer program could have a volunteer directing the operation and evaluating participants. Those found ineffective should be counseled out and shifted to other services. Just as we do not want to retain obviously poor teachers, so we should not retain inadequate volunteers and aides, although dismissals must be performed tactfully. The North Shore suburbs of Chicago organized and implemented such a model for many years and include a whole host of other organizations besides the schools in the enterprise. With social agencies, hospitals, and other organizations participating, volunteers were screened, assigned, supported by appropriate supervisory services, and evaluated.

Adult and Continuing Education and the Community School. Many districts have extensive programs in Adult and Continuing Education and some have developed Community Education programs as well, which provide additional opportunities to involve parents and the community in the schools. With the national average of people with children in the schools falling below 30 percent, it is imperative that schools involve and serve more parents and citizens as sensitively and thoughtfully as possible to develop support and commitment.

Citizens who partake of the huge number of offerings provided by a well-thought-out Adult and Continuing Education or Community School program generally learn to appreciate the schools. Adult Education may develop programs in academic areas such as courses in mathematics, computers, history, and English as a second language; or it may include programs in the arts, including sculpture, painting, ceramics, or piano. Good programs will also include a great range of recreational activities such as bridge, golf, dance, and model building. Such a program tends to appeal to middle class communities.

Another community group in need of service encompasses those who have not graduated from high school and who need a General Educational Development (GED) diploma. Still other people require help with basic literacy and arithmetic skills. Fortunately, state and federal help has been available to support such effort toward improving reading and mathematical literacy. Still another group of people is interested in adult vocational training in a wide variety of skills and fields such as auto mechanics, welding, TV repair, typing, drapery making, cabinetmaking, and sewing. Active school efforts in all these areas can both provide genuine help to meet people's needs and build the support schools need to solve their own problems effectively and creatively.

Community Education is a program sponsored for years by the Mott Foundation of Flint, Michigan, in which the schools are literally used day and night. A good Community Education structure develops a considerable variety of courses to "use all institutional forces in the education of the people" of the community (Seay and Associates 1974, 11). In this extended-day program, day care services may be provided for young children of working parents, perhaps along with breakfast, starting at 7:00 A.M. An after school program is then offered, both for the young children on a day care basis, and for regular students. Community-center-type programs with athletics, sports, arts and crafts, and camping may be developed for youngsters and adolescents. Similarly, evening programs may serve these and other age groups, including adults. Senior citizens may be offered school-based health clinics and a variety of other services in the school buildings. This location makes programs geographically convenient to nearly all. Programs, which tend to be avocational, include accounting, cake decorating, children's art, drawing, dog obedience, French, modern dance, painting, physical fitness, writing, and philosophy.

These programs, in any choice of combinations, link the schools and the community. Varied groupings have been developed in communities such as Little Rock, Arkansas (Shapiro 1981) and West Hartford, Connecticut. Continuing Adult Education and Community Education combine school facilities, town sites, park districts, and private facilities to offer programs which meet society's vast range of needs and interests. For example, park district fieldhouses or community centers may cooperate with the schools in establishing after school programs. Nursing homes may have community education programs for their residents.

Many communities are also establishing links between the schools and the community- and four-year colleges and universities to offer courses for college credit in the local schools. These can include offerings as diverse as Shakespeare, creative writing, contemporary moral problems, great books, speed reading, or real estate investment. Summer programs have also been worked out. Moreover, often shared funding has been arranged among schools, the city, park districts (community centers, golf courses), and the universities, depending on the program. All of these programs discussed above have been successful not only in involving the community, but also in using school facilities over a much longer day for twelve months of the year.

Programs such as these meet community needs; they also provide invaluable face-to-face contact among community members with the schools, and with other agencies. Extended use programs indicate clearly that the schools are for the community. One consequence of such programs has been that vandalism has been significantly reduced in a large number of sites.

A quality adult vocational education and/or community school program will also have its own boards with representatives from various publics carefully chosen. Such boards are helpful in eliciting realistic and supportive input from the business, professional, and working publics, and from teachers, the adult students themselves, city and/or park district representatives, and universities.

A Communications Coordinator. An active communications program between the schools and the community necessitates using competent skilled people to accomplish its goals. Often a board, in wishing to economize, tries to avoid the relatively modest expenses required to select a professionally trained person to accomplish such purposes even though it may be a part-time job in even moderately sized districts. Often the board asks the superintendent to do the work. Even if the superintendent is professionally prepared, it is a waste of the most expensive time and energy in the district. The superintendent was not selected to be a journalist, but rather to stand for and lead to excellence in the schools (Phillips 1963). Present-day problems are too complex and numerous for superintendents to have time or energy to produce the quality communications necessary to accomplish the job.

A better plan is to hire a professional publicist to communicate to the schools' publics. Such a professional should be directly responsible to the superintendent. Communications with the community, while it is every employee's responsibility, should not be delegated to an assistant superintendent.

As is true of any major function in the schools, a good deal of thought should be given to the functions of the person who is to develop and coordinate the school-community relations program. Leslie Kindred (1965) suggested seven major responsibilities for such a job.

1. Establishing and maintaining efficient channels of communication between personnel within the school system
2. Coordinating the public relations activities of all personnel employed by the board of education
3. Providing services on call which contribute either directly or indirectly to the strengthening of the school-community relations program
4. Working cooperatively with outside groups and organizations that have a constructive interest in public education
5. Undertaking assigned responsibilities in the school-community relations program
6. Involving citizens in the work of the school and in the solving of educational problems
7. Serving as a consultant to the superintendent, and through him, to the board of education on matters involving relationships with the community

Essentially, the schools need a person who can provide leadership in planning, developing, organizing, implementing, and evaluating the program, who is realistic in providing advice to the staff, superintendent, and board, and who coordinates all community relations efforts. A school community relations program does not imply a public relations program with its connotations of image manipulation and sleaziness. Rather, it is an attempt to inform the public honestly and straightforwardly about the schools. All too often public relations is viewed as manipulative and secretive, image building without solid substance. Such perceptions must be avoided by an administration and a board with integrity, who are trying to inform the community about the schools.

Other Vehicles. In this effort, then, the principals, central office, and board can be proactive in their support and guidance. School and district newsletters are prime examples of helpful practices. So is a yearly report, and special reports when necessary to deal with remodeling buildings, tax requests, and the like. Parent handbooks, staff newsletters, staff involvement, or high school and junior high school handbooks are other vehicles, as is provision of speakers for various community groups.

A number of ideas for improving school community relations can be noted. One is to determine and even to measure opinion on one or more issues. It is not necessary to survey an entire community completely to get an idea about this. Relatively small samples carefully drawn according to acceptable sampling approaches, and use of a randomized method, can determine attitudes on a variety of topics.

Relations with the press and community newspapers are crucial and should be attended to with special care. Relationships, once soured, can be sweetened again only with great difficulty and effort. It is easier and better to keep them breathing easily than to rescue them from the depths, half drowned or asphyxiated.

An important vehicle for this is to be honest and above-board with the press. Their trust is permanently impaired with anything less, so it is vital to be honest. Most reporters are fair and wish to be supportive; their help can be elicited to present stories and information objectively (McCormack 1983). A superintendent may wish to have lunch with the education editor of the city paper and with the editor of the community paper sporadically to let them know of impending developments and programs that are effective and interesting.

When appropriate, press conferences for important events plus features of successes and interesting programs are useful. All papers, as well as the community papers, should be called. Playing favorites is a sure way to produce needless negative feelings. It is also important to hold back publicity until a program is solid. Who wants to publicize programs that are not yet firmly based or successful? On the other hand, when programs do fail, handling criticism and complaints honestly and openly is probably the most useful approach. The papers will probably find out much of the truth about problems anyway and honesty is the best method of establishing one's openness to criticism and one's intention to do something about the problem.

Another relevant item is the role of nonteaching personnel in the community relations of the district and local school. Often this group is as numerous as the professionals. A wise system perceives everyone as a resource and a communicator, and involves the total staff in community relations.

A good number of problems may exist in developing effective school-community relationships. If the board of education and top executives do not perceive their roles (including honest, open communication) in this regard, and do not understand the nature and complexity of the process, such a program will hardly get off the ground, let alone be effective. It could even be counterproductive.

The Individual School Building

Similarly, local school building administrators have to understand their roles in communicating to the public and be supportive of district efforts. Nothing can be quite as effective as a school newsletter that highlights children's efforts and work, and that has photos of them. For both individual school and district, featuring children's accomplishments, recognizing teachers, custodians, secretaries, and other personnel including the administration and board is more crucial than featuring the superintendent's or principal's photograph in issue after issue. Schools that communicate with their parents often find much improved relationships and, of course, better understanding of the school's purposes, program, and operations.

In an individual school building, typically, a principal can call on a teacher or teachers for help. For the central or district effort, some school systems have found talent within their organizaton to do a professional and creditable job, while others have to go outside to professionals. A budget adequate to support the program and the skilled personnel is essential to the success of a quality and yet reasonably priced effort. These remarks should be construed as supporting a professional-appearing product to represent each of the schools and the district to its constituency. The National School Public Relations Association is a resource to help produce a better program.

Last, to make communications a priority it must *be* a priority. This may mean giving it force and impetus through an in-service program. The Great Neck, N.Y. school system yearly supported a weekend conference with the board and administration to discuss the school-community relations program. That is a statement of priority.

Teacher and Administrative Participation in the Community

If teachers, administrators, and boards want the community to participate in the schools, they have to be willing to participate in vital community activities and organizations. For years, in the DeKalb Community Unit Schools, DeKalb, Illinois, administrators participated in all the service clubs and organizations. This resulted in excellent relationships and support by the community. But like much that takes time to develop, a long period of persistent effort is required.

Adopt-a-School

A number of school districts (Pinellas County Schools, Clearwater, Florida; Little Rock Schools, Little Rock, Arkansas; Denver Schools, Denver, Colo.) have developed programs in which businesses support the district by adopting a school (Ozmon 1982). Banks, insurance companies, industries, and large corporations are prime prospects for such an enterprise. One vehicle for such an effort is the Chamber of Commerce.

The Kaffe (Coffee) Klatch is a key event to garner support, from passing a referendum, to developing positive attitudes, to a new major program. Parent visits to classroom innovations, carefully planned, can be an excellent way to let people see for themselves. Typically, educators do not see the schools as do persons outside the profession. Most people are impressed with the atmosphere of a school provided that it is peaceful and students are attending classes. One system even has developed a format having citizens function as a visiting team in one school a year (DeLucia and McCarthy-Miller 1983).

A Model of a Moderate-Sized Urban School Community Relations Program

The following model is one generated by the superintendent and staff of the Little Rock schools, Little Rock, Arkansas (1981). With some adaptation, most of these ideas are applicable to most systems.

As is typical of most urban districts, a changing school population and white citizens' apprehension over those changes led to a great deal of white flight in Little Rock. In the late 1970s a new superintendent, Paul Masem, was chosen to deal with these complex problems. Vigorous programs were established on several fronts, including making reading the first priority of the system to prevent drops in scores and eventually to improve them. Masem and his staff also focused on community relations, and undertook the following initiatives.

1. Developed a communications plan for the district complete with target publics and groups, including the contact person to do the job, and specifying time lines. Numerous meetings were generated for various purposes explained below.
2. Established a full time community relations position staffed by a person with considerable expertise and skill who could develop a quality product and approach.
3. Developed a logo for the schools (a student reading a book) (Figure 13-1).

The logo designed is an excellent example of how art, through right-brained perceptions, can reinforce the cognitive appeals a system is making; for it shows a balanced student body half Black and half white, reading equally integrated texts.

4. Established a theme for the district—"Continuing a Tradition of Excellence"—capitalizing on the opinion of the community that the schools were excellent in former years.
5. Started an Adopt-a-School program, with major organizations adopting schools and working in partnership with those schools.
6. Published an annual report pointing to the successes of the system.
7. Developed a publication, *Focus*, with a key theme for each issue, generally concentrating on students' accomplishments and interesting and different programs.
8. Implemented a Key Communicators group of attorneys, businessmen and businesswomen, and PTA leaders who were continually informed on all major issues so that they could communicate with their publics.
9. Adopted a slogan for the schools with bumper stickers, "My Heart Is in the Public Schools and So Are My Children."
10. Worked with the churches in supporting the schools not only from the pulpit but in having ministers enroll their own children in the schools.

Little Rock Public Schools

FIGURE 13-1 *Logo of the Little Rock (Ark.) Public Schools*

11. Implemented a special outreach program to attract white patrons, enrollment tent meetings with pledge cards committing patrons to go to the schools (to deal publicly with the decision usually made in isolation at home as to whether or not to enroll children in the public schools.)
12. Admitted senior citizens to all school events with free passes.
13. Developed a program in which the condition of the schools was explained to realtors, along with the programs for improving them. Printed packets of information were prepared to hand out to newcomers. (This is vital to any enterprise because realtors tend to reflect and shape community feelings about the schools. Any program that misses this key group will founder.)
14. Established a welcoming service for newcomers with volunteers and parents who explained the schools.
15. Implemented a speakers bureau to present talks with groups in the community.
16. Designed press releases for important events and press conferences at least twice a year to inform the papers about the directions for the year.
17. Met with newspaper editors and personnel from the TV stations at breakfasts.
18. Developed a program for parents to visit the schools.
19. Conducted museum events from the schools' archives with the State Historical Museum.
20. Developed brochures using the logo to explain the many programs above.
21. Implemented media events such as reading fairs and art fairs in shopping centers.

Summary

This chapter has reviewed the role of the school as an integral part of the community. The American tradition of localism has been explored briefly, together with the trends changing this long-established practice. Relevant changes in American communities and in education were explored with their implications for changing local control.

The roles of the board of education and the administration in communicating with the community were explored. Vehicles to establish effective programs were preferred, together with some guidance for their effective organization, development, and operation. An example of a far-reaching communications program was presented to provide a practical illustration that combined the critical elements discussed throughout the chapter.

References

Barnard, C. I. 1938. *Functions of the Executive.* Cambridge: Harvard University Press.

Becker, H. S. and **J. L. Epstein** 1981. *Parent Involvement: Teacher Practices and Judgments.* Baltimore: John Hopkins University, Center for the Social Organization of Schools.

Campbell, R. F. 1963. *Nationalizing Influences on Secondary Education.* Chicago: Midwest Administration Center.

Campbell, R. F., and **J. A. Ramseyer** 1955. *The Dynamics of School-Community Relationship.* Boston: Allyn and Bacon.

Cone, J. C. 1981. "How to Enlist and Keep Support of Your Constituency." In *Managing Schools in Hard Times,* edited by Stanton Leggett, 17–22. Chicago: Teach 'Em.

Cubberly, E. P. 1948. *The History of Education.* Boston: Houghton Mifflin.

DeLucia, J., and **G. McCarthy-Miller** 1983. "Community Validation: One Secret of Support for Schools." *The American School Board Journal* 170 (April): 40–41.

Else, D. 1983. "Ask Parents for Curriculum Advice." *The American School Board Journal* 170 (June): 34–38.

Hunter, F. 1950. *Community Power Structure.* Chapel Hill: University of North Carolina Press.

Kaye, S. 1981. "Keeping the Students on Your Side is Worth the Struggle" in *Managing Schools in Hard Times* edited by Stanton Liggett, 23–28. Chicago: Teach'Em.

Kindred, L. 1965. "The Public Relations Job Description." In National School Public Relations Association, *Public Relations Gold Mine.* Yearbook. 7: 15–16. Washington, D.C.. National Education Association.

McCormack, K. 1983. "What It Takes to be a Darling of the Media." *The American School Board Journal* 170 (May): 32-33.

Miller, J. C. 1963. "What Should a Superintendent Expect of His School Board?" *Journal of the New York State School Boards Association* 27 (March).

National School Public Relations Association. 1973. *Citizens Advisory Committees.* Washington, D.C.. National Education Association.

New York State School Boards Association. 1973. *Communications Public Relations.* Rev. Albany, N.Y.: New York State School Boards Association.

Olds, R. 1965. "Pitfalls in the School Public Relations Programs." In National School Public Relations Association, *Public Relations Gold Mine.* Yearbook. 7: 5-14. Washington, D.C.: National Education Association.

Ozmon, H. 1982. "Adopt-a-School." *Phi Delta Kappan* (January): 350-51.

Phillips, M. 1963. "What Should a School Board Expect From Its Superintendent?" *Journal of the New York State School Boards Association* 27 (March).

Rosenau, F. 1981. "Washington Report." *Phi Delta Kappan* (October): 85.

Seay, M., and Associates, 1974. *Community Education: A Developing Concept.* Midland, Mich.: Pindell Publishing Co.

Shapiro, A. 1981. "Community Use of Schools." In *Survey, Little Rock Schools,* edited by Stanley Leggett, et al. Little Rock, Ark.

Taylor, B. L., and **T. L. Groom.** 1971. *Social Studies Education Projects: An ASCD Index.* Washington, D.C.: Association for Supervision and Curriculum Development.

Tucker, H. J., and **L. H. Ziegler.** 1980. *Professionals vs. the Public: Attitudes, Communication and Response in School Districts.* Eugene, Ore.: Center for Educational Policy and Management, University of Oregon.

Wise, A. E. 1979. *Legislative Learning: The Bureaucratization of the American Classroom.* Berkeley: University of California Press.

14

In order to solve a problem, you've got to have guts. Most people pick around the edges at pieces of it and then don't have the guts to do things to really solve it. Fear is the great immobilizer.

- Judy Holbrook

Special Issues, Controversy, Conflict Resolution

Prologue: A Case Study/Scenario

When Mary Ann Payton, the principal at Quail Hollow Middle School, hustled in at 7:35 A.M. Monday morning, Ms. Luckman, her secretary, motioned her over to see a couple of items on the morning list of "Top Priorities." At the top of the list was Mr. Sam Harris's name. Ms. Luckman told Ms. Payton that Mr. Harris "was hoppin' mad." It seems that Mr. Harris's son, Marc, had just transferred from a nearby community into the eighth grade, and the father had learned over the weekend that there were no interscholastic sports in the middle school. Mr. Harris demanded to know why the school didn't have interscholastic football so his son could make the high school team next year as a freshman. The secretary indicated that Mr. Harris had threatened "to go to a business associate of mine" who also happened to be the president of the board of education. Ms. Payton briefly wondered how well this newly elected president understood and supported the middle school philosophy she and others had fought so hard to implement.

Item number two on Ms. Luckman's top priorities list was a session with the school board's attorney in preparation for the Friday meeting of the board's bargaining team, on which Ms. Payton served. She felt both a bit afraid and excited at the same time. Ms. Payton recalled that they were starting negotiations in another week, and knew that the teacher's building representative was displeased to have her on the board's team. She had even suggested that such action on Ms. Payton's part could impair her relations with the staff. Ms. Payton tried to figure out what the association's priorities might be.

The next item was a brief and informal meeting with the teacher association's building representative over other issues. In response to Ms. Payton's inquiry asking if the association representative had indicated what she wanted, Ms. Luckman shook her head, and then murmured a comment about "the choir and something else." Ms. Payton wondered what was on the building representative's mind, and briefly recalled the steps in the grievance procedure process initiated in last year's contract.

Another item on the agenda was a meeting for a staffing set for 1 P.M. Ms. Payton knew that the parents were terribly frightened at the prospect of having their child placed in a special education class; and she asked Ms. Luckman if the district staffing specialist would come in a half hour earlier to discuss ways of working with the parents to explain their rights and to reduce their fear and anxiety. She knew that the district was considering establishing a due process mediator, a sort of ombudsman (see p. 272) to help solve cases where the parents differed from the school's recommendation.

A tall, gaunt, well-dressed, but somewhat agitated parent clutching a Bible to his chest sat on one of the chairs in the corner of the waiting room. Ms. Luckman did not know what the man wanted and indicated that he had come in just a few minutes ago. Ms. Payton recalled that the board attorney's phone number was on her desk and the superintendent's instruction was to call the superintendent first, and then the attorney, if any legal issue arose, particularly as it related to Association contract or religious problems, or the family life education program just initiated.

She also remembered a letter from the attorney of another parent, Ms. Lu Anne Biggs, stating that under no circumstances were her two children to be sent home with their father, from whom she was separated, or with anyone else. The letter noted that Ms. Biggs had complete custody, and that Mr. Biggs was not to be permitted to see the children in school or on the school grounds. Ms. Payton recalled a conversation with her good friend, Gayle Sailors, principal of an elementary school, who had just mentioned over the past weekend receiving a similar letter, and who had been warned by the school attorney that kidnappings by parents who had lost custody battles were becoming more commonplace and were to be carefully guarded against.

Ms. Luckman reminded the principal that her note to Alana Michael, the choral and band director, had produced results. Ms. Michael had said that she would come in during the third period. Ms. Payton thought about the teacher representative's comment about the choir and then wondered how to help Ms. Michael see that having no black students in band and only one in choir (despite a 17 percent black enrollment in the school) was potentially explosive. She knew that Ms. Michael, a long-time teacher and the building representative's alternate, was powerful politically both with the teachers and with the community, and she decided to use a direct approach, asking Ms. Michael about the issue directly.

She wondered if she would want to call an emergency meeting of her cabinet should some of these problems and issues expand or develop sufficiently by the end of the day. She felt glad that she had asked the building representative to serve on the cabinet.

Ms. Payton's day had begun.

People in Organizations Deal with Conflict Daily

The preceding case study of a not-so-unreal school setting illustrates the daily issues, problems, and conflicts that swirl around practicing school administrators and supervisors. In the distant past, perhaps, the schools had fewer conflicts, fewer controversies, fewer landmines. But in an increasingly complex society, with conflicting expectations, purposes, and demands for the schools and for education, such conflict is not only to be expected, it is natural—indeed, it is normal. It is, in short, a condition of contemporary life with its multicultural strains from the pulling and hauling of different interests.

In truth, the kinds of controversies, problems, and conflicts the schools and their staffs face parade across the screens and pages of our media daily. The spectrum includes:

1. Questions about raising school taxes despite declining enrollments.
2. In the face of declining enrollments, what costs should be reduced?
    A. Personnel? Teacher associations and parents usually raise objections.
    B. Athletics? Parents and booster clubs get upset. (Mr. Harris would.)
    C. Academic and nonacademic programs? How does an administration establish priorities?
    D. Cut art, music, and physical education? Difficult to do in the face of parent objections and contract requirements to provide teachers with free periods.
    E. Maintenance and custodial services? These unions will object; and, besides, it is a truism that buildings do not heal themselves.
    F. Library? A small part of the budget at best.
3. Textbook selection and censorship: cases have reached the Supreme Court on First Amendment bases, meaning that administrators and boards have limitations on their behavior in eliminating texts or in removing books from library shelves.
4. Prayer in the school: a major controversy now perceived as a constitutional issue, more than two decades after the Supreme Court ruling. (Ms. Payton's visitor may be interested in this area.)
5. Sex, family life education, and the church: some parents feel that the family and church are the proper repositories for teaching this; others feel the schools are the only source for most children and youth. Generally, this issue produces inevitable problems unless great care is taken to develop heavy involvement, and escape hatches for objectors. (Ms. Payton's well-dressed visitor may possibly focus on her family life education program.)
6. Teaching evolution vs. creationism: controversies abound over the land even though recent court decisions have decided in favor of evolution. (Ms. Payton's visitor may also wish to examine this issue, a thorny one for our society presently.)

7. Collective bargaining: practiced in three-fourths of the states. The ultimate weapon is the strike or job action, particularly at the beginning of the school year. These are usually of great interest to the media. (Note that Ms. Payton has included the teacher association representative on her cabinet and meets with her to resolve issues.)
8. Teacher walkouts.
9. Students were accorded rights as citizens by the *Tinker v. Des Moines* and other decisions of the Supreme Court. (See chapter 8.) Increasingly, due process rights and procedures were established for students. Education became increasingly regarded as a property right and could not be removed arbitrarily, capriciously, or by whim. (Note that the principal has the board attorney's phone number on her desk.)
10. Parental concern over the adequacy of student discipline, for the last seven years ranked at the top of parent anxiety about the schools as reflected in Gallup polls on the schools (Gallup 1982).
11. The great increase in special education efforts to educate handicapped children brought on by court cases and federal law (94–142). Major changes in general procedures and in due process procedures were ushered in by these and other events. (The department has a staffing specialist and is contemplating a due process mediator.)
12. Overemphasis on sports. Even administrators "red shirt" their own children in junior high school: they hold their children back a year so that they can compete better with smaller boys in the same grade. (Ms. Payton's first agenda item lands in this domain and gives her a great deal of concern.)
13. Reading scores.
14. Mathematics scores.
15. Spelling skills.
16. Tax revolts. Propositions 13 in California and 2-1/2 in Massachusetts are outstanding examples.
17. Desegregation and busing: still having serious discussion by the public to the point of talking about limiting court jurisdiction or even having a constitutional amendment to prohibit busing.
18. Sex equity issues: coed physical education, equality of coaching stipends to both sexes.
19. A greater willingness to litigate by increasing numbers of people (Ms. Payton has specific instructions from the superintendent to call the school board attorney on any legal issue.)

The basic question any administrator, supervisor, teacher, and board member faces is how to deal constructively with such conflicts. Facing issues proactively rather than reactively, constructively rather than defensively is psychologically and strategically advantageous (Robbins 1974). As a matter of fact, Robbins notes, "Without conflict, there would be few new challenges: there would be no stimulation to think through ideas; organizations would only be apathetic and stagnant" (Robbins, 15). The question, of course, is how to do this effectively amidst the welter of demands and the busy schedules all administrators have (Nebgen 1978). Nebgen states, "Until recently, conflict has been considered a destructive force. The value of conflict in improving performance and helping to overcome staleness and inertia in organizations has only been recognized in the past decade" (Nebgen 2).

Procedures and Strategies: Alternative Approaches

The large number of conflicts and issues facing administrators, superintendents, and boards can be overwhelming. An atmosphere of crisis and excitement may be permitted to develop and control us. In such a setting there is a tendency to treat each issue as separate and independent. Each issue is handled on an ad hoc basis in the passing cascade of events and crises. While, indeed, some issues may be separate, many common elements prevail. It is more economical to see the commonalities and to develop structures, approaches, and processes that fit many and that help to produce calmness in dealing with problems.

Another common approach when people feel under fire is to treat each issue when it pops up and becomes a crisis, like "firemen" putting out brush fires. This approach, too, is reactive rather than proactive, and yet can be emotionally satisfying. The administration can come off as very effective for a while. Crises are met, flames are quenched, great effort is expended, much action occurs; and much complimentary recognition can result. Administrators can get the reputation of being tough minded, vigorous, and active in their firemen's role. Lack of planning is often unnoticed in the furor; but the absence of planning unfortunately precludes identifying and treating causes.

An alternative approach produces administrative and office styles that appear duller and more routine. It treats issues in the broad context of policy making, as thoughtfully as possible, and yet proactively.

Therefore, a structure for policy making is necessary as is a clearly understood process. Such a process and structure should include, where appropriate, key persons from the Board of Education and various levels of the administration, staff, community, and students. Typically, the superintendent utilizes a cabinet of top level executives in this manner, expanding to the previously mentioned groups when support and involvement are necessary. Teachers association representatives may also be involved, depending on the issue and the contract. In recent years principals also have developed expanded cabinets as advisory structures (as has Ms. Payton), and even community advisory boards of education.

Additional Approaches: Models of Conflict Resolution

In recent years, a good deal of time and effort have begun to be spent on approaches to resolving conflicts (Fillby 1975) to place such approaches in some perspective and in a conceptual construct. All that follow have had some wide dissemination and focus on third party roles in resolving conflict in organizations (Trusty 1982).

Legal Approaches

Legal approaches to conflict resolution are based on an adversarial relationship between the two parties and their respective attorneys. Rules are quite formal and often use a win-lose approach. Decisions reached are based on precedents, with conflicts sometimes mediated by a disinterested third party, the judge. Supposedly the process is free of publicity, pressure, and politics. Up to the early 1970s school boards rarely contracted with attorneys on a regular basis. Since then large numbers of boards have retained attorneys to handle the burgeoning load of litigation and legal issues the schools face.

(As Ms. Payton, the principal, is contemplating the issues of the day and her visitor, she is obviously thinking of the legal processes involved in a religion-in-the-schools case. The contract with the teacher association, a further vital issue in the back of her mind, is another legal matter, enforceable in court. Indeed, the board just purchased a liability policy for all administrators and board members as evidence of their concern about lawsuits.)

Note that a procedure has been established by the district to call the superintendent and then confer with the attorney in case any situation arises with the potential legal ramifications, a major change from the casual attitudes of most districts up to the 1970s.

Collective Bargaining

This, too, is a formal process that often leaves neither party fully satisfied. Its structure is adversarial and tends to polarize groups, often producing conflict and alienation. (Ms. Payton is directly involved in collective bargaining on the board's team; she will meet with the building representative to discuss issues, which is probably required by the contract. She may even be involved in the first step of a grievance procedure today. These procedures, now a part of many contracts, are a series of steps to resolve organizational disputes.)

Being on the board team not only binds Ms. Payton closer to the superintendent and subordinate administrators; it also provides her with a systemwide view of the negotiations process and economic and personnel factors. It also can split principals from the teachers associations and cause we-they rifts.

The Psychiatric, Clinical, or Counseling Model

In this approach a third party who is highly trained, certificated by proper authorities, and very knowledgeable uses approaches ranging from extremely directive to relatively nondirective. Typically, social workers and psychologists perform this function in the schools.

(As noted on page 298, Ms. Payton can call on the staffing specialist or the due process mediator to help with the staffing procedures of placing children with special education problems in the most appropriate educational setting for them.) Up to the enactment of Public Law 94-142, psychologists and social workers were seldom found in the schools to deal with special problems of exceptional children being educated in appropriate settings. The list of specialists and programs has grown considerably. The counseling model also applies in collective bargaining; if both parties have problems achieving a settlement, they can ask for a mediator who can only advise. If such mediation still fails to secure a contract, the parties can resort to yet another form of "counseling," called "binding arbitration."

The Administrative Model

In this process, conflict is solved by a high-level administrator who usually wants to resolve the problem of protecting the organization rather than solving the problem; the approach assumes that "rightness" belongs to the person with the higher status (the king's rule). Legitimization of the role depends on the level of the person in that organization; the higher up, the more legitimate. Established administrative rules and procedures are inadequate to handle the problem; they just paper it over. Often a "sample" of one is the basis for a good deal of generalizing by the administrator gathering data. The clients in this model are subordinates in the organization. Judgment is the primary basis of this decision-making, and favors the organization and the top echelons.

This model can become ritualized and move into a form of control of the employees. It is characterized by the top administrator using position power to solve the issues. Often the employee feels he or she has been taken advantage of; this, in turn, leads to the feeling that the organization is unjust but also unbeatable. (Ms. Payton doesn't use this model in the case study/scenario, except for letting the superintendent know that the father who wants interscholastic football may be in touch with the board president. She feels that this model exacerbates bad feelings and glosses over the real issues.)

Parental Model

In this model the father/mother (or the principal) is head of the structure and deals with problems and issues in a somewhat authoritarian mode, as parents may do with small children. This conflict management model is an integral part of the context of the organization. The unique aspect of this model is that the client changes (children and teachers grow), so the system changes. The model also has norms (standards) which can vary from social system (or group) to social system. In some schools principals have great influence and can operate as father or mother figures. Usually this system is protected by law, for the principal has a zone of indifference where she or he is free to function (Barnard 1938) and courts hesitate to intervene. The criteria are generally values, morality, and ethics.

The doctrine of *in loco parentis* used to be applied in the schools, but is used to a lesser extent at present because of legal rights which have been extended to students. Notwithstanding, the principal is often a father or mother figure and this approach may be helpful in resolving problems. (Ms. Payton does not seem to be employing this approach in the items presented. Possibly she is too young to be a mother figure to the 50 percent of the teachers who have been in the school ten or more years and who are older than she. She does use persuasion and influence at times.)

Role of the Administrator in Dealing with Controversy and Conflict

The role of the administrator in conflict deserves attention. We have mentioned earlier that the appropriate role is not to resist change, not to stand pat, not to be reactive. Rather, the administrator in the face of increasingly complex situations and problems has to deal constructively with change. In short, the role of the administrator is one of being a *change agent* to bring constructive and planned change to the organization she or he directs. A large number of administrators, however, do not see themselves as change agents. The very mention of the word "change" disconcerts some people. Their assumption is that they want to maintain the status quo. Chapters 13 and 15 deal with that set of assumptions, pointing to the immense changes affecting education in our society and noting the impossibility of resisting change. Such assumptions are simply unrealistic and unthinkable in the face of the ever-increasing rate of change and the number of changes society and the schools face now and in the future.

A great body of literature exists on the leadership role of administrators and supervisors, which generally points to the conclusion that the business of leadership is to lead. Reactive leadership doesn't fit the notion of leadership. Proactive approaches do. Management, however, is often conceived as keeping an uncluttered desk, rather than as providing inspiration, leadership, a goal, direction, or drive to the organization.

Katz (1955) has identified three skills of administration, of which the third is pertinent to this discussion and to the thesis of this chapter. (His first is Technical Skill, at the worker level; his second is Human Relations Skill. His last skill of administration is the Conceptual one, particularly relevant to top levels of organization leadership. It is an intellectual skill of having the capacity to perceive key, powerful trends and directions in society relevant to one's organization and then to take action to assure that several years hence the organization is in position either to take advantage of the trends, or to cope with them effectively. Lacking such a vital skill, the organization is subject to such unfortunate occurrences as competitive inadequacies, not perceiving changes affecting it, looking for wrong markets, and other equally disastrous results. The graveyard of administration is filled with organizational mastodons and brontosauri whose top leadership couldn't adapt to changing conditions. America's steel, auto, and motorcycle industries, as examples, are having troubles because foreign competitors have surged past them in a variety of domains.

Consequently, the administration has to develop processes and structures to deal with touchy items, with actual and potential conflicts and with future problems in a thoughtful and constructive way, or face disaster.

A variety of approaches does exist to obtain these results. Often an executive forms a team, a cabinet, a task force, or a citizen's advisory council (see Chapter 13) to discuss issues and to recommend action. Thorough, open, and honest discussion of all issues that may have major implications for the system is usually quite helpful, and develops more alternatives. The more options developed, the richer the array of potential solutions. Cabinets that joke a great deal, or that operate out of fear of punitive action by the leader and are "yes-men" or "yes-women" are usually ineffective in generating and evaluating options. Thus, once thoroughly discussed, issues and problems may be brought to the attention of the board along with appropriate analysis and recommendations. Not only that, but the administration is also responsible to recommend a policy-making process to the board. This will be discussed later. (Note that Ms. Payton has a cabinet that she can convene for emergencies, as well as regularly.)

Boards expect superintendents to bring issues to them with well-thought-out recommendations together with an analysis of the implications for each alternative course of action. Superintendents expect principals to do the same. If principals do not bring potentially "hot" issues to their superiors, superintendents often react emotionally.

Board Expectations for the Superintendent	Merrill Phillips, the widely recognized member of the Board of Education of Bedford—New Castle—North Castle—Pound Ridge, N.Y., for many years, was asked to ponder the board's expectations for the superintendent (Phillips 1963). His thoughtful response included as its most important point that the major "professional quality to be sought in a school superintendent is that of educational leadership. For with distinctions in this leadership role will be found the ability to affect significantly the education aspirations of a community, lifting its sights and helping it find justifiable reasons and motivations for support commensurate with broader areas and heightened goals."

In short, the role of the leader is, as Campbell (1977) notes, to develop goals and then organize to implement them. But establishing goals means impressing them on the minds and hearts of the community and the staff. To portray it even more vividly and realistically, the leader's foremost task is to establish a vision, a hope for the organization. As gasoline is the fuel of the automobile, so hope is the fuel of an organization. People in organizations, to be highly motivated, have to see a potentially better future. The leader is responsible for that vision, for involving people in developing and communicating it, and then planting it in the heart of the organization so that it is believed and begins to direct people's actions.

Without question, conceiving believable and achievable visions constitutes one of the most important tasks in any organization. The father of contemporary administration, Chester Barnard (1938) pointed to three essentials of any organization, the first of which is a common purpose. Establishing common purposes (such as achieving 100 percent literacy) sets priorities and energizes people. Petty problems are perceived as exactly that; a sense of urgency develops, and people can join their strengths. It is a pleasure to work in an organization with a sense of purpose, with a mission people believe in.

Role of the Board

In a companion article to that by Phillips, John Miller, superintendent of the Great Neck, N.Y., schools for more than a fifth of a century and widely recognized as a down-to-earth philosopher, tackled the superintendent's expectations of the board (Miller 1963). The first, of course, was its role in making policy on the recommendation of the superintendent. This, needless to say, includes cooperating to support the superintendent's recommendations in establishing policy-making structures and process.

In the process any wise board would seek background information as well as suggestions as to alternative courses of action from both the administration and the community. The board would also take into account the impact on the community, administration, teacher, and students of each policy alternative. In the process, the board has to work as a team. The board is a board only when it sits as a board legally. Individual board members cannot make decisions alone, although the temptation to make promises is a great one. Miller also notes that the board member is elected as a lay person who has to rely on the judgments of the professional the board selects (the superintendent) and the team the superintendent selects.

The Policy-Making Process and Structures

Policy making can be defined in more than one manner. Campbell and Mazzoni (1976) defined it as (a) decision(s) designed to give direction to a chosen course of action. Anderson (1975) considers policy making as the sum of processes in which all parties in and related to a social system shape the goals of the system.

Cunningham (1959) perceived policy making as very complex. "To understand the policy-making process, the observer must know the *setting* in which it takes place. The multi-dimensional. [*sic*] interrelatedness of institutions, individuals, and groups that are operative in the policy-making arena assume intelligibility only when cast in the background of populations, resources, topography, history, traditions, and economy."

Cunningham went on to note five steps of policy-making: Initiation, Definition, Deliberation, Enactment, and Consequences.

Initiation. Policy-making often occurs when a problem develops. Boards, administrators, teachers, students, and parents begin to be aware of a problem with various issues and ramifications for them. For example, Mary Ann Payton (p. 297), the principal of Quail Hollow Middle School, might call the superintendent to let him know that a parent might be raising the policy issue of interscholastic athletics with the president of the school board. If the well-dressed visitor raised issues relating to religion, it would be imperative for the chief administrator or a delegated subordinate to know of this case and of potential emerging support for it from others. Also, how would the board stick by its commitment to a middle school intramural policy rather than interscholastics should the very aggressive parent raise that issue?

Definition. As in medicine, the problem(s) and the issue(s) cannot be treated until they are accurately defined or diagnosed. Focusing on symptoms instead of the cause of the problem doesn't usually produce constructive action. It may often mislead. Consequently, the very basis of dealing with issues rests in defining them accurately. Without this, constructive action is often an accident. Trying to determine the teacher association's priorities in negotiations would be vital in preparing the strategy of counteroffers and in figuring out responses to make in negotiations in terms of the resources the board was willing to provide.

After serving as a professor of educational administration for a number of years, Jean Hills worked as an elementary principal for one year and had some strong words, worthy of full quotation, about administrators' inability to diagnose problems accurately (1975):

> Preparation programs for principals should place heavy emphasis on the development of critical-analytical and problem-solving skills [because C]asual observations across a wide variety of situations have led me to conclude that the problem-solving efforts of school administrators succeed less well than they might for want of the application of certain analytical skills and problem-solving techniques. The sorts of observations which have led me to draw that conclusion are illustrated by the following:
>
> 1. Administrators spend a great deal of time searching for solutions to un- or ill-defined problems.
> 2. Administrators spend a great deal of time debating irresolvable issues.
> 3. Administrators seldom question the problematic status of situations, or the desirability of stated objectives.
> 4. The search for solutions to problems tends to be a random, unsystematic process.
> 5. Solutions to problems tend to be highly generalized, unfocused, and ill-adapted to the problems to which they are applied.

6. The selection of a problem situation from among a number of alternatives tends to be an arbitrary, non-rational process.
7. Little effort is made to identify the conditions that permit (and/or cause) problematic situations to occur. Problems are seldom seen as symptoms of underlying causes.
8. Problems tend to be treated as discrete, independent, isolated phenomena. Relations among problems are seldom identified.
9. Problem-solving tends to proceed on a "putting out brush fires" basis with little attention given to systematic planning.

The root of these "problems" seems to lie in the administrator's (educators'?) tendency to deal with highly generalized, vaguely stated, diffuse problem statements, e.g., "home-school relations problems," "communication problems," "human relations problems," "emotional problems," etc. Given a vague, abstractly stated, diffuse problem of the sort identified above, items 3-9 on the list follow automatically. "Home-school relations" is a name, not for a problem, but for a class of problems, and it is difficult, if not impossible, either to question the importance of, or to find an effective solution for, a class of problems. One of the more obvious reasons for the difficulty of finding an effective solution is the fact that solutions for such vague, generalized problems tend to be as vague and generalized as the problems themselves. Furthermore, given a set of vague, generalized alternative solutions to a vague, generalized problem, one can only select what "feels like the best approach." (Hills 1975)

Hills makes the further point that frequently administrators rely on actions that have been successful in the past, even though such actions may be inappropriate for the present situation.

(It is noteworthy that Ms. Payton's day began with her trying to assess what most of her problems were, how they would affect the operation of the school, and how she could deal with them. She is thoughtful and does not appear to leap at simplistic solutions.)

Deliberation. This step involves looking at the issues or problems from as many aspects as possible, constructing alternative courses of action, and then examining the implication of each for the various reference groups, publics and resources of the school system. This is a difficult process, at times requiring the cooperative action of the board and the staff to look at the politics and dynamics of the system and the community.

Haste in this step can be a serious error, since backing off or undoing policy is generally somewhat more difficult than establishing one in a new area for the first time. Often, involvement of key publics and social systems for *advisory* purposes is useful and important. (See Chap-

ter 13 on Citizen Advisory Councils.) It provides input from a variety
of publics, prepares them for various courses of action, and generates
support for the initiative. This is where open and frank consideration of
the problems and courses of action available as options are indispensable.
Consequently it is also where an active Citizens Advisory Council can
be useful, and a quality administrative cabinet is indispensable. The
cabinet has to be able to generate the widest possible number of alternatives together with an accurate analysis of the implications of each alternative for each important reference group (Griffiths 1959).

Superintendents or principals who favor rubber-stamp cabinets do
not get the broadest possible range of options because the subordinates
lack the courage to offer suggestions or comments. (Ms. Payton had
formed a cabinet to give her the best possible analysis of the problems
and then to generate a wide range of options to deal with them. She
even includes the teacher association's board representative on the
cabinet. She hopes she will get issues and perceptions on the table
realistically and accurately.)

Enactment. It is here that the board role ceases, as does the committee's. The administrator implements the policy with the full advice of
the board, to be sure; but the administration is responsible for this phase,
no matter how complex. Consequently, once the board has determined
its policy in negotiating with the teachers, it is up to the administration
to determine how to negotiate and carry out the board's policy directives.

Does the board wish to reward teachers who have returned to
school and earned extra credits? Does the board wish to consider only
those courses in the field(s) in which the teacher is certificated? How much
of total resources should be allocated to this area? Once these decisions
have been made, the administration then has to implement them. Review of the implications of each course of action takes place in the previous step, deliberation. (Ms. Payton assumed that the board, administrator, and attorney would set policy guidelines for the negotiations and
that she and the other negotiators would carry them out. Similarly, the
hearing about special education placement that she would attend at the
staffing today was implementing the policies established by the courts
and the Congress. She too is implementing those policies. A teacher's
insensitivity to desegregation policies and minority students' and parents'
feelings also concerns Ms. Payton, who is taking action to avoid a serious
blowup.)

Consequences. The actual results of the policy are now to be perceived, digested, and evaluated for further action. At this point mid-course
corrections become possible; the entire line of action may be scrapped.
Most boards and administrators will want to make mid-course corrections where and when necessary. Scrapping a policy can be more difficult, particularly if people identify it as a part of themselves.

(Note that Ms. Payton was concerned that one parent might cause
the board to rethink its policy on having only intramural sports for the
middle school. It may be a useful practice for Ms. Payton to serve on
the board's negotiating team. She can speak with expertise on the consequences of any proposed contract provision on the actual functioning
of the school. Ms. Payton also handles the first step in the grievance

procedure and has to understand the consequences of her actions in administering the contract agreed upon by the board and union or association. Ms. Payton also may be dealing with the consequences of a national decision on school prayer over which controversy still abounds and over the implementation of a program of family life education. She is also involved in the implementation of Public Law 94–142 with the staffing procedures for handicapped children and is concerned to help produce the best possible result for anxious parents facing this emotion-laden situation.)

As for structures to facilitate policy making, Chapter 13 has a relatively full discussion of the uses, advantages, and disadvantages of Citizen's Advisory Councils (CACs). CACs of course, do not make policy. They can function to advise on policy making, including locating information, developing alternatives, and sorting out implications of the options for each public.

Another structure referred to earlier in the chapter is the superintendent's or the principal's cabinet. This body can function in a way similar to the CAC. Still other structures can be developed including special committees of citizens and/or faculty to function as task forces to study problems and make recommendations to the board and/or the administrator as appropriate. (Ms. Payton could approach the superintendent with such an idea should the need occur.)

Common Problems

One of the most common difficulties in dealing constructively with problems is the confusion of personal and professional roles by administrators, teachers, and board. In key situations such as censorship and desegregation this can inject more problems into already difficult situations. (Ms. Payton may be dealing with such a confusion in the case of Ms. Michael's choir and band.)

Confusing board and administrator roles can provide the same result. The board errs when it moves beyond policy into trying to run the schools, for which it has neither the time nor the expertise to perform on professionally acceptable levels (Phillips 1963; Miller 1963). The administration similarly can and should provide advice on policy making to resolve issues; but it does not make policy.

Community norms and beliefs have to be taken into account in board and administrator deliberation and problem solving efforts. Policies that could alarm the community have to be introduced thoughtfully and with the appropriate preparation in terms of informing or, better yet, involving the community. (Ms. Payton is sensitive to this in wondering if the parent is concerned about the family life education program.)

Staff views also have to be taken into account. Solutions and procedures that affect staff have to be examined in terms of their support, reaction, and capacity to carry out their share. (Ms. Payton's conference with Ms. Michael is an example of this.)

Administrators' views and skills must also be taken into account. Establishing a school-based budgetary system can work if the administrator knows how to build budgets and has the know-how to administer them. Administrators' knowledge, skills, and willingness to support courses of action are factors. In-service models can help accomplish some of these ends (Shapiro and Kirby 1981).

Last, if the board or administration identifies too strongly with a course of action or a policy, problems may develop in altering the behavior. Wise people try to hold policies flexibly unless, of course, the policies reflect basic beliefs or matters of principle. Even in this case, however, it may be prudent to proceed thoughtfully in areas of controversy. Resentment in those on whom policies are imposed may linger to poison other discussions. (Ms. Payton has developed a cabinet just to avoid causing rifts and problems unnecessarily.)

Postlogue

In a chapter on conflicts, issues, controversies, and modes of approaching conflict resolution, we have really touched only the tip of the iceberg in the prologue and discussion. The next chapter on change and change strategies examines proactive approaches to changing organizational practices, programs, and norms.

Ms. Payton faces a whole host of challenging issues, conflicts (both potential and actual), and controversy. They range from keeping intact the model of her middle school (Mr. Harris and football) to issues that are national in scope such as religion and prayer in the schools (her well-dressed visitor), a teacher's problem in facing up to her professional role in desegregation (Ms. Michael), and implementing the laws on educating the handicapped (the staffing at 1 P.M.).

She also will face the difficult and complex process of professional negotiations (a state matter), that could impair her relationships with her staff. She may be involved in the first step of a grievance procedure with the building representative.

Each of these issues has considerable consequences both for the school and for Ms. Payton personally. Many also have legal consequences (Ms. Bigg's requesting that her children not be sent home with anyone). Some of the consequences were noted as each issue was handled, and as the chapter dealt with the need for administrators to be accurate and perceptive diagnosticians to perceive problems realistically in order to take effective action.

The process of policy making was then analyzed and structures were suggested to assist in the process. Implications for Ms. Payton were frequently cited.

Conclusions

In this chapter a number of issues that abound in our society and in education were first portrayed in a case study/scenario and then in outline form. Several approaches to resolving or dealing with these were offered, ranging from treating each incident as separate, to being crisis oriented, to dealing with issues in the broad context of policy making. Conflict resolution approaches were suggested along with structures to make policy. The complementary roles of the board and superintendent were examined vis-a-vis the policy-making process, and steps in policy making were suggested. The last section dealt with common problems found in the policy-making process, and then concluded with a summary of the implications, and complexities of the case study/scenario.

References

Anderson, J. E. 1975. *Public Policy Making*, New York: Praeger.

Barnard, C. I. 1938. *The Functions of the Executive*. Cambridge: Harvard University Press.

Campbell, R. F., et al, 1977. *Introduction to Educational Administration*, 5th ed. Boston: Allyn and Bacon.

Campbell, R. F. and **D. H. Layton**, 1969. *Policy-Making for American Education*. Chicago: Midwest Administration Center.

Campbell, R. F. and **T. L. Mazzoni**, 1976. *State Policy Making for the Public Schools*. Berkeley, Calif.: McCutchan.

Cunningham, L. L. 1959. "The Process of Educational Policy Development." *Administrator's Notebook*, vol. 7, no. 5.

Duke, J. 1978. *Conflict and Power*, 2d ed. Provo, Utah: Brigham Young University Press.

Fillby A. C. 1975. *Interpersonal Conflict Resolution*. Glenview, Illinois: Scott, Foresman and Company.

Gallup, George H. 1982. "The 14th Annual Gallup Poll of the Public's Attitudes Toward the Public Schools." *Phi Delta Kappan* 64 (September): 37–50.

Griffiths, D. E. 1959. *Administrative Theory*. Englewood Cliffs, N.J.: Prentice-Hall.

Hills, J. 1975. "Preparation for the Principalship: Some Recommendations From the Field." *Administrator's Notebook*, vol. 23, no. 9.

Katz, R. L. 1955. "Skills of an Effective Administrator." *Harvard Business Review* 33 (Jan.-Feb.): 33–42.

Miller, J. C. 1963. "What Should a Superintendent Expect of His School Board?" *Journal of the New York State School Boards Association* 27 (March).

Nebgen, M. K. 1978. "Conflict Management in Schools." *Administrator's Notebook,* vol. 26, no. 6.

Phillips, M. 1963. "What Should a School Board Expect From Their Superintendent?" *Journal of the New York State School Boards Association* 27 (March).

Robbins, S. P. 1974. *Managing Organizational Conflict*. Englewood Cliffs, N.J.: Prentice-Hall.

Shapiro, A. S. and **K. C. Kirby**, 1981. "How to Retrain Your Staff to Improve Performance," in *Managing Schools in Hard Times*, edited by Stanton Leggett. Chicago: Teach 'Em.

Trusty, Frances 1982. Based on notes from lectures, seminar in Conflict Management.

15

Change is the primary social fact as surely as motion is the primary physical fact.

– John Dewey

Promoting Constructive Change

Introduction

Many administrators, scrambling daily to get on top of their routine work, finish reports on time, respond to emergencies, and deal with problems of students, parents, demands by superiors, and pressures from the community, scarcely have time to cope with the present, let alone plan carefully to implement future change. In these circumstances most administrators are happy just to maintain the existing order. In fact, most perceive themselves as maintainers and look upon change, at best, with trepidation. Current pressures and problems are at least somewhat predictable. Changes open up a world of uncertainty to many self-perceived harassed, harried administrators trying to run the schools and get by.

Are there problems with that strategy? Will it work?

Changes in Society in Recent Years

Indeed, even a brief look at the changes in our society leads us to conclude that enormous social drifts and major changes of which we have been scarcely aware have led to vast political, economic, and educational transformations. A brief review of the most important of these provides a perspective on how profoundly our daily lives have been affected.

Racial Equality Movement

The first major change to be discussed is the Racial Equality Movement, itself a part of the Human Rights Movement that has been developing by fits and starts for more than three centuries in Western civilization. The change, of course, for this country has been simply stupendous.

Black people are being accorded the rights and privileges of other citizens. They can live with whites, work with them, and even in the South socialize with them. This development has not been without a good deal of pain. There have been controversies and even litigation about racial quotas for jobs and changing neighborhoods. The alteration of political systems has occurred across the country, so that Black legislators, sheriffs, and other local, state, and national representatives are being elected and appointed.

Black pride has become a widespread phenomenon so that being Black is not automatically a badge of inferiority as it once was. As with all general or diffuse and gradual social movements (Blumer 1946), decades will yet pass before full equality begins to be approached.

Sex Equity: The Women's Movement

The Women's Movement brings other enormous changes to our society. Although women did fill the factories and many other jobs during World Wars I and II, they largely returned to the hearth after the war and to the relatively limited roles this society accorded them. In the market place, beyond secretarying, women taught and nursed. Starting in the late 1950s, women's attitudes changed. Women became more assertive, and legislation, executive orders, and court decisions began to emerge acknowledging women's rights. The impact on society has been at least as great as that of the Racial Equality Movement. Great numbers of both women and men are now perceiving women as persons, as having talents to develop and contributions to make, as being fully capable of performing virtually all jobs heretofore held by men.

The impact upon women in terms of job opportunities has been revolutionary. Women are moving in larger numbers into the legal profession, the full range of medical professions, the colleges, business, and industry, and administrative and supervisory positions. Seminars have been held for supervisors in jobs where women traditionally have been excluded, such as coal mining, oil drilling, and other nontraditional occupations.

Great numbers of women are more confident, more productive, more assertive, and more satisfied with their developing life-styles. Of course, as with any great social change, the progress is uneven and is characterized by setbacks, excesses, criticism, uneven movement, and by both opposition and encouragement.

Changes in Morality

Concurrent with the above change is one in basic morality. A look at the change in movie rating systems, in the success of a great variety of magazines such as *Playboy, Playgirl,* or *Penthouse* indicates fundamental changes in people's values and in customs (folkways) and mores (moral standards). Dress is more informal, and a variety of life-style options regarding remaining single, delaying marriage, or divorce and remarriage have been generated, from the late 1960s on.

Fundamental moral values, such as respect for others, have been changing, as evidenced by increases in child abuse, spouse abuse, and parent abuse cases. Similarly a decline in respect for authority has been occurring since the end of World War II, with even a president and vice president forced to resign for their disregard of law.

Hedonism is an ever-increasing element in our values, significantly changing younger middle-class Americans into being now-oriented, instead of future-oriented as their middle-aged parents are. Generational conflicts often result from this clash of basic values. For example, in the years before World War II, few people could take anything but brief vacations, if that. Vacations now are a major aspect of our lives and an entire industry has been built on this emerging value. Indeed, whole cities and states depend on tourism for their livelihood, and in economic recession suffer serious financial and social repercussions when the stream of tourists dries a bit.

The Moral Majority

The change in basic morality has generated its opposition in the form of the Moral Majority movement, itself declaring a wish to return to our former espoused value systems. Critical of the new freedoms for women, opposing busing to desegregate, upset at the greater emphasis on sexual liberty and perturbed at what they see as the elimination of religion from the schools, numbers of people have supported a return by legislation, court action, and constitutional revision, to the past principles and practices held by many.

Groups in the Moral Majority have actively defeated senators, and have had an impact on presidential elections. Many of these groups have raised large quantities of money for political action purposes, and are attempting to influence TV programming, school textbooks, and library book collections.

Tax Revolts

Tax revolts, beginning on a state level with Proposition 13 in California, have been major factors in American life. People across the country have been confronting the rising cost of various public services. In the presidential election of 1980 that factor was a major role in the campaign rhetoric and in the subsequent actions of the new administration. Massachussetts' Proposition 2-1/2 was a further extension of tax revolt and has had major impact on the schools and local governments.

Population Movements

Another social change of enormous proportions consists of major population shifts in the United States, in this case occurring for more than a century. The first major movement was from rural areas into the cities; after World War II the suburbs began to mushroom; and then in the late 1960s people began to move back to the rural areas to find more tranquility, roots, and different identities.

Concurrent with the last two moves has been the migration west in the 1950s, 1960s, and 1970s, and to the Sunbelt in the 1960s, 1970s, and 1980s. Huge numbers of people have moved accompanied by a shift in industry. The northeastern states have lost population and industry, as have some of their midwestern brethren. The west and the south have gained considerably. Our population is so mobile that by now a sizeable percentage of Americans lives more than five hundred miles from their birthplaces.

The Youth Revolt

Still another major change was the youth revolt of the 1960s and early 1970s. Sparked by college campus protests, youth in high schools began to assert themselves and in a good number of cases participate in protests of varying kinds, often to the dismay of numbers of adults. This topic leads directly to major changes in education, inasmuch as the youth revolt had a great deal of impact on the schools. As will be seen, the courts also contributed to this development.

Toffler

Toffler (1980) views the great social changes in human society over the last 12,000 to 15,000 years as occurring in three great waves. The first was the Agricultural Revolution, which ushered in the New Stone Age. The second wave was the Industrial Revolution, which entered our lives about 150 to 225 years ago. The third and last wave, which he calls the Post-Industrial Age, is now in process. In it, the importance of factories and heavy industry begins to erode; the service industries, computers and information systems, and communications begin to assume major proportions in the structure of the economy.

Great Changes in Education in Recent Years: Their Implications for our Fear of Change

The list of profound changes in education is so great that only a double handful will be mentioned.

Brown v. Board of Education of Topeka

The first, of course, was the Supreme Court's rulings in 1954 and 1955 that segregation is illegal, that separate schools in no way could be equal *(Brown v. Board of Education, 347 U.S. 483 [1954]).* As a consequence, Black students are now in formerly all-white schools, and discrimination against Black students is occurring to a considerably lesser extent. Once-separate schools and school systems have been abolished. (Indeed, in Delaware the state constitution mandated four separate school systems.) In the 1960s many schools housed their black students in such out-of-the way spots as basements and portables.

Unfortunately, resistance to the justice of this ruling still runs deep in the streams of American thought, with white flight persisting, and attempts to overthrow busing occurring as major political forces even in the early 1980s. The change, however, is so considerable as to affect the behavior of some white politicians. Governor George Wallace of Alabama, for example, who dramatically resisted integration by standing in front of a school's doors in 1964 in the early 1980s was courting and getting Black voter support for his candidacy.

Tinker v. Des Moines Independent School District

In its Tinker decision in 1969, (Chapter 8, pp. 180-181) the Supreme Court announced a new doctrine, that students had political rights that did not cease when they entered the school's gates (*Tinker* v.*Des Moines* 393 U.S. 503 [1969]). Shortly thereafter, a series of rulings and court decisions extended these to teachers and then expanded the rights of both teachers and students. In Tinker, students' freedom of speech in school was protected. In others such as Goss, due process was further expanded to include discipline and other areas (*Goss* v. *Lopez*, 419 U.S. 565 [1975], p. 182). The impact on the schools has been almost as profound as Brown because students now are perceived as having political rights, their education is seen as a property right, and they are not merely in the custody of the schools *in loco parentis* (in place of parents).

So students have all the rights provided adults by the Bill of Rights: they have the same freedom of speech as do adults; their publications cannot be interfered with (though in sections of the country this interference still persists); they can vote at 18; they can even sit on school boards. In short, they are political persons and citizens, not wards. Courts now listen to the wishes of children as young as twelve years of age with respect to the parent with whom they would prefer to live in divorce cases.

Changing School Populations

The school population is also changing, with more minority groups staying in high school to graduate. Many teachers now work with at least two groups of students, each coming from differing sociocultural roots. Logically speaking, at least one group will have roots in a sociocultural or socioeconomic world different from the teacher's own. Because of these differences, misunderstandings may result among students, between student and teacher, or between student and administrator. If such misunderstandings are not carefully handled, a good deal of hostility and conflict can be produced in the interaction of the confused participants.

The situations that result when two cultures meet have been anthropologically described as follows. At the first meeting, the participants experience conflict. Next, they undergo minimal accommodation or hostile cooperation. Then they achieve real cooperation. Finally they reach assimilation. We are apparently too often at the first two levels.

The probability of the problem disappearing in the near future is small. Our Black student population is still growing. The group of Latin students is also growing, and will be larger than the Black group by the early 2000s, according to conservative estimates. Despite movement toward an integrated society, our teaching and administrative staffs remain predominantly white. Of course, as these Black and Latin students move through our schools and into college, they will eventually enter the professions, including teaching and administration, in larger numbers (Hodgkinson 1983). Faculty and administration, like the student bodies, will become more diverse populations. Until then, and (in a different form) even after that happens, the schools will continue to be the meeting ground for these diverse cultural groups, including, by 2080, the white

Anglo-Saxon minority, as it will then be according to conservative estimates.

As we have been somewhat helpless observers to so many vast social changes, so have we watched helplessly and in dismay as the formerly expanding population, the growing school systems of this nation started to decline in the early 1970s. By the early 1980s systems in the northeast that once had twelve thousand students were down to six or seven thousand students. This has had catastrophic impact on employment for teachers, services for students, and on communities who have seen their neighborhood schools closed after they had operated for decades.

By 1974, New York State had 56,000 teachers unemployed. In the early 1980s teachers with eight years' and more of seniority were facing layoffs in many states.

The impact on the schools has been enormous. People seem frozen into positions they dare not leave. (This is reminiscent of the latter stages of the Roman Empire when, to stop farm labor from leaving the large corporate farms, the Emperor froze them into their jobs, creating serfs). With considerably decreased new blood entering the schools, a major former source of new ideas has virtually disappeared.

Psychologically, education, like all American industries, has been tied to an expensive philosophy. The unbridled optimism of the 1960s slowly faded by the early 1970s; by the late 1970s and early 1980s a sense of depression and gloom shadowed the field of education. Beset on all sides, the schools operated often as if they were in a state of shock, immobilized and retrenching into "Back to Basics" movements.

The Federal Aspect

As if the preceding were not enough, the new administration elected in 1980 espoused a philosophy that sharply reduced education as a national responsibility and announced its intention to reduce federal funds and programs equally devastatingly. The taxpayers' revolt and serious economic hard times reduced the contributions of local and state authorities to education's coffers at the same time that the federal government was making draconian cuts. So, any surcease of sorrow was to be denied, because local and state governments either were as hard-pressed as the federal government or had decided to join the budget-cutting and tax reduction by the national government.

The impact, while wide, fell particularly hard on the lower economic level of the populace served by education, as those programs and those districts who relied the most on outside help and who had the least resources were often the most hard hit. The results were increased teacher-pupil ratios, reductions in programs, and thousands of teachers and aides in virtually every state losing their jobs.

The Knowledge Explosion; Microcomputers

The vast increase in knowledge produces great opportunity, but spells problems to some teachers. Like physicians and airplane pilots, they must keep up. All across the country, junior high and high school students are crowding around the microcomputers beginning to dot the schools' landscapes. One problem is that the teachers and principals aren't crowding around the microcomputers. Students tend to be more accepting of the technical revolutions than are many educators.

The great gain in knowledge obviously implies that teachers must continue to try hard to keep up in their fields. Many approaches and models have been suggested (Shapiro and Kirby 1981). As for computers and education, a revolution of great force and power is occurring that has potential to increase teacher effectiveness tremendously, providing we capitalize on it.

Learning Styles: Left Brain, Right Brain, Whole Brain

Change in education, as in society, often appears on our doors much to our astonishment. The revolution in understanding teaching and learning has been knocking on our portals since the 1970s and offers opportunity to add precision and effectiveness to education (Dunn 1972; 1975; 1977). As we learn about the variety of ways in which people learn, we begin to be able to adapt our teaching styles to the learning styles. It takes flexibility and willingness to change and risk ourselves, challenges to any professional group facing major restructuring in the technological and conceptual base of their profession.

Similar to the potential impact of learning and teaching styles on our practice are the findings of research on left brain—right brain and the three levels of brain development or the triune brain (Herrmann 1981; Hart 1975). Unlike learning styles, which are relatively unchangeable, people can learn to develop the skills and approaches of both the right and left brains. (The left brain is sequential, ordered, logical, analytic; the right brain is creative, artistic, holistic, emotional, and capable of synthesizing and conceptualizing. Curricula in the schools and colleges, therefore, can be designed to teach these vital thinking skills and approaches, important to many occupations.

This set of examples of crucial changes could continue on and on. Women's Rights under Title IX and other regulations and legislation could be analyzed, as could other changes. The key point to consider is that major changes are inevitable and appear to be increasing in number, force, and impact (Toffler 1980). Consequently, the assumptions we have held so long, which support the notion that administrators and teachers must maintain the status quo, no longer operate. The status quo cannot be maintained. Like the pre-Civil War culture of the South, it is Gone With the Wind.

Additional Forces Promoting and Preventing Change: The Subcultures of Organizations Resist Change

Because of the American focus on the individual and our concern with individualism, we have not looked too closely at the organizations we live in, nor at the practices, the norms, and customs we develop in organizations. All formal and informal organizations develop customs, standards, and behavior shared by their members. Indeed, "shared, learned behavior" is one definition of culture. A slightly longer definition consists of the "commonly accepted and expected ideas, attitudes, values, and habits learned by individuals in connection with social living."

America has a culture, as does China, Italy, and Saudi Arabia. We begin to focus at subcultures, subsets of the larger culture, when we talk about the southern subculture and those of the New Englander, the Italian-American, the Polish-American, the Latin-American, and adolescents. Ethnic and minority groups, then, develop subcultures.

Organizations too, can develop a subculture, such as the U.S. Marines, the New York Stock Exchange, Harvard University, and different corporations such as Sears and IBM. A given newspaper has its own different standards and styles. So do individual schools. (Private prep schools have a subculture, as do suburban high schools and inner city schools; high schools' subcultures contrast markedly with those of elementary schools.) Each organization, then, develops commonly understood and accepted agreements to guide its participants regarding what is appropriate and inappropriate behavior.

Oscar Lewis (1959) writes of the subculture of poverty, pointing out that very poor people have common ways and expectations of dealing with the world, whether they are in Mexico City, San Juan, New York, or London.

The point to recognize is that the cultures of societies and organizations tend to resist efforts to change them. Just as adolescents are almost adult-proof, so are other subcultures. In part, they do not like to be changed; in part, they do not wish to change because they know no other way to behave. They like their customs, which are familiar to them. As a consequence, changing an organization is not the simplest thing to do. It takes thought, knowledge of a variety of strategies, careful planning, an ability to pull disparate forces to work together, plus a capacity to establish oneself.

Organizational Dynamics: Forces That Support Change

Max Weber

Virtually everyone recognizes that organizations tend to change over time, but most of us have not developed any generalizations about that process. Indeed, not too many theories of organizational change have been formulated.

Max Weber (1946), the late nineteenth and early twentieth century sociologist who developed the concept of bureaucracy, also set forth a two-stage theory of cyclical organizational change. Weber noted that organizations are started by men with charismatic or attractive, dynamic, powerful personalities. They are able to develop the loyalty and commitment an organization must have to get organized and started. He also pointed out that after the organization is on its feet, the charismatic leader will leave and a follower, "pale luminaries like the moon to the sun," will succeed to the leadership role. But the successor doesn't have the force, the dynamism, the powerful personality of the departed or deposed leader and is unable to hold the operation together; so it collapses.

We know now that many organizations will persist even with the poorest management, although in recent years bankruptcies of even large corporations have occurred in alarming numbers (for example, Braniff Airways, White Motor Company, Grant Stores) and only government

bailouts have kept others (Chrysler and Lockheed) from collapse. In Weber's day, with much smaller capital requirements to start up, companies rose and folded more rapidly and in much greater numbers (Kaufman 1975).

Consequently, Weber's two-stage cyclical theory of the phases of an organization's existence was based on a good deal of observation of empirical reality. He also noted that if the organization could get another charismatic leader, it could "rise from the ashes like a phoenix" and once again prosper.

The Tri-Partite Theory of Organization Change and Control

A more recent theory (Wilson et al. 1969) proposes that an organization, like a person, has a career that is more complex than a two-stage process. The Tri-Partite Theory states that organizations have three stages or phases in their career cycle. In the first, the organization is mired in red tape, is merely drifting, reacting to crises and trying only to get by. The organization then seeks a charismatic leader to revive it or to make it productive or to do something about how poorly it was operating. This leader captures the imagination of many members and infuses spirit and enthusiasm into the organization. The organization begins to hum with activity, with short range projects. Things happen! People like being in it. (This is similar to Weber's first phase.)

Charismatic leaders come to mind readily. Franklin Delano Roosevelt, Hitler, General Robert E. Lee, and Joan of Arc are examples. In education, Horace Mann, Robert Maynard Hutchins, and Father Theodore Hesburgh of Notre Dame may be named. After a time, the leader either leaves or is pushed out and goes to another organization wanting to lift itself out of an unsatisfactory condition.

The followers of the charismatic leader then have a problem: they need to act to keep their momentum. They generally seize upon the latest ideas of the leader and try to incorporate them into some form of a plan. Models of education plans can range from very simple in one building (such as developing a middle school, an ungraded school, or a basic school) to a more comprehensive plan involving a total system. The point is that a *Planner* succeeds the charismatic leader; and the followers, once *Person-Oriented* (oriented and loyal to the charismatic leader) become *Plan-Oriented*. Plans for the system can range from Progressive Education to open education to ungradedness to alternative education models. The people in the organization are loyal to the plan and try to ensure its success. They work at it. They are committed.

Planners can be found also. Lyndon Johnson, Ho Chi Minh, and General Omar Bradley were planners. A. S. Neill's Summerhill was a plan, as was B. Frank Brown's nongraded school in Melbourne, Florida.

Once we develop the plan we try to implement it by organizing, establishing clear roles and job descriptions, and building the bureaucracy to accomplish it. About three years down the road the plan begins to dim in people's memories. New employees enter with not much stake in the plan and after a while the details of the plan fade. It is forgotten.

After developing the Tri-Partite Theory one of the authors, who had earlier been a Core Demonstration teacher in a state laboratory school specifically designed for core, revisited the school after an eight-year absence. When he asked when core died, none of his former colleagues could understand his meaning.

The organization drifts, headed by a "bureaucrat," someone who does the nuts and bolts work but who has little charisma or planning ability. People are loyal to the *position* of the leader, but not to the individual. Bel Kaufman (1964) ably describes such a school and principal in *Up the Down Staircase* as focusing on details and not on any vision of the future or on any plan. This leader is a mechanic who gets details done, but little else. She or he is termed a Bureaucrat by the Tri-Partite Theory and the organization is Position-Oriented, with people loyal to the position, but not really to the administrator.

Figure 12-1 describes such a three-phase cycle of organizational change and succession.

The authors also note a fourth type of leader, one who is both a charismatic leader *and* a planner. They call this person a Synergist, a person who combines both charisma and the ability to plan. This person, obviously, has the potential to be even more effective in working with the organization. Synergists would be Dr. Martin Luther King, Jr., General Douglas MacArthur, Queen Elizabeth I, and Charlemagne, who had charisma *and* a plan. In education Horace Mann, Eugene Howard of Norridge High School, Consultant Stanton Leggett, and A. S. Neill are synergists.

Following the discussion of the Tri-Partite Theory the authors designed several change strategies to move the organizations into the two productive and more viable stages of their careers, which will be discussed in the section in "Change Strategies."

The hypothesis of this theory is somewhat disconcerting. It boldly states that organizations, like energy systems in the physical world, are entropic; that is, they run down. Indeed, Leggett's "Foreword" to *Sociology of Supervision* (1969) categorically affirms:

> Two facts about the American way of life are apparent to even casual observers. First, Americans live their lives in a sea of formal organizations. Secondly, Americans truly believe themselves to be free men—they do not consider themselves slaves. Yet, if the authors of this work are correct, we are all enslaved by an apparently invariable cycle through which our organizations must pass.

> This oppressive institutional cycle will prevail unless positive action is taken to alter its course. [The book] presents an in-depth study of the basic theory that institutional change is predictable. It further states that such change can be consciously managed and directed.

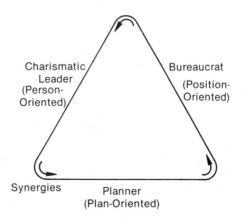

FIGURE 15-1 *Phases of Organizational Change: Tri-Partite Theory*

SOURCE: Adapted from Wilson, L. Craig; Byar, T. Madison; Shapiro, Arthur S.; and Schell, Shirley H.; *Sociology of Supervision*, p. 85. Newton, Mass.: Allyn and Bacon, 1969.

An understanding of the dynamics of institutional renewal and revitalization is obviously of strategic concern to education. This book is worthy of attention by all people who are concerned with social and institutional change. (Leggett 1969)

The Guba-Getzels Model

The model developed by Egon Guba and Jacob Getzels (1957) focuses more on understanding the structure of organizations, but does deal somewhat with their dynamics. Guba and Getzels focus on two dimensions in organizations, the Idiographic or personal and the Nomothetic or organizational. Figure 15-2 illustrates the model.

In the model, the authors describe the nomothetic dimension as follows. Institutions (organizations) have roles that are dynamic aspects of positions or offices (teacher, principal) people hold within the organization. Roles are defined in terms of expectations held for the actor regarding what she or he should and should not do.

The individual has a personality considered to be "the dynamic organization within the individual of need dispositions which govern his unique reactions to and with the environment" (Guba and Getzels 1957, 428). Need dispositions are "individual tendencies to orient and act with respect to objects in certain manners and to expect certain consequences from these actions" (Guba and Getzels 1957, 423). Such dispositions, in short, are motives for behavior.

Guba and Getzels then indicate three kinds of leadership in organizations: Nomothetic, Idiographic and Transactional, a mix between organization-focused and individual-focused.

The model does not deal with the social systems aspect nor the culture of the organization, among other shortcomings, although Getzels and Thelen (1960) collaborated in a later model to add these dimensions to the construct.

Richard Carlson (1962; 1972) focused on organizational change in his study of organizational succession and executive change. He noted that place-bound and career-bound superintendents differ in mandate for change, strategies for change, emphasis on innovation, career patterns, and proactive vs. reactive patterns.

Levin and Simon (1974) focused on studying new settings in which people come together to form new organizations. They proposed seven stages from their empirical study:

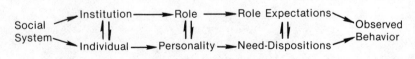

Nomothetic Dimension

Social System → Institution → Role → Role Expectations → Observed Behavior

Individual → Personality → Need-Dispositions → Behavior

Idiographic Dimension

FIGURE 15-2 *General model showing the nomothetic and the idiographic dimensions of social behavior.*

SOURCE: Reprinted from "Social Behavior and the Administrative Process." *School Review* 65 (1957): 429, by J. W. Getzels and E. G. Guba. By permission of The University of Chicago Press.

1. Getting together to define the discussion
2. Defining and obtaining support for the setting
3. Planning and assembling the setting
4. Getting started
5. Looking back and ahead
6. Starting again: stabilizing the setting
7. Looking ahead to next year

As can be easily seen, the focus is on the first year in this view of organizational dynamics; the Tri-Partite Theory on the other hand, takes a total cyclical or multiyear view.

Obviously, other formulations exist pointing to organizational dynamics. Other studies have focused on social, political, and social-psychological forces causing change in organizations. What is worthwhile to note is that organizations, like the solar system, individuals, and atoms, are in flux, are dynamic, and do not rest. This provides major support to anyone interested in changing an organization.

The Role of the Superintendent, Principal, and Staff in Dealing with Change

The key for any administrator is to realize the major purposes of the job; and it clearly is that the administrator's key role is to facilitate developing improved programs to enhance teaching and learning to meet student, staff, and community needs. Consequently, the role of the administrator is not to resist change, but to be a constructive change agent and facilitate change that enhances teaching and learning. The reason for the strong emphasis on this formulation is that this is not the present perception of their role by the majority of administrators. Moreover, it would hardly be useful to add large numbers of new administrators to the ranks who lack a basic understanding of their prime purpose, whose basic assumption is that they are stabilizers and must resist change.

The first issue is to determine change for what? Changes have to be made for a good reason, not for trivial ends.

1. Are goals needed for the organization?
2. Is the organizational structure not adequate?
   Is the structure too centralized?
3. Are instructional programs meeting student needs adequately?
   Are they sufficiently interesting?
4. Do long-established programs need a review?
5. Are new groups of students entering the schools?
   Are the existent programs appropriate for them?

We do not support making change for the sake of change. It has to be to accomplish major purposes.

How to Proceed?

Assessing the Situation

The first step, of course, is to assess the situation, detecting dissatisfactions by key social systems. Which situations and programs are perceived as inadequate? By whom? We have to ask, "What is the problem?" If we do not diagnose the problem correctly, we will develop the wrong solution.

Where does readiness for change exist? Where are key energy centers in the system, in the school? (Fabun 1972; Lewin 1947). What areas do key social systems and individuals perceive as needing change? Edwards (1977) developed an instrument that assessed faculty's readiness for change over a broad range of issues ranging from inconsequential (color of chalk) to major (structure of the school, basic programs of study).

Orlosky and Smith (1971) in their study of educational change found change to be complicated and difficult and administrators bound to find that "resistance arises regardless of the strong support an idea for change many have." One conclusion the authors developed was that many changes and attempts to change failed and that the reasons for success or failure were identifiable but complex.

Establishing Priorities

The administrator has to determine what can be changed and what is quite difficult to alter or replace. The next step is to decide what is most important and what has a relatively low priority, and should be dealt with later, if at all. Too many administrators want to rectify large numbers of situations, problems that took years to develop, in one major undertaking. One administrator known to the authors felt his mission meant that he had to replace eight or nine teachers out of fifty seven the very first year he was in charge of the school. Needless to say, a teacher and board revolt did him in. Another principal felt that if he could reduce the cost of the class ring by several dollars in a tradition-bound school, that would be a signal achievement. This was his priority, despite a high school program that no longer met the needs of a student body with an increasing number of minority students, and a guidance department that had "retired" and couldn't even give the superintendent's son realistic advice on college entrance.

To determine priorities requires a sense of what is important, and a sense of what is feasible with the school's key social systems; it requires a determination, once purposes and goals have been established, to stay with them and not to fritter away support by dealing with insignificant items. It really requires a good deal of self-discipline in the process because of the temptation in the day-to-day operation of the organization to right wrongs and correct problems. It also requires evaluating the alternatives developed in terms of their feasibility, usefulness, and priority.

Of course, establishing priorities also means involving key people and groups, which the next section will discuss.

Setting the Stage

In deciding on a course or multiple courses of action, and in determining what is possible and what will not work well, the administrator has to sort faculty, other administrators, the central office, and various key publics into those interested in change, those opposed to it, and those neutral. Where, then, does the administrator or supervisor go for support for a new idea? How does the administrator establish a base, and develop support in his or her function? Has all the key data been found to avoid unpleasant or lethal surprises in the change process?

Obviously, it takes time for a new administrator to be established. Even with a sense of being established, the administrator has to determine who will be, or could be, or actually is committed to a key enterprise or major initiative. Change is multifaceted and does not need to progress logically. The administrator goes with a program that is feasible and with those who are committed and interested, picking allies where they are.

Lewin's Basic Change Strategy

Kurt Lewin, who developed the concept of group dynamics, also designed a three-phase change strategy that is basic to almost any enterprise (1943) involving changing an organization or group or even oneself.

In Phase I Lewin notes that the old situation has to be unfrozen, changed. The question is, how to do this? Lewin sees the present situation as a series of forces opposing each other, which he calls a force field (Figure 15-3). Forces keeping the system, or program, or practice in a "quasi-stationary equilibrium" have to be changed. Lewin recommends that forces opposing the change be reduced, rather than that pressure favoring the change force it through. Increasing pressure leads to increased oppositional forces much as in an arms race. For example, if oppositional forces are based on teachers' anxiety that they do not know how to teach a new reading program, such fears can be reduced by establishing in the design process a carefully planned in-service workshop for those who are fearful of participating or trying out the new program. Consequently, we can reduce pressures and change the situation to a state of acceptance by effective in-service programs that actually help teachers and supervisors adjust to the newly developing situation.

The next step is to move to a new level by introducing the new program or practice, or skills, or knowledge. But this can't be left at this stage or people will regress.

Consequently, the third step is to refreeze the new program or skill into a new balance, so that the system does not return to the old practice. The administrator has to ensure the persistence of the change by facilitating its performance, by supporting it.

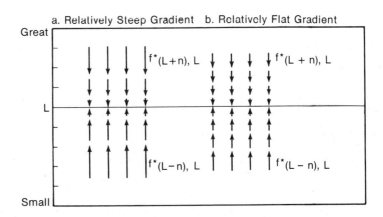

FIGURE 15-3 *Lewin's Force Field—Gradients of Resultant Forces*

SOURCE: K. Lewin, "Group Decision and Social Change," in *Readings in Social Psychology*, Rev. ed., 459-73, Edited by Guy E. Swanson, T. M. Newcomb, and E. L. Hartley (New York: Henry Holt and Co., 1952).

Other Change Strategies

PERT

Unfreezing can be done by a variety of approaches. PERT (Program Evaluation Review Technique) was a change strategy developed to design and build the first atomic submarine by Admiral Hyman Rickover (Cook 1966). Other systems approaches have also been designed. Previously mentioned conflict resolution approaches have been used to change existing practices and programs. A model PERT diagram is shown in Figure 15-4. For practice, you might wish to take a simple change such as buying a new car and PERT the process. Such an approach makes everything visible, diagrammed so that the process can be depicted visually.

A Curriculum Steering Committee Structure and Other Committees

Curriculum steering structures have been utilized to produce change in systems on a *routine* basis. This approach contrasts with treating each change as a separate item, a strategy takes enormous energy to change merely one course (Shapiro and Kirby 1981).

Figure 15-5 shows how the structure routinely introduces change into a system, so that changes in program are actually *expected*. An organization and a procedure are established that encourage people or groups to introduce change routinely into the system. Such a process would encourage any change to be supported by the necessary in-service arrangements. Of course, for such an arrangement to work it has to be supported by the top administrators—if in a building, the principal; if in a system, the superintendent and his or her staff. The same might be done for a pupil services program with a Pupil Personnel Services Steering Committee as its structure.

Committees, task forces, and Citizens Advisory Councils can initiate change into a system by recommending some alteration of the status quo. Their advantage is that they recommend *to* the administration, which is an important difference psychologically. (See Chapter 13 for more information on Citizen Advisory Councils and how to utilize them.)

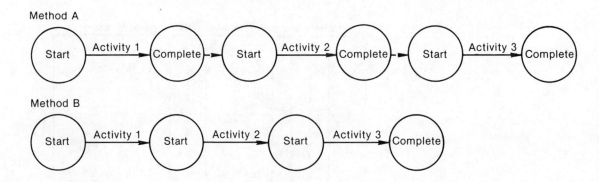

FIGURE 15-4 *Designation of Start and Completion of Activities for Network Clarity*
SOURCE: D. L. Cook, *Program Evaluation Review Technique: Application in Education.* Washington D.C.: University Press of America, 1979.

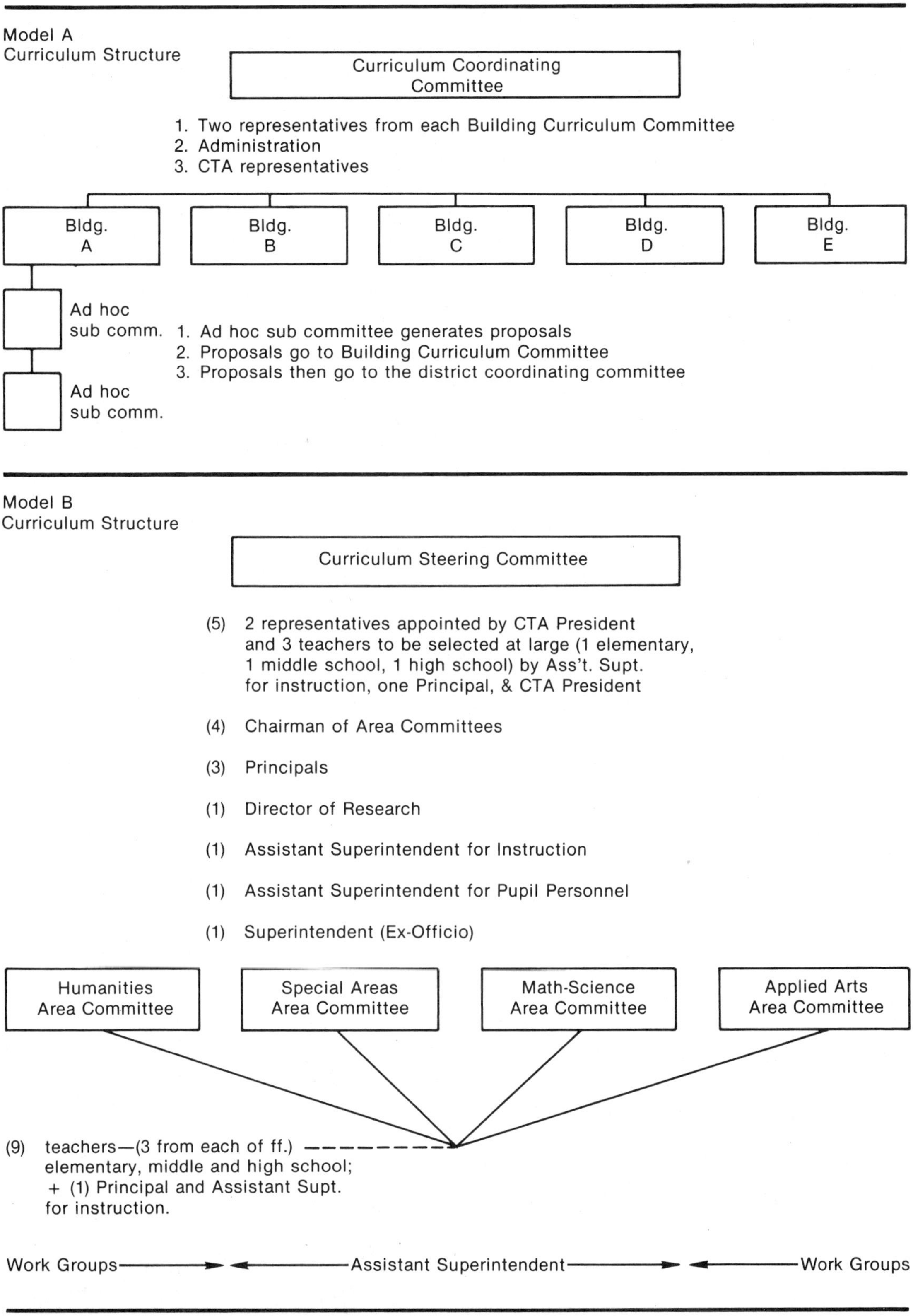

**Model A
Curriculum Structure**

```
┌─────────────────────────────────┐
│      Curriculum Coordinating    │
│            Committee            │
└─────────────────────────────────┘
```

1. Two representatives from each Building Curriculum Committee
2. Administration
3. CTA representatives

```
┌────────┐  ┌────────┐  ┌────────┐  ┌────────┐  ┌────────┐
│ Bldg.  │  │ Bldg.  │  │ Bldg.  │  │ Bldg.  │  │ Bldg.  │
│   A    │  │   B    │  │   C    │  │   D    │  │   E    │
└────────┘  └────────┘  └────────┘  └────────┘  └────────┘
```

Ad hoc sub comm.

1. Ad hoc sub committee generates proposals
2. Proposals go to Building Curriculum Committee
3. Proposals then go to the district coordinating committee

Ad hoc sub comm.

**Model B
Curriculum Structure**

```
┌─────────────────────────────────┐
│    Curriculum Steering Committee │
└─────────────────────────────────┘
```

(5) 2 representatives appointed by CTA President
     and 3 teachers to be selected at large (1 elementary,
     1 middle school, 1 high school) by Ass't. Supt.
     for instruction, one Principal, & CTA President

(4) Chairman of Area Committees

(3) Principals

(1) Director of Research

(1) Assistant Superintendent for Instruction

(1) Assistant Superintendent for Pupil Personnel

(1) Superintendent (Ex-Officio)

```
┌────────────┐  ┌────────────┐  ┌────────────┐  ┌────────────┐
│ Humanities │  │Special Areas│ │Math-Science│  │Applied Arts│
│Area Committee│ │Area Committee│ │Area Committee│ │Area Committee│
└────────────┘  └────────────┘  └────────────┘  └────────────┘
```

(9) teachers—(3 from each of ff.) – – – – – – –
     elementary, middle and high school;
     + (1) Principal and Assistant Supt.
     for instruction.

Work Groups ────▶ ◀──── Assistant Superintendent ────▶ ◀──── Work Groups

FIGURE 15-5 *Curriculum Steering Structure*
SOURCE: A Shapiro and K. C. Kirby, "How to Retrain Your Staff to Improve Performance." in *Managing Schools in Hard Times* edited by Stanton Leggett (Chicago: Teach 'Em, 1981), 103.

The Hawthorne Effect

The "Hawthorne Effect," is a change strategy in which the people involved are treated as special. A "halo effect" is produced as was done in studies of the Western Electric Hawthorne Plant outside Chicago (Mayo 1933). In that study the women in the experiment began to feel special with all the attention they received; so regardless of working conditions, they produced more. In practice, this means that because they are selected to share in a change, people feel special and support the change wholeheartedly, but the administrator has to be sincere.

Unilateral vs. Involvement Models

Another change strategy is for the administrator to make the change unilaterally. Often this authoritarian approach may result in opposition (as Lewin noted), building up subtle sabotage, reduced morale, and minimum compliance. In some circumstances and areas (calling fire drills), principals have the recognized and agreed-upon right to make changes; in some areas (transferring teachers) they do not (Barnard 1938; Lynam 1979).

Unilateral decisions are much faster to make. However, convincing people the decision was right may take a great deal of time after the fact. On the other hand, the time necessary to make the decision with staff involvement will take a good deal longer; but if properly done without forcing anyone and looking to meet everyone's concerns, no time is needed afterwards to convince anyone. The change is supported by those who made the decision. Figure 15-6 is drawn from an illustration from Thelen (1958).

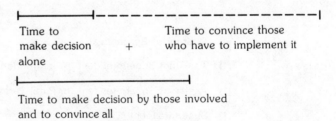

FIGURE 15-6   *Time Needed to Secure Acceptance of Decisions*

In the long run involvement is more effective and efficient.

Figure 15-7 illustrates another approach to strategy. Designed by Wilson and Shapiro (Wilson et al. 1969), it lays out stages of the change model with a great deal of precision.

As Figure 15-7 shows, phase I the normal diagnosing, mulling process is pointed up. Key decisions have to be made here such as what problem area(s) will and will not be attacked, and what area(s) are safe or approved to try to handle.

In the next major phase the structure to deal with the problem is to be designed in some form of study group or steering committee that has a job to do. The area to change has to be agreed upon first, *before* the steering committee is formed. Does the organization of the elementary division have to be looked at? Is the junior high no longer meeting pupils'

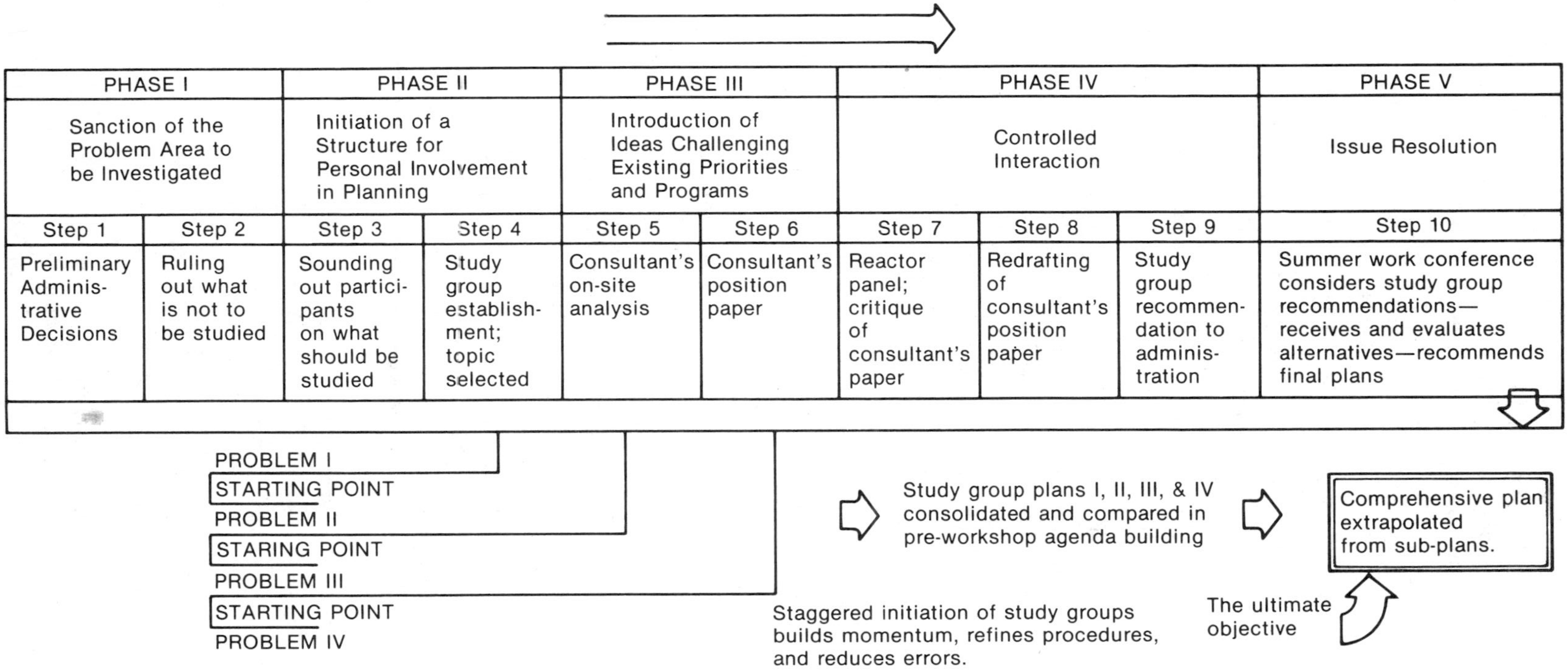

	PHASE I		PHASE II		PHASE III		PHASE IV			PHASE V
	Sanction of the Problem Area to be Investigated		Initiation of a Structure for Personal Involvement in Planning		Introduction of Ideas Challenging Existing Priorities and Programs		Controlled Interaction			Issue Resolution
	Step 1	Step 2	Step 3	Step 4	Step 5	Step 6	Step 7	Step 8	Step 9	Step 10
	Preliminary Administrative Decisions	Ruling out what is not to be studied	Sounding out participants on what should be studied	Study group establishment; topic selected	Consultant's on-site analysis	Consultant's position paper	Reactor panel; critique of consultant's paper	Redrafting of consultant's position paper	Study group recommendation to administration	Summer work conference considers study group recommendations—receives and evaluates alternatives—recommends final plans

Study group plans I, II, III, & IV consolidated and compared in pre-workshop agenda building

Staggered initiation of study groups builds momentum, refines procedures, and reduces errors.

Comprehensive plan extrapolated from sub-plans.

The ultimate objective

PROBLEM I
STARTING POINT
PROBLEM II
STARING POINT
PROBLEM III
STARTING POINT
PROBLEM IV

FIGURE 15-7 *Priority Determination: A Diagnostic Strategy*

SOURCE: L. C. Wilson, et al., *Sociology of Supervision* (Boston: Allyn and Bacon, 1969), 307.

needs? Does the system or school need to develop goals to drive it down certain directions? Does the junior high or high school need to revise its program or organization to meet student needs better? Does it need to develop achievable goals? The steering committee has to direct the change process, but is still advisory only.

In phase III ideas have to be introduced challenging existing practices. A consultant may be used or a small writing committee of three or four highly regarded faculty who are enthusiastic about making realistic changes.

Their position paper then has to be presented to the steering committee and to the rest of the faculty(ies) and administration involved in Phase IV. The PTA and minority groups should also be involved in the critique. If the changes are fundamental enough, the students might be involved. People who are a part of the process tend to support the end results.

The consultant or writing committee may then redraft the proposal in the controlled interaction phase. The steering committee then considers and recommends its final report to the administration for consideration and evaluation and final action.

In a brief overview of change in as limited a format as a single chapter, it is impossible to survey or even summarize the enormous literature on planned change in education. Eddy J. Van Meter in a recent paper (1980) on just that subject indicated that he was addressing five topics related to change, each formulated as a trend:

1. A trend toward increased clarification of strategies relating to planned change
2. A trend toward an increased sophistication concerning our understanding of change-related phenomena
3. A trend toward the publication of more reports of planned change efforts in educational settings using an intervention perspective
4. A trend toward greater awareness of the complexities of the dissemination and adoption of educational innovations
5. A trend toward increased concern for the ethical dimensions of planned change.

Organizational Development (OD) is an example of intervention approaches. The literature on OD strategies can fill shelves. (Schmuck 1977; Pfeiffer and Jones 1971–83). They consist of strategies to improve the operation of the organization and have been summarized as follows:

1. Diagnostic;
2. team-building;
3. intergroup;
4. survey-feedback;
5. education and training;
6. technostructural or structural;
7. process consultation;
8. grid organization development;
9. third party peacemaking;
10. coaching and counseling;
11. life and career planning; and

12. planning and goalsetting. These twelve approaches represent OD strategies that might be employed in working toward organization improvement and planned change within any organization, including school settings. (French and Bell 1978)

Approaches to change have to deal with methods for expanding positively viewed changes to other units and systems. Diffusion of change is an area where a great deal of work and thought have taken place in recent years. Successful implementation and adaptation of quality change concern all educators in a society trying to stay afloat and on the crest, rather than in the trough of the "third wave."

Caveats

For any administrator or supervisor to be successful, several conditions have to occur. First, one has to establish oneself. The new teacher making recommendations without knowing the complexity of the social systems, or the new administration rushing in without taking the time to discover "the lay of the land" probably will not accomplish their goals. Time is our greatest ally, although we act as if there is no time. (Lewin's model points to the value of time.)

Next, trust has to be built by any new administrator, a process that takes a long time. So does the process of building support systems. But if they are not built, little if anything constructive will take place.

The strategies chosen must be successful, or people who support the administrator the first time may not be inclined to take risks the next time. It is also useful to try an idea in more than one setting. One teacher trying a reading program will receive the normal slings and arrows. Three may get the barbs, but they can form a supportive or a protective subgroup or social system for each other. The value of having more than one person try a program lies in the fact that if one doesn't work too well because the teacher gets sick, there are two other teachers who are trying to make sure that it does work.

Next, designing the change so that it is implemented in three settings (three teachers in each of three schools) points up the value of that course of action. Even if one school fails, two others are operating the program.

Summary

We have examined the assumption of many administrators that they are stabilizers and are supposed to resist change (often fear underlies that strategy) by examining some of the enormous changes in society and education over the past decades. We have concluded, consequently, that it is impossible to resist change. In addition we have investigated forces in organizations resisting change (its subculture) and those promoting and supporting change (various formulations of the dynamics of the organization) and have arrived at the generalization that any organization inevitably changes.

Thereafter we briefly reviewed the role of the principal and superintendent and found it to be that of a change agent. The necessity of determining change to achieve purposes was discussed, as were a series of steps and procedures in making changes. Specific change strategies were next delineated. Last, some caveats were discussed for administrators to produce successful change.

References

Barnard, C. I. 1938. *The Functions of the Executive*. Cambridge: Harvard University Press.

Blumer, H. 1946. "Collective Behavior," in *New Outlines of Principles of Sociology*, edited by Alfred McClung Lee, 167–224. New York: Barnes and Noble.

Carlson, R. D. 1962. *Executive Succession and Organizational Change*. Chicago: Measurement Administration Center.

_____. 1972. *School Superintendents: Careers and Performance*. Columbus, Ohio: Charles E. Merrill.

Cook, D. C. 1966. *Program Evaluation and Review Technique*. Washington, D.C.: U. S. Office of Education, Cooperative Research Monograph No. 17.

_____. 1979. *Program Evaluation Review Technique: Applications in Education*. Washington, D.C.: University Press of America.

Dunn, R., and K. Dunn. 1972. *Practical Approaches to Individualizing Instruction*. West Nyack, N.Y.: Parker Publishing Company.

_____. 1975. *Educator's Self-Teaching Guide to Individualizing Instructional Programs*. West Nyack, N.Y.: Parker Publishing Co.

_____. 1977. *Administrator's Guide to New Programs for Faculty Management and Evaluation*. West Nyack, N.Y.: Parker Publishing Co.

Edwards, B., 1977. *The Development of the Edwards Receptivity to Change Inventory*. Unpublished doctoral diss. Nashville, Tenn.: George Peabody College.

Fabun D., 1972. "The Corporation as a Creative Environment." *Kaiser News*. No. 1. Oakland, Calif.

French, W. L., and C. H. Bell. 1978. *Organization Development*, 2d ed. Englewood Cliffs, N.J.: Prentice-Hall.

Getzels, J. W., and H. A. Thelen. 1960. "The Classroom Group as a Unique Social System," in *The Dynamics of Instructional Groups*, edited by Nelson Henry. The Fifty-ninth Yearbook of the National Society for the Study of Education. Part II. Chicago: University of Chicago Press.

Guba, E. G., and J. W. Getzels. 1957. "Social Behavior and The Administrative Process." *School Review* 65.

Hart, L. 1975. *How the Brain Works*. New York: Basic Books.

Herrman, N. 1981. "The Creative Brain." *Training and Development Journal* (October): 11–16.

Hodgkinson, H. L. 1983. "Guess Who's Coming to College." *Academe* 69 (March-April): 13–20.

Kaufman, B. 1964. *Up the Down Staircase*. Englewood Cliffs, N.J.: Prentice-Hall.

Kaufman, H. 1975. *The Limits of Organizational Change*. University, Alabama: University of Alabama Press.

Leggett, S. 1969. "Foreword" to *Sociology of Supervision*, by L. C. Wilson, et al. Boston: Allyn and Bacon.

Levin, M. A., and R. I. Simon. 1974. "From Ideal to Real: Understanding the Development of New Educational Settings." *Interchange* (Ontario Institute for the Study of Education) vol. 5, no. 3.

Lewin, K. 1943. "Group Decision and Social Change," in *Readings in Social Psychology*, edited by T. M. Newcomb and E. D. Hartley. 2d ed. New York: Henry Holt and Company, 1952.

_____. 1947. "Frontiers in Group Dynamics: Concept, Method and Reality in Social Science; Social Equilibria and Social Change." *Human Relations* 1 (June): 5-41.

Lewis, O. 1959. *Five Families*. New York: Basic Books.

Lynam, R. 1979. *An Exploratory Investigation of the Relationships Between Teacher Morale, Attendance Pressure and Absenteeism*. Unpublished doctoral diss. Nashville, Tenn.: George Peabody College.

Mayo, E. 1933. *The Human Problems of an Industrial Civilization*. New York: Macmillan.

Orlosky, D. E. and B. O. Smith. 1972. "Educational Change: Its Origins and Characteristics." *Phi Delta Kappan* 53 (March): 412-14.

Pfeiffer, J. W., and J. E. Jones. 1971-83. *Annual Handbook for Group Facilitators*. La Jolla, Calif.: University Associates.

Schmuck, R. A., et al. *The Second Handbook of Organization Development in the Schools*. Palo Alto. Calif.: Mayfield Publishing.

Shapiro, A. S., and K. C. Kirby. 1981. "How to Retrain Your Staff to Improve Performance." In *Managing Schools in Hard Times*, edited by Stanton Leggett. Chicago: Teach 'Em.

Thelen, H. 1958. Conversation with A. S. Shapiro.

Toffler, A. 1980. *The Third Wave*. Toronto: Bantam Books.

Van Meter, E. J. 1980. "Planned Change in Education." *Administrator's Notebook*, vol. 28, no. 7.

Weber, Max. 1946. *From Max Weber: Essays in Sociology*, edited by H. H. Gerth and C. W. Mills. New York: Oxford University Press.

Wilson, L. C., T. M. Byar, A. S. Shapiro, and S. H. Schell. 1969. *Sociology of Supervision*. Boston: Allyn and Bacon.

Donald E. Orlosky is professor of education at the University of South Florida, where he has served on the faculty since 1969. Between 1959 and 1969 he was a visiting lecturer in educational research and educational psychology at Indiana University. Concurrent with his lectureship at Indiana University he was on the faculty at DePauw University and served as head of its education department. He has taught mathematics in public schools and has served as an administrator in secondary schools and in higher education. He was co-director of the National Leadership Training Institute for Educational Personnel with B. Othanel Smith from 1970 to 1977. He has authored, edited, or co-authored 25 books, including Socialization and Schooling: The Basics of Reform, Curriculum Development: Issues and Insights, and Introduction to Education. He has consulted throughout the United States and presented workshops and lectures in Great Britain, Germany, and France.

Lloyd E. McCleary is professor of educational administration at the University of Utah. There he also directs the research and development lab of the college of education, chairs the board of the NASSP Intermountain Assessment Center, and heads a long-term project to develop learning modules for field-based training in education and related fields. He has been an assistant principal, principal, and assistant superintendent in the public schools and has served as department chairman in two universities.

McCleary has directed more than thirty funded projects, over half of which were overseas. His projects include work with the U.S. Department of State, the Agency for International Development, the U.S. Department of Defense, Dependent Schools, UNESCO, and the Academy for Educational Development.

McCleary chaired the research team of the recent NASSP National High School Principal Study. He leads a national task force on administrative in-service education and works with a large U.S. corporation in management training. He has authored and co-authored seven books and numerous monographs, articles, and research reports.

Arthur Shapiro has been professor of education and chairperson of the department of educational leadership at the University of South Florida since 1982. Previously, he directed the University of Tennessee at Knoxville Graduate Center at the University of Tennessee, Chattanooga, and was professor of education and chairperson of education faculty at George Peabody College.

Dr. Shapiro is a practicing administrator, having been superintendent of schools in Long Beach, New Jersey, and an assistant superintendent, director of secondary education, high school principal, and a teacher in nationally visible districts in rural, urban and suburban areas.

He has authored and co-authored a number of books and articles including the first theory of supervision in Sociology of Supervision. He has also published a number of simulations that have been utilized at the national conventions of the Center for the Study of Educational Personnel Policies and Regional Conventions of the Teacher Corps, and various universities.

L. Dean Webb is a professor of educational administration at Arizona State University. Formerly a public school teacher and administrator, she has participated in numerous state and local school finance studies. She has served on the board of directors of the American Education Finance Association (AEFA), and is co-editor of the 1983 and 1984 AEFA yearbook. Dr. Webb has written extensively in the area of school finance and school law, is co-author of a book on Arizona school law, and edits the Journal of Educational Equity and Leadership.

INDEX